MW00817912

Freedom on the Offensive

A VOLUME IN THE SERIES

THE UNITED STATES IN THE WORLD

Edited by Benjamin A. Coates, Emily Conroy-Krutz, Paul A. Kramer, and Judy Tzu-Chun Wu

Founding Series Editors: Mark Philip Bradley and Paul A. Kramer

A list of titles in this series is available at cornellpress.cornell.edu.

Freedom on the Offensive

Human Rights, Democracy Promotion,
and US Interventionism in the Late Cold War

William Michael Schmidli

Cornell University Press
Ithaca and London

First published 2022 by Cornell University Press

Library of Congress Cataloging-in-Publication Data

Names: Schmidli, William Michael, 1979– author.
Title: Freedom on the offensive : human rights, democracy promotion, and US interventionism in the late Cold War / William Michael Schmidli.
Description: Ithaca [New York] : Cornell University Press, 2022. | Series: The United States in the world | Includes bibliographical references and index.
Identifiers: LCCN 2021057943 (print) | LCCN 2021057944 (ebook) | ISBN 9781501765148 (hardcover) | ISBN 9781501765179 (pdf) | ISBN 9781501765162 (epub)
Subjects: LCSH: Human rights—Political aspects—United States—History—20th century. | Cold War—Influence. | Intervention (International law) | United States—Foreign relations—1945–1989. | United States—Foreign relations—Nicaragua—Case studies.
Classification: LCC JC571 .S3695 2022 (print) | LCC JC571 (ebook) | DDC 323—dc23/eng/20220318
LC record available at https://lccn.loc.gov/2021057943
LC ebook record available at https://lccn.loc.gov/2021057944

Contents

Acknowledgments

This book has had numerous institutional homes. Many thanks to colleagues in the Department of History at Bucknell University, especially Claire Campbell, David Del Testa, John Enyeart, Jay Goodale, and Ann Tlusty. This book was also shaped by the Bucknell Brigade to Nicaragua program, a wonderful service-learning opportunity for students. Special thanks to Janice Butler and Paul Susman for generously inviting me to participate and to the Center for Development in Central America for hosting the brigades. This book also benefited from research funding from the Bucknell Institute for Public Policy.

A residential fellowship at the Institute for Advanced Study in Princeton, New Jersey, with funding provided by the Herodotus Fund, gave me much-needed time to work through the documentary record in a deeply inspiring academic setting. Thanks to Michael van Walt van Praag for his interest in the book and to María Mercedes Tuya, who did a wonderful job turning annotated documents into a database of digital note cards. As I began the writing process, a fellowship at the Helsinki Collegium for Advanced Studies provided a lovely space to think, talk, and write. Special thanks to Katja Ritari, Mikko Saikku, and Florencia Quesada Avendaño for their feedback and engagement in the book.

As this book entered the final stretch, in 2018 I joined the Institute for History at Leiden University. I am especially thankful to Joke Kardux and Eduard van de Bilt for their unflagging patience and advice as I acclimated to Dutch academic culture, and to colleagues in the master's program in

North American Studies including Dario Fazzi, Damian Pargas, Sara Polak, and Giles Scott-Smith. At the tail end of the book, a fellowship at the Netherlands Institute for Advanced Studies provided much-needed time and funding to make final revisions.

Numerous colleagues and organizations have provided opportunities to present my work and receive valuable feedback. Thanks to the Danish Institute for International Studies, the Helsinki Collegium for Advanced Studies, the Latin American Studies Association, the London School of Economics International History Research Seminar, the Modern International Relations Seminar at the Institute for Advanced Study, the Netherlands American Studies Association, the New Diplomatic History Network, the Society for Historians of American Foreign Relations, and the Transnational Studies Association. Many colleagues have helped me to clarify the book, in both formal and informal settings. In particular, I thank Mario Del Pero, Petra Goedde, Jonathan Hunt, Andrew Kirkendall, Simon Miles, David Painter, Roger Peace, Robert Pee, Joe Renouard, Flora Roberts, Brad Simpson, Sarah Snyder, Rasmus Sinding Søndergaard, and Eline van Ommen.

I wish to acknowledge Cornell University Press for granting me permission to adapt portions of my chapter "Reframing Human Rights: Reagan's 'Project Democracy' and the US Intervention in Nicaragua" in *The Reagan Moment: America and the World in the 1980s*, eds. Jonathan Hunt and Simon Miles (2021), 237–59. Additionally, I adapted portions of my chapter "Recreating the Cold War Consensus: Democracy Promotion and the Crisis of American Hegemony," in Robert Pee and William Michael Schmidli, *The Reagan Administration, the Cold War, and the Transition to Democracy Promotion* (2019), 75–92, with permission from Palgrave Macmillan.

At Cornell University Press, Michael McGandy saw potential in the book at an early stage, and the manuscript benefited from his editorial expertise. The book was greatly improved by insightful comments from the anonymous readers and The United States in the World editorial team: Benjamin A. Coates, Emily Conroy-Krutz, Paul A. Kramer, and Judy Tzu-Chun Wu. Thanks also to Sarah E. M. Grossman, who took the editorial reins at the tail end of the book and shepherded it to completion.

Throughout writing this book, I have drawn on a deep well of support from my family. My daughters, Sibyl and Sonya, are my greatest source of joy and inspiration. When I started the book, Sibyl was just learning to walk; over the following years she seemed equally at home in central Pennsylvania and Princeton, Helsinki and South Holland. Sonya was only three months old when we arrived in Finland; watching her grow to be a bright and thoughtful young person has been both humbling and exhilarating. I am deeply indebted to my wife, Elisa Da Vià, who endured innumerable conversations about US Cold War foreign policy and strengthened the manuscript with sharp feedback and a careful editorial eye. Finally, this book is dedicated to my parents, Dave and Sharlie Schmidli, whose support, advice, and encouragement have been invaluable.

Abbreviations

ADST	Foreign Affairs Oral History Program of the Association for Diplomatic Studies and Training, Arlington, VA
AFL-CIO	American Federation of Labor and Congress of Industrial Organizations
AMNLAE	Association of Nicaraguan Women Luisa Amanda Espinoza
APF	American Political Foundation
ARDE	Alianza Revolucionaria Democrática (Democratic Revolutionary Alliance)
CDM	Coalition for a Democratic Majority
CDS	Sandinista Defense Committee
CIA	Central Intelligence Agency
CNFP	Coalition for a New Foreign Policy
CNWS	Concord Naval Weapons Station
COHA	Council on Hemispheric Affairs
COSEP	Council of Private Enterprise
CPD	Committee on the Present Danger
CSCE	Conference on Security and Cooperation in Europe
EPS	Ejército Popular Sandinista (Sandinista Popular Army)
FAO	Frente Amplio Opositor (Broad Opposition Front)
FBI	Federal Bureau of Investigation
FDN	Fuerza Democrática Nicaragüense (Nicaraguan Democratic Force)
FDP	Popular Democratic Front

FMLN	Frente Farabundo Martí para la Liberación Nacional (Farabundo Martí National Liberation Front)
FSLN	Frente Sandinista de Liberación Nacional (Sandinista National Liberation Front)
GDP	gross domestic product
GRN	government of Nicaragua
IBRD	International Bank for Reconstruction and Development
ISIS	Islamic State in Iraq and Syria
MDN	Nicaraguan Democratic Movement
NACLA	North American Congress on Latin America
NAM	Non-Aligned Nations Movement
NATO	North Atlantic Treaty Organization
NBC	National Broadcasting Corporation
NED	National Endowment for Democracy
NEPL	National Endowment for the Preservation of Liberty
NGO	nongovernmental organization
NPR	National Public Radio
NSC	National Security Council
NSDD	National Security Decision Directive
PATCO	Professional Air Traffic Controllers Organization
PBS	Public Broadcasting Corporation
Prodemca	Friends of the Democratic Center in Central America
SALT I	Strategic Arms Limitation Treaty I
SALT II	Strategic Arms Limitation Treaty II
S/LPD	Office of Public Diplomacy for Latin America and the Caribbean
UCLA	University of California, Los Angeles
UNITA	União Nacional para a Independência Total de Angola (National Union for the Total Independence of Angola)
UNO	Unión Nacional Opositora (National Opposition Union)
USAID	United States Agency for International Development
USIA	United States Information Agency
WFP	Witness for Peace
WOLA	Washington Office on Latin America

Introduction

"The Most Important Place in the World": The Reagan Administration, Democracy Promotion, and the Nicaraguan Revolution

In ringing tones, on March 14, 1986, the fortieth president of the United States set forth a vision for US foreign policy in a world defined by the global Cold War. Speaking to a joint session of Congress, Ronald Reagan lauded US engagement with the world in the decades since the Second World War. The United States, the president declared, had consistently worked to resolve regional conflicts and decrease the possibility of nuclear war. Striking a distinctly Wilsonian register, Reagan continued, "We have sought to defend and advance the cause of democracy, freedom, and human rights throughout the world" and "to promote prosperity and social progress through a free, open, and expanding market-oriented global economy."[1]

After more than three decades of waging the Cold War, however, the United States faced a dire national security threat. In the 1970s, Reagan warned, the Soviet Union and its clients had projected military power as never before into so-called wars of national liberation. "The Soviets appeared to conclude that the global 'correlation of forces' was shifting inexorably in their favor," the president asserted. The results, he continued, were horrific: genocide in Vietnam and Cambodia, mass famine in Ethiopia and South Yemen, tens of thousands of Soviet-backed Cuban soldiers in Angola, the Red Army waging a brutal counterinsurgency war in Afghanistan, and communism spreading across Central America. Soviet foreign policy adventurism in the 1980s, Reagan gravely concluded, was "the most important obstacle to the future spread of freedom."[2]

Yet, amid the carnage, the president sensed opportunity. Even as Moscow extended its influence abroad, Reagan asserted, a "democratic revolution" was brewing. "In this global revolution, there can be no doubt where America stands," the president proclaimed. "The American people believe in human rights and oppose tyranny in whatever form, whether of the left or the right." Lauding the wave of democracy sweeping Latin America and emphasizing his administration's recent support for democratic transitions in the Philippines and Haiti, Reagan declared that "American support will be ready, in these countries and elsewhere, to help democracy succeed." Significantly, Reagan positioned anticommunist fighters in the developing world as central players in the global democratic revolution. "Growing resistance movements now challenge Communist regimes installed or maintained by the military power of the Soviet Union and its colonial agents—in Afghanistan, Angola, Cambodia, Ethiopia, and Nicaragua," the president asserted. Calling on congressional legislators to extend US support to "freedom fighters," Reagan pointedly concluded, "We did not create this historical phenomenon, but we must not fail to respond to it."[3]

Reagan's embrace of democracy promotion signaled one of the most important developments in US foreign relations in the late Cold War. In the late 1960s, the bipartisan Cold War consensus among American policymakers had collapsed amid domestic opposition to the Vietnam War.[4] Combined with Watergate and revelations in the 1970s of illiberal US actions abroad, the détente era was defined by a crisis in US Cold War leadership. Competing visions of how the United States should engage the world roiled the US political landscape, and the realist approach of the Richard M. Nixon and Gerald R. Ford administrations was attacked by domestic critics with increasing intensity over the course of the decade.

In an era defined by the breakdown of the Cold War consensus, Reagan's vision of a US victory over the Soviet Union harked back to the bipartisan anticommunism of early Cold War US foreign policy. Yet, as Reagan was well aware, implementing a muscular US approach to the Cold War would require confronting the inroads liberal internationalists had made into the heart of the US foreign policy establishment over the previous decade. Reagan's Cold War victory, in other words, would require a dual containment strategy: containing liberal internationalists at home and the spread of communism abroad.

In this process, human rights would increasingly—and unexpectedly—take center stage. At the outset of the 1980s, the Reagan campaign had lambasted the human rights policy of his predecessor, Jimmy Carter, as defeatist and self-abasing. In the months following Reagan's inauguration in January 1981, the new administration quickly took steps to curtail Carter-era pressure on right-wing regimes with poor human rights records. "We must change the attitude of our diplomatic corps so that we don't bring down governments in the name of human rights," Reagan told the National Security Council (NSC) in early February. "None of them is as guilty of human rights violations as are Cuba and the USSR. We don't throw out our friends just because they can't pass the 'saliva test' on human rights. I want to see that stopped."[5]

By the end of 1981, however, the Reagan administration was shifting gears. Stiff resistance from Congress and intense lobbying by human rights advocates raised concerns in the White House that the effort to downgrade human rights was becoming a costly liability. With strong influence from liberal Cold War hawks—increasingly referred to as neoconservatives—the administration orchestrated a dramatic shift, embracing human rights as consistent with both traditional US moral concerns and the United States' policy priorities in the global Cold War. Human rights, an influential internal memo asserted in October 1981, "is not something we tack on to our foreign policy but is its very purpose: the defense and promotion of freedom in the world."[6]

By the time Reagan stepped to the podium for the joint address to Congress in March 1986, human rights had assumed a defining role in the administration's foreign policy approach. The Reagan team articulated human rights, however, in accordance with its political and economic goals, casting human rights as anticommunism, neoliberal economic policies, and democracy promotion. Social and economic rights, which had been championed throughout the Cold War by the communist world, and in the 1960s and 1970s by many third-world nationalists, were intentionally excluded from the Reagan administration's human rights framework.

The centerpiece of Reagan's human rights policy was democracy promotion. In a major address to members of the British Parliament at Westminster in June 1982, the president emphasized the need "to foster the infrastructure of democracy, the system of a free press, unions, political parties, universities, which allows a people to choose their own way to develop their own culture, to reconcile their own differences through peaceful means."[7] The following year, White House lobbying for "Project Democracy" convinced lawmakers on Capitol Hill to legislate seed money for the National Endowment for Democracy (NED), a bipartisan, nonprofit, private organization that would be annually funded by US government appropriations. Closely aligned with the Reagan administration's foreign policy priorities, the NED emerged over the course of the decade as the flagship purveyor of US democracy promotion, connecting a growing number of stakeholders including think tanks and academics, funding organizations, and nongovernmental organizations (NGOs). In turn, the NED facilitated the transfer of democracy promotion training and material assistance to hundreds of pro-US political organizations and projects overseas.

Like the human rights policy as a whole, the administration's definition of democracy and the mechanisms it developed to promote democracy abroad were interwoven with ideas aimed at advancing US political and economic interests. The essential ingredients for a functioning democracy, Reagan officials concluded, were regular elections, the protection of civil liberties, and a free market economy protecting the interests of corporate capitalism. Dovetailing with the Reagan administration's neoliberal economic agenda, this model of democracy de-emphasized questions of social and economic inequality and posited a direct relationship between market logic and democratic process.

The evolution of Reagan's approach to human rights was widely recognized as a political milestone. The president had undertaken a "turnaround on human rights," an influential article in *Foreign Affairs* asserted shortly after Reagan's joint address to Congress, "a 150- if not a 180-degree change."[8] More importantly, the melding of Reagan's call to roll back communism with a more general emphasis on supporting democracy won bipartisan support on Capitol Hill. By early 1986, Congress had continued to allocate funding for the NED, augmented US support for anti-Soviet fighters in Afghanistan, repealed the congressional prohibition on covert operations in Angola, legislated military assistance to noncommunist resistance in Cambodia, and approved nonlethal aid to counterrevolutionaries in Central America.[9] By 1986, in other words, the administration's emphasis on democracy promotion, as the core of its human rights policy, had made significant steps toward recreating the bipartisan Cold War consensus between the executive and legislative branches that had foundered in the late 1960s on the shoals of the Vietnam War.

Reagan's human rights policy would have important implications for the administration's aggressive approach to the Cold War. Revolutionary Nicaragua, in particular, would play a defining role in US foreign relations during the 1980s. With US backing, the small, impoverished Central American nation had been run since the 1930s by members of the corrupt and nepotistic Somoza family dynasty. Extreme inequality fueled unrest; after years of rising tension, at the end of the 1970s political opposition escalated into a full-fledged war between insurgent forces with strong popular support and Anastasio Somoza Debayle's National Guard. The human and material costs of the 1979 Nicaraguan revolution were immense. In a nation of three million, the conflict cost an estimated fifty thousand lives and left one-fifth of the population homeless and another forty thousand orphaned.[10] But the revolutionaries won. And as tens of thousands of Nicaraguans celebrated the triumph over Somoza in July 1979, there was a palpable sense of hope for the future. The revolutionaries "appeared scrawny, heroic, unbelievably young," wrote the journalist Alma Guillermoprieto. "They embodied the best of everything that three and a half million people who were used to seeing their nation treated as a fourth-rate banana republic could dream of."[11]

The power vacuum left by Somoza's overthrow was quickly filled by the leftist Frente Sandinista de Liberación Nacional (Sandinista National Liberation Front), or FSLN. Assuming the role of a political vanguard, the Sandinistas sought to transform Nicaragua according to a vision of social and economic justice. The FSLN dramatically increased state social spending, sending tens of thousands of young Nicaraguans into the countryside on literacy brigades and building scores of schools, clinics, and houses. Touting a mixed economy model that would operate according to the "logic of the poor," the revolutionary government sought to limit the power of private producers by using the levers of state to serve the needs of the majority. Correspondingly, through mass-based political organizations, the FSLN hoped to provide non-elites with avenues to participate in the nation's political life. Authentic democracy, FSLN officials maintained, flowed from the promotion of social and economic rights and was maintained through daily engagement in grassroots political organizations. In foreign policy, inspired by socialist Cuba, the FSLN aimed to serve as a model for third-world nations seeking to break free from the legacies of colonialism and underdevelopment; covertly, the FSLN quietly funneled Cuban-supplied weapons to leftist revolutionaries in neighboring El Salvador.

The Sandinista revolutionary project was incompatible with Reagan's effort to reassert US power in the global Cold War. The Reagan administration perceived the FSLN as a defining challenge; as the influential UN ambassador Jeane J. Kirkpatrick asserted, Central America was "quite simply the most important place in the world." Viewing the revolution in Nicaragua and the blossoming leftist insurgency in neighboring El Salvador through the lens of the East-West confrontation, the Reagan administration emphasized Nicaragua's proximity to both the continental United States and geostrategically vital sea-lanes. A Soviet satellite in Central America, top administration officials repeatedly warned, would pose a distinct threat to US security interests. Moreover, in light of Cuban involvement in major military operations in the Horn of Africa and Angola, and the strong ties between the Cuban dictator Fidel Castro and top Sandinista officials, the Reagan administration was deeply worried that a joint Cuban-Nicaraguan operation, armed and supplied by the Soviets, could threaten the entire region. "We must not let Central America become another Cuba on the mainland," Reagan warned the NSC in February 1981. "It cannot happen."[12]

The administration also viewed Central America as an opportunity to roll back perceived Soviet gains in the third world. In what would become known as the Reagan Doctrine, administration hard-liners sought to turn the tables on the Soviet Union by supporting anticommunist wars of national liberation.[13] Finally, the administration understood Central America as a test case for defeating the perceived inroads of post-1968 liberalism in US foreign policy, particularly the Carter administration's emphasis on multilateralism, noninterventionism, and a human rights policy that, in the Reaganites' view, targeted right-wing allies but gave communist adversaries a free pass.

By the end of 1981, the Reagan administration had established the framework for a destabilization policy toward Nicaragua that would span the remainder of the decade. Within two years, US-funded counterrevolutionary forces, known as the Contras, had grown to a force of seven thousand combatants and were regularly attacking targets in northern Nicaragua. Eventually marshaling some fifteen thousand fighters, the Contras systematically used assassination, torture, rape, and kidnapping to demoralize Sandinista sympathizers and targeted clinics, schools, and cooperatives to drain the revolutionary government of scarce resources and sow disillusionment among FSLN rank and file.

The Reagan administration's undeclared war on Nicaragua illuminated how human rights could serve US Cold War goals. Reagan officials used the language of human rights to criticize the Sandinistas for denying political rights and civil liberties. Eliding the FLSN's social and economic achievements, the administration castigated the revolutionary government for censoring the opposition newspaper *La Prensa*, accused the FSLN of cracking down on democratic labor federations and the Catholic Church, and dismissed Nicaraguan mass organizations as mechanisms for political coercion. Correspondingly, the administration energetically utilized the lexicon of human rights to portray the Contras as anticommunist democrats, despite evidence of extensive human rights abuses. Intertwined with the Reagan administration's democracy promotion initiative, in other words, were deeply *undemocratic* practices that misled the US people, violated US law, and contributed to immense human and material destruction in Nicaragua and the destabilization of the Sandinista political project.

A growing number of scholars have turned their attention to the history of human rights since the early 2000s. As the first wave of pioneering studies gives way to a new generation of scholarship, it is an exciting time to be a human rights historian.[14] This is also a propitious moment for scholars of US foreign relations during the Reagan era. Thanks to a growing availability of archival sources, historians are now reassessing the 1980s on the basis of fresh archival research.[15]

This study contributes to this body of scholarship by examining the Reagan administration's democracy promotion initiative. Infused with exceptionalism, Americans have long understood the US engagement with the wider world in relation to democracy. As the historians Daniel Bessner and Jennifer M. Miller write, "'Democracy' is one of the most potent keywords of the so-called American Century, consistently referenced as both a goal and critique of U.S. foreign affairs."[16] Yet, unlike political scientists and international relations scholars, historians are only beginning to examine the US emphasis on democracy promotion in the late Cold War era.[17] In part, the limited visibility of democracy promotion in the historiography stems from its very success; in the heady aftermath of the Cold War, the development of a distinct epistemic community focused on democracy promotion, led by "experts" who approached the issue as a value-free technical program, obscured the power relations and ideological assumptions underpinning US programs.[18] Yet, as pioneering critical theorists have pointed out, US democracy promotion was (and remains) aimed at fostering a specific model of liberal democracy that would, in turn, advance specific kinds of power relations.[19]

This book examines how and why democracy promotion emerged as the centerpiece of the US human rights agenda during the 1980s. It does so by exploring the multifaceted conflict between the United States and Nicaragua in the final decade of the Cold War.[20] The book asks three central questions: How did the breakdown of the bipartisan Cold War consensus in the late 1960s shape the emergence and evolution of human rights in US foreign policy in the 1970s and 1980s? How did the Reagan administration's confrontation with revolutionary Nicaragua illuminate a defining struggle over the contours of US foreign policy? And how did Reagan's emphasis on democracy promotion set the stage for the United States' unique engagement with human rights in the post–Cold War era?

On the US political landscape in the late twentieth century, nothing loomed as large as the Vietnam War. Americans of all political stripes operated in the 1970s and 1980s in the shadow of the ignominious US defeat. Chapter 1 explores the collapse of the bipartisan Cold War consensus in the late 1960s as a result of the Vietnam War and its impact on US foreign relations in the following decade. During the détente era, the Nixon and Ford administrations' realist approach to international relations was assailed by domestic critics. On one flank, liberal internationalists criticized the White House for its support of repressive right-wing allies in the developing world and increasingly turned to the language of human rights as a framework for legislation aimed at curtailing US political, economic, and military support for anticommunist dictatorships. On the other flank, liberal cold warriors denounced détente as thinly veiled appeasement of Soviet totalitarianism. Like their liberal internationalist counterparts, congressional hawks embraced the politics of human rights, but focused their attention on the plight of captive peoples of the communist world. Carter's victory in the 1976 presidential election underscored the extent to which Americans had shifted against the realist approach of the Nixon-Ford era. Yet Carter's emphasis on nonintervention-ism, multilateralism, and human rights in US foreign policy ultimately failed to forge a new and durable foreign policy consensus, setting the stage for Reagan's victory in the 1980 election.

The Reagan administration took office intent on removing human rights as a US foreign policy priority. Chapter 2 examines Reagan's efforts to normalize relations with repressive allies, an approach dubbed the Kirkpatrick Doctrine, and deepening US involvement in Central America. Rejecting evidence that pointed to socioeconomic inequality, rather than external subversion, as the principal cause of conflict in Central America, the Reagan administration moved quickly to increase US military and economic support for the Salvadoran government's effort to eradicate leftist insurgents. The Reagan team also initiated a major covert effort to destabilize Nicaragua's revolutionary government. Correspondingly, in the face of fierce congressional and nongovernmental opposition to its effort to downgrade human rights, beginning in late 1981 the Reagan administration increasingly embraced a narrow definition of human rights that justified the Cold War imperatives at the heart of the Kirkpatrick Doctrine.

Chapter 3 shifts the focus from Washington to Managua. Assuming power in Nicaragua following the bloody 1979 revolution, the FSLN dramatically increased state social spending and emphasized international nonalignment and a mixed economy model. Drawing inspiration from socialist Cuba and the Non-Aligned Nations Movement (NAM), these initiatives were rooted in a vision of extending social and economic justice to ordinary Nicaraguans and providing a model of participatory democracy for third-world nations seeking to break free from the legacies of colonialism and underdevelopment. In the early 1980s, the FSLN could boast significant achievements in social sector spending, with dramatic improvements in education, health care, and urban reform. Yet by the time Reagan entered the White House, the Sandinistas were nearing a crossroads. Facing severe economic challenges in the foreseeable future, the FSLN could not ignore the clamor of opposition from the private sector or popular frustration with the revolution's unmet aspirations. Rather than seeking to negotiate a security agreement with Nicaragua, however, the Reagan administration initiated a major covert operation utilizing counterrevolutionary forces to destabilize the FSLN. In response, the Sandinistas dug in their heels, clamping down on civil liberties and reflexively falling back on a mix of nationalism, anti-imperialism, and anti-Americanism. The result was a protracted and bloody conflict that forced the FSLN to divert scarce resources to defense and placed an enormous burden on the Nicaraguan people.

Chapter 4 details the emergence of democracy promotion as a defining feature of US foreign policy. Building on neoconservatives' embrace of human rights to advance US political and economic interests, Reagan's 1982 address at Westminster established democracy promotion as a core US goal and set the stage for the creation of the NED. Secretary of state George P. Shultz played a particularly important role in fusing the Reagan Doctrine's vision of rolling back communist gains in the developing world with the liberal internationalist appeal of the democracy promotion initiative, aligning the United States rhetorically behind democratization processes in Latin America, while dismissing the 1984 Nicaraguan national elections as a "Soviet-style sham." This approach won bipartisan support on Capitol Hill; by 1986, the administration's emphasis on democracy promotion, as the core of its human rights policy, had made significant steps toward re-creating the bipartisan Cold War consensus.

As the US intervention in Central America intensified, Nicaragua emerged as a pivotal site of right-wing solidarity activism in the late Cold War. Chapter 5 explores the loose alliance between administration actors including the White House Outreach Working Group on Central America and the Office of Public Diplomacy for Latin America and the Caribbean (S/LPD) and nonstate actors such as the adventurer and right-wing activist Jack Wheeler. Fusing a grassroots anticommunism with the rising tenor of New Right nationalism, right-wing activists played an important role in popularizing the Reagan Doctrine's vision of rolling back communist gains in the developing world. Yet, even as the Reagan administration was fashioning a new Cold War consensus, top administration officials disregarded the checks and balances at the heart of US democracy by engaging in a web of illegal operations—later revealed in the Iran-Contra scandal—that aimed at maintaining the Contras as a fighting force in the absence of congressional funding. Such efforts illuminated the extent to which undemocratic practices were intertwined with Reagan's democracy promotion initiative.[21]

Chapter 6 shifts the focus to US left-wing activism in opposition to the Reagan administration's intervention against the Sandinistas. For US activists, with the painful memory of the US defeat in the Vietnam War still fresh, Reagan's repeated condemnations of the Sandinistas, support for the Contras, and the extensive US military maneuvers in the region raised the specter of US soldiers fighting and dying on Nicaraguan soil. As the Contra war intensified, the widespread abuses of the Contras against civilian targets elicited a rising chorus of criticism from US-based human rights organizations, churches, and Latin America–focused solidarity groups. By mid-decade, US activists had established a powerful voice in the Central America debate.[22] Yet they faced an uphill battle as Reagan's efforts to reconstruct the bipartisan Cold War consensus around the democracy project appealed to moderate liberals and sowed discord within the US Left.

Chapter 7 examines the denouement in US-Nicaraguan Cold War relations. Following the 1988 presidential election, the George H. W. Bush administration sought to maintain US pressure on Nicaragua without Reagan's incendiary and divisive rhetoric. Underscoring the power of the democracy initiative, secretary of state James A. Baker III adeptly shifted the focus inside the Washington Beltway from the Contras to the 1990 Nicaraguan election. Portraying the Sandinistas as a retrograde totalitarian regime in a vibrant age of democratization, the White House won bipartisan support in its effort to maintain the Contra threat and US economic pressure as well as provide an infusion of funds for the electoral opposition.

The FSLN's defeat in the February 1990 national election was viewed by many in Washington as a fitting coda to the dramatic and largely peaceful end of the Cold War in late 1989. By the late 1980s, it was evident that the Reagan administration's embrace of democracy promotion had led to a greater institutionalization of human rights—albeit narrowly defined—in US foreign policy. Human rights promotion had become increasingly accepted as a legitimate US foreign policy goal among the many players shaping foreign policy in the

Washington Beltway and in US diplomatic posts overseas. Yet, as US policy toward Nicaragua made clear, the emphasis on democracy promotion also served to legitimate a distinctive form of interventionism—pursued through civil society or low-cost military interventions and rooted in the neoliberal imperatives of US-led globalization—a development with major implications for post–Cold War US foreign policy.

Chapter 1

Competing Visions

Human Rights and US Foreign Policy in the Era of Détente, 1968-1980

In late January 1977, the influential Republican strategist Richard V. Allen met with former governor Ronald Reagan. It was an inauspicious moment for the Republican Party, and for Reagan in particular; after a bitter campaign for the Republican presidential nomination over the first eight months of 1976, Reagan had been narrowly defeated at the Republican National Convention in August by the incumbent, Gerald R. Ford. In turn, Ford had lost to Jimmy Carter in the November general election. As Allen and Reagan talked politics over sandwiches at Reagan's California residence, the Carter administration, flush with success, was entering its second week in the White House.

After wide-ranging discussion of foreign policy issues, Reagan shifted the conversation to US grand strategy. "Look, we've been talking all morning. I find it very interesting, but I'd like to now tell you my basic theory about the Cold War," he told Allen. "Some people say I'm very simplistic, but there's a difference between being simplistic and simple. A lot of very complex things are very simple if you think through them," Reagan continued. "Keeping that in mind, my theory of the Cold War is, we win and they lose. What do you think about that?"[1]

Allen was shocked. The impact of Reagan's words was like a "ton of bricks," he recalled many years later. "I couldn't believe it. Hair went up on the back of my neck." In disbelief, Allen pressed Reagan. "Do you mean that? Do you actually mean that?" Reagan responded with characteristic certainty. "Of course. I said it. I mean it, of course I mean it."[2]

Allen recognized that in the tumultuous decade of the 1970s Reagan's vision of winning the Cold War was perhaps unique among mainstream American politicians. Indeed, in the late 1960s, the bipartisan Cold War consensus among US policymakers had collapsed. The foundation of US foreign policy since the late 1940s, the Cold War consensus embodied a shared commitment among centrist liberals and conservative internationalists to project US political, economic, and military power abroad to contain the spread of Soviet communism. The containment strategy had undergirded the Harry S. Truman administration's robust framework of security and economic assistance to Western Europe at the onset of the Cold War; by the early 1950s, US policymakers were taking an increasingly global approach to containment following the successful Soviet detonation of an atomic bomb, the communist victory in the Chinese Civil War, and the outbreak of war on the Korean peninsula. Put simply, as the containment strategy emerged as the lodestar of US foreign policy, the Cold War consensus among US policymakers facilitated aggressive efforts to prevent communist inroads in the developing world, underpinning extensive US security and economic assistance to anticommunist allies and justifying a pattern of expansive US military and covert interventionism.

In the late 1960s, however, the Cold War consensus among US policymakers fell apart amid the United States' failed intervention in Vietnam. On the left, the Democratic Party fractured under the strain of widespread domestic opposition to the war and rising New Left political activism, leaving liberal cold warriors increasingly overshadowed by "New Politics liberals" who rejected the Cold War logic of the previous two decades. On the right, the White House under Richard M. Nixon emphasized the gains that could be achieved by separating ideology from strategic interests. Guided by secretary of state Henry Kissinger's realist approach to international relations, Nixon's effort to decrease tension and increase cooperation between the United States and the Soviet Union, dubbed détente, defined US–Soviet relations throughout the turbulent 1970s. Accordingly, in a decade defined by images of overcrowded US helicopters escaping Saigon as the defeated city fell to the advancing North Vietnamese, "I never heard anybody say, 'win the Cold War,'" Allen remembered. "I heard 'manage the Cold War.'" In the détente era, he continued, Kissinger's approach was merely to "get the best deal you can."[3]

If Kissinger claimed significant achievements in the Nixon-Ford era, the taciturn secretary's realist approach to foreign policy was attacked by domestic critics with rising intensity over the course of the 1970s. On one flank, a rising chorus of liberal internationalists increasingly turned to the language of human rights as a framework for legislation aimed at curtailing US political, economic, and military support for anticommunist dictatorships. On the other flank, liberal cold warriors, led by senator Henry M. "Scoop" Jackson (D-WA), denounced détente as thinly veiled appeasement of Soviet totalitarianism. Like their liberal internationalist counterparts, congressional hawks embraced the politics of human rights, but they focused their attention on the plight of captive peoples of the communist world.

Competing visions of how the United States should engage the world thus roiled the US political landscape in the 1970s. And in a decade defined by the breakdown of the Cold War consensus, Reagan's simple vision of a US victory over the Soviet Union harked back to the bipartisan anticommunism of early Cold War US foreign policy. Yet, as Reagan was well aware, 1976 was not 1946; implementing a muscular US approach to the Cold War would require confronting the inroads that New Politics liberals had made into the very heart of the US foreign policy establishment. Reagan's Cold War victory, in other words, would require a strategy of dual containment: rolling back Soviet gains abroad while containing the US Left at home.

In his 1976 meeting with Reagan, Allen sensed a rare opportunity. Electrified by Reagan's words, he made a decision. "Well, Governor," Allen told Reagan, "I haven't the faintest idea what you're going to do with the rest of your life, but if you intend to run for President of the United States, you just signed me up right now, because that's been my objective for a long time."[4]

At the end of the 1960s, the rationale for détente had been clear. More than half a million US soldiers were fighting an enormously costly war in South Vietnam, and the 1968 Tet Offensive belied the Lyndon B. Johnson administration's regular assurances of light at the end of the tunnel. At home, antiwar demonstrations surged. Abroad, as the US ground war in Vietnam expanded, the United States' relations with Western European allies eroded, undermining the foundation of containment. Across the Iron Curtain, the Soviets had reached effective parity with the United States in nuclear weapons, enhancing the Soviet Union's credibility as a major power, mitigating US coercive capabilities, and opening the door to greater Soviet power projection in the developing world.[5]

The Nixon administration's strategic pursuit of détente emerged in response to the breakdown in the domestic Cold War consensus as well as the unique foreign policy challenges of the late 1960s. Guided by a much-vaunted realist approach to international affairs, Nixon and Kissinger hoped direct engagement with the USSR—lubricated with the promise of lucrative trade deals and transfers of much-needed technology—would moderate Soviet behavior in the international arena, slow the arms race, and facilitate a graceful US exit from Vietnam. Indeed, détente underpinned the administration's most important foreign policy successes. In July 1971, Kissinger's secret meeting with Chinese premier Chou En-lai, followed by Nixon's formal visit to Beijing the following year, laid the groundwork for the reestablishment of US-Chinese diplomatic relations. It was a remarkably rapid reorientation of US policy and an instance of clear-sighted strategic vision.[6] As Nixon bluntly told the White House staff, "Where vital interests are involved, great powers consult their vital interests—or else they're played for suckers by those powers that do."[7]

The White House claimed other successes as well. In the late spring of 1972, Nixon and Soviet premier Leonid Brezhnev signed the twelve-point Basic Principles of Relations statement at a summit in Moscow. Underscoring the administration's realist approach, the document declared that "differences in ideology and in the social systems of the USA and the USSR are not obstacles to the bilateral development of normal relations based on the principles of sovereignty, equality, non-interference in internal affairs and mutual advantage."[8] More concretely, the Strategic Arms Limitation Treaty, known as SALT I, and the Anti-Ballistic Missile Agreement were milestones in the effort to halt the nuclear arms race. The following year, as détente neared its apogee, the two powers signed the Prevention of Nuclear War Agreement and began preparing for SALT II.

The Nixon administration also ended the US war in Vietnam. There was little to celebrate in the administration's handling of the war; the White House intensified bombing campaigns over civilian targets and expanded the conflict into neighboring Laos and Cambodia, while tens of thousands of South Vietnamese were assassinated in the Central Intelligence Agency (CIA)–sponsored Phoenix Program.[9] Between 1969 and 1973, 20,553 US soldiers lost their lives, and the US government estimated that a staggering 107,504 South Vietnamese and more than a half million North Vietnamese and National Liberation Front soldiers died in combat.[10] Yet Nixon praised the January 1973 Paris Peace Accords as a "peace with honor," permitting the rapid withdrawal of the last US soldiers from Vietnam.[11]

If Nixon claimed significant foreign policy achievements, the administration's realist approach was increasingly attacked in the 1970s from both sides of the US political spectrum. For liberal internationalists, the war in

Vietnam took center stage. Liberals denounced the US intervention as epitomizing the misguided and destructive logic of the US containment strategy, while Nixon's secret expansion of the war and indiscriminate bombing campaigns showcased an imperial presidency's shameful abdication of US traditional values. Although liberals were generally supportive of the Nixon administration's pursuit of détente, opposition to the Vietnam War propelled them toward a broader vision of reform, and the 1970s witnessed a remarkable surge of congressional efforts to scale back the primacy of the president in US foreign policy. For the first time, in 1972 the Congress rejected Nixon's foreign aid request, an unmistakable flexing of legislative muscle that was repeated the following year. More substantively, the November 1973 War Powers Act, passed over Nixon's veto, required the executive branch to consult with Congress before involving the United States in military interventions abroad and, significantly, gave the legislative branch the power to force a US troop withdrawal.[12]

The immense popular outcry following the Watergate scandal accelerated congressional liberals' efforts to rein in the executive branch. In the November 1974 congressional elections, seventy-five new Democrats joined the Ninety-Fourth Congress, the largest freshman class since 1948. Intent on enacting major legislative reform and expanding the power of Congress, the "Watergate Babies" upended the traditional relationship between the legislative and executive branches by undermining the power of committee chairs, providing individual members with a greater role in legislative initiatives. As one new member of the House asserted, "Everyone—whether they were liberal, moderate, or conservative—felt they were here to do congressional reform."[13]

The determination of liberal Democrats on Capitol Hill to redirect US foreign policy reflected a defining development of the 1970s: the rising influence of human rights. It was a development fueled by global transformations. As the rapid advance of globalization reshaped state power, new openings emerged for nonstate actors to shape the international arena. Correspondingly, technological advances facilitated the exchange of people and ideas across national borders and increased flows of migrants and refugees stimulated interest in labor exploitation and human trafficking. These sweeping developments contributed to a "new global affect toward power and territoriality," writes the historian Mark Philip Bradley. In an era of thriving social mobilization ranging from environmentalism to anti-apartheid activism, "individual consciousness, lived experience, moral witness, and a testimonial turn became the keywords for activists of this era and began to reshape the contours of global politics and morality."[14]

The emphasis on the individual in the 1970s shaped Americans' understanding of human rights. Whether championing anti-Soviet dissidents or condemning Latin American military regimes' use of torture against perceived subversives, US human rights activists focused their attention on the violation of political rights and civil liberties. In an era defined by privatization, deregulation, and economic liberalization, few US human rights activists advocated social and economic rights.[15] Moreover, as the historian Kenneth Cmiel has written, human rights organizations eschewed "thick descriptions" of local culture and context in favor of simple and direct "thin" messages.[16] Although thin descriptions could both make human rights violations visible and drive human rights activism, they came at a cost, rendering less visible unique local conditions and structures that contributed to rights abuses.[17] Finally, Americans who gravitated toward human rights activism typically did so out of a sense that human rights violations occurred overseas; in a movement that appealed primarily to white, middle-class activists, the far-reaching domestic challenges the United States faced in the 1970s were rarely perceived as *human rights* problems.[18]

Over the course of the decade, rising interest in human rights led to the emergence of dozens of human rights lobbying groups. Consisting of an "amorphous yet multifaceted aggregate," in the words of an early assessment, the human rights movement ranged from organizations focused on awareness raising, political lobbying, and media outreach to solidarity organizations advocating on behalf of human rights in particular nations.[19] Underscoring the rising interest in human rights, membership of the US branch of Amnesty International jumped from six thousand to thirty-five thousand between 1970 and 1976. Leveraging both grassroots activism and Washington-based political lobbying, Amnesty had branch offices in five US cities and an operating budget of more than $1 million by the end of the decade.[20]

In the effort to reform US foreign policy, liberal internationalists increasingly embraced the politics of human rights. Led by senators James Abourezk (D-SD), Alan Cranston (D-CA), Hubert H. Humphrey (D-MN), and Edward Kennedy (D-MA) and representatives Donald M. Fraser (D-MN) and Tom Harkin (D-IA), liberals charged that Nixon's strategic vision meant turning a blind eye to the political prisoners, torture victims, and state-sanctioned murders carried out by repressive allies, such as the brutal military juntas in Greece and Brazil.[21] The Nixon administration's "secret blockade" of Chile following the 1970 election of socialist president Salvador Allende—culminating in the vicious Chilean military coup d'état of September 1973—was especially significant in accelerating the momentum of congressional human rights advocates. As the newly installed Chilean military dictatorship engaged in a massive campaign of repression against Allende supporters, torturing thousands in Santiago's soccer stadium and sending "caravans of death" into the countryside, US congressional lawmakers increasingly articulated their opposition in the language of universal human rights.[22]

Human rights lobbying bolstered the efforts of liberal internationalists in Congress to pass legislation binding US economic and security assistance to human rights considerations. Fraser's successful inclusion of section 502B into the 1974 Foreign Assistance Act set the tone. A pathbreaking amendment, 502B asserted that "except in extraordinary circumstances, the President shall substantially reduce or terminate security assistance to any government which engages in a consistent pattern of gross violations of internationally recognized human rights." Initially a nonbinding "sense of Congress," Fraser's amendment nonetheless provided a foundation for subsequent efforts to use congressional legislation to bind US foreign policy to human rights considerations.[23]

Liberal internationalists were not the only ones to use the issue of morality to criticize the Nixon and Ford administrations' realist foreign policy approach. Liberal cold warriors, led by senator Jackson, also embraced human rights as a blueprint for downgrading détente in favor of robust US support for the captive peoples of the communist world. Combining hardline anticommunism with support for a generous welfare state modeled on the New Deal, Jackson's political outlook was ideologically consistent with the centrist "Vital Center liberalism" that had guided traditional Democratic Party politics since the Truman administration. The rise of the New Left over the course of the 1960s, however, placed traditional liberals squarely on the defensive as activists associated with the anti–Vietnam War movement, counterculture, and a range of progressive rights-based movements pushed the Democratic Party to the left. As the chaotic spectacle of the 1968 Democratic National Convention in Chicago made starkly evident, New Left activism—channeled into mainstream Democratic Party politics as "New Politics liberalism"—threatened to sever the Cold War moorings that had anchored US liberalism for two decades.

Traditional liberals' unease with the direction of their party turned to a sense of betrayal when senator George McGovern (D–SD) secured the Democratic Party nomination in the 1972 presidential election. As the head of the Commission on Party Structure and Delegate Selection in 1969, Mc-Govern had overseen significant changes in the nomination process, which, in the eyes of traditional liberals, privileged New Politics liberals at the expense of the white working class.[24] Worse, McGovern's anti–Vietnam War platform, spelled out in his "Come Home, America" acceptance speech at the Democratic National Convention in Miami, appeared infused, recalled Ben J. Wattenberg, a former speechwriter for Johnson, with the "countercultural, pro-Vietnamese, and neoisolationist ideas" of the New Left.[25] The South Dakota senator's crushing defeat in the November election—Nixon won forty-nine states—reinforced a sense that the Democratic Party had been hijacked by activists whose agenda lacked appeal for centrist voters.[26]

The following month, Wattenberg and a small group of disaffected Democrats formed the Coalition for a Democratic Majority (CDM). The CDM was intended to provide a political home for liberal anticommunists, and the organization quickly became a lightning rod for a growing number of liberal intellectuals who were increasingly described as "neoconservatives." In the early 1970s, "there were many active, public-spirited people who felt quite isolated politically, knowing that something was going very wrong in their Democratic Party," Wattenberg recalled. "As individuals they felt politically homeless and weak. . . . They knew they weren't Republicans. But they were deeply offended by the message of the McGovern anti-war Democrats and by the highly publicized counterculture." The CDM, Wattenberg concluded, "offered a way to stay in the game and remain true to long-held principles."[27]

If liberal anticommunists viewed the McGovern wing of the Democratic Party with disdain, they were also deeply opposed to the Nixon administration's support for détente. First, liberal Cold War hawks viewed détente as a betrayal of the United States' traditional democratic values. They recognized, as the historian Arthur M. Schlesinger Jr. wrote in an early assessment, "that foreign policy must be founded on national interest but considered ideals an indispensable constituent of American power."[28] Second, in the eyes of Cold War liberals the US pursuit of détente was misguided and dangerous. Duplicitous Soviet leaders might pay lip service to détente, the hawks argued, but their ultimate aim was to use a relaxation in Cold War tension to advance their own strategic aims abroad.

Significantly, liberal cold warriors attacked the Soviet Union's human rights record to bolster their case against détente. Drawing on the language of the Universal Declaration of Human Rights, Jackson and his colleagues worked to publicize the plight of prominent Soviet dissidents, such as the physicist Andrei Sakharov and the Nobel laureate Aleksandr Solzhenitsyn, whose immense *Gulag Archipelago*—described by eminent statesman George Kennan as the "most powerful single indictment of a political regime to be levied in modern times"—was first published in the West in December 1973.[29] Similarly, Jackson emerged as a champion of Soviet citizens facing emigration restrictions, particularly the thousands of Jewish "refuseniks" seeking exit visas to Israel. Along with his cosponsor, representative Charles Vanik (D-OH), Jackson successfully passed the Jackson-Vanik Amendment to the Trade Act of 1974, making normal US trade relations with nonmarket countries conditional on unrestricted emigration. The amendment's success in convincing the Soviets to release greater numbers of refuseniks is debatable; indeed, given the Soviets' deeply hostile response to the Washington senator's highly publicized demands, it may have been counterproductive. Yet Jackson-Vanik was an unmistakable broadside fired over the bow of détente, revealing both congressional lawmakers' opposition to Kissinger's realism and the accelerating momentum of human rights politics on Capitol Hill.[30]

Throughout the first half of the 1970s, however, the White House waged a relentless rearguard action to derail, dilute, or delay congressional human rights legislation. At the center of the battle was the stalwart Kissinger, whose tenure in the National Security Council (NSC) and as secretary of state bridged the tumultuous Watergate era.[31] Kissinger dismissed congressional human rights initiatives as a manifestation of the political turf war between Congress and the White House over the prerogatives of power in the post–Vietnam era. Privately, the secretary worried that human rights legislation would tie the president's hands, undermining the ability of the executive branch to effectively pursue US interests in the international arena. If the attention on human rights continued, the secretary complained in October 1974, "we are going to see a precipitant slide of the American position in the world that is totally unprecedented."[32]

Kissinger perceived congressional efforts to inject a dose of morality in US foreign policy as missing broader US strategic objectives. In his view, the benefits of anticommunist allies in the third world outweighed the cost to US credibility of associating with unsavory regimes. More importantly, détente, the secretary argued, had the potential to decrease tension between the two superpowers. What better way to promote human rights than by stepping back from the brink of thermonuclear war? As Kissinger told reporters after Nixon and Brezhnev signed the Basic Principles of Relations, "It is an event of considerable significance that the countries whose seemingly irreconcilable hostility has characterized the entire postwar period, and the two countries which, between themselves or, indeed, individually have the capacity to destroy humanity are making an effort . . . which would reduce the dangers of war and which would enable them to promote a more stable international system."[33] By contrast, pressing the Soviets on domestic human rights abuses would, in Kissinger's view, simply put the Kremlin on the defensive. "I don't think it is proper for you to start lecturing them about freedom of speech," the secretary of state had advised Nixon in the lead-up to the Moscow Summit. Nixon concurred. "Oh no," the president responded, "no, no, no, no, no, no."[34]

Yet by mid-decade, domestic opposition to Kissinger's realist approach to foreign policy closed in on the White House. For their part, liberal internationalists expanded their efforts to distance the United States from repressive allies. In late January 1975, the Congress refused to approve the Ford administration's budgetary requests for South Vietnam. Less than three months later, congressional lawmakers again defied White House efforts to prop up the beleaguered government in Saigon, denying the Ford administration's request for a $722 million supplemental spending package. Bereft of US support, on April 30 the South Vietnamese capital fell to the North Vietnamese.[35]

Congressional restrictions on security assistance were not limited to Vietnam. Lawmakers on Capitol Hill also passed a raft of human rights legislation. US economic assistance was linked to human rights by section 116 of the 1975 International Development and Food Assistance section of the Foreign Assistance Act. Known as the Harkin Amendment after its sponsor, freshman representative Harkin, the amendment stipulated that no US aid be provided "to the government of any country which engages in a consistent pattern of gross violations of internationally recognized human rights," unless it could be shown that the aid would benefit the "poor and needy."[36] Legislators also attached country-specific legislation to security assistance authorization bills, prohibiting the Chilean dictatorship from receiving any US military aid in 1975 and significantly reducing assistance to South Korea.[37] Frustrated with Kissinger's foot-dragging on the issue, liberal internationalists also bombarded the Foreign Service with information requests. In 1975, for example, Fraser pressed the State Department regarding implementation of 502B and, over the course of the year, requested updates on specific human rights cases in Brazil, Bulgaria, Chile, Indonesia, Iraq, Kenya, Mexico, Namibia, South Africa, South Korea, and Taiwan.[38]

Correspondingly, the White House faced a damaging round of congressional investigations that further deepened the animosity between the legislative and executive branches of government. Using his chairmanship of the Senate Select Committee to Study Governmental Operations with Respect to Intelligence Activities, senator Frank Church (D-ID) initiated a broadbased investigation of US intelligence agencies over the past fifteen years. Eventually releasing fourteen reports over the course of 1975 and 1976, the Church Committee revealed CIA assassination attempts on numerous foreign leaders over the previous fifteen years, manipulation of foreign elections, and the Federal Bureau of Investigation's (FBI) examination of hundreds of thousands of suspected subversives. Viewing the episode as part of the larger power struggle with Congress, Kissinger described the investigations as "worse than in the days of McCarthy."[39]

If the Ford administration struggled over the course of 1975 to contain liberal internationalists' human rights initiatives, it faced an even greater threat on its opposite flank. In 1975, attacks on détente by congressional cold warriors, led by Senator Jackson, reached a fever pitch. At the center of the uproar was the Ford administration's decision to participate in the Conference on Security and Cooperation in Europe (CSCE). A series of negotiations involving thirty-five nations, the CSCE talks began in 1972 and culminated three years later with the signing of the Helsinki Final Act. With the talks divided into three "baskets" of issues, the motivations of the participants varied significantly; the Soviets hoped Basket I, emphasizing the "territorial integrity of states," would legitimate Soviet control over Eastern Europe, while Basket II promised greater economic and scientific cooperation. By contrast, many Western European leaders recognized that Basket III, pledging to expand East-West cooperation and affirming the signatory nations' protection of human rights, had the potential to undermine the Iron Curtain. Ever the realist, Kissinger viewed the nonbinding accords with a mix of disinterest and skepticism and considered President Ford's signing of the Final Act of the CSCE in Helsinki on August 2, 1975, as little more than a sop to Western European allies. "No matter what goes into the final act," Kissinger had dismissively confided to the Soviet foreign minister Andrei Gromyko, "I don't believe the Soviet Union will ever do anything it doesn't want to."[40]

In fact, over the subsequent decade the Helsinki Final Act would spur the development of a powerful transnational movement focused on monitoring Soviet compliance with the agreement's human rights provisions. In summer 1975, however, Ford's decision to sign the Helsinki Final Act was excoriated as an act of appeasement by cold warriors in the United States. Jackson led the charge. "For three decades, the Soviets have sought formal Western recognition of their domination of Eastern Europe, just as they have sought international recognition of their quest of the Baltic states," he declared. "The President's signature on the CSCE declarations will be invoked by the Soviets as a sign of the West's retreat from this crucial point of principle."[41] Ford's refusal to meet with Solzhenitsyn in July made matters significantly worse; opposition to détente mounted on Capitol Hill, while the spurned dissident denounced the CSCE agreement in widely publicized remarks as "a betrayal of Eastern Europe."[42] The administration, Ford glumly admitted to Kissinger, had taken "a lot of flak."[43]

Caught in a cross fire between cold warriors and liberal internationalists, the secretary of state went on the rhetorical offensive. Beginning in mid-1975, Kissinger gave speeches in nearly a dozen cities emphasizing the Ford administration's commitment to balancing national security considerations with moral concerns.[44] Indeed, according to one study, Kissinger gave more speeches on human rights in 1976 than any other major political figure.[45] It was a remarkable—albeit rhetorical—about-face for the consummate realist, underscoring how far the issue of morality in US foreign policy had penetrated the domestic political landscape over the past half decade. It was not sufficient, however, to buoy the administration's flagging political fortunes. Struggling to regain the initiative, Ford undertook a major cabinet shake-up in late October that included removing Kissinger as NSC adviser. Although Kissinger's like-minded deputy, Brent Scowcroft, took the helm at the NSC, and Kissinger continued to serve as secretary of state, the president's demotion of the chief architect of détente—the press dubbed it the "Halloween massacre"—was an unmistakable sign of the shifting political landscape.[46]

The changes, however, did little to mollify the administration's critics. In December, the White House suffered another foreign policy setback when senators John Tunney (D-CA) and Dick Clark (D-IA) successfully sponsored legislation cutting off all US foreign assistance to anticommunist military forces operating in Angola, ending a yearlong US effort to counter a Cuban intervention—backed by the Soviets—in the former Portuguese colony.[47] Kissinger took it as a sign of the times, telling the president, "We are living in a nihilistic nightmare. It proves that Vietnam was not an aberration but our normal attitude."[48] With the 1976 election season underway, a beleaguered Ford struggled to stay ahead of the curve, banning the use of the word "détente" by members of his administration.[49] Yet the White

House had no viable alternative to the defining feature of US Cold War strategy since the late 1960s. As a result, "by early 1976," writes Kissinger biographer Jussi Hanhimäki, "the bipartisan attacks and Ford's growing concerns over his election campaign had virtually frozen the administration's ability to conduct meaningful foreign policy."[50]

Ford still hoped to win the 1976 general election. Before he could square off against his Democratic opponent, however, Ford faced an insurgency in his own party. In November 1975, Reagan announced his bid for the Republican presidential nomination. Championing the virtues of small government and low taxes, social conservatism, and a muscular approach to the Cold War, Reagan hoped to capitalize on Ford's low poll ratings and Americans' dissatisfaction with a federal government that had become, Reagan asserted, "more intrusive, more coercive, more meddlesome, and less effective."[51]

Reagan's path to politics had taken an unusual route. A staunch supporter of the New Deal in the Roosevelt era, Reagan enjoyed a successful Hollywood film career in the late 1930s and the 1940s. By the end of the decade, however, Reagan was shifting to the political right. He had become a fierce opponent of federal taxes, particularly the progressive income tax, which he considered a disincentive to productivity. "You could only make four pictures and then you were in the top bracket," Reagan recalled of his film career many years later. "So we all quit working after four pictures and went off to the country."[52] Correspondingly, as president of the Screen Actors Guild during a period of protracted, and at times violent, labor disputes, Reagan developed an intense anticommunism. Communist labor activists in Hollywood, Reagan later asserted, used "lies, deceit, violence, or any other tactic that suited them to advance the cause of Soviet expansionism."[53]

Reagan emerged as a nationally recognized conservative figure in the 1950s. With his acting career on the wane, Reagan accepted an offer in 1954 to host a television series sponsored by the General Electric Corporation. The experience propelled Reagan further to the political right. With a salary that placed him in the top marginal tax rate of 94 percent and regularly exposed to the concerns of US businesspeople, Reagan's opposition to federal government taxes and regulation of private enterprise intensified, and he became a rising star in a growing conservative movement that loosely coalesced around opposition to New Deal liberalism.[54] And as he met thousands of General Electric workers and headlined hundreds of speaking engagements, Reagan developed an effective message that combined scathing criticism of the inefficiency and bureaucratic bloat of big-government liberalism with an optimistic rendering of the individual freedom and economic opportunity at the heart of US greatness. Tapped to serve as co-chairman of Republican Arizona senator Barry M. Goldwater's quixotic 1964 presidential campaign against Johnson, Reagan electrified conservatives with a thirty-minute address that packaged his core ideas into a powerful stump speech for a national television audience. Although Goldwater lost in a landslide, Reagan's reputation soared, propelling him to victory in the November 1966 California governor's race.[55]

After serving two terms in Sacramento, the sixty-five-year-old Reagan set his sights on the White House. At the beginning of the 1976 primary season, however, Reagan floundered as Ford swept to victory in the first five primaries. With his campaign on the ropes, Reagan focused on foreign policy, attacking the Ford administration's pursuit of détente as "a one-way street that simply gives the Soviets what they want with nothing in return."[56] Ford had presided over a period of dramatic communist adventurism, Reagan charged, with Soviet-backed proxies threatening Africa, Central America, and Southeast Asia. Reagan also began repeatedly accusing the White House of planning to give away the Panama Canal, telling cheering crowds, "We built it, we paid for it, it's ours, and . . . we are going to keep it."[57] The strategy paid off; tapping into the nationalism and anticommunism of the Republican rank and file in the South, Reagan won a string of primary victories in North Carolina, Texas, Alabama, and Georgia, as well as in his home state of California.

Ford eked out a victory at the Republican National Convention in August, beating Reagan by 117 votes out of 2,257. But the Reagan challenge illuminated widespread right-wing disillusionment with the realist policy prescriptions undergirding US foreign policy during the Nixon-Ford era. Indeed, Reagan's supporters successfully introduced a plank into the Republican Party platform titled "Morality in Foreign Policy," praising Solzhenitsyn as a "great beacon of human courage and morality" and asserting that "we must not grant unilateral favors [to the Soviets] with only the hope of getting future favors in return."[58] A clear repudiation of détente (and Ford's refusal to meet Solzhenitsyn the previous year), the incident brought to center stage a rising chorus of conservative voices demanding that the United States pursue aggressively anticommunist foreign policies consonant with US moral traditions.

The importance of moral concerns in US foreign policy was made further evident in Carter's narrow victory over Ford in the 1976 general election. A virtual unknown at the outset of the campaign, the former Georgia governor turned an outsider status to his advantage, championing a homegrown brand of reformist politics that resonated with liberal voters in the post-Vietnam, post-Watergate era. Carter compensated for a lack of foreign policy experience by repeatedly criticizing the lack of transparency shrouding Kissinger's diplomacy.[59] "Under the Nixon-Ford Administration, there has evolved a kind of secretive 'Lone Ranger' foreign policy—a one-man policy of international adventure," Carter told the New York Foreign Policy Association in a June 1976 luncheon address. "This is not an appropriate policy for America."[60]

To be sure, such criticism reflected Carter's moralism and deeply held religious beliefs. But Carter also recognized that in order to win the election, he would need to appeal to both wings of the fractured Democratic Party. Although he had opposed McGovern's "Come Home, America" campaign in 1972, Carter wooed New Politics liberals four years later by denouncing the Nixon and Ford administrations' support for repressive allies and interventionism abroad.[61] Americans, Carter asserted, felt a "sense of shame" for illiberal US actions taken in the name of the global Cold War, and he emphasized the need to align US foreign policy with traditional US values. "I have always felt that, to the extent that government in all its forms can equal the character of the American people—to that extent, our wrongs can be redressed, our mistakes corrected."[62]

Carter also needed to win the support of liberal cold warriors. Accordingly, he attacked the Nixon-Ford approach to détente as soft on the Soviets and criticized the president's refusal to meet with Solzhenitsyn. "The policy of East-West détente is under attack today because of the way it has been exploited by the Soviet Union," Carter told the Chicago Council on Foreign Relations in March 1976. Meanwhile, Kissinger had wagered his own reputation on the success of détente, Carter asserted, and as a result "he is trumpeting achievements on paper while failing to insist on them in practice."[63]

More significantly, Carter began using the term "human rights" to describe his approach to international affairs. The candidate's own understanding of human rights was distinctly limited and nationalist, a loose synthesis of his belief in US exceptionalism, Christian faith, and experiences as a white Southern liberal with the civil rights movement.[64] Yet Carter increasingly recognized the potential for deploying human rights rhetoric in the 1976 presidential campaign. As Carter's campaign speechwriter Patrick Anderson asserted, "It was seen politically as a no-lose issue. Liberals

liked human rights because it involved . . . getting liberals out of jail in dictatorships, and conservatives liked it because it involved criticisms of Russia."[65]

The importance of the human rights issue in papering over the rift between liberal internationalists and cold warriors was made clear at the 1976
Democratic National Convention. As the delegates began drafting the party
platform, in foreign policy "there was almost no agreement, except, as it
turned out, about human rights," recalled Daniel Patrick Moynihan, a former US representative to the United Nations and a staunch cold warrior.
"On this the two sides shared a humanitarian impulse, although they cer-
tainly didn't see the issue in the same way." Although the Jackson Democrats envisioned human rights as a weapon against Soviet totalitarianism,
and the McGovern Democrats sought to curtail US ties to right-wing dictatorships, there was, Moynihan asserted, "enough common ground to allow a meeting of the minds." Like the broader US human rights movement,
both sides focused on political rights and civil liberties; little consideration
was given to social and economic rights. As Moynihan told fellow delegate
Sam Brown, a former leader in the anti–Vietnam War movement and a dedicated New Politics liberal, "We'll be against the dictators you don't like the
most . . . if you'll be against the dictators we don't like the most."[66]

Appealing to a broad-based constituency, human rights thus played a
signal role in Carter's narrow victory over the Ford administration. To be
sure, at points in the campaign Ford appeared to be his own worst enemy,
such as his baffling assertion during the October presidential debate in San
Francisco that "there is no domination of Eastern Europe, and there never
will be under a Ford Administration."[67] But human rights was the "perfect
unifying principle" for the Carter campaign, as the historian Schlesinger
wrote in an early assessment, connecting with "the most acute contemporary concerns as well as the finest American traditions."[68]

Although Carter embraced human rights late in the campaign, the issue
fit neatly with his administration's vision of forging a new approach to US
foreign policy. A graduate of the United States Naval Academy and a former naval officer, Carter was committed to maintaining the US containment
strategy. Yet Carter also brought to the White House a focus on deepening
global interdependence, and the administration aspired to pursue strategic
objectives without being constrained by the Cold War logic of the previous
quarter century, which had underpinned US support for repressive allies
and interventionism overseas. "For too many years, we've been willing to
adopt the flawed and erroneous principles and tactics of our adversaries,

sometimes abandoning our own values for theirs," Carter declared in a remarkable critique of containment in his May 1977 commencement address at the University of Notre Dame. "We've fought fire with fire, never thinking that fire is better quenched with water. This approach failed, with Vietnam the best example of its intellectual and moral poverty."[69]

Instead, Carter emphasized a striking shift away from the realpolitik of previous administrations. Having declared that the US commitment to human rights "must be absolute" in his inaugural address in January, Carter at Notre Dame asserted that "we can already see dramatic, worldwide advances in the protection of the individual from the arbitrary power of the state."[70] While ignoring this pattern would result in the dissipation of US global influence and moral authority, "to lead it will be to regain the moral stature that we once had." Correspondingly, Carter championed a multilateral approach to international issues. Emphasizing the importance of nuclear nonproliferation and "North-South problems of poverty, development, and global well-being," Carter promised US engagement with "newly influential nations" around the world "to create a wider framework of international cooperation suited to the new and rapidly changing historical circumstances."[71]

The Carter administration's commitment to human rights, noninterventionism, and multilateralism underpinned the thirty-ninth president's signal achievements in foreign affairs. Carter's deep commitment to advancing peace in the Middle East played a signal role in the September 1978 signing of the Camp David Accords by Egyptian president Anwar el-Sadat and Israeli prime minister Menachem Begin. Establishing a framework for a bilateral peace treaty that would be signed the following year, the intense thirteen days of negotiations showcased Carter's diplomatic skills, endurance, and attention to detail.[72] Similarly, the successful signing of the Panama Canal treaties on September 7, 1977, setting a fixed date for returning the Canal Zone to the Panamanian government, showcased Carter's willingness to tackle a politically unpopular issue in the interest of the greater good. For Carter, the treaties were "the ideal fusion of morality and politics," recalled national security adviser Zbigniew Brzezinski. Carter was "doing something good for peace, responding to the passionate desires of a small nation, and yet helping the long-range U.S. national interest."[73]

The Carter administration's most important foreign policy initiative, however, was the effort to institutionalize human rights in US foreign policy. Carter's choice of Patricia Derian to act as assistant secretary of state for human rights and humanitarian affairs signaled an unmistakable sea change from the Nixon-Ford era. A fiery former civil rights worker in Mississippi and a Washington outsider, Derian undertook a sustained effort to insert human rights considerations into the day-to-day workings of US foreign policymaking. In a stark shift from Kissinger's "quiet diplomacy," Derian regularly used strident rhetoric and public forums to cast opprobrium on human rights violating regimes—elating human rights advocates while setting off a firestorm of criticism among career diplomats who understood their primary mission as maintaining a close working relationship with foreign counterparts. Derian was "an activist if there ever was one," noted NSC member Lincoln Bloomfield, and the Human Rights Bureau "soon acquired the opprobrium throughout the buttoned-down elements of the bureaucracy as 'the Human Rights Mafia.'"[74]

The results were mixed. Bureaucratic opposition to the human rights initiative, combined with the Carter administration's lack of a clear strategy, distinctly limited the integration of human rights into US policymaking. Nonetheless, the Carter administration made significant achievements in the field of human rights, especially in US policy toward right-wing dictatorships in Latin America. Carter cut US military assistance to the region from $210 million in 1977 to $54 million in 1979, and, particularly toward the brutal military juntas of the Southern Cone, the administration used the threat of aid cutoffs and No votes in international financial institutions as leverage to encourage human rights improvements, while orchestrating highly visible meetings with local human rights activists.[75] Although clear-cut human rights successes were few and far between, Carter's human rights policy nonetheless provided an unprecedented government-sanctioned arena for human rights advocacy.[76] As one editorial writer accurately noted in the *New York Times*, "By elevating human rights to a prominent, though selective role in U.S. foreign policy, Carter created a new and refreshing situation in which victims of repressive governments do not everywhere assume, as they once did, that Washington is on the side of the jailers and the torturers."[77]

But if Carter succeeded in weaving human rights more fully into the fabric of US foreign policy, the administration failed to create a domestic political consensus around its foreign policy priorities. Restive liberal internationalists protested that Carter's lofty human rights rhetoric failed to translate into across-the-board policy changes. While supportive of the efforts of Derian, congressional human rights advocates pointed to the administration's maintenance of close ties to strategic allies such as South Korea, the Philippines, and Iran as demonstrations of the low priority of the human rights policy in comparison to other strategic goals. Carter's praise for the repressive Iranian leader

Mohammad Reza Pahlavi during a formal visit to Tehran in December 1977, for example, was perceived by liberal internationalists as pandering to a strategic ally.[78] Even in US relations with Latin America—by all accounts the region where human rights considerations had the greatest impact on the formulation and implementation of US policy—the Carter administration was criticized as halfhearted. As Representative Harkin complained in 1978, "One thing that bothers me in this whole human rights thing is that we seem to be projecting a policy in the United States right now through the Carter Administration that I see as more form than substance."[79]

Liberal cold warriors, by contrast, perceived Carter's effort to construct a post–Cold War foreign policy as unrealistic and dangerously shortsighted. Neoconservatives, Wattenberg recalled, were "outraged" by what they perceived as Carter's outright dismissal of the containment strategy in his Notre Dame speech.[80] More to the point, although Carter had worked assiduously to appeal to the Jackson wing of the Democratic Party during the election campaign, "when it came to staffing his administration," wrote Jackson aide Joshua Muravchik, "he included only the McGovernites."[81] Indeed, the Carter administration ignored a list of personnel recommendations from the CDM, and its only member to receive an ambassadorship was assigned to Micronesia.[82] The Carter administration, Jackson aide Elliott Abrams bluntly put it, "froze us out completely."[83]

The Carter administration's apparent lack of a clear strategy in US–Soviet relations further infuriated liberal cold warriors. Carter initially believed he could press the Soviets on human rights without jeopardizing the broader détente framework. Human rights, the president told the press in February 1977, could be "legitimately severed from our inclination to work with the Soviet Union, for instance, in reducing dependence upon atomic weapons and also in seeking mutual and balanced force reductions in Europe."[84] By the summer of 1977, however, the visceral Soviet reaction to the White House human rights offensive had sent a chill through US–Soviet relations. Pressing the Soviets on human rights *and* successfully cooperating pursuing the core elements of détente turned out to be a circle that proved impossible to square, fueling a growing perception among the administration's critics of a president suffering from diplomatic näiveté and an inability to prioritize among competing foreign policy goals.[85]

Deepening Soviet political and military involvement in the Horn of Africa added to the Carter administration's difficulties. As a result, by mid-1978 the administration was under a sustained political attack by cold warriors on both sides of the political spectrum. Revealing the frustration of the Jackson wing of the Democratic Party, the CDM in late June published a report on Carter's foreign policy bluntly titled "Unilateral Restraint: The Experiment That Failed." Having filled his administration with appointees "whose careers are heavily invested in the most hopeful propositions about Soviet behavior," the CDM declared, Carter had proceeded to systematically weaken the US position vis-à-vis the Soviet Union.[86]

Simultaneously, Carter's approach to foreign policy was assailed by a resurgent right wing, with Reagan leading the attack. Two weeks after Carter's commencement address at Notre Dame, Reagan emphasized the importance of applying human rights "with consistency" in an address to the Foreign Policy Association in New York. "With the exception of some earlier and highly publicized comments about the Soviet Union's treatment of dissenters," Reagan continued, "the new administration's foreign policy has aimed most of its human rights criticisms at governments that are no threat to others and that, despite not always behaving as we might like, have nevertheless been our friends."[87] Similarly, in November, Reagan chastised the White House for failing to focus on human rights abuses in the communist world. "We express concern that human rights are being denied to some in Rhodesia, S[outh] Africa & Chíle," Reagan told listeners on his widely circulated daily radio commentary. "But where are the indignant voices protesting the hundreds of thousands of S[outh] Vietnamese, Laotians & Cambodians who are dying of torture & starvation in N[orth] Vietnam[']s concentration camps?"[88]

Reagan was especially critical of the Carter administration's emphasis on human rights in its policy toward right-wing dictatorships in Latin America. "There is an old Indian proverb: Before I criticize a man, may I walk a mile in his moccasins," Reagan told radio listeners in mid-1978. "Patricia Derian and her minions at Mr. Carter's human rights office apparently never heard of it. If they had, they might not be making such a mess of our relations with the planet's seventh largest country, Argentina, a nation with which we should be close friends."[89] Reagan also assailed the Carter administration's restrictions on US assistance to the Chilean dictatorship. Augusto Pinochet "set out to restore the economy of the nation. He promised to restore democratic rule also and to allow elections," Reagan argued. "True they haven't taken place as yet," Reagan admitted, "but there is reason to believe that if & when they do the Gen[eral] might just be the favorite candidate if he chooses to run." In Chile, "prosperity is coming back, inflation has dropped to a fraction of what it was and the food shortages are gone," Reagan concluded. "Sounds like a nice country to be friends with." Sidestepping a growing body of evidence indicating that tens of thousands of perceived subversives had been kidnapped, tortured, and murdered at the hands of Argentine and Chilean state security personnel, Reagan decried Carter's human rights policy as demonstrating an "inability to forgive any character flaws at all in those nations which have been our friends & allies back through the years."[90]

It was the Carter administration's strong support for the Panama Canal treaties, however, that brought right-wing opposition to center stage. Although opposition to the treaties ultimately failed to prevent Senate ratification, by framing the debate in nationalist terms that characterized treaty supporters as defeatist sellouts, right-wing activists such as Richard A. Viguerie mobilized a massive campaign of grassroots opposition, accelerating the coalescence of disparate strains of conservative activism into the blossoming New Right political movement. "The New Right came out of the Panama Canal fight with no casualties, not even a scar," Viguerie later asserted.[91] The brouhaha over the treaty debate also propelled Reagan further into the conservative limelight. Dismissing Panamanians as ungrateful beneficiaries of US development assistance and assailing the Carter administration's support for the treaties as a callow abdication of the United States' global leadership, Reagan concluded that the "logical and honorable course" would be "for Panama to offer to buy the canal. How do we reconcile yielding to a demand that we hand it over free of charge plus giving them $70 mil[lion] a year for taking it off our hands?"[92]

As domestic political opposition to the Carter administration's foreign policies intensified, Cold War tension surged. In the Horn of Africa, the Soviet intervention continued; by 1979, there were more than seven thousand civilian and military experts from the Soviet bloc in Ethiopia.[93] The Carter administration also faced the nearly simultaneous implosion of long-standing client regimes in Iran and Nicaragua. In Tehran, undeterred by the imposition of martial law, a wave of mass demonstrations, strikes, and riots forced the shah to flee the country in January 1979. By early spring, under the guidance of the radical Islamic nationalist Ayatollah Ruhollah Khomeini, Iran had shifted from a geostrategically critical US ally to a deeply hostile theocratic republic.

Almost simultaneously, eight thousand miles away in Managua, Nicaragua, the Carter administration's tepid efforts to broker a nonviolent political transition between a loose coalition of moderates and the teetering authoritarian regime of Anastasio Somoza Debayle collapsed. The small Central American nation quickly devolved into a grisly war zone between Somoza's brutal National Guard and tens of thousands of homegrown revolutionaries, who filled the ranks of the leftist Frente Sandinista de Liberación Nacional (Sandinista National Liberation Front [FSLN]). Six months later, thousands of ecstatic Nicaraguans crowded the central plaza of the largely destroyed capital to celebrate the overthrow of the Somoza dictatorship, setting off alarm bells in Washington as top US policymakers worried that the political sea change could lead to leftist revolutionary upheaval throughout the region.

In the face of aggressive Soviet initiatives in Africa and the deepening crises in Iran and Nicaragua, Carter shifted toward a more traditional US Cold War posture. Illuminating the rising influence in the administration of National Security Adviser Brzezinski, human rights during the second half of Carter's term moved to the back burner as a US policy priority. The Soviet invasion of Afghanistan in late December 1979 accelerated Carter's transition to a hard-line Cold War stance. "My opinion of the Russians has changed most drastically in the last week than even the previous two and a half years before that," Carter told the press. Describing the invasion in his State of the Union address as "the most serious threat to peace since the Second World War," the president moved with alacrity to establish an updated version of the containment doctrine. "An attempt by any outside force to gain control of the Persian Gulf region will be regarded as an assault on the vital interests of the United States of America," Carter declared, "and such an assault will be repelled by any means necessary, including military force."[94] More concretely, Carter shelved the SALT II treaty negotiations and increased US aid to Pakistan and Afghan insurgents, while also restricting US high-technology transfers to the Soviet Union, curtailing Soviet fishing rights in US waters, embargoing US grain exports to the USSR, and boycotting the 1980 Moscow Olympics.[95]

The Carter administration's newfound toughness in US-Soviet relations did little, however, to assuage domestic critics. Led by the Committee on the Present Danger (CPD), cold warriors on the right lashed out at the White House for its perceived weakness in the face of a growing Soviet threat. Co-founded by Richard Allen in 1975 as a pressure group to oppose détente, the CPD championed a robust US commitment to confronting the Soviet Union. As the committee asserted in its founding document, "The principal threat to our nation, to world peace, and to the cause of freedom is the Soviet drive for dominance based upon an unparalleled military buildup."[96] Following the 1976 election the CPD quickly emerged as a biting critic of Carter's foreign policies, publishing detailed policy briefs that exaggerated Soviet strategic and conventional military superiority and Moscow's expansionistic ambitions in the interest of galvanizing domestic support for a rapid US military buildup.[97]

In the aftermath of the Soviet invasion of Afghanistan, the committee's criticism reached a fever pitch. The Carter administration "has, by words and acts of restraint, taken one unilateral step after another in the hope that the Soviet Union would accept such a policy of restraint for itself. The results of these efforts have been uniformly negative," the CPD declared in mid-January 1980. "Pursuing a policy built on illusion, we have been adrift and uncertain while the Soviet Union expanded its power and empire on every continent and on all the seas." Whether the United States could rapidly and substantively increase its military strength, the committee gravely concluded, "will determine whether the 1980 crisis is the forerunner of catastrophe for the non-Communist world or whether it marks a turning point toward restoring peace with security and freedom."[98]

The CPD also emerged as a key source of information for Reagan. As the 1980 presidential campaign got underway, Allen was meeting regularly with Reagan and the CPD was sending foreign policy material to the candidate "three or four times a week, if not daily."[99] Indeed, Reagan's withering attacks on the Carter administration's foreign policies in the lead-up to election day bore the unmistakable imprint of the committee's alarmist Cold War rhetoric. "Mr. Carter has failed in his most fundamental duty as President," Reagan asserted on the campaign trail in late January 1980. "His continual failure to give the Soviet Union clear and unmistakable signals concerning our vital strategic interests is driving the country closer to military confrontation and the risk of nuclear war."[100] Moreover, Carter had presided over a dramatic weakening of the United States vis-à-vis the Soviet Union, Reagan repeatedly told listeners. The USSR "surpasses us in virtually every category of military strength," the candidate told the Chicago Council on Foreign Relations in March.[101] "The Soviets keep outspending us in strategic arms by nearly three to one," Reagan asserted in a stump speech the following month. "And, in conventional arms, their investment continues to be nearly twice as large as ours." US national security, Reagan warned, "will not, and cannot, be found in some rhetorical doctrine, or in deceptive manipulation of the defense budget."[102]

More broadly, Reagan portrayed the Carter administration as demonstrating the defeatism, isolationism, and self-abasement characteristic of New Politics liberalism. Carter's weak-kneed and woolly-headed policy initiatives, Reagan contended, had alienated allies and emboldened enemies. "The unwillingness of the Carter Administration to make our case is pervasive," Reagan told listeners at a campaign rally in March. "We apologize, compromise, withdraw and retreat; we fall silent when insulted and pay ransom when we are victimized."[103] Reagan sounded a similar theme at the Republican National Convention in July. "America's defense strength is at its lowest ebb in a generation, while the Soviet Union is vastly outspending us in both strategic and conventional arms," he told cheering supporters. Dismissing the Carter administration as living "in the world of make-believe," Reagan asserted that "the rest of us . . . live in the real world. It is here that disasters are overtaking our nation without any real response from Washington."[104]

Significantly, by 1979 liberal cold warriors were sounding a similar theme, especially in the pages of the neoconservative magazine *Commentary*. Jeane J. Kirkpatrick's seminal article "Dictatorships and Double Standards" was a particularly influential example of liberal hawks' frustration with the Carter administration. A lifelong Democrat and a founding member of the CDM, Kirkpatrick had gained a reputation over the course of the 1970s as a fierce opponent of the McGovern wing of the Democratic Party. Taking up her pen in response to ongoing revolutionary upheaval in Iran and Nicaragua, Kirkpatrick argued that the contradictory impulses behind Carter's emphasis on noninterventionism and opposition to right-wing authoritarians had resulted in distinctly misguided US policies. On a practical level, by withholding US assistance and pressing for political liberalization in Iran and Nicaragua at precisely the moment the two regimes faced intensifying guerrilla insurgencies, the Carter administration had played a key role in weakening the authority of the shah and Somoza. "Hurried efforts to force complex and unfamiliar political practices on societies lacking the requisite political culture, tradition, and social structures not only fail to produce desired outcomes; if they are undertaken at a time when the traditional regime is under attack, they actually facilitate the job of the insurgents," Kirkpatrick asserted. "Vietnam presumably taught us that the United States could not serve as the world's policeman"; she continued, "it should also have taught us the dangers of trying to be the world's midwife to democracy when the birth is scheduled to take place under conditions of guerrilla war."[105]

On a deeper level, Kirkpatrick argued that the Iran and Nicaragua episodes illuminated the ill effects of the Carter administration's "progressive liberalism," characterized by "a posture of continuous self-abasement and apology vis-à-vis the Third World." In an effort to move beyond the binary logic of the Cold War, Kirkpatrick argued, Carter had accepted "at face value the claim of revolutionary groups to represent 'popular' aspirations and 'progressive' forces—regardless of the ties of these revolutionaries to the Soviet Union," and had weakened long-standing US allies at the very moment they faced existential crises. The president was convinced, Kirkpatrick argued, "that the U.S. had, as our enemies said, been on the wrong side of history in supporting the status quo and opposing revolution." Yet this approach, she continued, was entirely misguided, since "there is no instance of a revolutionary 'socialist' or Communist society becoming democratized," while right-wing autocracies, by contrast, "do sometimes evolve into democracies." The Carter administration's policy toward Iran and Nicaragua, Kirkpatrick concluded, failed to recognize that "if victorious, violent insurgency headed by Marxist revolutionaries is unlikely to lead to anything but totalitarian tyranny."[106]

Tension between liberal cold warriors and the Carter administration culminated in a January 1980 breakfast meeting between Carter and a dozen leading members of the CDM. Perhaps not surprisingly, the meeting was a dismal failure. In a later interview, Kirkpatrick put it mildly: "We found that our conceptions of the Soviet Union and Soviet strategy and intentions and actions were just very substantially different than his, and they remained that way."[107] Indeed, dismissing the CDM members' appeal for an aggressive US human rights campaign against the Soviet Union, Carter turned to US efforts to promote human rights in South America—a region of distinct disinterest to the Soviet-focused CDM contingent. Recalling the incident nearly three decades later, Wattenberg was still dumbfounded. "Carter went on about a difficult human rights situation in Ecuador. (Ecuador!) Perhaps we could help there. Perhaps we could. But we were interested in human rights not only for idealistic reasons but because it was an issue with which to hammer our superpower adversary, the Soviet Union."[108]

As liberal cold warriors' frustration with Carter reached the breaking point, Richard Allen sensed opportunity. From his position at the CPD, Allen recognized that Reagan's single-minded focus on confronting the Soviet Union combined with his determination to reverse the gains made by New Politics liberals over the course of the 1970s placed the former California governor at the center of a constellation of Republican and Democratic hawks seeking to re-create the bipartisan consensus that had guided US foreign policy in the early Cold War era. Indeed, by 1980, the Reaganites and the liberal cold warriors were offering almost identically negative critiques of the Carter administration; in an analysis strikingly similar to neoconservative critiques in the pages of *Commentary*, for example, Reagan speechwriter Tony Dolan assailed the Carter administration for filling the State Department and the NSC with "McGovernites and compulsive defeatists."[109]

Acting as an "intellectual impresario and talent scout for Reagan," as one journalist later put it, Allen began deftly working to convince members of the CDM to join the ranks of the CPD.[110] As Allen recalled in a later interview, "Knowing Reagan's thinking and seeing where the committee was going, I thought to myself, *well this would be an extraordinary opportunity to build a bipartisan coalition.* So I set my sights on bringing the committee over a bridge that I would construct to meet with Reagan."[111] The strategy worked. Over the course of 1980, thirteen members of the CDM's foreign policy task force joined the CPD.[112] Jeane Kirkpatrick was one of the erstwhile Democrats to make the transition. Allen had given Reagan a copy of "Dictatorships and Double Standards" to read on a transcontinental flight in late 1979. "I'm going to borrow some of her elegant phraseology," Reagan told Allen the following day on the phone from California. "Who is she?" Allen moved into action, setting up a series of meetings and ultimately convincing Kirkpatrick to join the Reagan camp. "I took her down to the Potomac," Allen told the *Washington Post*, "and baptized her."[113]

The defection of Cold War liberals from the Democratic Party was a signal victory for the Reagan campaign. "One cannot overemphasize the importance of this historic coalition," Allen later wrote. "It assisted in the process of Reagan's mastery of subjects such as arms control, military hardware, force structure, budgeting for national security, intelligence capabilities and the like, and assisted him in testing and honing his views on grand strategy."[114] More to the point, the neoconservative exodus underscored how far the US political terrain had shifted over the course of the fraught 1970s. It was a development few could have predicted at the outset of the decade, when the Nixon administration's support for détente defined the US engagement with the international arena. Yet the openly realist approach of the Nixon-Ford-Kissinger era ultimately proved short-lived. By 1975, the White House was struggling to keep an even keel amid a storm of congressional human rights activism, as liberal internationalists sought to curtail US ties to anticommunist dictatorships and hawks worked to shine an international spotlight on the plight of captive peoples of the communist world.

In an uncertain decade defined by the US defeat in Vietnam, the importance of moral considerations in US foreign policy was particularly evident in Carter's slim victory in the 1976 presidential election. A Washington outsider completely lacking foreign policy experience, Jimmy Carter emphasized a transparency and honesty that appealed to US voters in the post-Vietnam, post-Watergate era, while his embrace of loosely defined human rights rhetoric served to bridge (albeit temporarily) the deeply divided Democratic Party. Reagan's landslide victory in 1980, however, made it starkly clear that Carter's emphasis on noninterventionism, multilateralism, and human rights in US foreign policy had failed to create a lasting foreign policy consensus.

To be sure, foreign policy considerations were only one of the defining issues in the 1980 election. Economic worries, in particular, were a key factor in Carter's defeat.[115] Yet Cold War fears loomed large in the 1980 campaign. As the Carter administration struggled to secure the release of the Americans held hostage in Iran and with the Red Army ensconced in Kabul, Reagan's tough Cold War rhetoric resonated with an American people increasingly concerned with an apparent erosion of US power and rising Soviet adventurism. Indeed, polls over the course of the Carter presidency showed a dramatic uptick in the percentage of Americans who believed the Soviet Union had grown stronger than the United States.[116] Effectively portraying Carter as embodying a defeatism and näiveté emblematic of post-1968 New Politics liberalism, Reagan offered a vision of a rejuvenated United States in the titanic battle against Soviet totalitarianism—with US military superiority regained, confidence restored, and the trauma of Vietnam forgotten. It was an image the majority of voters found appealing. Despite a low voter turnout—only 52 percent of voting-age Americans went to the polls—the sixty-nine-year-old former governor of California decisively defeated Carter in the November 1980 election, winning forty-six of the fifty states.[117] Moreover, on Capitol Hill, Republicans gained a Senate majority for the first time since 1954 and picked up thirty-three seats in the House—their biggest gain in more than a decade.[118]

Four years after sharing his vision of a US Cold War victory with Allen, Ronald Reagan stood poised to be sworn in as the United States' commander in chief. The détente era had ended—"buried," as Brzezinski had memorably declared, "in the sands of the Ogaden."[119] Relations between the United States and the Soviet Union were on a razor's edge; an end to the Cold War was nowhere in sight. Yet members of the incoming administration were optimistic. As Kirkpatrick later remarked, the election of 1980 "marked the end to a national identity crisis."[120]

Chapter 2

"A Hostile Takeover"

The Reagan Administration and US Cold War Policy, 1981-1982

In his first press conference as the fortieth president of the United States, Ronald Reagan's sunny optimism was clouded by the existential threat posed by the Soviet Union. The United States, Reagan warned, was in danger. The Cold War—that twilight struggle for hearts and minds punctuated over the past three decades by bloody Chosins and Khe Sanhs—threatened the United States as never before. The Soviets were dedicated to "the promotion of world revolution and a one-world Socialist or Communist state, whichever word you want to use," Reagan told reporters. Détente in the 1970s had failed; it was a "one-way street that the Soviet Union has used to pursue its own aims." In this grim contest the West could expect no quarter; Soviet leaders, the president acidly concluded, had "openly and publicly declared that the only morality they recognize is what will further their cause, meaning they reserve unto themselves the right to commit any crime, to lie, to cheat."[1]

Reagan's tough talk came as no surprise. He had delivered the same message hundreds of times over the course of the 1980 election campaign in stump speeches and interviews across the nation. The Soviets were "monsters," he repeatedly declared, dedicated to an implacable and unending crusade to spread "Godless communism" throughout the world.[2] "Let us not delude ourselves," he told an interviewer in June 1980. "The Soviet Union underlies all the unrest that is going on. If they weren't engaged in this game of dominoes, there wouldn't be any hot spots in the world."[3]

Now as the United States's commander in chief, Reagan hailed his sweeping victory in the November election as a mandate to reverse the perceived failures of US policy during the détente era. Reagan's priorities were clear. The president aimed to strengthen the US economy vis-à-vis the Soviet Union through a major package of supply-side economic reforms. Correspondingly, Reagan believed a significant military buildup would give the United States the leverage to engage the Soviets from a position of strength, while also ramping up the pressure on the faltering Soviet economy by forcing the Kremlin to allocate additional scarce resources to toward defense.[4] The administration also aimed to raise the costs of Soviet expansionism. In what would later become known as the Reagan Doctrine, the administration was poised to aid anticommunist militants battling the Soviets and their proxies in the third world.

In the Reagan administration's struggle against communism, Central America took center stage. The White House viewed both the leftist Frente Sandinista de Liberación Nacional (Sandinista National Liberation Front [FSLN]), which had assumed power in Nicaragua following the bloody 1979 revolution, and the blossoming insurgency in neighboring El Salvador through the lens of the East-West confrontation. Emphasizing Nicaragua's proximity to the continental United States and geostrategically vital sea-lanes, top administration officials warned that a Soviet satellite in Central America would pose a distinct threat to US security interests. The administration also viewed Central America as a defining test case of the Reagan Doctrine. Finally, underscoring the importance of domestic politics in foreign policy, the Reagan team understood Central America as a battleground for defeating the inroads of post-1968 liberalism in US foreign policy, particularly the emphasis of Jimmy Carter's administration on multilateralism, noninterventionism, and human rights.

But what role should human rights play in US Cold War policy? Over the course of the previous decade, human rights had emerged as a flashpoint in a fierce struggle over the direction of US foreign policy in the aftermath of the Vietnam War. Embraced for different reasons by both liberal internationalists and Cold War hawks, human rights conditionality had been inserted piecemeal into the US foreign policymaking process by congressional lawmakers over the opposition of the Richard M. Nixon and Gerald R. Ford administrations and further advanced by Carter's effort to bring "competence and compassion" to the White House. Correspondingly, dozens of nongovernmental human rights advocacy groups had taken up residence inside the Washington, DC, Beltway and had established a reputation for influential lobbying and effective mobilization. At the time of the 1980 election, in other words, despite a resurgence of Cold War tension, human rights remained a powerful issue in shaping US foreign policy.

Viewing human rights as a Carter-era holdover, the Reagan administration entered the White House determined to reaffirm ties with Cold War allies regardless of their human rights records. With top Reagan officials focused on convincing Congress to back the president's economic plan and increased defense spending, and with secretary of state Alexander M. Haig Jr. increasingly mired in White House infighting, the newly minted US ambassador to the United Nations, Jeane J. Kirkpatrick, played an influential role in defining the administration's approach toward the developing world. Dubbed the Kirkpatrick Doctrine, Reagan's efforts to normalize relations with repressive allies along with deepening US involvement in Central America sent a clear signal that Cold War concerns would trump human rights considerations.

Yet, by mid-1981, the Reagan administration was battling a stiff political headwind on the issue of human rights. In the face of bipartisan opposition on Capitol Hill and from nongovernmental human rights advocates, White House officials increasingly recognized that the effort to downgrade human rights was becoming a costly liability. In response, the administration pivoted. Embracing human rights as central to the United States' traditional moral concerns as well as US leadership in the Cold War, Reagan officials claimed the mantle of defending human rights in a world defined by the struggle against totalitarian communism. But from the outset, the Reagan administration's political worldview shaped its understanding of human rights. Emphasizing political rights and civil liberties and excluding social and economic rights, the White House advanced a human rights policy that was infused with American exceptionalism and served to justify aggressive US Cold War policies.

Reagan's victory in the 1980 election, recalled Robert M. Gates, precipitated the "most extraordinary transition period of my career." From his vantage point at the CIA, Gates watched as the Reagan team "orchestrated a comprehensive battle plan to seize control of a city long believed to be in enemy hands." Throughout the election campaign, Reagan had echoed the alarmist assessments of the influential Committee on the Present Danger (CPD), depicting Carter's emphasis on multilateralism, noninterventionism, and human rights as alienating allies and emboldening enemies. Following the November 1980 election, the Reagan administration took office determined to dramatically redirect US foreign policy. The Reaganites "saw their arrival as a hostile takeover," recalled Gates, and they unleashed "a political blitzkrieg."[5]

The result was a wrenching transition. Top Reagan officials dismissed the Carter administration's offer of exit briefings on national security issues. "You'd better be out of that office at noon on January 20," Reagan's national security adviser Richard V. Allen warned Robert A. Pastor, the director of Latin American and Caribbean affairs on Carter's National Security Council (NSC), "or police are going to come and take you out of that office."[6] Rumors of impending purges at the Departments of State and Defense as well as the CIA created a mix of "resentment and anger, dread and personal insecurity," Gates remembered.[7]

If the Reaganites viewed the State Department as a battleground, the Bureau of Human Rights and Humanitarian Affairs was ground zero. Sporting a bold pinstripe in his first press conference, Secretary of State Haig bluntly informed reporters that "international terrorism will take the place of human rights" as the priority of the Reagan administration.[8] Significantly, such statements echoed the president's own view. "We must change the attitude of our diplomatic corps so that we don't bring down governments in the name of human rights," Reagan told the NSC in early February. "None of them is as guilty of human rights violations as are Cuba and the USSR. We don't throw out our friends just because they can't pass the 'saliva test' on human rights. I want to see that stopped."[9]

Accordingly, the Reagan administration moved quickly to distance itself from Carter's human rights agenda. Top US policymakers repeatedly emphasized in early 1981 that human rights concerns would be pursued through quiet diplomacy rather than instances of public remonstrance—"private arm-twisting," as one administration official put it.[10] Correspondingly, formal invitations to Washington were extended to US allies with poor human rights records, such as South Korean president Chun Doo-Hwan. "In the short time you've had, Mr. President, you've done much to strengthen the tradition of 3,000 years' commitment to freedom," Reagan told Chun, whose repressive military regime, according to the State Department's 1980 human rights country report, deprived Koreans of most "basic political freedoms and rights."[11]

More worryingly for liberal internationalists, Reagan nominated Ernest Lafever for the position of assistant secretary of state for human rights and humanitarian affairs. A conservative political theorist and founder of a right-wing think tank, Lafever had taken a distinctly oppositional position toward congressional human rights legislation. In testimony before a subcommittee of the House Foreign Affairs Committee in July 1979, Lafever asserted, "In my view the United States should remove from the statute books all clauses that establish a human rights standard or condition that must be met by another sovereign government before our government transacts normal business with it, unless specifically waived by the President."[12] Moreover, Lafever had openly encouraged dismantling the Human Rights Bureau during the 1980 presidential campaign.[13]

It was economic policy, however, not foreign policy, that took center stage during the Reagan administration's first months in office. The administration had "three priorities," chief of staff James A. Baker III told Reagan: "economic recovery, economic recovery, and economic recovery."[14] Reagan agreed. The president "had a greater sense of urgency about his economic program than any item on the foreign policy agenda," writes veteran journalist Lou Cannon.[15] Armed with a certainty that a combination of high interest rates, tax cuts, deregulatory measures, and cuts to welfare programs would reinvigorate the US economy, the Reagan administration waded into a bitter struggle with congressional legislators. After very nearly being killed by a crazed would-be assassin only six weeks after the inauguration, Reagan enjoyed an outpouring of public support, and during his rapid recovery the president kept up the pressure on Capitol Hill to pass his budget. By late summer, the White House had achieved a major victory; legislators had agreed to slash taxes over five years by $750 billion—the deepest tax cut in previous US history. Correspondingly, the administration secured a $25 billion cut from welfare programs and was aggressively pursuing a wide range of deregulatory measures.[16]

If economic policy was the top priority in the opening months of 1981, increasing US defense spending was a close second. Reagan was convinced that Soviet defense spending during the 1970s had dramatically outpaced the United States. Only a rapid US military buildup, the president believed, would allow the United States to confront the communist world from a position of strength. Sidestepping the significant rise in military spending during the Carter administration—constant-dollar defense spending rose from $216.4 billion in 1977 to $229.4 billion in 1980—the Reagan administration claimed the 1980 election as a mandate to dramatically increase the defense budget.[17] "What is new is that Americans, last fall, reasserted their belief that our nation must restore its military strength as President Reagan promised," secretary of defense Caspar Weinberger boldly declared. "What is new is that we have decided that America can, and in fact must, remain a great power if we are to keep peace and freedom."[18]

With the Red Army still occupying Afghanistan, congressional legislators shared the administration's concern about Soviet foreign policy adventurism. The White House secured a defense budget increase of 12 percent in fiscal year 1981 and 15 percent the following year. Awash in funds, the Pentagon went on a spending spree that included high–sticker price items such as dozens of B-1 bombers, Trident submarines, and MX intercontinental ballistic missiles, as well as research and development funding for the B-2 Stealth bomber and the Trident II missile.[19]

As the White House worked overtime to secure the president's economic agenda and accelerate the US defense buildup in the first half of 1981, Reagan's inner circle of advisers—the so-called troika consisting of Chief of Staff Baker, counselor to the president Ed Meese, and deputy chief of staff Mike Deaver—worked to tamp down aggressive Cold War rhetoric to avoid ruffling congressional feathers. When anticommunist hard-liner Richard E. Pipes, the NSC director of East European and Soviet affairs, was quoted in the press declaring that "Soviet leaders would have to choose between peacefully changing their communist system in the direction followed by the West, or go to war," the administration quickly backtracked.[20] Similarly, the troika derailed Secretary of State Haig's proposal in early 1981 to put down a "marker" in the Western Hemisphere against communist subversion. Testifying before the House Foreign Affairs Committee in March, Haig made front-page news by charging that the Soviets were training "thousands of terrorists" and, using Cuba as a proxy, had a "hit list" of nations to be taken over in Central America.[21] The former four-star general wanted to strike first. "Give me the word and I'll make that island a fucking parking lot," Haig fulminated at one White House meeting. Instead, an alarmed Deaver used his control over the president's schedule to prevent Haig from ever meeting alone with Reagan.[22]

With the president focused on domestic policy and infighting between Haig and White House insiders escalating, Kirkpatrick emerged over the spring of 1981 as a leading voice defining the Reagan administration's approach toward the developing world. From the outset of her term at the United Nations, Kirkpatrick characterized the 1980 election as constituting a decisive and historic political shift in US politics and society, ushering in a new era of hardheaded realism in US foreign policy. "We have taken off our 'kick me' sign," Kirkpatrick asserted, when questioned at the United Nations on how the Reagan administration would differ from its predecessor. "Does that mean that if you're kicked, you'll kick back?" she was asked. "Well, not necessarily," Kirkpatrick replied, "but it sure means that if we're kicked, we won't apologize."[23]

Indeed, Kirkpatrick moved quickly to reassert US standing in the UN General Assembly, where the United States was regularly subjected to bruising criticism from third-world nationalists and ambassadors from the communist world. It was "an almost obsessive goal" Kirkpatrick recalled in a later interview, "to secure decent treatment for the United States." Following in the footsteps of President Ford's fiery ambassador Daniel Patrick Moynihan, Kirkpatrick attacked foreign criticism head-on. "I always said that my goal for the U.S. at the U.N. was that we should be treated with as much fundamental respect and consideration as any small third world country, which we were not," Kirkpatrick asserted.[24] Accordingly, she rejected outright politically charged terms such as "North-South" and "nonaligned" on the basis that such groups were "not a monolithic, integrated whole," but "disparate nations with disparate interests."[25] In the fall of 1981, Kirkpatrick would send letters to forty third-world ambassadors, accusing them of disseminating "base lies" and engaging in "malicious attacks upon the good name of the United States." She also worked to raise the risk of opposing the United States at the United Nations for nations receiving US foreign aid by pointedly sending their UN voting records to the US Congress.[26]

Kirkpatrick's ascent to the United Nations was a remarkable feat for a woman with no policymaking experience and lacking the almost de rigueur degrees from an Ivy League institution. Stranger still was Kirkpatrick's self-identification as a liberal, even as she made a defining imprint in the most conservative presidential administration since Calvin Coolidge. Excoriated by liberal internationalists as a conservative reactionary, in reality Kirkpatrick's anticommunism had deep roots in the hard-line approach to the Soviet Union that had defined US liberalism in the early Cold War era. The daughter of a marginally successful oil well driller, Kirkpatrick—born Jeane Duane Jordan in 1926—spent a bookish childhood in quiet Duncan, Oklahoma, 160 miles northwest of Dallas, Texas. She was a motivated, studious child who taught herself to read and, at age ten, saved three dollars from her allowance to buy a thesaurus. Kirkpatrick was also exposed early on to the crosscurrents of Midwestern political life. Her father imbued the family with an entrepreneurial spirit and an aspiration for upward mobility. "The free enterprise system really worked for my father," Kirkpatrick's brother, Jerry Jordan, later asserted. "Through hard work and saving he was able to have an interest in his own rig by the time he was 26. Then he bought an interest in a second rig. He was able to borrow $60,000—a lot of money in the 1930s—to convert his rigs from steam to diesel, and follow the oil boom into Illinois." Her grandfather, by contrast, was a founder of the Socialist and Populist Parties in his county, and Kirkpatrick claimed to have populist leanings throughout her life.[27]

Indeed, Kirkpatrick considered herself a socialist as an undergraduate in the mid-1940s. After attending Stephens College in Missouri for two years, Kirkpatrick transferred to Barnard College in New York, graduating in 1948. By the time she had finished a master's degree in political science from Columbia University two years later, Kirkpatrick's political worldview had been transformed by revelations of the immensity of Nazi and Soviet atrocities. "I was impressed by the capacity of politics and government to create human misery on a massive scale," Kirkpatrick later recalled. "I became interested in totalitarianism."[28] She also became deeply anti-Stalinist.

Taking a position in 1950 as a research analyst at the Intelligence and Research Bureau of the State Department, she met the political scientist Evron Kirkpatrick, who had served as assistant director for research and analysis in the Office of Strategic Services during the Second World War. They married in 1955. A deeply committed Democrat, Evron Kirkpatrick had played an active role in Minnesota politician Hubert H. Humphrey's successful 1944 merging of Minnesota's left-wing Farmer-Labor Party and the state's Democratic Party and as an adviser during Humphrey's successful bid for mayor of Minneapolis in 1945. Kirkpatrick subsequently helped draft Humphrey's landmark address advocating expansive domestic action on civil rights at the 1948 Democratic National Convention in Philadelphia. Over the subsequent decade, while serving as the director of the American Political Science Association, Kirkpatrick continued to actively support Humphrey through three terms in the US Senate and a failed 1968 presidential election bid.[29]

In the process, Jeane Kirkpatrick was integrated into her husband's close-knit circle of Cold War liberals and quickly emerged as a political intellectual in her own right, teaching part-time and raising three children while honing her ideas on the differences between authoritarian and totalitarian regimes in a PhD dissertation on the political legacy of Argentine dictator Juan Perón.[30] "She had a tremendous capacity for work," recalled one of Evron Kirkpatrick's colleagues. "It was evident she would succeed." After the housework was done, he continued, "about 10 o'clock at night Jeane would say, 'You'll have to excuse me. This is when I do my work.'"[31] A deep engagement in Democratic Party politics permeated the Kirkpatricks' family life; on one occasion, one son related that the children at his nursery school had been discussing "what we are." Asked what he meant, the child replied, "Well, you know, Jimmy said he was a Catholic, and Annie said she was a Jew, and Tim said he was a Quaker—and I told them we were Democrats." Recounting the incident, Jeane Kirkpatrick noted, "It takes a family of serious Democrats to produce a response like that."[32]

Accordingly, the fracturing of the Democratic Party amid opposition to the Vietnam War and New Left political activism made the 1960s and 1970s a deeply disturbing era for Kirkpatrick. It was a period, she later asserted, in which the United States confronted a "national identity crisis" centering on the "notion that we were a sick society presided over by a repressive government whose motives were base and whose methods were immoral and whose soul was corrupt." In Kirkpatrick's view, "radical liberalism" fueled a period of "self-hatred . . . which swept through our institutions—sweeping aside the lessons of history and common sense and wreaking havoc, of course, with our schools, our families, our economy and our politics."[33] Characteristically, Kirkpatrick was also a biting critic of the women's liberation movement. "She believed that she herself was a successful feminist, but also thought her accomplishments had value precisely because they had been achieved without the institutional brace of a movement, the ululations of victimhood, or maudlin sympathy from the media," writes the biographer Peter Collier. "Obtusely, she also couldn't see why her path—that of rugged female individualist plowing through what the new feminism saw as insuperable structural obstacles—shouldn't be regarded as a default option for women."[34]

It was foreign policy, however, that remained Kirkpatrick's primary area of interest. Accepting a tenured position at Georgetown University in 1968, Kirkpatrick was a fierce opponent of the anti–Vietnam War movement, which she viewed as an attack "on the integrity of our government and culture." As she later asserted, "I always believed in the importance of truth, law and authority. Military kids grow up with such values. So do Oklahoma kids."[35] Appalled at George McGovern's antiwar platform in the 1972 presidential campaign, Kirkpatrick voted for Nixon and cofounded the Coalition for a Democratic Majority (CDM), a political lobbying organization for traditional liberals.[36]

Although Kirkpatrick voted for Jimmy Carter in 1976, she became an outspoken critic of Carter's foreign policy approach, particularly the administration's emphasis on nonintervention, multilateralism, and human rights. Kirkpatrick's article "Dictatorships and Double Standards," published in November 1979 in the neoconservative magazine *Commentary*, quickly became a seminal critique of the Carter administration's response to the political crises leading up to the revolutions in Iran and Nicaragua. It also propelled Kirkpatrick into then-candidate Ronald Reagan's inner circle. The Carter administration, she acidly wrote shortly before the election, "has given us a brand of McGovernism without McGovern that is, at best, only slightly less objectionable than the authentic, original product."[37]

Reagan's subsequent decision to appoint Kirkpatrick US ambassador to the United Nations was a remarkable achievement for the bookish native of Duncan, Oklahoma. She was the first woman to serve as the United States' UN ambassador and the only woman to serve as a member of Reagan's NSC, as well as the president's smaller National Security Planning Group. As the *New York Times* noted many years later, "No woman had ever been so close to the center of presidential power without actually residing in the White House."[38] Kirkpatrick herself projected an image of staid equanimity. "Once one moves into the upper levels of decision-making in this society, one moves almost exclusively into masculine domains," she told a journalist. "I think there are some resistances to women, usually easily overcome once one demonstrates that one is serious and competent, and willing to work hard."[39]

If Kirkpatrick's sudden rise was a "Cinderella story," in the words of fellow neoconservative Norman Podhoretz, it also revealed the extent to which Reagan—himself a former Democrat—recognized Kirkpatrick as a kindred spirit in his effort to reverse the inroads of "New Politics" liberalism and advance an aggressive approach to the global Cold War.[40] Indeed, following Reagan's victory, Kirkpatrick emerged as a leading voice in identifying the 1980 election as a defining turning point in US history. Reagan's election reflected a "new consensus" among American voters, she told listeners in an April 1981 address, marking "a return to the norm after the episode of self-doubt that surrounded the Vietnam War." The US electorate had rejected the defeatism and isolationism that had permeated the late 1960s and the 1970s, Kirkpatrick continued, revealing a conviction "that the United States government should once again reflect the views and values of ordinary Americans, should once again affirm the fundamental success of the American experience, and that the principal task of American foreign policy should be the defense of the American national interest."[41] Kirkpatrick saw her own tenure in the Reagan administration in similar terms; as she told a journalist the following July, her goal was to help put "an end to the period of retreat."[42]

Accordingly, in early 1981 Kirkpatrick offered an influential prescription for the Reagan administration's foreign policy approach. The Carter administration's human rights policy had been "utopian," Kirkpatrick asserted in a March 1981 interview in *U.S. News and World Report*, "because it was conducted outside of the political and historical context, and because it didn't work." By establishing a human rights standard that was impossible for most nations to achieve, Kirkpatrick maintained, Carter's policy had devolved into an arbitrary series of judgments that targeted right-wing allies to the detriment of US national security. "The principal function of the policy has been to make us feel good about ourselves," Kirkpatrick continued. "But that is not an appropriate foreign-policy goal."[43]

By contrast, Kirkpatrick emphasized that the Reagan administration would take the "cure of history." As she rather hubristically told members of the Council on Foreign Relations in New York: "The cure of history is nothing more or less than the cure of reality. And if we take the cure of history, we will, I think, discover something about the very essence of freedom and the very essence of human rights. . . . We will discover that the freedom of the American people is based not on the marvelous and inspiring slogans of a Thomas Paine but, in fact, on the careful web of constraints, of permission, of interests, of tradition woven by the founding fathers into the Constitution and explained in the Federalist papers."[44] American freedom, in other words, was rooted in the checks and balances that limited the power of the state and preserved the liberty of citizens rather than in political radicalism manifested as moral claims.

Correspondingly, Kirkpatrick emphasized the existential threat to the United States posed by global communism. "No matter how ill-fed, ill-housed, ill-clothed; no matter how illiterate, no matter how miserable the people . . . have been under their traditional governments, they will be more miserable under communist government," she told listeners at the Conservative Political Action Conference in mid-March 1981. Extrapolating on a central thesis of her article "Dictatorships and Double Standards," Kirkpatrick repeatedly emphasized that totalitarian regimes were categorically different from their authoritarian counterparts. "Nobody doubts that the government of Kaiser Wilhelm, although an autocracy, was less hard on the German people than the government of Adolf Hitler." Like the totalitarianism of Nazi Germany, communism "doesn't produce an economic order than can support a population. It does not produce a social system that provides equal opportunity or a good life for anyone," Kirkpatrick concluded. "It does not work as a human system and . . . the number of refugees which pours out of communist countries decade after decade after decade proves the inhumanity of these systems and their incompatibility with human survival and human realization."[45]

In response to the Soviet challenge, Kirkpatrick championed a muscular US approach to the Cold War. National security, not moral considerations, she contended, should be the foundation of US foreign policy in the 1980s.

"We're not free to have relations *only* with the democratic countries of this world," Kirkpatrick maintained in the *U.S. News and World Report* interview. "And in governments, as in life, there are degrees of evil. To say that measles is less bad than meningitis doesn't make you pro-measles, does it?" To be sure, the UN ambassador concluded, the United States was "revolted" by torture. "But the central goal of our foreign policy should be *not* the moral elevation of other nations, but the preservation of a civilized conception of our own self-interest."[46]

Not surprisingly, Kirkpatrick's criticism of the Carter administration's human rights policy and her emphasis on protecting US national security sparked fierce opposition from liberal internationalists. Her parsing of authoritarian and totalitarian regimes—frequently essentialized by critics as advocating across-the-board support for friendly authoritarians—made the UN ambassador a lightning rod for criticism that her policy prescriptions were unmoored from the United States' moral traditions. Yet Kirkpatrick's hard-line position was far from novel; as her continued self-identification as a liberal in the deeply conservative Reagan administration made clear, her ideas were rooted in the hard-line anticommunism that defined Vital Center liberalism from the late 1940s to the 1960s.

Indeed, national security concerns had dominated US foreign policy in the first quarter century of the Cold War, and American policymakers had used generous transfers of military equipment and extensive counterinsurgency training programs to cultivate close ties with anticommunist authoritarians throughout the developing world.[47] In advocating US support for right-wing allies in the 1980s, Kirkpatrick was, in effect, echoing John F. Kennedy, who confided his fear of communist revolutions to his advisers after the 1961 assassination of the brutal Dominican dictator Rafael Trujillo: "There are three possibilities in descending order of preference: a decent democratic regime, a continuation of the Trujillo regime, or a 'Castro' regime. We ought to aim at the first, but we can't really renounce the second until we are sure that we can avoid the third."[48] Like the Cold War liberals of the Kennedy-Johnson era, Kirkpatrick was a staunch proponent of American exceptionalism, perceiving the United States as the bedrock of the Western alliance, indispensable to the fragile array of political systems that preserved individual liberties and advanced through reformist politics. Given the stakes, supporting unsavory allies was, at times, a necessary evil. "The defense of a civilized conception of the American national interest is not only morally acceptable," Kirkpatrick maintained, "but is in our time a moral imperative."[49]

Significantly, Kirkpatrick's emphasis on US national security tacked closely to Reagan's own belief in American exceptionalism and understanding of the relationship between human rights and US power in the international arena. Kirkpatrick was "without doubt one of the finest Ambassadors to the United Nations this country's ever had," Reagan maintained in January 1983. In a revealing statement illustrating Reagan's own thinking on the issue, the president approvingly noted that Kirkpatrick had delivered a clear message to the United Nations: "The defense of American interests is tantamount to the defense of national independence, liberal democracy, and human rights throughout the world, and our defense of these principles must be considered a moral imperative."[50]

Over the course of early 1981, the Kirkpatrick Doctrine, as the UN ambassador's policy prescriptions came to be known, served as the blueprint for the Reagan administration's reorientation of human rights in US foreign policy. In March, in a major address to the Trilateral Commission, Secretary of State Haig reiterated Kirkpatrick's emphasis on the need to distinguish between authoritarian and totalitarian regimes in US human rights policy, while military leaders from Chile, Brazil, and Argentina were invited to Washington for meetings with top US policymakers.[51] More concretely, in June 1981, the administration approved a $3.2 million sale of jeeps and trucks to Guatemala. In the midst of a vicious, scattershot campaign against leftist insurgents in the predominately Maya-populated western highlands, the Guatemalan government was considered by many human rights advocates to be the worst human rights violator in the Western Hemisphere. Roughly one hundred thousand peasants would be illegally executed over the next two years, many after being tortured.[52] The "great majority," the Inter-American Human Rights Commission reported the following October, were victims of state-sanctioned violence.[53] In a slap to the face of liberal internationalists on Capitol Hill, the White House signed off on the sale by simply removing the trucks from a list of nonmilitary items categorized as security assistance and therefore restricted by congressional human rights legislation.[54]

The following month, Haig announced the United States would no longer oppose loans on human rights grounds in the multilateral development banks to the military governments of Argentina, Chile, Paraguay, and Uruguay. Reported in the press as the Kirkpatrick Doctrine in action, the decision was an unmistakable shift away from the Carter administration, which had made curtailing abuses in the Southern Cone the centerpiece of its human rights policy and had frequently abstained or opposed loans to the four nations from the World Bank and the Inter-American Development Bank.[55] Haig justified the Reagan administration's about-face by emphasizing "dramatic, dramatic reductions" in human rights violations.[56] Levels of state-sanctioned abuses had indeed decreased considerably in all four nations since the peak of the kidnapping, torture, illegal incarceration, and murder of perceived subversives in the previous decade. Yet ongoing repression and a near-total refusal by the Argentine and Chilean military governments to provide an accounting of thousands of disappeared, combined with a spike in abuses over the previous eighteen months in Paraguay and Uruguay, led Amnesty International to quickly release a report repudiating the Reagan administration's claim that the human rights situation in the Southern Cone had markedly improved.[57] Liberal internationalists in Congress were dismayed; the administration, representative Henry S. Reuss (D-WI) asserted, "has played fast and loose with the law."[58]

The most unmistakable display of the Kirkpatrick Doctrine's reorientation of US relations with right-wing allies, however, was undertaken by Jeane Kirkpatrick herself. In August, Kirkpatrick chose Latin America for her first major trip overseas as US ambassador to the United Nations. On a six-nation tour that included Argentina, Uruguay, and Chile, Kirkpatrick emphasized with characteristic candor the Reagan administration's desire for warm relations with anticommunist allies. Carter's human rights policy, she told reporters in Buenos Aires, was based on "a selective negative focus on Latin America."[59] By contrast, the Reagan administration had tried not to "push people around," Kirkpatrick asserted. "And we won't." Similarly, in Santiago, Kirkpatrick pointedly declined to comment on Chile's human rights record and emphasized that the Reagan team intended to "normalize completely its relations with Chile in order to work together in a pleasant way."[60]

Not surprisingly, the UN ambassador was warmly received by the region's military leaders. Chilean dictator Augusto Pinochet was "particularly gratified that Ambassador Kirkpatrick had not come with the intention of offering advice to the military on internal Chilean affairs," the US Embassy cabled Washington. Kirkpatrick's visit, the embassy concluded, "was extremely valuable in accelerating the return to cooperative relations."[61] Others were less sanguine. "A lot of us in the career [foreign] service had the feeling that we were being whip-sawed by a pendulum," recalled George S. Jones, who was assigned to accompany Kirkpatrick on her Latin American tour. "On the one hand we had gone through the Carter administration which in its worst moments and its worst people were pressing to have the most moralistic kind of foreign policy regardless of the interest of the United States, [and] it wouldn't have anything to do with countries it didn't like, even if we had very strong reasons for having something to do with them. Then the pendulum swung to the opposite extreme and here we were with people who seemed to have no moral distinctions at all." Kirkpatrick's determined embrace of repressive right-wing allies, Jones concluded, "was the most severe test possible of our professionalism."[62]

If adapting to the precepts of the Kirkpatrick Doctrine left members of the US diplomatic corps reeling, for Latin American democrats and human rights activists the shift in US foreign policy was decidedly grim. Apparently emboldened by the sea change in US-Chilean relations, Chilean security personnel forced four prominent opposition politicians into exile only two days after Kirkpatrick's departure, including Jaime Castillo Velasco, the president of the Chilean Commission on Human Rights. Castillo had hoped to discuss ongoing abuses in Chile with the UN ambassador during her four-day visit; his efforts to set up a meeting, however, were rebuffed. The result, one opposition member subsequently declared, was a "tragedy for the democratic opposition in Chile."[63]

In tandem with her effort to rebuild relations with the right-wing allies in the hemisphere, Kirkpatrick placed special emphasis on confronting leftist revolutionaries in Central America and the Caribbean. The region was "quite simply the most important place in the world," she asserted at the Conservative Political Action Conference in March 1981. The United States' ability to shore up the Western alliance and project its power across the developing world, Kirkpatrick continued, depended on keeping the cost of maintaining security in the Western Hemisphere low. In Kirkpatrick's view, the successful 1979 Nicaraguan revolution and the rising challenge posed by leftist revolutionaries in neighboring El Salvador threatened to metastasize into a regional communist threat that would place enormous demands on US attention and resources.[64]

Since the late 1970s, the political situation in Central America had indeed developed with dizzying speed. In Nicaragua, the relatively limited violence between small revolutionary groups and state security forces that had punctuated the 1960s and early 1970s had transformed by 1978 into a mass-based protest movement. Nicaraguan businesspeople, politicians, and union leaders rallied to demand the resignation of the ageing dictator Anastasio Somoza Debayle, whose family dynasty had ruled the Central American nation since the 1930s. Even the influential archbishop Miguel Obando y Bravo publicly denounced Somocismo. Non-elite opposition to Somoza rose as well, and

antigovernment violence flared in working-class neighborhoods of Estelí, Ji-
notepe, León, Masaya, and Matagalpa. In response, the government unleashed
a brutal campaign of repression, including bombings of civilians and execu-
tions of men aged eighteen to twenty-five. The nation teetered on the brink of
total civil war; following nationwide insurrections in September, at least fifteen hundred people had been killed, and the International Committee of the
Red Cross estimated that twenty-five thousand people had been displaced and
nearly ten thousand had fled to Costa Rica and Honduras.[65]

As the situation in Nicaragua deteriorated, the Carter administration reluctantly assumed the lead role in mediations between Somoza and the Frente
Amplio Opositor (Broad Opposition Front [FAO]), an umbrella organization
of moderate, nonstate actors who sought to undertake democratic reform.
Carter hoped to spearhead the peaceful resolution of the Nicaraguan crisis
while also upholding a policy of US nonintervention. It proved an impossible
challenge; rather than facilitating political reform or insulating the United
States from accusations of meddling in Nicaragua's internal affairs, the Carter
team's halfhearted efforts played into Somoza's calculated obstructionism,
which succeeded in breaking down the mediation. As the moderates' influence waned, the ranks of the FSLN, a leftist revolutionary organization with
strong ties to Cuba, swelled with new recruits. By early 1979, the US Embassy
reported that "there [were] two poles of strength in Nicaragua, the GON [So-
moza] and the FSLN," and in successive months Somoza's brutal Guardia Nacional squared off against a radicalized revolutionary opposition with rising
support from regional allies, including Costa Rica, Panama, and Venezuela.[66]

Cold warriors in the United States viewed the revolutionary triumph in
Nicaragua in July 1979 as a critical flashpoint in the global Cold War and
were quick to pin the blame for Somoza's defeat squarely on Carter. Kirkpatrick set the tone. "What did the Carter administration do in Nicaragua? *It
brought down the Somoza regime*," Kirkpatrick hyperbolically asserted in *Commentary* magazine. The White House, she continued, had declared "open season" on Somoza, cutting US arms shipments to the Nicaraguan government
on human rights grounds, inhibiting the Somoza regime's ability to respond
to FSLN violence, and encouraging the opposition through the mediation
effort. Meanwhile, as Cuban arms shipments flowed into Nicaragua the
FSLN had carefully played down its "anti-democratic tendencies" by forging
alliances with moderate anti-Somocistas and rhetorically supporting a democratic political transition.[67]

Following Somoza's ouster, the Sandinistas, Kirkpatrick contended, had
betrayed their true intentions. The FSLN Directorate—which had assumed

political power when Somoza fled the country—postponed national elections and restructured the Council of State to give themselves a permanent majority. The revolutionary government, Kirkpatrick warned, was taking over banks, industries, and television and radio stations, while muzzling the press, forcing trade unions into state-affiliated workers' associations, and redesigning public education to indoctrinate revolutionary ideals. Guided by rising numbers of Cuban advisers, the FSLN's actions, Kirkpatrick concluded, "reflect the characteristically totalitarian desire to absorb the society into the state, to transform social groups into agencies and instruments of the government."[68]

Moreover, Kirkpatrick warned that Nicaragua's slide toward communist totalitarianism threatened to carry over into neighboring El Salvador. With five and a half million inhabitants, tiny El Salvador was the most densely populated nation in the region—a nation so small, US ambassador Robert White observed, that one could see the entire country from a helicopter at nine thousand feet.[69] It was a land of stark inequality. Long-standing socioeconomic disparity had deepened over the past two decades, as the nation's arable land had become increasingly concentrated in the hands of a small number of powerful families who dominated the nation's banking, manufacturing, and export agriculture. With 60 percent of the population living in the countryside, by the early 1970s more than 40 percent of Salvadoran families were landless. For the rural poor, illiteracy and malnutrition were endemic; the infant mortality rate was four times that of the United States. "Hundreds of thousands of peasants live in hovels made of packed mud; naked children with swollen bellies and open sores wander among the grunting pigs, garbage and flies," wrote the journalist Raymond Bonner. "Their mothers and sisters trudge for an hour or more to the nearest well for water, carried in gourd-shaped plastic containers balanced on their heads." By contrast, in the wealthy neighborhoods of San Salvador, he continued, "brick walls hide $500,000 houses."[70]

Closely tied to local elites, the Salvadoran state was led for decades by military governments relying on terror and repression to maintain control. In the 1930s, General Maximiliano Hernández Martínez stamped out a peasant insurrection by killing perhaps thirty thousand people. In the early Cold War, extensive US counterinsurgency training and aid enhanced the repressive capacity of the Salvadoran security forces and fueled the radical anticommunism that permeated much of the nation's right wing.[71] By the 1970s, El Salvador had reached the breaking point. The fraudulent 1972 election betrayed moderates' hope of political reform and sparked a wave of political violence by the Left. In response, state and paramilitary groups resorted to repression.

"The regimes of the 1970s repeatedly hoped that massacres would produce the desired silence, but their attempts contributed instead to the radicalization of significant sectors of the once reformist or inactive opposition," writes the historian Aldo A. Lauria-Santiago. "For the early years of the conflict, those expectations were repeatedly disappointed: the increasingly frequent massacres led only to an escalation of the confrontation and the successful creation of rebel recruits."[72]

Fearing a replay of the Sandinista victory in neighboring Nicaragua, the Carter administration threw its support behind a reformist junta that took power in mid-October 1979. In the coup's aftermath, however, right-wing violence intensified. "Bodies turn up regularly with their heads or limbs severed by machete, the traditional weapon of the land that is still carried by troops in full battle dress" one journalist noted in the *Washington Post.* "Other cadavers have been found charred by a torturer's blowtorch or with their skin peeled off their faces or with steel spikes driven through their ears."[73] In 1980 alone, military forces and death squads murdered perhaps eight thousand people. Watching the situation unfold, the Carter administration was caught in a bind: on the one hand, recognizing that the majority of killings were carried out by the Salvadoran right-wing, the White House hoped to use US aid as leverage to curtail human rights abuses in El Salvador. On the other hand, as the Cold War intensified in the second half of the Carter presidency and conservative criticism mounted in the lead-up to the 1980 election, human rights moved increasingly to the back burner as a policy priority. As a result, although the Carter administration briefly halted US military aid to San Salvador following the rape and murder of four American churchwomen and a lay missionary in early December 1980, the White House feared a rebel victory and reopened the aid spigot shortly before leaving office.[74]

Nonetheless, cold warriors in the United States attacked the Carter administration for failing to adequately support a Cold War ally facing a communist insurgency. Jeane Kirkpatrick led the charge. Although admitting that socioeconomic inequality in El Salvador was a problem, Kirkpatrick argued that the same conditions had existed "in El Salvador and in Central America generally forever, throughout their history." Revolutions, she contended, did not occur because local conditions worsened, but because they improved, raising people's hopes for positive change and thereby paving the way for radical insurgents to establish a following. Revolutions "are caused by revolutionaries and revolutionaries are people," Kirkpatrick claimed. "They are not social forces, they are people with guns. Revolutions are caused by violence and terrorism that brought about the popular fronts and they utilize in our times in El Salvador and in Central America, the instruments of terror to destroy the already weak societies and institutions of government and to undermine the already weak bases or order that exists in those societies."[75]

The upheaval in Central America, Kirkpatrick argued, was a clear-cut case of communist foreign policy adventurism. Weapons and supplies were flowing from Cuba to El Salvador via secret transit points in Nicaragua, and leftist revolutionaries of the Frente Farabundo Martí para la Liberación Nacional (Farabundo Martí National Liberation Front [FMLN]) were gaining ground against the increasingly demoralized Salvadoran army. Events were nearing the tipping point; a communist victory in El Salvador would threaten the entire Central American isthmus—with enormous implications for US security in the Western Hemisphere. It was, Kirkpatrick ominously concluded, like "the point in a chess game where, if a move is successfully completed, the whole character of the game changes."[76]

Kirkpatrick was hardly the first cold warrior to voice concern over the perceived spread of communism in Central America and the Caribbean. As Secretary of State Haig wrote in his memoirs, at the outset of the 1980s "the fires of insurrection, fed by the Soviets and fanned by their surrogates, the Cubans, spread unchecked in Central America."[77] Reagan concurred. "The Caribbean is rapidly becoming a Communist lake in what should be an American pond," he had declared in 1979, "and the United States resembles a giant, afraid to move."[78] Following Reagan's inauguration, the new administration continued to view political developments in Central America through the lens of the US Cold War confrontation with the Soviet Union and its proxies. "It is important to mention at the outset that Cuba's role in the area is a central fact," National Security Adviser Richard Allen asserted at an NSC meeting on February 6. The secretary of state agreed. Central America was in "turmoil," Haig emphasized. "Yet these countries could manage if it were not for Cuba." The Cuban dictator Fidel Castro, Haig continued, "exploits internal difficulties in these states by exporting arms and subversion."[79]

El Salvador was a case in point. US intelligence reports estimated that hundreds of tons of arms were flowing from Cuba to the FMLN, including captured US arms left behind in Vietnam. The discovery of these weapons, Haig told his NSC colleagues, was unmistakable evidence of significant Soviet involvement in Central America, since "not even the Cubans are capable of orchestrating such complicated arms transactions alone." Underscoring the gravity of the issue, the secretary of state had already raised the issue with the Anatoly Dobrynin, the Soviet ambassador to the United States. The two superpowers needed to "establish an acceptable code of international behavior,"

Haig told Dobrynin. "The first order of the day was Soviet activity in Afghanistan and the use of Cuban proxies in troubled areas. The U.S. would not stand by and permit the Cubans to draw us into another Vietnam."[80]

Apprised of the deteriorating situation in El Salvador, the members of the NSC were in consensus that the United States needed to adopt a hard line against Cuban adventurism. "To stop the Cubans and help others stop them, we need better intelligence, a psychological warfare program, and an ability to impede guerrilla activities," recommended General David C. Jones, the chairman of the Joint Chiefs of Staff. Secretary of Defense Weinberger took a similar view. "With some covert aid, we could disrupt Cuban activities," he argued. The president agreed. "We can't afford a defeat. El Salvador is the place for a victory," Reagan asserted at the tail end of the meeting. "For too many years, we have been telling adversaries what we can't do," he added a moment later. "It's time we make them start wondering what we will do."[81]

Galvanized by the possibility of a revolutionary victory, the Reagan administration worked vigorously in late February to shore up domestic and foreign support for expanded US assistance to the Salvadoran government. The centerpiece of the administration's effort was a widely publicized State Department white paper titled "Communist Interference in El Salvador" and made public on February 23. Drawing on dozens of captured rebel documents, the report described the conflict in the tiny Central American nation as "a textbook case of indirect armed aggression by Communist powers through Cuba." Detailing an arms-soliciting trip to the Soviet Union and six other communist countries by a Salvadoran rebel leader, the report asserted that some eight hundred tons of "the most modern weapons and equipment" had been promised to the insurgents. "The situation in El Salvador presents a strikingly familiar case of Soviet, Cuban, and other Communist military involvement in a politically troubled Third World country," the report concluded. "By providing arms, training, and direction to a local insurgency and by supporting it with a global propaganda campaign, the Communists have intensified and widened the conflict. . . . Their objective in El Salvador as elsewhere is to bring about—at little cost to themselves—the overthrow of the established government and the imposition of a Communist regime in defiance of the will of the Salvadoran people."[82]

The white paper effectively set the tone of the domestic debate over US assistance to El Salvador. The US media initially accepted the Reagan administration's claims at face value and gave the report considerable coverage. On Capitol Hill, the white paper's implicit call for a resolute US response to the communist threat in Central America was welcomed by cold warriors, while liberal internationalists, reeling from the Republican gains the previous November and buckling down for the impending budget battle with the White House, gave the Reagan administration considerable latitude on US policy toward El Salvador. As a result, "from February 1981 onward, the issue was not whether the United States should provide military aid to El Salvador," writes the historian William M. LeoGrande, "but how much should be given and under what conditions."[83] By the end of the month, Reagan had more than doubled the number of US military advisers in El Salvador—bringing the total number to fifty-four—and approved a $25 million military aid package for the Salvadoran government. Underscoring the sense of urgency surrounding the issue, the president used special emergency powers to immediately dispatch 80 percent of the aid—bypassing potential congressional delays.[84]

Holding the line in El Salvador, however, would require halting the clandestine flow of arms from abroad. US intelligence revealed that most of the weapons passed from Havana to Nicaragua en route to the Salvadoran insurgents. Significantly, in February 1981 the CIA believed only a quarter of the estimated eight hundred tons of arms dispatched to the insurgents by communist nations in late 1980 and early 1981 had reached Salvadoran soil—the remaining six hundred tons were dispersed in secret holding sites in central Nicaragua awaiting transshipment by air, land, or sea to rebel strongholds across the border.[85]

Accordingly, the administration moved quickly to step up pressure on Managua to curtail arms transfers to the Salvadoran rebels. In January, Reagan had placed a temporary freeze on the final $15 million installment of a $75 million aid package to Nicaragua secured by the Carter administration the previous June. Now the administration debated whether to enact a total cutoff. Called to Washington for consultations in early February, the US ambassador to Nicaragua, Lawrence A. Pezzullo, was cautiously optimistic. Having repeatedly raised the issue of FSLN support of Salvadoran insurgents with top Nicaraguan officials in previous weeks, Pezzullo believed the aid funds could be used as leverage.[86] "I'm not saying they're going to turn Nicaragua into Connecticut, but I think we can deal with these fellows," he told Secretary of State Haig. "And I think we can prevent them from doing stupid things, and causing problems in the hemisphere."[87] Haig gave his approval. Give the Sandinistas an ultimatum, the secretary of state recommended at an NSC meeting on February 11: halt all support for the FMLN within 30 days or suffer an immediate US aid cutoff. After a brief discussion, Reagan approved the plan.

But the president also emphasized that the stakes were high. "We must not let Central America become another Cuba on the mainland," Reagan warned. "It cannot happen."[88]

Back in Managua, Pezzullo delivered the Reagan administration's message to the FSLN leadership. The threat shook the Sandinistas. With an annual balance of payments deficit of $65 million, the Nicaraguan treasury was virtually empty; the revolutionary government, the CIA estimated, did not have the necessary currency reserves to pay for a single month's imports. At the same time, private investment had plummeted and foreign banks were holding off on providing new loans until Nicaragua's foreign debt had been rescheduled.[89] Facing impending shortages, the Sandinistas were "almost frantic in their search for additional help," Pezzullo had reported in late January.[90] Indeed, after an extensive internal debate following the Reagan administration's ultimatum, the FSLN Directorate had concluded that it was "essential to maintain good relations" with the US government, directorate member Daniel Ortega Saavedra informed the US ambassador in an evening meeting on Valentine's Day. "We understand your concerns about El Salvador," Ortega maintained, and "we will not risk our revolution for an uncertain victory in El Salvador." Emphasizing the daunting internal problems confronting the revolutionary government, Ortega insisted that the FSLN sought to diffuse tension with the United States. The FSLN had decided to "not permit use of our territory for the transit of arms to El Salvador." The ambassador pressed Ortega: Could the Sandinistas sever their "emotional ties to the FMLN and their operational ties to the Cubans"? The Nicaraguan leader's response was simple. "The future of our revolution is at stake," he replied curtly.[91]

Over the following weeks, the US threat seemed to be working. In an effort to mollify the Reagan administration, the Sandinistas had undertaken a series of efforts to reach accommodations with domestic critics, including the influential figures in the Catholic Church, the opposition newspaper *La Prensa*, non-FSLN political leaders, and members of the private sector.[92] More importantly, after receiving the ultimatum, the FSLN Directorate had instructed all commanders to cease any support for Salvadoran guerrillas. "Not a single round will move through Nicaragua hereafter," Ortega told the US ambassador. Admitting that the FSLN had been "very permissive in allowing the FMLN to mount operations in Nicaragua," Ortega emphasized that both the Salvadorans and the Cubans had been notified that such operations were terminated and that commanders had been strictly prohibited from supporting guerrilla operations on their own.[93] Significantly, US intelligence—rapidly stepped up to track aircraft, vehicles, and ships moving from Nicaragua to El Salvador—indicated that the Sandinistas were as good as their word: by late February, the clandestine flow of arms from Nicaragua to El Salvador appeared to have stopped.[94]

It was the Reagan administration's overriding emphasis on confronting the communist world, however, that would determine US policy toward Nicaragua. In late January, Haig set the tone by dramatically confronting the Nicaraguan ambassador, Rita Delia Casco, at a White House reception. With the Honduran ambassador in tow, the secretary of state "stuck his finger in her face" and asserted that US assistance to Nicaragua would be suspended, "because Nicaragua had been converted into a base for Soviet operations in Central America."[95] A few days later, Haig confided to the Honduran foreign minister that the United States had "absolutely firm evidence of massive Cuban intervention in El Salvador via Nicaragua." The president, Haig added, "considers this intervention totally unacceptable and is prepared to take whatever steps necessary to terminate it."[96]

The US aid ultimatum, as it turned out, was little more than a ruse—a stalling tactic to buy the Reagan administration enough time to provide the Salvadoran government with an injection of US military aid. To convince the Sandinistas to halt their support for the FMLN, the $15 million "should be held out like the Holy Grail," Haig asserted at the NSC meeting on February 11. "Of course," he added, "they will not get it."[97] Pezzullo was left out in the cold. At the same time that Haig had promised to give the Sandinistas a thirty-day grace period, the ambassador later recalled, "What I didn't know, was that he was . . . agreeing to begin this covert program."[98]

Indeed, in February 1981, the Reagan administration was moving quickly toward a secret war with the Sandinistas. Determined to roll back communist gains in the third world, the Reagan team viewed Central America as a defining test case. Yet widespread opposition among the public and members of Congress to sending American soldiers into conflict zones overseas—the "Vietnam Syndrome" as Reagan put it—forced the White House to seek alternative means of achieving its Cold War goals. "Can we use the Argentines?" Kirkpatrick asked at the NSC meeting on February 18. "The Argentine military has a very good training capability and [is] active in Bolivia," she continued, referring to Argentina's role in the so-called cocaine coup of July 1980 that brought to power the ruthless and corrupt general Luis García Meza. The Argentine military junta, she concluded, "might help if given the right signal."[99] Haig agreed and quickly dispatched General Vernon Walters to make inquiries in Buenos Aires.

In fact, the Argentines were already active in Central America. After a series of meetings with top military leaders, Walters cabled Washington that Buenos Aires was "clearly engaged in major activity and would do more." In addition to hosting forty Honduran officers in intelligence training courses ranging from five to eight months, the Argentine military had opened two military attaché offices in Central America, and fifty antiguerrilla specialists were training Salvadoran officers in counterinsurgency tactics. The Argentine top brass took the opportunity to lecture Walters on the näiveté of the Carter administration, which had made the military junta's abuses—including regularly disposing of perceived subversives by tossing them alive from airplanes into the South Atlantic—a defining test case of the US human rights policy. Nonetheless, the generals enthusiastically agreed to work with the Reagan administration to expand Argentine training programs for anticommunist forces in Central America and offered to provide arms, ammunition, and even financial assistance.[100] "All we have to do is tell them what to do," Walters tersely concluded.[101]

Less than two weeks later, Reagan signed a secret presidential finding on Central America providing $19.5 million to train, equip, and assist Central American efforts to "counter foreign-sponsored subversion and terrorism."[102] In the following weeks, dozens of CIA operatives made contact with anti-Sandinista paramilitary groups in Florida and Central America and assisted Argentine advisers to expand their counterinsurgency training programs.[103] On April 1, the administration officially terminated all US economic aid to Nicaragua. In addition to the $15 million that had been frozen since January, the Reagan team suspended $20 million in food aid, $35 million in economic aid, and $7.4 million in food aid budgeted for the following fiscal year.[104] Significantly, the decision was taken despite evidence that the ultimatum was working. "There is no hard evidence of arms arriving in El Salvador from Nicaragua since February 1," Haig admitted in a memorandum to the president.[105] Viewing revolutionary Nicaragua through the prism of the Kirkpatrick Doctrine, the Reagan administration, however, rejected negotiating with the Sandinistas out of hand. "For the moment, Nicaragua is a proto-totalitarian system in which the mob is used more often than the secret police to frighten and then eliminate opposition. Nicaragua, however, should mature rapidly as a full-blown totalitarian state in the coming months," predicted Roger Fontaine, the hard-line anticommunist NSC director of Latin American affairs. In seeking aid from the United States, Fontaine concluded, the FSLN was trying to "have the best of both worlds, i.e. foster a totalitarian revolution, and have the democracies pay for it."[106]

As the White House policy toward Nicaragua was taking shape, the Reagan administration stumbled into stiff congressional opposition over its handling of human rights. Viewing the State Department Bureau of Human Rights and Humanitarian Affairs as epitomizing the failures of the Carter administration, the Reagan team had set out to downgrade human rights as a US foreign policy priority. In mid-May 1981, however, the Senate Foreign Relations Committee refused to confirm Ernest Lafever to lead the Human Rights Bureau, a surprise setback that forced the Reagan administration to reevaluate its human rights policy. The culmination of an intense lobbying campaign by liberal human rights advocates, the Lafever fiasco was a clear demonstration of the human rights community's ability to mobilize effectively as well as the abiding bipartisan interest in human rights on Capitol Hill—raising concerns within the Reagan administration that the effort to downgrade human rights was becoming a costly liability.[107] As a six-page "eye-only" memo to Secretary of State Haig asserted in late October, "Congressional belief that we have no consistent human rights policy threatens to disrupt important foreign policy initiatives. Human rights has been one of the main avenues for domestic attack on the Administration's foreign policy."[108]

The memo recommended a dramatic shift in the administration's approach. Human rights, the authors asserted, "is not something we tack on to our foreign policy but is its very purpose: the defense and promotion of freedom in the world." Moreover, human rights were at the heart of the US-Soviet confrontation; the US emphasis on political rights and civil liberties, the memo contended, "conveys what is ultimately at issue in our contest with the Soviet bloc. The fundamental distinction is our respective attitudes toward freedom. Our ability to resist the Soviets around the world depends in part on our ability to draw this distinction and to persuade others of it."[109]

Reportedly approved by both Haig and Reagan, the memo, drafted by assistant secretary for international organizations Elliott Abrams and signed by deputy undersecretary of state William P. Clark and undersecretary of state for management Richard T. Kennedy, served as a blueprint for a reorientation of the administration's human rights policy in late 1981.[110] Reagan signaled the shift by nominating Abrams to head the Human Rights Bureau on October 30; in an unusual statement accompanying the nomination, the president emphasized human rights as "important in all aspects of our foreign policy."[111] Abrams, a hard-nosed neoconservative with a law degree from

Harvard, had worked in the 1970s for senators Henry M. Jackson (D-WA) and Daniel Patrick Moynihan (D-NY)—two of the most influential politicians for the budding neoconservative movement.[112] Reputed to be the youngest person in the twentieth century to become an assistant secretary in the State Department, the thirty-three-year-old Abrams had followed the migration of liberal cold warriors into the Reagan camp. During his confirmation hearings, Abrams deftly balanced anticommunist rhetoric—describing the Soviet Union as "an enemy of the United States"—with a pledge to honestly report on human rights conditions abroad and to choose tactics "with a practical goal in mind."[113] In stark contrast with the Lefever episode, he easily won unanimous confirmation. Abrams's nomination, chairman Charles H. Percy (R-IL) told reporters, "signals a real commitment by the administration to seek the high road" on human rights.[114] Or, as senator Paul E. Tsongas (D-MA) put it, "Being a neoconservative does not disqualify you from the job."[115]

The Reaganites' political worldview, however, would make a distinctive imprint on the administration's human rights policy. Put simply, Reagan's human rights policy was grounded in the basic assumptions of the Kirkpatrick Doctrine, US exceptionalism, and the Cold War containment strategy. From the outset, the administration took a narrow approach to human rights that emphasized political rights and civil liberties. Allen had set the tone shortly after the Lafever nomination, asserting that human rights "include, most fundamentally, the rights not to be deprived arbitrarily of life, liberty, or property, and the right not to be subjected to humanly degrading treatment such as torture or exile under brutal conditions."[116]

By contrast, social and economic rights, which had been championed throughout the Cold War by the communist world and in the 1960s and 1970s by many third-world nationalists, were intentionally excluded from the Reagan administration's human rights framework. In the communist world, "from the government's point of view, the reason its subjects receive free education and medical care is in no way different from the reason its tractors receive mechanical care: if the services weren't provided, the machine—either animate or inanimate—wouldn't work," wrote Joseph Shattan, a neoconservative who served as an influential speechwriter for both Kirkpatrick and Abrams. "In such circumstances, the economic 'rights' of citizens under communism makes about as much sense as to speak of the economic 'rights' of automobiles to gasoline."[117] Moreover, the communist world used human rights rhetoric to hide totalitarianism's quotidian depredations. "The notion of economic and social rights is a dilution and distortion of the original and proper meaning of human rights, and we need to identify it as such," Allen argued. "It serves as a convenient excuse for those regimes and movements which do not respect ordinary civil and political rights; not surprisingly, it has been taken up by the Soviet Union and its allies and surrogates as a way to defend the dismal human rights record of most communist governments."[118] Abrams held a similar view. "You could make the argument that there aren't many countries where there are gross and consistent human rights violations," the Human Rights Bureau chief told a reporter, "except the communist countries because they have the system itself."[119]

Corresponding with the Reagan administration's dismissal of social and economic rights claims, the White House promoted US exceptionalism and justified aggressive US Cold War policies as essential to the protection of human rights. Underscoring the influence of domestic politics on foreign policy, the administration articulated human rights as part of its effort to reverse liberal internationalists inroads in US foreign policy in the 1970s, particularly the emphasis on noninterventionism abroad. In a mid-1983 foreign policy address, for example, Abrams would tell listeners that "the lesson of Vietnam" was that "where democracy and human rights are threatened . . . American power provides the necessary deterrent to aggression." Sidestepping both consistent US support for repressive and unelected governments in Saigon and the horrific human and material costs of the US military intervention in Southeast Asia, Abrams maintained that "where that shield is in place—as in Western Europe—democracy and human rights can flourish. Where that shield is removed—as in Vietnam—the prospects for democracy are destroyed."[120] Moreover, Soviet and Cuban adventurism, not socioeconomic factors, the Reagan administration consistently argued, fueled insurgencies in peripheral locales like El Salvador; as Kirkpatrick controversially asserted, "Revolutions in our times are not caused by social injustice."[121]

As the Reagan administration's human rights policy took shape over the second half of 1981, the White House also established the framework for a concerted effort to destabilize revolutionary Nicaragua. Following the US aid cutoff to Managua in April, US intelligence had revealed that arms shipments were once again flowing from Nicaragua to Salvadoran revolutionaries.[122] The FSLN was also engaged in a major military buildup; US intelligence agencies estimated that the FSLN army numbered between twenty thousand and twenty-five thousand soldiers, along with a rapidly expanding militia that could grow to as many as eighty thousand members by the end of the year—force numbers far in excess of neighboring military establishments. Correspondingly, perhaps two thousand Cuban military advisers were active in Nicaragua, and, in early June, Managua received a shipment of T-55 tanks from Algeria. It was "impossible to discount [the] more ominous implications of [the] Cuban/Soviet supported military build-up in Nicaragua," the NSC's Latin America specialists Fontaine and William L. Stearman asserted.[123] Reagan administration officials worried that time was running out. The United States "cannot allow the Soviets to militarize Central America with sophisticated systems which radically change the balance and threaten neighboring countries as well as the Panama Canal," Allen emphasized in a top secret memo to the president on June 6.[124]

As tension between the United States and Nicaragua deepened, the newly confirmed assistant secretary of state for inter-American affairs, Thomas O. Enders, flew to Managua in early August for a round of high-level talks with Sandinista leaders. The discussions were tense. "You can do your thing, but do it within your borders, or else we're going to hurt you," Enders told FSLN Directorate members Bayardo Arce, Humberto Ortega Saavedra, and Jaime Wheelock. "All right, come on in," Arce fired back. "We'll meet you man to man. You will kill us, but you will pay for it. You will have to kill us all to do it."[125]

Diplomatic fireworks aside, Enders came away from the meeting believing the Nicaraguans were willing to work toward an accommodation with the United States. The assistant secretary "found that you could hit these guys right between the eyes with a bat, and they'd come right back and talk to you," recalled Pezzullo. Sensing a potential breakthrough, the ambassador encouraged Enders to lay the groundwork for a mutual security agreement in which the Sandinistas would agree to curtail support for revolutionary groups abroad and limit the size of their military, while the United States would make a commitment "that we will not mount any attack on them." According to Pezzullo, both sides accepted the deal in principle; "I'll buy it," Daniel Ortega told Enders in a one-on-one meeting.[126]

But back in Washington, Enders's initiative collided with the Reagan administration's determination to destabilize revolutionary Nicaragua. As a secret intelligence estimate issued in September by CIA director William J. Casey made clear, the stakes were too high. "Communist exploitation of trends in Central America constitutes the most serious challenge to U.S. interests and freedom of action in the hemisphere since Cuba became allied with the USSR," the report maintained. As a flashpoint in the East-West confrontation, there could be no modus vivendi with the FSLN. "The principal objectives of Cuba and the USSR in Central America are to consolidate the Sandinista revolution in Nicaragua, and to use Nicaragua as a base for spreading leftist insurgency in the region," the report continued. "Indeed, by virtue of its location, cooperation with Communist and other radical advisers, and support for Central American insurgencies, Nicaragua has become the hub of the revolutionary wheel in Central America."[127]

Although congressional constraints forced the White House to articulate its goal as interdicting arms flowing from Nicaragua to revolutionaries in El Salvador, from the outset top Reagan administration officials conceived the real mission as sponsoring the overthrow of the FSLN. Casey was a particularly strong advocate for covert action against Managua. In the fall of 1981, the sixty-eight-year-old CIA director was "absolutely delighted" that Argentine security personnel were training former members of the Nicaraguan National Guard, recalled CIA deputy director Admiral Bobby Ray Inman. "He knew that the Argentines' hope was to unseat the Sandinistas. And that was farther than the U.S. Congress was ready to let us go."[128]

Moreover, for Central American revolutionaries and counterrevolutionaries alike, as the United States quickly monopolized control of the operation following Argentina's spectacular defeat in the Falklands War, the Reagan administration's ultimate goal was never in doubt. "I speak in the name of Ronald Reagan," the aggressive CIA operative assigned to run the operation, Duane R. "Dewey" Clarridge, told his Honduran and Argentine counterparts in autumn 1981. "We want to support this effort to change the government of Nicaragua." More concretely, the agency facilitated an August 11 merging of two counterrevolutionary groups that had materialized following Somoza's overthrow, creating the Fuerza Democrática Nicaragüense (Nicaraguan Democratic Force [FDN]). For all intents and purposes, the FDN was a CIA creation; "The name of the organization, the members of the political junta, and the members of the general staff were all chosen or approved by the CIA," former FDN leader Edgar Chamorro later revealed.[129]

Undermined by top Reagan administration officials, Assistant Secretary Enders's effort to negotiate a deal with the FSLN quickly fell apart. "Enders couldn't get anything through the administration in Washington, that resembled anything like the beginning of a negotiation," recalled a disillusioned Pezzullo, who left his post in Managua shortly thereafter. Rather than a quid pro quo, the final version of Washington's proposal "was really an insulting attack."[130] Not surprisingly, Enders's subsequent efforts to negotiate with the Sandinistas in fall 1981 fell victim to mutual recriminations. It was "an impossible situation for a diplomat: to have two policies in effect," recalled Pezzullo's successor, Anthony Quainton. Enders's initiative went nowhere, Quainton continued, because "in the White House, there was no deal. There the domino theory was much in vogue and many White House officials believed that if we did not get rid of the Sandinistas, revolutionary Marxism would roll from Sandinista Nicaragua through Salvador to Guatemala and into south Texas."[131]

In an NSC meeting on November 10, Reagan's top advisers reiterated the fear that the situation in Central America was deteriorating. "If we wait much longer to act, then the price will be much higher," Secretary of State Haig asserted. The United States needed to send an unmistakable message to the Cubans that "we mean business," albeit short of invading Cuba. "Invasion is the trigger for a serious Soviet response. Up to that point there is a free play area," Haig added with characteristic swagger. There was disagreement in the NSC regarding US priorities in Central America. Kirkpatrick advised focusing first on El Salvador; Casey argued that the United States should move aggressively against the Sandinistas; Haig warned against creating a counter-revolutionary insurgency in Nicaragua "unless you are prepared to go all the way." But none of Reagan's top advisers questioned the underlying logic that Nicaragua posed a significant national security threat to the United States, and no one spoke out against ratcheting up the pressure on Managua. The decision to intervene had already been made; with the Rubicon behind them, the November 11 discussion remained firmly in the realm of the tactical. As Ed Meese, counselor to the president, put it, "The key element is whether U.S. land forces and naval actions are to be contemplated."[132]

Reagan supplied the answer. Escalating US actions against Nicaragua, the president warned, entailed risks at home. With the legacy of the Vietnam War fresh in the minds of the public, the media, and the Congress, invading Nicaragua with American soldiers, the president argued, was "an impossible option." It would also negatively affect inter-American affairs. "How do we deal with the image in Latin America of the Yankee colossus?" the president asked. Yet Reagan also emphasized the need to move aggressively against the FSLN. "I don't want to back down," he told his advisers. "I don't want to accept defeat."[133] With the option of a US military intervention off the table, the discussion turned to black operations. The president was keen: the United States needed to find covert actions, Reagan asserted, "that would be truly disabling and not just flea bites."[134]

Two weeks later, the framework of the US destabilization policy toward Nicaragua was put into place. Reagan approved covert financial support for domestic opponents of the Sandinistas on November 23, along with a CIA plan to train a force of five hundred Latin American commandos. The president also signed National Security Decision Directive (NSDD) 17, an eleven-point plan for Central America emphasizing the imperative of defeating the insurgency in El Salvador and halting Cuban and Nicaraguan interventionism.[135] Publicly, Haig, Weinberger, and Meese made the rounds of the news outlets, warning of Nicaragua's slide toward totalitarianism and emphasizing that a US response was imminent. "We have not given up on Nicaragua, but the hours are growing rather short," Haig ominously proclaimed.[136] On Capitol Hill, congressional doves reacted with alarm. "If I were a Nicaraguan I would be building my bomb shelter this afternoon," representative Michael Barnes (D-MD) declared.[137]

Barnes's comment was hardly an exaggeration. At the CIA headquarters at Langley, the person running the covert war on Nicaragua, Clarridge, had established a plan of action. "It didn't take superior intellectual ability to figure out that we needed an offensive approach to containing Nicaraguan aggression," Clarridge recalled in a subsequent memoir. He continued, "My plan was simple: 1. Take the war to Nicaragua. 2. Start killing Cubans."[138]

By the end of 1981, the Reagan administration could claim significant achievements. In the aftermath of Reagan's success in securing sweeping tax cuts and slashes to social spending, the administration's "first hundred days" quickly acquired an almost mythical quality among conservatives.[139] Reagan's handling of a major strike in August by the Professional Air Traffic Controllers Organization (PATCO)—the president fired eleven thousand federal employees—further burnished the president's reputation for decisive action in the domestic political arena.[140] Among congressional Democrats the mood was dour. Speaker of the House Thomas P. "Tip" O'Neil (D-MA) captured the tone: "I'm getting the shit whaled out of me," he told one constituent.[141]

In foreign policy, too, the Reagan administration had taken significant steps to reverse the perceived failures of US policy during the détente era. Convinced that the United States could outspend the Soviet Union, the White House had secured a massive increase in defense outlays. Over the next five years, the US military budget would double; by 1985, the Department of Defense was spending an average of $28 million per hour.[142] Correspondingly, the administration had moved quickly to confront perceived Soviet expansionism in the developing world. Backed by the February white paper's claim that El Salvador was "another case of indirect armed aggression against a small Third World country by communist powers acting through Cuba," the White House dramatically deepened US involvement in Central American affairs, rapidly expanding military training programs for Salvadoran soldiers and infusing the Central American nation with $25 million in military aid—more than US military aid to the rest of Latin America and the Caribbean combined in 1981.[143]

By the end of 1981, the Reagan administration's effort to destabilize revolutionary Nicaragua was also proceeding apace. Dismissing Ambassador Pezzullo's recommendation that Washington could achieve a modus vivendi with the Sandinistas, the White House established the framework for a secret war on Nicaragua that would run through the remainder of the decade. The United States provided "an extraordinary sum of money," a former Argentine trainer revealed in a 1982 interview. US funds, he continued, paid for the "setting up of various camps, the arming of thousands of men (as well as their provisions), salaries and economic assistance to those leading the counterrevolution, [and] the salaries of the Argentine paramilitary advisers, who, as in my case, collect sums ranging from $2,500 to $3,000 monthly."[144]

Finally, the Reagan administration's human rights policy had undergone significant evolution over the course of 1981. Viewing the issue as a defining feature of Carter's failures in the international arena, the White House initially sought to simply remove human rights as a policy priority. The Reagan administration "came to office without a conception of human rights policy except the view of the Carter administration," recalled Elliott Abrams. "That conception was viewed as flawed from a pragmatic point of view and leftist from an ideological point of view."[145] With Kirkpatrick providing the blueprint, the administration moved quickly to shore up relations with authoritarian allies. As Reagan told Argentine general Roberto Viola in mid-March, there would be "no public scoldings and lectures" and "anything we ask for will be with a *por favore* [sic]."[146]

Despite the Reagan administration's initial resistance, human rights did not disappear, however, as a US foreign policy concern. Galvanized by Lafever's failed confirmation bid, the White House by the end of 1981 had embraced human rights as a defining feature of its foreign policy approach. Significantly, this shift was not a repudiation of the Kirkpatrick Doctrine's emphasis on national security; by emphasizing political rights and civil liberties, the Reagan team increasingly justified aggressive US Cold War policies as essential to the protection of human rights. As undersecretary of state for political affairs Walter Stoessel Jr., succinctly put it, "Our objective is to make our security interests and our human rights concerns mutually reinforcing so that they can be pursued in tandem."[147]

But if Reagan could boast significant achievements in 1981, by the end of the year it was also evident that the administration's framework for deepening the US intervention in Central America was built on a shaky foundation. White House accusations that the FMLN was closely tied to Cuba were accurate; Castro's relationship with the Salvadoran guerrillas, writes the historian Andrea Oñate, "was extensive and consequential."[148] Yet, in June, journalists examining the captured rebel documents that had formed the evidentiary basis of the February white paper were shocked to discover that few of the Reagan administration's claims were substantiated. In a remarkably candid interview, the Foreign Service Officer who first examined the trove, Jon D. Glassman, admitted to the *Wall Street Journal* that the white paper was "misleading" and that the State Department had "over-embellished" the evidence to strengthen the administration's case for deepening US military support to El Salvador.[149]

Significantly, none of the material supported the assertion that the rebels were armed with 200 tons of communist-supplied weapons. "In document after document, there are reports of rebels short of arms, or looking for ways to buy arms, or exhorting comrades to produce home-made arms, or plotting to kidnap wealthy Salvadorans to have access to private arsenals," reported the *Washington Post*. The claim that 800 tons of weapons were stored in Nicaragua awaiting transshipment to the rebels was also unsubstantiated. Journalists discovered that one of the documents indicated 130 tons of arms were stored at a secret site in Nicaragua; to estimate the total tonnage of arms, Glassman had simply multiplied that number by six. It was an extraordinary revelation; although few observers denied that arms were reaching the Salvadoran insurgents from Cuba via Nicaragua, given that weapons interdiction was a central justification for the Reagan administration's growing covert operation against the Sandinistas, the white paper's expansive claims were based on astonishingly thin evidence.[150]

Similarly, the documents failed to support the Reagan administration's assertion that the conflict in El Salvador was a product of Soviet adventurism. Aid from the communist world to the insurgents had been a trickle, the documents revealed, not a deluge. More to the point, even the Salvadoran government—although desperately seeking US aid—refused to accept the characterization of the war as Soviet inspired. "This is a history of people starving to death, living in misery," José Napoleón Duarte, the leader of the Christian Democratic Party and president of the ruling junta told the journalist Raymond Bonner. "For 50 years, the same people had all the power, all the money, all the opportunities," Duarte continued. "Those who did not have anything tried to take it away from those who had everything. But there were not democratic systems available to them, so they have radicalized themselves, they have resorted to violence. And of course this second group, the rich, do not want to give up anything, so they are fighting."[151] As Duarte made clear, notwithstanding the Reagan administration's repeated claims to the contrary, it was El Salvador's extreme inequality, not foreign subversion, that had sparked the insurgency.

Moreover, by blending the Kirkpatrick Doctrine into its human rights policy, the Reagan administration had concocted a heady brew. Almost immediately, the White House confronted the challenge of justifying expanded US military assistance to San Salvador on human rights grounds in light of evidence that the vast majority of the killings in El Salvador were perpetrated by the Salvadoran military and paramilitary groups. In 1981, right-wing death squads killed three hundred to five hundred Salvadorans a week in what Americas Watch Committee vice-chairman Aryeh Neier delicately described as a "human *abattoir*."[152] At the end of the year, the slaughter showed no signs of abating. Indeed, on December 11, 1981, the US-trained and US-equipped Atlacatl Rapid Deployment Infantry Battalion massacred more than eight hundred peasants in the village of El Mozote. The bodies were left unburied.[153] Yet underscoring the centrality of the Kirkpatrick Doctrine's emphasis on confronting totalitarianism, Elliot Abrams, the assistant secretary of state for human rights and humanitarian affairs, subsequently informed a congressional committee that reports of the massacre were "not credible."[154]

As 1981 drew to a close, the Reagan administration had made major strides in establishing a framework to advance its Cold War goals. In Managua, the Sandinistas braced for the impending storm. For the FSLN, in the spring of 1982 the real battle would begin.

Chapter 3

"Is This Not Respect for Human, Economic, and Social Rights?"

Nicaragua and the United States, 1979-1984

On September 27, 1983, Comandante Daniel Ortega Saavedra stepped to the podium of the United Nations General Assembly. The coordinator of Nicaragua's Junta for National Reconstruction and a member of the Directorate of the Sandinista National Liberation Front (FSLN), Ortega addressed the assembled diplomats in his characteristic military fatigues—an unmistakable symbol of his leadership in the bloody revolution that had successfully overthrown the Anastasio Somoza Debayle dictatorship four years earlier. With his thick-rimmed glasses, Ortega, the novelist Salman Rushdie would later write, "looked like a bookworm who had done a bodybuilding course; his manner, too, combined a bespectacled blinking, mildvoiced diffidence with an absolutely contradictory self-confidence. You wouldn't kick sand into his face any more."[1]

For more than a century, Ortega declared, the United States had consistently intervened in Central American affairs to promote its own economic and political interests. Starting with the US filibuster William Walker in the mid-nineteenth century, "there has been one landing of U.S. soldiers after another, direct interventions aimed at propping up tyrannical governments and drowning the people's blood in struggle." As a result, Washington "became the greatest enemy of our peoples," Ortega asserted, and US democracy "has meant hunger and exploitation for the peasants and workers in our region. And it has meant fabulous wealth for the exploiting minorities." Only the 1979 Nicaragua revolution, with its enormous human and material destruction, Ortega asserted, had allowed Nicaragua to decisively end the continuous US domination dating back to Walker's filibusters.[2]

As Ortega's extraordinary address made clear, the revolution marked a decisive moment in Nicaraguan history. Filled with a triumphalist sense of possibility, the FSLN set out to transform the deeply impoverished and unequal Central American nation by using the power of the state to extend social and economic rights to ordinary Nicaraguans. In the revolution's first two years, the regime dramatically expanded spending on health, education, and pensions; built hundreds of schools; and sponsored a nationwide literacy campaign that lowered the illiteracy rate from 50 percent to 13 percent.[3] On the political front, the FSLN envisioned a balance between top-down vanguardism and a form of direct democracy in which non-elites could participate in the nation's political life through newly created mass-based organizations. A multitude of new FSLN grassroots organizations emerged, including peasant and worker associations, women's organizations, and community defense committees. By the time Ronald Reagan entered the White House, Nicaragua remained in the foundational stages of post-conflict recovery but could nonetheless boast significant achievements.

Reagan's election, however, ushered in a new chapter in US aggression against Nicaragua. Beginning in the spring of 1982, the rising tenor of Washington's undeclared war on Nicaragua was unmistakable evidence that, in the Reagan administration's aggressive effort to roll back perceived communist gains in the developing world, the ousting of the FSLN took center stage. Enumerating a list of US acts of aggression since Reagan entered the Oval Office, Ortega in his United Nations address cited 203 violations of Nicaraguan airspace by US spy planes, nearly three dozen violations of Nicaraguan territorial waters by the US Navy, and unprecedented US land and sea military maneuvers in neighboring Honduras involving tens of thousands of American soldiers. Correspondingly, US-backed counter-revolutionaries operating on the Honduran border had killed 717 Nicaraguans and kidnapped 529 others since January 1981. The Contras had destroyed or damaged ports; bombed airports, fuel tanks, and production facilities; and razed health centers and schools—some $108 million in damages, representing one-quarter of Nicaragua's annual investments. "Once more it was the policy of the Big Stick, the policy of gunboats, the policy of terror," Ortega avowed.[4]

Indeed, Reagan was deeply committed to defeating the Sandinistas; over the course of two terms in the Oval Office, the president would devote more speeches to Nicaragua than any other single topic.[5] Far from a peripheral issue handed off as a sop to the hard Right, the administration's policy toward Nicaragua was a central concern for top Reagan officials throughout the administration's eight years in office. "It's difficult to remember that Nicaragua was an absolute foreign policy focus of the Reagan administration," asserted Harry W. Shlaudeman in a later interview. A career Foreign Service Officer who served as the president's special envoy to Central America, Shlaudeman continued, "Nothing was more important, except the Soviet Union itself."[6]

Competing visions between Washington and Managua thus fueled a fierce conflict. As Ortega's UN address made clear, the deeply anti-imperialist Sandinistas viewed the US government as the source of filibusters, decades of gunboat diplomacy, and, ultimately, the Somoza dynasty. By creating a revolutionary nation that was nonaligned, and maintaining a mixed economy but dedicated to social and economic justice, the FSLN aspired to provide a new model of democracy for third-world nations seeking to break free from the legacies of colonialism and underdevelopment. By contrast, the Reagan administration saw Nicaragua as the proving ground in its effort both to reverse the inroads in the US foreign policymaking process made by liberal internationalists in the 1970s and to roll back Soviet gains in the developing world. The result was a grim struggle between Reagan and the Sandinistas that would span a decade.

The 1979 Nicaraguan revolution was a popular uprising against a brutal and sclerotic dictatorship. Founded in 1961 and drawing on the inspiration of the successful 1959 Cuban revolution, the FSLN struggled unsuccessfully over the 1960s to ignite an insurgency that would oust the Somoza dictatorship. Over the course of the decade, hundreds of FSLN recruits were killed in firefights with the National Guard or captured and deposited in one of Somoza's medieval prisons. By the end of the decade, the FSLN had been reduced to perhaps a dozen militants. "The struggle the FSLN carried out was an armed and clandestine struggle," recalled Jaime Wheelock, who joined the Sandinista Front in 1969. "The members didn't live long, and lines of formal leadership were very unstable. Quite often the actual leadership of the Sandinista Front was made up of those cadres still alive in the country."[7]

Worsening economic conditions, however, fueled popular opposition to Somoza. In the 1950s and 1960s, the Somoza family and a small number of Somocista elites increasingly dominated the Nicaraguan economy. The number of landless peasants swelled as big landowners aggressively expanded their holdings to produce for export markets. An influx of US funding for agricultural development during the Alliance for Progress initiative in the 1960s accelerated the production of export crops such as cotton and coffee at the expense of staple foods. Yet Nicaragua's rapidly rising gross national product obscured extreme inequality. By the early 1970s, although half the population lived in rural areas, less than 2 percent of the population controlled 41 percent of the land; the average life expectancy—fifty-five years—was the lowest in the region. Ruling the nation like a fiefdom, Somoza owned roughly 15 percent of the nation's land and could boast a fortune of perhaps $300 million.[8] By contrast, less than 2 percent of Nicaraguans had access to potable water; diarrhea was the principal cause of illness and death among children under five years of age.[9]

Opposition to Somoza accelerated in the 1970s. When a massive earthquake flattened Managua in 1972, Somoza diverted much of the international relief aid into his own bank accounts and left large swaths of the destroyed capital to languish.[10] "Block after block of buildings lay in ruin, with weeds sprouting up among the debris," wrote the journalist Stephen Kinzer, who arrived in 1976. Such enormous destruction, Kinzer continued, "defied description and begged only for comparison, perhaps to Dresden after the Allied bombing."[11] On a visit to Nicaragua more than a decade after the disaster, Rushdie was equally shocked at ruin on such scale. Managua, he wrote, "sprawled around its own corpse."[12]

By the end of the 1970s, political tension in Nicaragua reached the boiling point. Somoza's blatant fraud in the 1974 national election had fueled support for the FSLN—particularly after the Sandinistas kidnapped a group of government officials late in the year, forcing the dictatorship to pay $5 million in ransom and release more than a dozen political prisoners.[13] The brutal assassination of the well-known political opposition leader Pedro Joaquín Chamorro in early 1978 was taken by many Nicaraguans as further evidence that political reform was impossible in the face of Somoza's intransigence. Correspondingly, the Sandinistas' reputation soared following the stunning takeover of the Nicaraguan National Palace on August 22 by twenty-five FSLN guerrillas, forcing the dictatorship to pay $500,000 in ransom and to run an anti-Somoza communiqué in the press and on the radio. Crystallizing popular opposition to the dictatorship, the takeover sparked a wave of popular insurrections that paralyzed Nicaragua in early September.[14]

Frustrated at their exclusion from political power by the Somoza regime and fearing a left-wing revolution, Nicaraguan middle-class producers increasingly joined the political opposition. In March 1978, the Nicaraguan Democratic Movement (MDN) was formed by private-sector leader Alfonso

Robelo. The MDN initially hoped to wrest democratic reforms from the Somoza regime and took a lead role in bringing together a political coalition of anti-Somoza parties known as the Broad Opposition Front (FAO). The failure of the US-led mediation effort between Somoza and the FAO in late 1978 and early 1979, however, convinced the MDN that stronger measures were necessary. As Robelo later recalled, "We soon became convinced that in order to topple a right-wing dictatorship three things were necessary: a strike with the participation of the private sector, a people's insurrection where the citizens would take to the streets upon the calling of their leaders, and military action per se."[15]

The resulting explosion of insurgency that culminated in the government's overthrow in mid-1979 was overwhelmingly popular. As the fighting between the revolutionaries and government soldiers intensified in 1979, state-sanctioned abuses reached an unprecedented scale. Entire neighborhoods became targets for the National Guard, and thousands of unaffiliated Nicaraguans were caught in the cross fire. "They left the bodies here for 27 days then allowed them to be burned in front of the house. All that was left of my father was his head," Miria Ochoa told a reporter in the destroyed city of Estelí, where fifty-five hundred residents died in the first half of 1979 from National Guard mortar fire, rocket fire, incendiary bombs, and street shootings.[16] Likewise, in Managua, indiscriminate government bombings in June killed nine thousand civilians.[17]

The resulting politicization engendered widespread support for the revolution. Impoverished, terrorized by government agents, and pushed to action by revolutionary propaganda, few of the young men and women who transformed working-class neighborhoods into barricaded strongholds and ultimately defeated the hated National Guard could have articulated the lofty goals outlined in the Sandinistas' *Historic Program*.[18] Indeed, most Nicaraguans were pushed by government brutality rather than pulled by FSLN ideology to rally beneath the revolutionary banner. "The new recruits of 1978 and 1979 were attracted to the FSLN because they wanted to fight against Somoza," writes the historian Matilde Zimmermann, "not because they wanted to debate the fine points of strategy with other revolutionaries."[19]

Yet the FSLN played a critical leadership role in the Nicaraguan revolution. Dividing the nation into six fronts, each with a FSLN general staff, the Sandinistas demonstrated themselves to be skillful tacticians in the bloody months leading up to Somoza's overthrow. As the Latin Americanist Thomas W. Walker noted in an early assessment, "In the end, it was superior organization and extensive grass-roots support that made it possible for the small insurgent forces to defeat the corrupt and demoralized, yet more numerous and better-armed, National Guard."[20] As a result, when the fighting ended, the FSLN's leadership role paved the way for the Sandinistas to assume political control. "As the only armed force in the country and as the undisputed leader of the effort that finally forced Somoza out," US ambassador Lawrence A. Pezzullo later reported, "the FSLN found itself in an unexpectedly predominant position with a clear path to exercising nearly unrestrained power."[21] Indeed, as tens of thousands of Nicaraguans celebrated the revolution's final victory in Managua's main square on July 19, 1979, it was clear that the Sandinistas enjoyed a powerful popular mandate. One observer in Managua estimated that 75–80 percent of the population supported the FSLN.[22]

Yet rebuilding Nicaragua would be a challenge of herculean proportions. The revolution had cost an estimated fifty thousand lives—nearly 2 percent of the population—and left another forty thousand orphaned. One-fifth of the population was homeless. Nicaragua's gross domestic product (GDP) dropped by 25 percent in 1979, and capital flight before and during the conflict exceeded $0.5 billion. In addition to secretly transferring over $100 million to his own overseas accounts, Somoza left a foreign debt of $1.6 billion—a sum equivalent to nearly 80 percent of GDP. When the fighting ended, the national banking system contained only $3 million—a sum sufficient to pay the government's bills for two days.[23] "After eighteen months of rapid economic deterioration and massive financial and human capital flight, culminating in the last months of open warfare," the US Embassy cabled Washington, "the country is broke and in a shambles."[24]

With the fighting over, the FSLN turned to the task of rebuilding Nicaragua. At the top of the structure of the provisional government, nine individuals with the title of *comandante de la revolución* made up the FSLN Directorate, a consensus-based body representing the three distinct revolutionary movements that, until uniting against Somoza in early 1979, had viewed one another with enmity. Beneath the directorate, the Junta for National Reconstruction—initially composed of five members but subsequently reduced to three—formed the executive branch. The junta took the lead in carrying out the day-to-day tasks of running the country in coordination with the Council of State, an advisory body representing a range of political, social, and economic organizations. Four of the comandantes were also given control of key government ministries, and Ortega emerged as the "coordinator" of the junta, resulting in a complicated and often opaque interplay of power and personalities.[25] With the exception of Tomás Borge—the only founding member of the FSLN to have survived the Somoza era—none of the comandantes was older than forty. Observing the raucous celebration in Managua, the intellectual Regis Debray enthused, "Nicaragua in the year zero restores an air of youth . . . to ideas that were thought to be worn out, as if the end of our century had suddenly lost its wrinkles here."[26]

If the revolutionary triumph gave Nicaraguans hope for a bright future, from the outset the FSLN's policies were shaped by the historical legacy of US interventionism. In the mid-nineteenth century, the infamous William Walker briefly ruled Nicaragua, reinstating slavery and, before being overthrown and executed, razing the elegant city of Granada. By the early twentieth century, US economic leverage, intertwining with the political power of local elites, played a signal role in Central America's dependence on a handful of export crops. Correspondingly, Washington repeatedly resorted to gunboat diplomacy in the effort to maintain a system amenable to US interests; between 1900 and 1920, the United States carried out nearly two dozen military interventions in the circum-Caribbean.[27] Nicaragua was no exception; the United States underwrote the overthrow of nationalist president José Santos Zelaya in 1909, and US Marines occupied Nicaragua from 1912 to 1925 and from 1900 to 1933. In their wake, the Marines left the newly formed National Guard, a constabulary organized by the United States to maintain domestic order under the command of General Anastasio Somoza García. Two years later, Somoza carried out a successful coup d'état, laying the foundation for the family dynasty that would rule Nicaragua—with significant US backing—for more than four decades.[28]

The United States continued to wield an outsize influence in Nicaragua during the Somoza dynasty. Franklin Delano Roosevelt supposedly defended his support for Anastasio Somoza García by famously asserting that "Somoza may be a son of a bitch, but he's our son of a bitch."[29] Both of Somoza's sons, Luis Somoza Debayle and Anastasio Somoza Debayle, were educated in the United States; the latter described himself as a "Latin from Manhattan" and peppered his English with US colloquialisms from the 1940s.[30] More to the point, by the 1950s the Nicaraguan economy was almost totally dependent on the United States, which accounted for as much as 70 percent of Nicaraguan trade.[31] Similarly, in the early Cold War era more Nicaraguans received military training at the US-run School of the Americas in the Panama Canal Zone than any other Latin Americans, and by the late 1960s Washington was supplying 13 percent of Nicaragua's annual defense budget. Washington's military relations with Managua, writes the historian Walter LaFeber, "were perhaps the closest in the hemisphere."[32]

Following the 1979 revolution, the Sandinistas were determined to escape Nicaragua's historically subordinate role vis-à-vis the United States. "What guides *Sandinismo* is the conviction that our country, Nicaragua, has never been a country with real sovereignty or national independence," agriculture minister Wheelock told the journalist Kinzer. Nicaragua, Wheelock continued, "has been an appendage of the United States. We have been abused and humiliated. Nicaragua was kept dependent and backward, a country of illiterate farm laborers. Our function was to grow sugar, cocoa, and coffee for the United States. We served the dessert at the imperialist dinner table."[33] Moreover, FSLN leaders emphasized that Nicaragua's perpetual dependence on the United States had arrested the nation's political development. US domination of Nicaragua "presupposed the draining of all our national identity and ideas, of any hopes of creating a political model or developing our own creative capacity," junta member Sergio Ramírez asserted in a mid-1983 address. Echoing the critique of imperialism by dependency theorists, Ramírez continued: "The almighty, strong, and wise Yankees owned all initiative and the future; we, the cause and product of underdevelopment, could only own our misery, our poverty which created more poverty, condemned to live off the ideological leftovers of the perfect model of Yankee democracy that elects a President every four years among colored balloons, willing nonetheless to tighten the screws of domination in our countries in the name of the bankers and financiers whose claws neither Jefferson nor Madison envisioned."[34]

If the Sandinistas looked to the United States as the source of more than a century of Nicaraguan suffering, in the eyes of the FSLN, Fidel Castro's socialist Cuba was the revolutionary model par excellence. For the Sandinistas, the 1959 Cuban revolution was the sole example of a successful anti-imperialist struggle in the hemisphere; moreover, since the FSLN's founding in 1961, the Cuban dictator had provided the fledgling organization with arms, training, and a much-needed safe haven. The Sandinistas were "old friends of the Cuban revolution," Castro informed Bulgarian leader Todor Zhivkov in April 1979. Cuba continued to be the Sandinistas' most important benefactor in the months leading up to the Nicaraguan revolution. Castro personally facilitated an agreement unifying Nicaragua's three revolutionary factions in early 1979 and played a critical role in funneling clandestine weapons to the FSLN.[35]

Castro retained his special relationship with the FSLN following the triumph of the revolution in July. The Cubans had an inside track with the Sandinistas "that nobody was going to compete with," recalled US ambassador Pezzullo. Castro was "bigger than life to them."[36] Moreover, when the fighting subsided, FSLN leaders saw Cuba as the lodestar for reconstructing post-conflict Nicaragua. "Many of us wanted to adopt the Cuban model in its entirety, even in the most banal matters. It was a question of blind faith," wrote Ramírez in a later memoir. Such emulation stretched beyond the bounds of mere governance; FSLN officials would frequently bring Cuban advisers to government meetings as a sign of distinction, and the island nation's accent and colloquialisms, Ramírez remembered, "were imitated so much that it seemed like a new language that you had to learn."[37]

If FSLN leaders were smitten with Cuban revolutionary chic, Cuba's influence on Nicaragua was also deepened by Castro's singular willingness to assist with post-conflict reconstruction.[38] By late 1981, 2,045 Cuban teachers were living and working in Nicaragua, alongside 240 technicians, 159 doctors, and 66 nurses. Correspondingly, the CIA estimated that 1,800 Cuban military and security advisers were operating in the Central American nation; the Cubans claimed the actual number was limited to "several dozen."[39] Yet such figures only partially reveal the depth of Castro's commitment to Sandinista Nicaragua. Cuba's generosity, "was absolute, to the point of abuse," Ramírez later wrote. Reflecting on the decade of FSLN rule, he continued: "Because we asked for everything and we were never denied anything: teachers; doctors; construction brigades for highways, schools, and homes; scholarships for every level of education and specialization imaginable; irrigation equipment and farming equipment; herds of cattle; insecticides; fertilizers; vaccinations; medicines; book publishing; a turnkey sugar plantation; and even doctors' visits for the leadership and their families in hospitals in Havana, along with vacations in Varadero."[40]

Top Sandinista officials' close ties to Castro were also indicative of the strong current of Marxist-Leninism running through the FSLN. "The Sandinistas rebels are mature revolutionaries, sharing Marxist-Leninist beliefs," Castro told Zhivkov in 1979. "Cuban comrades advise them against giving publicity to their beliefs and speaking publicly about Marxism-Leninism. They should be raising other slogans for the time being—for democracy, revival of the nation, etc. So far they are heeding the advice." Indeed, in an effort to rally broad-based support against Anastasio Somoza Debayle, FSLN leaders worked to maintain an image as moderates. In early 1979, Humberto Ortega Saavedra maintained in a secret missive that some FSLN militants lacked an awareness of the need for "tactical alliances." Emphasizing the need to avoid alienating conservative allies in the struggle against Somoza, Ortega asserted that "the fact that we cannot establish socialism immediately after Somoza's collapse does not mean that we are creating a capitalist-developmentalist type of social-democracy; what we propose is a broad, democratic and popular government which, even if the bourgeoisie is involved, is a means and not an end, in order to make the leap toward truly popular forms of power and guarantee the process toward socialism."[41]

Following Somoza's defeat, the FSLN's political worldview gathered form in September 1979, when some four hundred Sandinista militants gathered to draft a strategic blueprint for the nation's future over the course of three days. The result, known as the "72-Hour Document," defined the FSLN as a vanguard party charged with uniting Nicaraguans in a revolutionary society. Emphasizing the need to build state-sanctioned mass organizations, consolidate the military, and establish an economy "independent of the system of extortion and subordination imposed by imperialism worldwide," the "72-Hour Document" called for a concerted effort to isolate "the traitorous bourgeoisie, which blindly persists in trying to keep our country subject to the economic dependence of imperialism."[42] Reflecting on the document many years later, Ramírez emphasized its radical vision. "In full splendor of Marxist terminology, we declared that our objective was to achieve a Socialist society based on a proletarian dictatorship, after a period of alliances with the bourgeoisie, the shorter the better."[43]

Significantly, the FSLN's Marxist-Leninism was tempered, however, by a pragmatic recognition that rebuilding the shattered nation would require tactical alliances at home and abroad. The Sandinistas desperately needed international relief aid from Western donors, along with new foreign loans to replenish the nation's empty treasury and debt restructuring on existing loans. Domestically, gaining the trust of the Nicaraguan private sector would be crucial in rebuilding the economy—there could be no recovery if fields lay fallow and factories idle. In the spiritual arena, too, the Sandinistas needed to tread lightly. To be sure, progressive priests and Catholic lay workers advocating the teachings of liberation theology—with its emphasis on the "option of the poor"—had played an important role in the 1970s in fueling opposition to Somoza. The vast majority of Nicaraguans, however, embraced a traditional brand of Catholicism; shepherded by conservative members of the Church hierarchy, particularly Archbishop Manuel Obando y Bravo, most Nicaraguan Catholics were ingrained with a deep distrust of Marxism-Leninism and its derivatives. Significantly, even the Sandinistas' closest ally counseled pragmatism; watching events unfold from Havana, Castro emphasized the political differences between Cuba and Central America and warned that the FSLN could expect only limited assistance from the socialist bloc.[44]

Accordingly, the FSLN consistently emphasized a platform of political pluralism, international nonalignment, and a mixed economy. As the Jimmy Carter administration and the Organization of American States debated whether to dispatch a peacekeeping force to Nicaragua in the late spring of 1979, "the Sandinistas were astutely reassuring the world about their democratic intentions," recalled Robert A. Pastor, director of Latin American and Caribbean affairs on the National Security Council (NSC).[45] Indeed, provisional recognition of the anti-Somoza forces by the Organization of American States on June 23 was made contingent on the promise that the post-Somoza regime would hold free and fair elections, establish an independent media, protect the rights of trade unions, and maintain religious freedoms; with the revolutionary victory drawing near, on July 12 the Sandinistas dispatched a written communiqué to the organization explicitly promising to guarantee democratic freedoms and to hold free elections.[46] The Sandinista leadership continued to follow this approach in the months following Somoza's ouster; when Humberto Ortega declared that "Sandinismo, without Marxism-Leninism, cannot be revolutionary" in a September 1981 address, he was privately rebuked by the FSLN Directorate, and a revised version of the speech was quickly printed—with the offending phrase omitted—and top Sandinista officials awkwardly declared that the original copy had been "maliciously altered" by opponents of the revolution.[47]

Yet there was more behind the FSLN's emphasis on political pluralism, nonalignment, and a mixed economy than mere deception. The most important influence on Nicaragua in the 1980s was the early twentieth-century nationalist Augusto Sandino, whose legacy the FSLN claimed with intense devotion. A fierce anti-imperialist, Sandino led a rebellion between 1927 and 1933 against the US military occupation of Nicaragua in the rugged region of Segovia. Sandino also excoriated Nicaraguan political and economic elites as traitors whose self-interested collaboration with the North Americans created a perpetual state of Nicaraguan impoverishment. Lured to attend peace talks with the Nicaraguan government following the withdrawal of US Marines, Sandino was assassinated in 1934 by members of the National Guard, led by Anastasio Somoza García.

Sandino's legacy played a profound effect in shaping the FSLN. Resurrected as a patriot and martyr in the 1960s by the Nicaraguan revolutionary Carlos Fonseca Amador, Sandino developed into a powerful symbol in the struggle for national sovereignty and social and economic justice.[48] Following Somoza's overthrow, these same ideas papered over the ideological rifts between the three revolutionary factions and emerged as the central features of the public expression of the FSLN's political platform. And while the Marxism-Leninism undergirding the Sandinistas' *strategic* vision was an open secret, there were no constraints on the *tactical* reiteration of Sandino's underdog nationalism and rough-and-tumble egalitarianism. As Ramírez writes, "The ideas always most rooted in everyone's conscience were those that came from Sandino himself—national sovereignty, authentic democracy, social justice—because they were the most simple and clear."[49]

The result was a remarkable effort to transform Nicaragua in the post-Somoza era. On the whole, the FSLN increased social sector spending from 18 percent of the total budget in 1977 to 29 percent in 1981.[50] In the field of education, the Sandinistas confronted a grim legacy of Somoza's neglect. More than half of Nicaraguans were functionally illiterate, nearly twice the average across Latin America. In response, in early 1980 the FSLN launched a massive literacy campaign. Some sixty thousand volunteers fanned out across the country to teach basic reading skills to four hundred thousand people over a five-month period, reducing illiteracy to 12.9 percent.[51] It was an enormous effort for a nascent government struggling to confront the revolution's massive destruction. Yet the campaign itself was understood as just the beginning of a dramatically expanded national education system. In much of the countryside, education facilities were nonexistent, and for Nicaraguans fortunate enough to attend primary school, the dropout rate was 60 percent. Of the remaining 40 percent who finished primary school, less than half were able to attend high school.[52] In response, the revolutionary government set out to infuse the education system with new classrooms and new teachers. The number of children attending preschool programs jumped from 9,000 to 66,850 between 1978 and 1984; primary school enrollment over the same period increased from 369,640 to 635,637; and more than 15,000 new teachers entered classrooms between 1980 and 1984.[53] By 1981, continuation programs for adult learners enrolled nearly 144,000 people; three years later the program's enrollment neared 200,000; remarkably, by the end of the year, one-third of Nicaragua's population was enrolled in formal or technical higher education programs.[54]

The Sandinistas made similar advances in health care. Within a month of Somoza's overthrow, the FSLN had inaugurated a national health system that promised free medical attention to all Nicaraguans. By the end of 1980, the Health Ministry accounted for 14 percent of the national budget, a higher percentage than in any other Latin American nation and more than double the regional average.[55] Between 1980 and 1984, 309 new primary care facilities were constructed, as well as Nicaragua's first children's hospital. As a result, the number of medical visits jumped from 2.4 million in 1977 to 6.4 million in 1983, dental visits more than doubled, and the number of pregnant women under medical supervision increased from 23 percent in 1977 to 93 percent in 1983. Correspondingly, 1.2 million Nicaraguans received vaccinations against polio, measles, and tetanus in 1980; four years later, polio had been eradicated, and only 110 cases of measles were reported. Government-sponsored health campaigns, involving some 78,000 volunteers, spared Nicaragua from a regional outbreak of dengue in 1981 and reduced the number of Nicaraguans who contracted malaria from an annual average of 20,000 to only 505.[56] "We are a very poor country, a very underdeveloped country and a devastated country," admitted Xabier Gorostiaga, an official at the Ministry of Planning. "Yet we are showing the world that education and health are not a matter of economic resources; they are a matter of political will."[57]

The FSLN also tackled urban reforms. Under Somoza, parasites, typhoid, and dysentery were endemic in a nation where 94 percent of the rural population lacked safe drinking water and illegal garbage dumps, inadequate sewage facilities, and stagnant water pockmarked urban slums. "Shacks were built on the edge of the lake [Lake Managua], next to garbage dumps and drainage causeways and beneath electricity wires; 30% of the urban population received no services," noted an FSLN press release. "The great bulk of the housing was improvised and did not fulfill the basic human right to a roof over one's head."[58] In its first two years in power, the revolutionary government enacted a flurry of legislation, halting sales of subdivisions lacking basic services, setting rent ceilings, and placing regulations on landlords' ability to terminate rental agreements. More than 1,000 houses were constructed in 1980, a number that had grown to 3,698 by the end of 1982. The FSLN also confronted Nicaragua's dilapidated infrastructure. In the first three years following the revolution, 135 kilometers of new water and sewage lines served 43,541 people, 484 kilometers of new electric lines brought power to nearly three dozen communities, and 1,000 kilometers of new telephone wires connected 15,900 new users.[59]

The FSLN's most ambitious initiative, however, was an attempt to fundamentally restructure the Nicaraguan economy. Following Somoza's overthrow, the FSLN immediately expropriated the landholdings of the dictator and his associates, giving the revolutionary government ownership of roughly 25 percent of Nicaragua's 3.6 million hectares of arable land. Combined with nationalization of the domestic banks and insurance companies, and the mining and forestry sectors, the FSLN increased the public sector's share of GDP from less than 10 percent in 1978 to 40 percent by 1981.[60] Although the FSLN retained a mixed economy model—the private sector retained control of 80 percent of agriculture and 75 percent of manufacturing—the revolutionary government aimed to aggressively employ the levers of the state to benefit the majority rather than the top tier of income earners.[61] The FSLN had adopted the "logic of the poor," Gorostiaga asserted in 1981. "Our strategy differs from other models of economic development whose first priority is to establish a model of accumulation," Gorostiaga continued. "Our first objective is to satisfy the basic needs of the majority of the population."[62]

In the effort to reorder Nicaraguan economic life, land reform took center stage. The exploitation of peasants under the Somoza regime had drawn bitter FSLN criticism since the revolutionary organization's founding. "The Popular Sandinista Revolution outlines an agrarian policy that will realize an Authentic Agrarian Reform," proclaimed the FSLN's *Historic Program*, "immediately enacting a massive redistribution of the land by liquidating large landowners for the benefit of the workers (small producers) of the land."[63] Indeed, the nationalization of Somoza's landholdings transferred a huge expanse of Nicaraguan soil to the revolutionary government. Combined with subsequent government expropriations of large property owners' holdings deemed insufficiently exploited, the FSLN by 1984 had reduced the amount of property in large estates from more than 50 percent to a mere 13 percent.[64]

Rather than distributing the expropriated land to landless peasants, however, the Sandinistas ambitiously set out to enact a far-reaching agrarian transformation centered on state-run agricultural projects. With new legislation guaranteeing access to land, technical assistance, and financing, the number of agricultural cooperatives in Nicaragua grew from less than two dozen in 1979 to 3,800 at the end of 1981, with a total of 62,359 members.[65] Through cooperatives, the Sandinistas aimed to enhance Nicaraguan peasants' economic and sociopolitical status, raising them to the level of the urban working class. Correspondingly, the FSLN hoped state-run farms would facilitate high levels of export production without bowing to US pressure and, through strategic state investment, promote local production over imports. By 1984, the government was running sugar, milk, tobacco, palm oil, and cacao projects, while the nationalization of Nicaragua's timber and mining industry, the FSLN maintained, had revived "Nicaragua's right to decide the use of its economic resources."[66]

In the Sandinistas' ambitious vision of transforming the Nicaraguan economy to serve the needs of the majority, the power of large-scale producers would necessarily be severely circumscribed. The defining feature of capitalism, agriculture minister Wheelock asserted in a 1984 interview, was the power of the bourgeoisie "to do whatever they have to do, including breaking the rules of the game whenever necessary." Yet, with 60 percent of the economy remaining in private hands, the FSLN faced a serious dilemma: how to ensure that the private sector would serve the goals of the revolution rather than advancing its own self-interest. There was no easy solution; as Borge noted in July 1981, "We are struggling to create a society in which the workers are the fundamental power driving things forward, but in which other social sectors also play a role, always insofar as they identify with the interests of the country, with the interests of the majority."[67]

In an effort to encourage private enterprise, the FSLN would attempt to employ both the carrot and the stick, plying producers with ample incentives to maintain productivity while punishing decapitalization with fines or even expropriation. In 1982, for example, the private sector received nearly two-thirds of the credits approved by the state-run banking sector, as well as 68.8 percent of the authorized foreign exchange. In effect, the revolutionary government was engaged in a high-stakes gamble, in Wheelock's words, to determine "whether it is possible that the bourgeoisie simply produce, without power, that they limit themselves as a class to a productive role. That is, that they limit themselves to exploiting their means of production and use these means of production to live, not as instruments of power, of imposition."[68] FSLN officials admitted that it would not be an easy transition. "In this process you step on a few corns," conceded the foreign minister Miguel D'Escoto. "But you just step on the corns of the people who have shoes."[69]

The FSLN's social and economic initiatives were part of a larger effort to establish a unique form of participatory democracy in revolutionary Nicaragua. The FSLN envisioned a balance between top-down vanguardism and a form of direct democracy in which non-elites could participate in the nation's political life through newly created mass-based organizations at the grassroots level. In the heady aftermath of Somoza's overthrow, a multitude of new FSLN-sponsored grassroots organizations emerged, ranging from peasant and worker associations to the 60,000-member women's organization Association of Nicaraguan Women Luisa Amanda Espinoza (AMNLAE). The Sandinista Defense Committees (CDSs), in particular, were conceptualized as both a verticalist mechanism to carry out FSLN directives and a means for ordinary citizens to actively participate in the nation's day-to-day political life. The CDSs were charged with civil defense; grassroots political consciousness-raising; participation in the FSLN's education, health, and related social welfare projects at the community level; and monitoring activities ranging from food distribution to unveiling corruption. Significantly, the CDSs also allowed direct political participation in the revolutionary government through representation at the Council of State. The FSLN envisioned the CDSs as a decisive break with the past, providing non-elite Nicaraguans with a new pathway for political activism. By the end of 1982, a remarkable four hundred thousand Nicaraguans—16 percent of the nation's population—had joined one of the 9,915 CDSs that had been formed across the nation.[70]

The FSLN's dramatic increase in social sector spending and effort to instill a popular democracy rooted in grassroots political organizations reflected a vision of a new Nicaraguan society rooted in a specific conception of human rights. In the realm of political rights and civil liberties, the Sandinistas immediately abolished the death penalty and curtailed the use of state torture and disappearances. Confronting a crowd of Nicaraguans demanding the execution of captured members of the National Guard, Borge—himself a survivor of imprisonment and torture during the Somoza years—illuminated the FSLN's vision of making a decisive break with the brutal Somoza dictatorship. "So why did we make this revolution if we are going to do the things they used to do? If that's the way it is going to be, we would be better off not having made this revolution," Borge declared.[71]

If the Sandinistas succeeded in setting an important marker differentiating the revolutionary government from its predecessor and state-sanctioned violence, the paternalism characteristic of the FSLN's vanguardism led from the outset to constraints on Nicaraguan civil liberties. Indeed, following Somoza's overthrow, the FSLN moved quickly to consolidate political power. In April 1980, the FSLN expanded the membership of the Council of State from thirty-three to fifty-seven members, giving the FSLN a clear majority. The move "converted the FSLN into a steam roller," recalled business leader Robelo, who served on the five-member junta. "This was technically a coup d'état, since the basic structure of one of the branches of government is being altered." In the opening salvo of a bitter confrontation with the FSLN that would last more than a decade, Robelo and the publisher Violeta Barrios de Chamorro resigned from the junta and became outspoken opponents of the FSLN.[72]

The Sandinistas continued to consolidate political control in the subsequent months. "It soon became apparent that all significant lines of power were converging on the members of the National Directorate," wrote the Latin Americanist Dennis Gilbert in an early assessment. "They dominated the junta and the Council of State, controlled the military, and personally held the most important cabinet portfolios, including Defense, Interior (police), Planning, and Agriculture."[73] Correspondingly, the FSLN placed limits on civil liberties and prohibited the publication of information that could compromise national security as well as material pertaining to economic shortages; from late 1980 to early 1982, the government temporarily shuttered the opposition newspaper *La Prensa*—run by Chamorro—on three occasions for violating the new media laws. The government also turned a blind eye when mobs of Sandinista youth known as "turbas" shut down a rally by Robelo's newly formed opposition party, the MDN, and denied Archbishop Obando y Bravo—an increasingly sharp critic of the regime—permission to hold Sunday mass on state-run television. Outspoken opponents on both ends of the political spectrum risked FSLN retaliation; in the first three years of revolutionary rule, the leaders of both a communist labor union and the Council of Private Enterprise (COSEP) were briefly imprisoned.[74]

To be sure, such constraints were a far cry from the intense political repression that characterized neighboring El Salvador and Guatemala, where political activists and perceived subversives were kidnapped, tortured, and murdered in the tens of thousands. In Sandinista Nicaragua, opposition political parties continued to operate, and criticism from the Church, the media, and non-Sandinista labor unions was publicly aired. Even in the Council of State, the private sector and political opposition were significantly overrepresented in light of their small number of supporters. More significantly, in April 1980 the Sandinistas promised to hold national elections in 1985 (later moved up to late 1984), in part as a concession to the demands of the domestic political opposition.[75]

Yet the constraints on Nicaraguan civil society nonetheless illuminated the FSLN's dim view of unfettered political liberties and, in particular, electoral institutions as a mechanism of popular political participation. Sandinista officials were quick to point out that during the Somoza dynasty, Nicaragua maintained the pretense of formal democracy. The dictatorship, asserted Ramírez, "imported the political model of elections every four years, and elections existed here, a bi-partisan system existed here, and there was a two-chamber legislative system, a supreme court, and a constitution with laws. And it was all a bloody hoax."[76] More broadly, the Sandinistas dismissed "democratism" as a "liberal bourgeois ideology" that championed abstract notions of liberty in order to hide structural inequalities. "Bourgeois freedom has nothing to do with popular freedom that reflects the people's own objective interests in terms of their right to organize and to arm themselves (politically, militarily, and ideologically) *as a class*, in order to imbue the historical project of society in a way that corresponds with their interests as the majority," the FSLN asserted in the government-run daily *Barricada* in March 1980.[77] For the majority of Nicaraguans, in other words, formal political equality in the Somoza era had been a chimera; ballots meant little in a society where 90 percent of the health facilities served 10 percent of the population.

By contrast, for the Sandinistas, authentic democracy and economic and social justice were inextricably linked. Setting the tone, Borge in a 1982 address on human rights asserted that "it is not true that all persons are born free and equal in dignity and rights, as is stated in the Universal Declaration of Human Rights of the United Nations." Borge continued, "This equality ends when one child receives a specialized diet and the other is the victim of malnutrition. In Nicaragua now all children are born free, but they are still not born equal. They will only be equal when they have the same opportunity to live; when 100 of each 1000 children who are born do not die; when linen diapers and rag diapers do not exist at the same time; when mangers and cradles of gold do not exist at the same time."[78]

For the FSLN, *authentic* democracy flowed from the promotion of social and economic rights and was maintained through daily participation in grassroots political organizations. Revolutionary Nicaragua aimed to create a "a permanent dynamic of the people's participation in a variety of political and social tasks," Ramírez maintained, shaped by "the people who suggest, construct, and direct, organize themselves, who attend to community, neighborhood, and national problems." By creating a "daily democracy," Ramírez concluded, the FSLN was advancing a model of popular sovereignty far more democratic than electoral systems in which candidates were selected "like a soap or deodorant" and voters routinely "manipulated by an advertising agency."[79]

Corresponding with the FLSN's emphasis on social and economic justice at home, the Sandinistas aspired to serve as a model of national liberation in the international arena. Although the shadow of US interventionism loomed over the Sandinista political project, the revolutionary triumph imbued FSLN leaders with a sense of unbridled possibility. "You know, you are very fortunate to be here at this time. Because you can see from us, you know, how things are going to play out all through Latin America," one of the comandantes told US ambassador Pezzullo shortly after the revolutionary triumph. "We're going to be the model all through Latin America." Support from a diverse range of leftist groups and nonaligned governments enhanced the FSLN's sense of revolutionary Nicaragua as a unique source of inspiration abroad. According to Pezzullo, after the revolution, "every cuckoo nut around the world" took up temporary residence in Managua. "We had extremists from Peru. We had the Montoneros from Argentina. Miristas from Chile. The Tupamaros from Uruguay. We had the PLO [Palestine Liberation Organization]. We had North Koreans; it was the first time I saw the North Koreans. We had revolutionaries from Africa," the ambassador remembered. Filled with visiting international delegations, Managua's Intercontinental Hotel, Pezzullo noted, "looked like some sort of a Hollywood stage."[80]

More concretely, from the moment of the Nicaraguan revolutionary triumph, the Sandinistas supported the leftist insurgents of the Farabundo Martí National Liberation Front (FMLN) in neighboring El Salvador. Publicly, top FSLN officials repeatedly emphasized Nicaraguan "solidarity" with the Salvadoran rebels, while denying that Nicaragua was providing material aid.[81] Privately, illicit military aid flowed from Cuba via Nicaragua to Salvadoran rebels in the lead-up to the failed "final offensive" in January 1981. After stepped-up US pressure forced the Sandinistas to halt C-47 flights, a fleet of hardy canoes—small enough to avoid US detection—regularly plied a nightly passage across the Gulf of Fonseca, ferrying arms to the Salvadoran insurgents. Although the actual amount of weapons that moved through Nicaragua to El Salvador in the early 1980s was probably far less than the hundreds of tons estimated by US intelligence agencies, by early 1981 the support itself was an open secret. "They don't really deny it," Pezzullo reported in February. "They only say it's less than we assume it is."[82] Indeed, at the national ceremony commemorating the Nicaraguan revolution's second anniversary five months later, the FSLN brashly seated the canoeists on the stage in a place of honor surrounded by the assembled dignitaries.[83]

Yet the trickle of arms to Salvadoran revolutionaries was the exception, not the rule, in Sandinista foreign policy. The FSLN's principal aim was to be a model for third-world nations seeking to break free from the legacies of colonialism and underdevelopment. The revolution, Wheelock asserted, had made it possible for the nation to "exist as *Nicaragua*, in a way that it never existed before in the sense of a sovereign state."[84] Similarly, Sandinista leaders emphasized that their dedication in promoting social and economic justice was the signal contribution of the Nicaraguan revolution for other struggles of national liberation. "We export ideas, ideas of change and renovation, ideas that provide a foundation for a new world being born, we export the proven possibility that an armed people, when they set about to do so, can overthrow tyranny and establish a nascent and innovative world on the wastes of that tyranny; we export the news that in Nicaragua the revolution has brought with it literacy, agrarian reform, an end to poliomyelitis, the right to life and hope," Ramírez eloquently declared in 1983. "How can one prevent a peasant from another Central American country from hearing, from finding out, from realizing that in Nicaragua land is given to other poor and barefoot peasants like him? How can you avoid his realizing that here children—not his children—are being vaccinated while his children still die of gastroenteritis and polio?"[85]

Accordingly, the revolutionary government staked out a nonaligned foreign policy approach that aimed to avoid the orbit of either the US-led Western alliance or the Soviet-led communist bloc. Immediately following Somoza's ouster, the Sandinistas successfully petitioned for membership in the Non-Aligned Nations Movement (NAM). Sparked by the efforts of Asian and African leaders at the Bandung Conference in 1955, the first summit of NAM countries had been held in Belgrade six years later. By the 1970s, NAM had developed into a heterogeneous bloc of nearly one hundred developing nations utilizing the United Nations General Assembly as a sounding board to advocate third-world solidarity and a political path independent of either the first or second world; in practice, NAM's opposition to imperialism, colonialism, apartheid, and Zionism frequently brought it into alignment with the socialist world. Algerian president Houari Boumedienne's 1974 declaration of a New International Economic Order was a defining moment in NAM's evolution. Denouncing the divide between rich and poor nations and the unequal terms of exchange that hindered third-world development, Boumedienne offered a blueprint for a statist, anti-Western approach to development predicated on state expropriation of natural resources and the creation of new international mechanisms to support third-world development.[86]

Five years later, the FSLN quickly embraced the nations of the nonaligned movement as "natural allies," in the words of Sandinista diplomat Alejandro Bendaña. "We saw the overall economic and political limitations that exist for any small independent country seeking liberation and respect for human rights in all their dimensions," Bendaña asserted. "So we stressed the need for a new international economic order, a new international political order, so that when people come to power, even if they're from small nations, they can carry out their social transformations free from foreign intervention."[87] NAM reciprocated, holding an extraordinary session in Managua in January 1983, including 116 delegates from forty-one nations, to discuss the Central American situation.[88] In the resulting communiqué, the ministers reiterated their support for the Sandinista project, emphasizing "the historic significance of the democratic, popular, anti-imperialist, anti-colonialist and anti-racist struggles that the Latin American and Caribbean people are waging for national liberation and the consolidation of their independence."[89] More importantly, support from the nonaligned nations was critical in Nicaragua's successful 1983 bid for the rotating seat on the UN Security Council, which the Central American nation won with 104 votes, despite intense opposition from the United States.[90]

The Soviet Union, by contrast, initially had little influence over the Sandinistas. The FSLN had been formed in 1961 following a split between its founding members and the pro-Moscow Nicaraguan Communist Party, and in the nearly two decades that followed, the USSR maintained almost no contacts with the organization.[91] In the months following Somoza's overthrow, the Kremlin kept its distance from the revolutionary regime, offering Nicaragua only symbolic economic and humanitarian aid between 1979 and 1981, including two shipments of medical supplies and children's food and a donation of twenty thousand tons of wheat. Moreover, in the year and a half after Somoza's overthrow, the Soviet Union offered no military assistance to Nicaragua.[92]

If the FSLN saw itself as a model for third-world national liberation, Sandinistas viewed the military as a tool to consolidate the Nicaraguan revolution, not as a mechanism to export it. The "72-Hour Document," for example, placed greater emphasis on domestic policy than on military matters. "Without downplaying the need for a strong army capable of assuring national defense, it should be noted that at present there are no clear indications of an armed counterrevolution by Somocista forces from abroad which actually threatens our stability," the FSLN's strategic blueprint for post-Somoza Nicaragua asserted. "Actually, what merits our attention, from this point of view, are domestic matters."[93] Indeed, at the beginning of the 1980s, the quality of the newly formed Ejército Popular Sandinista (Sandinista Popular Army [EPS]) was dismal. A force of roughly fifteen thousand in 1980, the EPS lacked standardized equipment and specialized training; the following year, FSLN chief of staff Joaquín Cuadra Lacayo admitted that one well-trained soldier was equal to three EPS regulars. Under such conditions, it was "inconceivable" that Nicaragua would invade another country, Cuadra asserted.[94]

Instead, FSLN leaders were dedicated to safeguarding the Nicaraguan revolution by making the military a bastion of Sandinista support. In particular, the lessons drawn from the 1973 Chilean military coup significantly shaped the Sandinista political project. Unlike Nicaragua, where Somoza's National Guard had been thoroughly destroyed, Chilean socialist president Salvador Allende had confronted a largely antagonistic military establishment. When the US-backed political and economic destabilization campaign had created propitious conditions for a coup, "the military was used for the final blow and brought about the removal of the government in a matter of four hours," Wheelock noted in a 1984 interview. As a student in Santiago, Wheelock had watched firsthand the violent destruction of Allende's democratic experiment. A decade later, he underscored the necessity of maintaining a pro-Sandinista military to avoid Allende's fate: "Our case is different. The axis of aggression against Nicaragua is military because they are trying to overthrow an armed people's revolutionary government. It can't be destabilized by economic or political measures alone, because we can counteract those. They have to overthrow us militarily, impede the consolidation of our process, impede the consolidation of our people's armed forces. That's why they are resorting to Somoza's army [the Contras], which is what they have closest at hand for the task."[95] Predictably, in response to the rising US-backed counterrevolutionary threat, the Sandinistas moved to expand Nicaragua's military establishment. In February 1981, the FSLN created the Sandinista People's Militia to defend against cross-border attacks that had claimed dozens of Nicaraguan lives in the previous months. The militia's capacity was limited; consisting of male and female volunteers as young as thirteen years old, it was conceived as a reserve organization that could be mobilized in a national security crisis. Yet, combined with the increase in the size of the regular army, the total number of Nicaraguan full-time and reserve forces reached forty thousand in 1981.[96]

Correspondingly, the FSLN solicited military aid from abroad. In late 1981, the FSLN signed a $17.5 million contract with France for a pair of helicopters, one hundred air-to-ground rocket launchers, forty-five trucks, and two patrol boats. Friendly Arab states offered aid as well, with Algeria shipping small arms and Libya's mercurial Mu'ammar Gadhafi offering helicopters. Most of the aid, however, came from behind the Iron Curtain. By the end of 1981, the FSLN had received an estimated nine hundred metric tons of military assistance from the Soviet bloc, mostly from East Germany, which sent more than 150 trucks, and tens of thousands of small arms, helmets, mess kits, backpacks, and uniforms.[97]

Taken as a whole, the FSLN succeeded in making major steps toward transforming Nicaragua in the first phase of the post-Somoza era. The massive increases in social spending, combined with an emphasis on popular political participation, were unprecedented in the Central American nation's history, leading many to conclude that the Sandinistas had indeed embarked on a remarkable political project. More to the point, many thousands of Nicaraguans experienced tangible improvements in their day-to-day lives. Capturing the unique sense of possibility that permeated revolutionary Nicaragua in the early 1980s, the journalist Stephen Kinzer described a visit to a newly created government agricultural cooperative:

> Although only 35, Eduardo Rojas looked withered and played out. His leathery face was deeply lined and many of his teeth were missing. All his life, starting when he was five years old, he had worked on a small plot of land in the fertile hills outside his village in the northern province of León. Half the produce was sent to an absentee landlord; Rojas, when he grew up, had to keep himself, his wife and their five children alive on what remained. That was how his father and grandfather had lived. That is how his children would live. Poverty, ignorance, illness and backbreaking toil have been the lot of hundreds of thousands of Nicaraguan peasants.

The revolution, however, had changed that. Rojas was now working with two dozen other peasant families on a state-run farm, with credit and technical help from the Agrarian Reform Ministry and fixed prices for their surplus produce at a government food distribution agency. A maternity ward had opened in a nearby village. For Rojas, such a dramatic transition was hard to believe. "My children are going to school—can you imagine it?" he enthused. "They will get other ideas. Perhaps they will not be poor peasants. They will be able to choose a different life for themselves—whatever they want. This is a total change. Without the revolution, it would never have happened." Reflecting on the visit, Kinzer realized he was witnessing an extraordinary moment in Nicaraguan history. The Sandinistas, he astutely concluded, "have given many downtrodden Nicaraguans something as precious as it is rare for the poor people in Latin America: hope for the future."[98]

Yet the revolution had also created enormous expectations that went far beyond the FSLN's capacity to fulfill. In the first two years following Somoza's overthrow, Nicaragua received more than $1 billion in loans and trade credits from international and bilateral agencies, equivalent to $135 per year for every Nicaraguan. Yet the FSLN ended 1980 with a deficit of some $170 million. The problem was threefold. First, after assuming power, the Sandinistas agreed to pay off all external debts inherited from Somoza. It was an enormous sum: at the end of 1980, public debt stood at $1.7 billion—a figure nearly three times the size of Nicaragua's annual exports. Although the revolutionary regime managed to negotiate favorable terms of repayment with bilateral and multilateral creditors, public debt remained an immense burden on the fragile Nicaraguan economy.[99]

Second, in addition to simply rebuilding Nicaragua's war-torn infrastructure, ballooning social sector and state-run agriculture programs required a major infusion of scarce government resources. At the same time, the FSLN's demand that private producers cooperate in meeting the "needs of the people" was met with skepticism. COSEP president Enrique Dreyfus set the tone, grimly predicting that Nicaragua's foreign debt was leading to a "crisis of incalculable proportions" and assailing the FSLN for "wasting the money obtained from this indebtedness on unproductive activities while the private sector is being starved for foreign exchange that it needs for raw materials and spare parts."[100] Following COSEP's lead, between 1980 and 1981, Nicaraguan entrepreneurs rapidly decapitalized; private-sector investment dropped from roughly 85 percent of total Nicaraguan investment in the mid-1970s to a mere 15 percent in the early 1980s, as producers removed as much as $140 million from the nation's economy. With the revolutionary government controlling only a quarter of Nicaragua's material production, the result was a massive hole in the economy that state investment was unable to fill.[101]

Third, the Sandinistas confronted the twin challenges of an economy focused on raw material exports and a legacy of economic dependence on the United States. For every dollar of production, the Ministry of Planning estimated that Nicaragua needed $0.60 in imported raw materials, a problem compounded by a drop in sugar and coffee prices and a rise in import costs at the outset of the 1980s.[102] By February 1982, Nicaragua was "at best a marginally creditworthy country," an International Bank for Reconstruction and Development (IBRD) report noted. "The level of assistance Nicaragua needs in the short term is even larger than the unprecedented aid the country has received in the last few years," the IBRD concluded. "It is unlikely that this level of very preferential aid will continue much longer."[103]

As a result, Nicaragua experienced limited economic growth and deepening instability in the early 1980s. In 1981, the Nicaraguan GDP was only 80 percent of the 1977 level, exports were 16.8 percent lower than in 1978, and industrial growth was 35 percent lower than the government's projected goal. Despite overall agricultural increases, Nicaragua for the first time in many years was forced to import rice, oil, beans, and chickens. Rising prices squeezed ordinary Nicaraguans' pocketbooks; the US Embassy estimated that private consumption dropped 12 percent in 1982, while FSLN officials admitted that efforts to conserve exports by exhorting Nicaraguans to shift from white to brown sugar and to substitute beef with chicken, pork, and fish had confronted "a lot of popular resistance."[104]

Correspondingly, a combination of bureaucratic inefficiency and limited resources left the FSLN's social promises unfulfilled. Hospitals lacked medicine, equipment, and doctors. In the countryside, the much-vaunted land reform proceeded at a snail's pace, with less than 20 percent of the lands seized under the Agrarian Reform Law distributed to government-sponsored cooperatives by June 1982. "The GRN [government of Nicaragua] wants to give land only to cooperatives it sponsors, but is constrained by lack of organizational, financial, and technical resources needed to support them," the US Embassy reported. "It could speed the pace of reform by giving more land to individual farmers, who have no claim on state resources (but also who do not have to answer to the state). So far it has chosen not to do that."[105]

By the time Reagan entered the White House, the fortieth president of the United States confronted a revolutionary regime in Nicaragua that remained in the foundational stages of post-conflict recovery but could boast significant achievements. Yet the Sandinistas were also nearing a crossroads. Facing severe economic challenges in the foreseeable future, the FSLN could hardly ignore the clamor of opposition from the private sector. Popular frustration with the revolution's unmet aspirations added to the Sandinistas' difficulties. "The FSLN is getting full blame for the revolution's failure to satisfy all of the aspirations awakened in the victory over Somoza," Ambassador Pezzullo cabled Washington in May 1981. By limiting non-FSLN political participation, Pezzullo reported, the Sandinistas were reaping the lion's share of public criticism for Nicaragua's problems. Moreover, while the Sandinistas retained significant popular support, many Nicaraguans viewed the FSLN with skepticism. "As a leftist guerrilla movement inspired by Castro's example and fuzzy Marxist-Leninist ideas, the FSLN came to power encumbered by an ideology in conflict with the way of life of most Nicaraguans," the ambassador asserted.[106]

But would Nicaragua's mounting problems force the FSLN to widen the political playing field and deepen its cooperation with the domestic opposition? Pezzullo was cautiously optimistic. With strong support from the Nicaraguan middle and upper classes, opposition leaders, he wrote, were confident that they could eventually "bring the Sandinistas to their senses." Significantly, Pezzullo recognized, however, that such a development was by no means inevitable. With the Reagan administration's accusations of Sandinista support for Salvadoran revolutionaries intensifying, the ambassador presciently warned that "one factor that domestic opposition groups cannot control and that may rescue the FSLN from having to make common cause with non-Sandinista forces is an external threat to the revolution. Any threat to the achievements of the past two years—especially one linked to Somocismo—would quickly turn the tide of public opinion back to the FSLN."[107]

In Washington, however, Pezzullo's warnings went unheeded. Viewing Central America through the lens of the global Cold War, the Reagan administration was deeply concerned by political developments in Nicaragua. "We are now at a watershed in U.S. foreign policy," national security adviser William P. Clark began at a NSC meeting on February 10, 1982.[108] The Soviet threat to the Caribbean "is unprecedented in severity and proximity and complexity," Clark continued. Remarkably, according to the national security adviser, even "the Nazi threat in the 1930s and 1940s and the Castro threat in the 1960s were more limited in scope, with fewer resources being expended. The strategies were of a less sophisticated nature, and were employed for a shorter period of time."[109]

Clark's alarm was underscored by a grim assessment of Cuban foreign policy adventurism from the director of the CIA, William J. Casey. With seventy thousand military and civilian advisers operating in nearly thirty countries, Cuba "has displayed a remarkable reach on a worldwide scale," reported the CIA background paper prepared for the NSC meeting. Moreover, Soviet support for its Caribbean proxy had increased significantly since Reagan had entered the White House; in 1981 the Kremlin shipped more than $1 billion in arms to Cuba—sixty-six thousand tons of equipment, compared to an annual average of fifteen thousand tons over the previous decade—augmenting the island nation's fighting forces with sophisticated tanks, attack helicopters, and MIG fighter jets. Moscow's support, the CIA report continued, was underwriting a systematic Cuban effort to destabilize the circum-Caribbean by unifying, training, and supplying guerrilla leftist groups "in virtually every Latin American country."[110]

Revolutionary Nicaragua was the tip of the lance. "There is every indication that Nicaragua is being built up to [be] a superpower on the Central American scale," the CIA report warned. Managua had become the nerve center for nearly two thousand Cuban military and security advisers and dozens of Soviet personnel, as well as a handful of East Germans, Bulgarians, Vietnamese, North Koreans, and radical Arabs. Domestically, the FSLN was drawing heavily on Castro's political template to establish a totalitarian regime, systematically silencing opposition political parties, private-sector leaders, and the press. Internationally, the Sandinistas were dedicated to exporting revolution abroad. As a result, the insurgency in El Salvador, the CIA claimed, was "being directed, trained, and supplied" by the Sandinistas and their allies. Yet clandestine aid to the Salvadoran revolutionaries was only the beginning.

The Sandinistas were poised to dominate the entire Central American isthmus. "When Nicaragua receives Soviet MIGs it can threaten the Panama Canal. Tanks can roll into Honduras and also through Costa Rica to the borders of Panama," the CIA concluded. "In short, Nicaragua will be able to intimidate its neighbors by military force."[111]

Echoing the report's findings, Reagan's top advisers reiterated the need for aggressive US action to confront deepening communist inroads in the hemisphere. "This is *our* border we are talking about, and *our* security, and *our* vital national interests," UN ambassador Jeane J. Kirkpatrick emphasized, "interests which are very immediate and very concrete and are very different from the sorts of interests that may have been threatened in the past."[112] Reagan concurred. Recognizing significant domestic opposition to increased US military involvement in the region, the president underscored the need to avoid beating the drums of war. Nonetheless, Reagan was determined to stem the tide of communist interventionism. "I would not want history to record that there was a time when we could have headed off this hemisphere becoming an extension of the Warsaw Pact," he confided. "Lenin may then turn out to have been right when he said that someday the Western Hemisphere would be ripe fruit after Europe."[113]

Washington's response was not long in coming. In late 1981, Reagan had approved a CIA plan to train five hundred Latin American commandos, and on Capitol Hill, in secret briefings with the House and Senate Intelligence Committees, CIA director Casey mollified skeptical legislators by emphasizing that the operation was focused entirely on interdicting clandestine shipments of weapons. In reality, from the outset the Reagan administration's goal was to wage guerrilla warfare on the Sandinistas; in no small irony, the CIA officer running the operation, Duane R. "Dewey" Clarridge, drew inspiration from the FSLN's own namesake. "It dawned on me that we needed to mimic Sandino and his tactics," Clarridge recalled in a 1997 memoir.[114] By the time Reagan met with the NSC in February 1982, the Contras had grown to a guerrilla force of more than one thousand.

A month later, the Reagan administration's intervention began in earnest when a US-trained and US-equipped demolition team destroyed the Rio Negro bridge and badly damaged the Ocotal bridge in northern Nicaragua. Although the administration assured the House Intelligence Committee that the bridges were essential conduits for arms trafficking, the evidence that the White House was engaged in a much broader destabilization campaign was mounting. "It is much easier and much less expensive to support an insurgency than it is for us and our friends to resist one," CIA director Casey told a student group the day before the attacks. "It takes relatively few people and little support to disrupt the internal peace and economic stability of a small country."[115]

In Nicaragua, the FSLN response to the attacks was swift. Having declared 1982 the year of "Unity in the Face of Aggression," the Sandinista Directorate denounced the "CIA plan to overthrow [the] revolutionary government" and immediately imposed a state of emergency—a preparatory period "previous to a war," according to Sergio Ramírez—suspending political rights and clamping down on civil liberties.[116] As Tomás Borge grimly asserted, "We can only conclude that the U.S. government, for all practical purposes, has declared war against us, and that a logical consequence of this could be open confrontation."[117]

Over the following months, Contra attacks intensified. In the 100-day period following the bridge attacks, counterrevolutionaries filtering across the porous Honduran border carried out more than one hundred actions in northern Nicaragua, ranging from assassinations of low-level government officials and sniper attacks on FSLN military patrols to the sabotage of bridges and the burning of crops.[118] By October 1982, more than one hundred Sandinista soldiers had been killed in combat, and US ambassador Anthony Quainton reported that "while the contras do not have the ability to displace the GRN they are an ever-present irritant which exerts constant pressures on the Sandinista system." The counterrevolutionaries were forcing the FSLN to divert scarce resources to defense, Quainton concluded, and "serve to provide encouragement to those opponents of the regime who are convinced the survivability of the GRN is at risk."[119]

Yet the Contra threat also provided the FSLN with a means to rally its supporters in the face of a rising national security threat. As Pezzullo had predicted, the FSLN dug in its heels, reflexively falling back on a mix of nationalism, anti-imperialism, and anti-Americanism to denounce the Somocista threat. "The FSLN uses the presence of the contras as a powerful propaganda tool. GRN leaders consistently seek to link [the] contras with Somoza's despised National Guard," the US Embassy reported. "The Sandinista press gives extensive publicity to contra attacks, and funerals for slain Sandinistas are routinely turned into politicized spectacles. The Sandinistas emphasize the purported US connection. They then appeal to Nicaraguan patriotism and nationalism by calling for unity in the face of external aggression."[120]

The Contra threat also prompted the Sandinistas to dramatically expand Nicaragua's armed forces. Soviet bloc military deliveries jumped from nine hundred metric tons in 1981 to sixty-seven hundred metric tons in 1982, and the EPS received deliveries of Soviet-made small arms, as well as 57-millimeter antitank guns and 152-millimeter howitzers, SA-7 surface-to-air missiles, East German artillery trucks, and armored personnel carriers. By the end of the year, Nicaragua had also obtained nearly fifty Soviet-made T-55 tanks—thirty-year-old behemoths weighing thirty-six metric tons and armed with a 100-millimeter gun. Although the Nicaraguan air force remained basically nonexistent, Nicaraguan pilots began training on Soviet MIGs in Cuba and Bulgaria, and the FSLN began quietly expanding four airfields to handle advanced fighter aircraft.[121] When US secretary of state George P. Shultz warned Nicaragua not to obtain MIG fighters, the Sandinistas responded with defiance. The United States was "committing open aggression" against Nicaragua, Daniel Ortega declared, and the secretary's demand that Nicaragua limit its arsenal was "cynical and immoral." Drawing parallels between the Vietnam War and the US intervention in Central America, Ortega offered a grim riposte: "Like Vietnam," the comandante avowed, "Nicaragua would ultimately triumph."[122]

Meanwhile, in Washington, opposition among congressional lawmakers and a majority of the US people threatened to constrain the scale of the Reagan administration's intervention in Central America. In December 1982, representative Edward P. Boland (D-MA), the chairman of the House Intelligence Committee, successfully offered an amendment to the House Appropriations Bill—subsequently referred to as the Boland Amendment—prohibiting the Department of Defense or the CIA from using US funds to overthrow the FSLN or incite a war between Nicaragua and Honduras.[123] Correspondingly, public opinion polls consistently revealed that most of the American public opposed a US military intervention in Central America. In April 1983, for example, only 10 percent of respondents polled by the *Los Angeles Times* supported US covert operations in Nicaragua, and nearly half believed that US involvement in El Salvador was not essential to US national defense.[124]

In the aftermath of the successful passage of the Boland Amendment, the Reagan administration upped the ante, describing the Contras as "freedom fighters" while insisting that the goal of US pressure was to curb Sandinista support for insurgencies abroad.[125] "We are not doing anything to try to overthrow the Nicaraguan government," Reagan assured reporters in mid-April.[126] Correspondingly, top administration policymakers emphasized the threat of spreading communism in the Western Hemisphere. "The whole scenario sounds like a grade B movie from the 1950s, but that, alas, does not mean it is not true," Kirkpatrick asserted in a *Washington Post* op-ed. "It's almost unbearably unfashionable to say so, but there is a plan to create a communist Central America which, if successful, will have momentous consequences for our security and that of our European allies, for Israel's international position, and for the unfortunate people of Central America."[127] Similarly, in a major policy address, Secretary of State Shultz claimed that "all of Central America" had become a target of Nicaraguan subversion and expressed concern that Nicaragua could become a base for Soviet missiles.[128]

At the end of the month, Reagan underscored the signal importance of Central America in an address to a joint session of Congress. Emphasizing the geographic proximity of Central America to the continental United States, Reagan warned that US inaction would allow communism to spread unchecked across the isthmus. "The Sandinista revolution in Nicaragua turned out to be just an exchange of one set of autocratic rulers for another, and the people still have no freedom, no democratic rights, and more poverty," Reagan declared. "Even worse than its predecessor, it is helping Cuba and the Soviets destabilize our hemisphere." Calling on congressional legislators to support economic and security programs in Central America, Reagan drew parallels to the Truman Doctrine at the onset of the Cold War and cast the region as vital to US interests. "The national security of all the Americas is at stake in Central America," the president warned. "If we cannot defend ourselves there, we cannot expect to prevail elsewhere. Our credibility would collapse, our alliances would crumble, and the safety of our homeland would be put at jeopardy."[129]

Privately, hard-liners in the administration worried that the US position was rapidly deteriorating. "We are losing in Central America. Within a year, perhaps earlier, there is a good chance that the national security and geopolitical position of the United States will have been permanently worsened," CIA director Casey bluntly informed the president in a top secret letter on June 25. "This would represent a historic failure."[130] Similarly, as the NSC prepared an update on Central America the following month, deputy assistant to the president for national security affairs Robert C. "Bud" McFarlane wrote, "As to the status report, I want the President to know that: 1. We are losing. 2. A principal reason we are losing is too little resources."[131]

Reagan agreed. In a top secret memo on July 12 to the secretaries of state and defense, the CIA director, and the chair of the Joint Chiefs of Staff, the president of the United States reiterated his commitment to confronting Sandinista Nicaragua. "The security situation in Central America is deteriorating," Reagan began. Emphasizing a lack of public awareness and insufficient resources, Reagan gave the green light to an extensive "public affairs / legislative action plan" and charged his top deputies to convene a presidential commission aimed at building bipartisan support for US policy toward Central America. The president further ordered that the US military presence in Central America be strengthened. These steps, Reagan concluded, "are designed to improve, as quickly as possible, our ability to deter the consolidation of a Marxist/Leninist state in Central America which could serve as a base for Soviet power projection and/or destabilization of other states in the region."[132]

But at the Nicaraguan revolution's fourth anniversary celebration later that month, there was little evidence of communism on the march. Instead, the strain of war on a deeply impoverished nation pervaded the festivities. A crowd of eighty thousand people sang revolutionary ballads and danced to salsa music, while FSLN leaders wore T-shirts depicting the revolution as a happy child, inscribed with the words "I am in love with a little girl who is four years old." Yet the tension with Washington was palpable. "She's terrified of the thunder from Washington," one official told a reporter for *Newsweek*. "She's afraid Ronald Reagan won't let her grow to be five."[133]

Indeed, over the first half of 1983, the Contra war had intensified. The Contras had mushroomed to a force of ten thousand combatants by early 1983 and were regularly hitting targets across northern Nicaragua.[134] By July, the CIA estimated that the counterrevolutionaries had destroyed $24 million worth of Nicaraguan infrastructure and had cost the FSLN $21 million in military expenditures and $7.2 million in "opportunity costs" from mobilizing military reserves and militia forces. The FSLN had been forced to commit nearly half of the nation's active-duty military forces to the Honduran border area, and Nicaraguan soldiers faced grueling deployments lasting as long as five months. The human cost was rising as well: in the first half of 1983 alone, 350 Nicaraguan civilians and 250 soldiers were killed at the hands of counterrevolutionary forces, while the Contras' systematic use of assassination, torture, rape, and kidnapping cut swaths of trauma and suffering across the countryside.[135] The Contras "gang-raped me every day," one survivor of a March 1983 kidnapping later reported. "When my vagina couldn't take it any more, they raped me through my rectum. I calculate that in five days they raped me 60 times."[136]

CIA-sponsored dirty tricks threatened further destabilization. In June, Marlene Moncada, a thirty-year-old Nicaraguan double agent, exposed a plot to assassinate foreign minister D'Escoto with a poisoned bottle of wine, replete with coded messages written in invisible ink and hidden in a hollow figurine. The wine "would give a good blow to the communists and facilitate the liberation of my people," the agent running the operation had assured Moncada, who promptly handed it over to the FSLN's security services.[137] Yet the foiled plot was hardly an isolated incident; a few months later the CIA would begin distributing dozens of copies of a Spanish-language manual titled *Psychological Operations in Guerrilla Warfare*, which encouraged "neutralizing" low-level FLSN officials, engaging in extortion, and provoking mass demonstrations.[138]

As the Contra war intensified, Nicaragua's economic situation deteriorated. By July 1983, the FSLN had rationed thirteen basic commodities, including gasoline, sugar, beans, corn, cooking oil, soap, chicken, and bread. Although the Sandinistas accurately claimed that staples were far more equitably distributed than during the Somoza era and that overall consumption had increased significantly since 1979, the food system was badly hampered by a combination of poor distribution, government regulations, hoarding, and speculation, as well as the accumulating effects of the Contra war. The result was widespread shortages, and, for many Nicaraguans, waiting in line to buy basic items—often unsuccessfully—became a daily ordeal.[139] "We have not had any bread in my house for a week," one opposition politician complained in mid-1983. "In the supermarket, people fight one another for chickens."[140]

As Nicaragua's economic challenges increased, the Contra war accelerated political polarization. Tension between the FSLN and the Catholic Church increased, culminating in a much-anticipated visit by Pope John Paul II in March. In a serious setback to the FSLN, the pope reprovingly shook his finger at the minister of culture, Father Ernesto Cardenal, then publicly expressed support for the outspoken FSLN critic Archbishop Obando y Bravo. Shouting Sandinista militants subsequently drowned out a portion of the pontiff's televised mass, a remarkable development that many religious Nicaraguans found deeply offensive.[141] Two months later, the FSLN began expropriating private property to punish individuals who had "either failed to support the government on a particular policy or who had provided assistance to counter-revolutionary forces," the US Embassy reported, and in June the government began handing out weapons to state cooperatives to defend against Contra attacks.[142]

Frustrated with food shortages, concerned about the FSLN's relationship to the Church, and experiencing the daily pressure of the Contra war, many Nicaraguans by mid-1983 were deeply disillusioned. The immense sense of expectation that had accompanied the revolutionary triumph, US ambassador Quainton reported, had been replaced by "grim reality." Emphasizing the erosion of political pluralism and increased restrictions on civil liberties, the shrinking private sector and the dire state of Nicaragua's economy, Quainton saw little cause for optimism. "The revolution's original goals still receive lip-service," the ambassador wrote. "But they generally have been abandoned in practice."[143]

In response to the rising tenor of accusations emanating from Washington and facing a burgeoning guerrilla threat, the FSLN adamantly rejected the Reagan administration's claims of deepening Soviet influence in Nicaragua. It was the United States, not the USSR, Sandinista leaders regularly asserted, that had historically dominated Nicaragua. As Ramírez maintained, "When they speak about copying models, we must remember that during half a century Somocismo slavishly copied the model imposed by the United States." Ramírez continued, "Nicaragua was branded with the most radical capitalist model, a market economy which impoverished the country and ravished the possibilities for its true development. With this destructive capitalist model came the destructive dependency on markets, raw materials, and financial resources; Nicaragua became a satellite of the United States; Nicaragua was behind a true iron curtain with a solid, triple-locked bar."[144] Having overthrown the Somoza dictatorship, FSLN leaders repeatedly declared, revolutionary Nicaragua sought international nonalignment, not a new form of dependence. "If we were nincompoops, if we were so dishonorable as to sell out to somebody, there can be no doubt whatever that it would be much easier and much more comfortable to sell ourselves to the government of the United States," asserted Borge in late July 1983. "We Sandinistas have never been, are not and never will be anybody's satellites."[145]

Indeed, it was the FSLN's determination to serve as a model for national liberation, Sandinista leaders believed—not its purported communist ties—that accounted for Washington's singular aggression. In mid-1982, the Ministry of Planning's Gorostiaga speculated whether the actual goal of US pressure was to *accelerate* Nicaragua's entry into the Soviet orbit, in order to "delegitimize its originality and prevent this model of mixed economy and political pluralism from succeeding, and to prevent the economic success of the Nicaraguan Revolution from demonstrating that it is possible to maintain an efficient popular economy." Similarly, FSLN Directorate member Carlos Núñez Tellez attributed Reagan's actions to the United States' long-standing drive to dominate the hemisphere. For the US president, Núñez asserted, "in his global strategy and ruling philosophy, the hegemony of the United States, especially in a continent like Latin America, must not be damaged by any country seeking independence."[146]

More broadly, the Sandinistas viewed Washington's aggression as an assault on their effort to create an authentic democracy rooted in social and economic justice. "The achievements in health care during the last four years have been greater than the accomplishments during the previous 150 years," Borge wrote in a July 1983 op-ed in the *Washington Post*. Revolutionary Nicaragua offered free education and health care, Borge continued, and had achieved remarkable success in eliminating polio and dramatically reducing tuberculosis, malaria, and infant mortality. Illuminating the fundamental divide over human rights at the core of the conflict between Reagan and the Sandinistas, Borge asserted, "Is this not respect for human, economic, and social rights? Is the Reagan administration fighting against this? What other country in Latin America has accomplished so much in such a short period of time, in spite of sabotage and opposition of the most powerful country of the planet?"[147]

By the time Daniel Ortega addressed the United Nations General Assembly in late September 1983, however, the Contra war had entered a new phase. In the north, the Nicaraguan Democratic Force (FDN) went on the offensive, sending guerrilla columns deep into Nicaragua's interior to cut power lines, destroy bridges, sabotage oil tanks and pipelines, and raze health clinics, schools, and cooperatives. On the Caribbean coast, the FSLN's overreaction in 1980 and 1981 to a bid for greater autonomy by a coalition of ethnic minority groups had sparked an insurgency; by 1983, Managua had lost control of much of the sparsely populated department of Zelaya.[148] And along Nicaragua's southern border with Costa Rica, the Alianza Revolucionaria Democrática (Democratic Revolutionary Alliance [ARDE]), formed in 1982 by former Sandinista guerrilla leader Edén Pastora Gómez, was accelerating attacks along the San Juan River.[149] The CIA stepped up activity as well. Using the expanded Contra operations as a cover, the agency deployed specially recruited operatives of Latino origin to carry out attacks on high-level targets. Puerto Sandino reported attacks by speedboats on September 8, and an air raid on Corinto the following day narrowly missed oil storage facilities. Meanwhile, as thousands of US troops engaged in military maneuvers in Honduras—including a landing of US Marines on the Caribbean coast—the Department of Defense operationalized a "perception management program" intended to stoke Nicaraguan fears of a US invasion.[150]

Yet the Contras confronted a rapidly expanding Sandinista military establishment. Soviet bloc military deliveries to Nicaragua in 1983 more than doubled over the previous year to fourteen thousand metric tons.[151] Correspondingly, the EPS grew to an estimated twenty-four thousand soldiers in 1983, and reserves and militia mushroomed to more than fifty thousand members.[152] As the fighting intensified, the FSLN responded by enacting a military conscription on September 14 for all Nicaraguan males between the ages of eighteen and forty, touching off intense outcry from the political opposition, the private sector, and the Church.[153]

At the United Nations, Ortega demanded an end to Washington's war on Nicaragua. Calling on the international community of nations to support a peaceful solution to the Central American conflict, Ortega emphasized that "Nicaragua has won its right to be free, and this right must be respected." Nicaragua "is building its democracy," the comandante defiantly concluded, "and its sovereign right to choose its own internal system, its own brand of democracy, is a right of our people that cannot be negotiated, cannot be discussed, and must be respected."[154] Yet the relentless pace of Contra and CIA attacks continued. Speedboat strikes on Port Benjamín Zeladón set a pair of fuel tanks ablaze on October 2, destroying 380,000 gallons of fuel—a month's fuel supply for the entire Mosquito Coast. Eight days later, the FSLN suffered an enormous blow when CIA air and sea attacks on oil tanks in Corinto destroyed more than 3.2 million gallons of fuel, and on October 14, CIA assets blew up the underwater oil pipeline at Puerto Sandino. Reeling from the attacks, the Sandinistas tightened fuel rations and declared plans to further expand the size of Nicaragua's military reserves and militia.[155]

Fittingly, amid the attacks the twelve-member National Bipartisan Commission on Central America arrived in Managua as part of a weeklong fact-finding mission. Created by Reagan in July, the commission was charged with generating a blueprint for US policy in the region that would appeal to congressional legislators on both sides of the political aisle. Yet when Reagan tapped Henry Kissinger to lead the proceedings, the Sandinistas accurately perceived the commission's mandate, in Ortega's words, as "more propagandistic than otherwise." Not only was Kissinger the architect of US efforts to destabilize Allende's presidency a decade earlier, but his disinterest in Latin America was almost legendary. Indeed, for the Kissinger Commission, as the group quickly became known, Cold War considerations took center stage. As Kissinger told an interviewer shortly after the commission was formed, "If we cannot manage Central America, it will be impossible to convince threatened nations in the Persian Gulf and in other places that we know how to manage the global equilibrium."[156] As a result, the commission's conclusions were largely predetermined. "I already know what we want to say," Kissinger bluntly informed lead consultant Howard J. Wiarda at the opening meeting.[157]

Indeed, during the commission's one-day visit to Nicaragua, Kissinger's antipathy toward the Sandinistas was evident. "You don't mean I have to shake hands with the son of a bitch?" Kissinger complained to US ambassador Quainton after a briefing on protocol before meeting with Ortega. At the meeting itself, with the commissioners wearing simultaneous translation headphones, Kissinger began by abruptly demanding, "Well, Commandante, what do you have to say?" Ortega obligingly launched into a forty-minute lecture on US interventionism in Nicaragua dating back to William Walker's filibusters. Watching the spectacle unfold, Quainton recalled: "As this is going on, all the Commission members, one by one, take their headphones off and stop listening. Dr. Kissinger listens until the end. He then turns to Ortega and says, 'Commandante, I did not like the tone or the substances of your remarks. Any further discussion between our two governments will be in writing.'" The meeting was over. The Kissinger Commission, Quainton concluded, was "not about to be lectured to by someone as unprepossessing as Daniel Ortega."[158]

Then, on October 25, 1983, the United States invaded the tiny island nation of Grenada. The previous week, prime minister Maurice Bishop had been assassinated in a military coup led by the deputy prime minister, Bernard Coard. Claiming that Grenada had become a forward staging base for Cuban adventurism in the circum-Caribbean, and emphasizing the threat posed to US citizens on the island—particularly eight hundred US medical students—Reagan dispatched two thousand Marines and US Army Rangers. Within seventy-two hours the United States took control of the nation. Havana had intended to use Grenada to "export terror and undermine democracy," Reagan declared after the fighting subsided, while McFarlane emphasized that the United States had discovered a vast cache of Cuban weapons. "It was clear from the scale of things that were discovered, we got there just in time," McFarlane assured the press.[159]

Watching events unfold from Managua, the Sandinistas saw the US intervention in Grenada as a test run for an impending US invasion of Nicaragua. Like the FSLN, after taking power in a 1979 coup, Bishop's New Jewel Movement had made impressive gains extending social and economic rights to ordinary Grenadians, including free health care and education, and had embarked on reducing unemployment through agricultural diversification and state-run cooperatives. Bishop also advanced a nonaligned foreign policy but maintained close ties with Cuba, and, at the time of the US invasion, dozens of Cuban advisers were in residence on the island. Moreover, since taking power, the Reagan administration accused Havana of turning the island into a springboard for foreign policy adventurism, and the CIA was reportedly carrying out political and economic destabilization operations.[160]

Fearing a US invasion, the FSLN embarked on a major civil defense campaign. Billboards sprouted along Nicaraguan highways emblazoned with the words "We will never surrender" and "They shall not pass," and regularly scheduled television programs were interrupted with instructional films on guerrilla warfare. Tens of thousands of Nicaraguans received civil defense training on depressing topics such as how to treat skin seared by napalm. Evacuation drills at factories became increasingly routine, weapons and ammunition were secretly stockpiled in private homes, and thousands of Nicaraguans dug defensive trenches.[161] "It is up to us to assure that in Nicaragua there will not be another Chile or another Grenada," one militia member told a journalist. "Our two weeks of training is not much compared with the years the Yankees spend at West Point, but there are enough of us to bury them."[162]

The invasion never materialized. But an end to the Contra war was nowhere in sight. In early December, the White House wrested a victory from Congress by securing a $24 million assistance package for the Contras as part of the Intelligence Authorization Act for fiscal year 1984, ensuring that the counterrevolutionaries would continue operations in the near future. Although the Reagan administration assured legislators that the funds would not be used to orchestrate a regime change in Managua, FDN leaders made little effort to hide their intention to oust the Sandinistas.[163] Correspondingly, the Reagan administration paid lip service to regional negotiations while quietly dismissing the FSLN's efforts to reach an accommodation. In a late 1983 meeting, for example, US ambassador Quainton informed Borge that ending FSLN aid to Salvadoran rebels was a sine qua non for improving US-Nicaraguan relations. Borge was skeptical. "I don't believe you. I don't think that could change anything," he told the ambassador. "But, for the moment, let's assume that there is such aid and that we would stop it. What would you do if we did?" When Quainton replied that Washington would react positively, Borge responded, "Well, consider it done. Your government has the capacity to monitor everything that goes in and out of this country and El Salvador. Come back in a month's time and tell me how things are going." According to Quainton, who quickly forwarded Borge's message to Washington, in the following weeks US intelligence discovered no trace of FSLN support for the FMLN. The Sandinistas' conciliatory gesture, however, was met with silence by the Reagan administration. After a month had passed, Borge phoned the ambassador. "What did I tell you?" the Interior minister demanded. "This was just a pretense." Reflecting on the incident many years later, Quainton emphasized the lost opportunities for negotiation that resulted from Washington's hard-line approach toward Nicaragua. By the end of 1983, the Sandinistas, the ambassador noted, were certain that "it was going to take a great deal more than just accommodation of the Salvadoran issue before we would live with their regime."[164]

Similarly, in a December meeting in Managua with State Department assistant secretary for inter-American affairs Langhorne A. Motley, Ortega emphasized that the FSLN was "willing to discuss all U.S. concerns in order to achieve a framework of security for the U.S. and Nicaragua." Expressing a willingness to negotiate limits on arms and foreign advisers, Ortega rejected the accusation that totalitarianism was taking root in Nicaragua. "The revolution's biggest victory would be if it could achieve a democratic system," the comandante asserted, "but [U.S.-backed] aggression had not helped."[165] Such efforts, however, made little headway. "The end game was to prevent the consolidation of the Sandinista regime," Motley admitted in an interview years later. US policy, Motley continued, "did not lend itself to a timetable. But we knew that sometime in the future . . . the Sandinistas would be removed from office."[166]

Indeed, by the end of 1983, the confrontation with Washington had taken a severe toll on the promise of the Nicaraguan revolution. As defense spending ballooned and the economy stagnated, Nicaraguans found the FSLN's lofty promises of social and economic justice increasingly out of reach. Correspondingly, although the FSLN retained significant popular support in the face of Contra threat, the intensification of the war polarized the political landscape and left many Nicaraguans increasingly disillusioned. As Marta Patricia Baltodano, the coordinator of the independent Nicaraguan Commission on Human Rights, told a journalist in mid-1983, "Under Somoza, who was unimaginably bad, you could at least avoid politics. Now it seeps into all levels of life. You cannot escape it. Both systems are bad. Asking which is worse is like saying, 'What rope should I hang myself with?'"[167]

The real victims, however, were those caught in the cross fire of the brutal Contra war. In late August, in one of the hundreds of attacks that largely went unreported outside of Nicaragua, a task force of 350 heavily armed FDN counterrevolutionaries slipped into the rugged Paiwas mountains in Nicaragua's central department of Zelaya. The Contras murdered six residents of the township of Anito, bragging to the residents that they enjoyed Reagan's support while burning houses and destroying a boat used by a state-run cooperative. In neighboring Ocaguas, the Contras gouged out the eyes of one villager, hung another from the beam of his house, and murdered the local militia leader's wife before burning the inventory of a cooperative selling clothing.

The task force murdered nine residents of tiny Guayabo the following day, including a fourteen-year-old who was gang-raped and then decapitated, her severed head deposited at the entrance to the village as a macabre warning to FSLN supporters. The municipal center of Bocana de Paiwas, however, was hardest hit. In a surprise attack, the Contras killed twenty civilians, raped three women, and burned eighteen houses. A ten-year-old, Cristina, watched the men kill two of her uncles. As she screamed, "Don't kill me! Don't kill me!," recalled the local parish priest, one of the men fired four bullets into her body.[168]

Miraculously, Cristina survived. Yet her fate, like that of the Nicaraguan revolution itself, was far from clear.

Chapter 4

"Global Revolution"

The Ascendance of Democracy Promotion
in US Foreign Policy, 1982-1986

Flanked by solemn beefeaters brandishing eight-foot spears, on June 8, 1982, Ronald Reagan delivered a landmark foreign policy address to five hundred members of the British Parliament. Speaking in the majestic Royal Gallery of the Palace of Westminster beneath massive paintings of British military victories at Trafalgar and Waterloo, Reagan called for a "crusade for freedom" in the Cold War struggle against communist totalitarianism. "From Stettin on the Baltic to Varna on the Black Sea, the regimes planted by totalitarianism have had more than 30 years to establish their legitimacy," Reagan asserted, revising Sir Winston Churchill's famous 1946 declaration that Eastern and Western Europe stood divided by an "iron curtain." "But none—not one regime—has yet been able to risk free elections. Regimes planted by bayonets do not take root." Emphasizing both the weakness exposed by the Soviet Union's moribund economy and the threat posed by communist subversion across the globe, Reagan championed democracy as the defining strength of the United States and its allies.

Reagan's Westminster address contained the seeds of a democracy promotion initiative that would grow to become a defining feature of the administration's approach to international affairs. Overshadowed in the press by Reagan's pronouncement that "the march of freedom and democracy . . . will leave Marxism-Leninism on the ash-heap of history," the president also declared that "it is time that we committed ourselves as a nation—in both the public and private sectors—to assisting democratic development."[1] These efforts bore fruit; after a prolonged and rancorous debate, lawmakers on Capitol

Hill legislated annual congressional funding for the National Endowment for Democracy (NED), a bipartisan, nonprofit, private organization to aid democratic groups overseas.

The Reagan administration embraced the NED with enthusiasm. By mid-decade, the democracy initiative had emerged as the defining feature of the Reagan administration's human rights policy and the lynchpin of the administration's effort to re-create the bipartisan Cold War consensus that had foundered in the late 1960s on the shoals of the Vietnam War. By simultaneously aligning the United States behind democratization processes abroad and ratcheting up the pressure on the communist world, the Reagan administration sought to seize the political high ground with a project that would protect national security without losing sight of moral considerations. The initiative won bipartisan support on Capitol Hill, as congressional legislators lauded Reagan's withdrawal of support for US-backed dictators in Haiti and the Philippines and increasingly supported the White House call for aid to anticommunist militants in Afghanistan, southern Africa, Cambodia, and, to a limited extent, Central America. By 1986, the democracy promotion initiative had succeeded in making steps toward re-creating the foreign policy bipartisanship of the early Cold War.

Yet, as the administration was orchestrating a new foreign policy consensus, the interventionism at the heart of the Reagan Doctrine's support for anticommunist militants in the third world illuminated how human rights and democracy promotion could be used to advance US Cold War goals. Nowhere was this more evident than in the White House's covert war on Nicaragua. Framed as support for "freedom fighters," Reagan's intervention in Central America was undertaken in the spirit of a democracy promotion initiative that sought to orchestrate a regime change in Managua. Respect for human rights, Reagan asserted in 1985, meant standing "side by side with those who share our ideals, especially in Central America." Underscoring his commitment to supporting the Contras' efforts to overthrow the Sandinistas, the president continued, "We must not permit those heavily armed by a faraway dictatorship to undermine their neighbors and to stamp out democratic alternatives at home. We must have the same solidarity with those who struggle for democracy as our adversaries do with those who would impose Communist dictatorship."[2] The message was clear: as Reagan's democracy initiative accelerated, the US covert war on Nicaragua intensified.

Reagan's call for a democracy initiative at Westminster grew out of the administration's shifting position on human rights over the previous year and a half. After initially attacking human rights as embodying the worst of Jimmy Carter's weak-kneed liberalism and, more broadly, the national self-abnegation of the McGovernite wing of the Democratic Party, the Reagan White House by the end of 1981 had undertaken a remarkable about-face. Stung by the Senate Foreign Relations Committee's refusal to confirm Ernest Lafever to lead the Human Rights Bureau and concerned that the festering issue could poison the president's relations with Congress, the Reagan team had embraced a narrow human rights framework emphasizing regular elections, the protection of civil liberties, and a free market economy protecting the interests of corporate capitalism. Social and economic rights, by contrast— stalwarts of human rights rhetoric in the communist world and embraced by many third-world nationalists—were intentionally excluded by the Reagan administration. As UN ambassador Jeane J. Kirkpatrick told members of Congress in March 1982, "Rights should not be confused with wishes, or goals . . . the list of human rights cannot be indefinitely lengthened like a shopping list in a global supermarket." Instead, Kirkpatrick continued, rights such as "free speech, press, religion, freedom of assembly, freedom from arbitrary arrest, and the right to due process are the fundamental rights: they are the prerequisites to other social and economic goods."[3]

Kirkpatrick's emphasis on civil and political rights ran parallel with Reagan's own views. On one level, Reagan's understanding of human rights flowed from a belief in US exceptionalism. "I think human rights is very much a part of our American idealism. I think they do play an important part," the president told Walter Cronkite in a March 1981 interview on CBS Evening News. On another level, Reagan's perceived human rights as inextricably linked to the East-West confrontation. "My criticism of them, in the last few years, was that we were selective with regard to human rights," he continued. "We took countries that were pro-Western, that were maybe authoritarian in government, but not totalitarian . . . and we punished them at the same time that we were claiming détente with countries where there are no human rights."[4]

By the time Reagan mounted the podium at Westminster, the president's criticism of the US human rights policy under previous administrations had started to evolve into a strategy of democracy promotion as the centerpiece of the US human rights policy. The product of weeks of preparation, the speech bore the imprint—at points awkwardly—of State Department officials, the National Security Council (NSC) staff, White House speechwriters, and the conservative columnist George F. Will.[5] Including the emphasis on democracy, however, was reportedly Reagan's personal decision; as presidential speechwriter Tony Dolan later noted, "The president believes that we in the West for too long have expressed our foreign policy goals in the negative: i.e. resistance to Soviet expansionism. More is needed to rally the world than a negative formulation."[6] Indeed, it was the president who penned one of the Westminster speech's most memorable lines: "Day by day democracy is proving itself to be a not-at-all-fragile flower."[7] More importantly, after reminding the audience that free elections were enshrined in the Universal Declaration of Human Rights, Reagan announced one of the most important US foreign policy initiatives of the late Cold War. "The objective I propose is quite simple to state: to foster the infrastructure of democracy, the system of a free press, unions, political parties, universities, which allows a people to choose their own way to develop their own culture, to reconcile their own differences through peaceful means."[8]

Reagan had nailed his colors to the mast of democracy promotion. But what would the initiative actually mean in practice? In the weeks following Westminster, the White House itself offered little guidance, as disagreements over the issue flared between the State Department and the NSC, as well as representatives from the national US political parties and congressional committees. It was hardly a unique situation for a president who, as the journalist Lou Cannon noted, "managed by indirection when he managed at all."[9] Indeed, Commonweal reported that "no one in the administration had a clear idea what Reagan's words meant, least of all the president."[10]

If the Reagan administration initially struggled to translate the president's lofty rhetoric at Westminster into concrete policy initiatives, the idea of promoting democracy abroad had deep roots in American political culture. Amid the carnage of the First World War, Woodrow Wilson perceived a mix of capitalism, democracy, and collective security as the lifeblood of a peaceful, prosperous postwar world. Wilson's efforts had foundered on the shoals of European nationalism, his own intemperate leadership, and intractable resistance in the US Senate. Yet the tenets of Wilsonian internationalism served as a framework for subsequent policymakers seeking to harness US power in the interest of international stability and security.[11]

In the 1940s, having experienced both the Great Depression and the Second World War, the administrations of both Franklin Delano Roosevelt and Harry S. Truman envisioned a democratic, market-oriented postwar world order consistent with US interests. And unlike under Wilson, the exigencies of the Depression and the Second World War combined with Roosevelt's deft cultivation of support among Republicans on Capitol Hill created a window of opportunity to fashion Wilsonian ideas into concrete policy initiatives.[12]

Indeed, the liberal internationalist impulse defined US foreign policy in the early postwar era. The United States took a lead role in the creation of the Bretton Woods system, the United Nations, and the drafting of the Universal Declaration of Human Rights. More concretely, support for democratic institutions was a core component of the US effort to mold Germany and Japan into peaceful players on the postwar world stage. Significantly, this approach carried over into the early Cold War; the key features of the containment strategy in Europe—the Truman Doctrine, the Marshall Plan, and the creation of the North Atlantic Treaty Organization (NATO)—were largely consonant with the liberal internationalist goal of fostering open markets and democratic political systems.[13]

The globalization of the Cold War in the 1950s, however, gave the containment strategy added weight and reduced US support for democracy overseas. To be sure, even at the high-water mark of US support for Western European democracies in the late 1940s, American policymakers defined democracy in decidedly narrow terms, eschewing more participatory forms of democracy in favor of the perceived stability of a republican political structure. "The New England town meeting is the idea of democracy, and all they do is talk," Truman asserted with characteristic bluntness. By contrast, he continued, "a republic is one that has checks and balances in it, as ours is set up for that purpose . . . there can be a continuing form of government carried out by men who are responsible to the people and yet who can't be thrown out every fifteen minutes if something goes wrong."[14] Viewing communism as a fundamental threat, US policymakers "had little patience for democracy as it was practiced and defined by other states and peoples," writes the historian Jennifer M. Miller. The result was a "dialectic process, whereby obsession with democratic qualities fueled an almost antidemocratic democracy," Miller concludes.[15]

Indeed, in the early Cold War, US support for democracy in Western Europe and Japan envisioned elections dominated by political elites from the pro-capitalist center-right of the political spectrum. American policymakers worked assiduously to use economic aid, covert operations, and political pressure to exclude left-wing political parties from gaining power through the ballot box. The US intervention in the 1948 Italian general election offered a case in point; fearing a victory of the left-wing coalition of the Popular Democratic Front (FDP), the CIA in the lead-up to the election blanketed the Italian peninsula with anticommunist propaganda to discredit the FDP, while top US policymakers threatened to deny Marshall Plan aid in the event of a left-wing victory. Although the Christian Democrats' success at the polls was heralded by the Truman administration as a triumph for the free world, the election illuminated distinctly *undemocratic* characteristics of a foreign policy ostensibly aimed at promoting democracy abroad.[16]

As the Cold War globalized at the tail end of the 1940s, the balance between liberal internationalism and containment tilted in favor of the latter. The shift was first felt in Latin America. In the mid-1940s, a democratic tide had swept across the region, supported by US diplomats during the war years in local contexts as varied as Guatemala, Paraguay, and Argentina. By the end of the decade, however, the rising influence of containment led to an overriding US emphasis on anticommunism in inter-American affairs. This shift resulted in deepening US ties to Latin American militaries and conservative political and economic elites.[17]

By the mid-1950s, the overriding emphasis on global containment in US foreign policy was evident throughout the developing world. Viewing nationalist and anticolonialist political movements with suspicion, the Dwight D. Eisenhower administration feared that local communists might play upon deep-seated grievances to create inroads for advancing Soviet influence. In 1953, the administration successfully dispatched the CIA to foment a military coup against Iranian leader Mohammad Mosaddeq, whose nationalization of British oil holdings and ties to the communist Tudeh Party had raised warning flags in Washington and London. A similar enterprise the following year led to the overthrow of Guatemalan president Jacobo Arbenz, a progressive reformist with members of Guatemala's communist party in his advisory circle. Hailed by the Eisenhower administration as cost-effective Cold War victories for the West, the operations closed off avenues of reformist politics and propelled both nations down a path to decades of state-sanctioned repression, political violence, and eventual revolutionary upheaval.[18]

Less spectacularly, Eisenhower quietly solidified US support for friendly authoritarians. In Latin America, US support for conservative military and political leaders contributed to a resurgence of authoritarianism: by mid-decade more than half of the nations of Latin America had returned to dictatorial rule.[19] In Asia, the administration ramped up support for the autocratic Chiang Kai-shek, backed the French effort to retain control of Indochina, and committed the United States to supporting South Vietnam under the repressive leadership of Ngo Dinh Diem.[20] In the Middle East, the United States worked to offset the regional influence of Egyptian leader Gamal Abdel Nasser's pan-Arab nationalism by strengthening ties to conservative monarchies in Saudi

Arabia, Jordan, and Iran.[21] In the effort to create a web of security alliances in the developing world, the Eisenhower administration paid scant attention to democratic institutions.

Fearing the possibility of communist influence in the developing world and willing to use US political, economic, and military power to shape events overseas, successive US administrations supported repressive allies at the expense of democracy. Although US assistance earmarked for political development abroad increased substantially during the 1960s, the John F. Kennedy and Lyndon B. Johnson administrations' overriding emphasis on preventing communist subversion also led to a surge in US counterinsurgency training and aid programs in the developing world. Particularly in Latin America, despite the lofty rhetoric surrounding Kennedy's Alliance for Progress, Washington's fear of communist insurgencies tempered support for regional democratic reforms and ultimately strengthened local conservatives and military leaders at the expense of moderate democrats. "The Alliance for Progress" writes the historian Stephen G. Rabe, "proved a notable policy failure of the 1960s, superseded only by the U.S. debacle in Vietnam."[22]

As Johnson deepened the US commitment to South Vietnam, US funding for building democracy abroad fell by the wayside. US support for private-sector groups abroad suffered a major setback following revelations of secret CIA funding for a host of organizations ranging from the Congress for Cultural Freedom to the US National Student Association. First published by *Ramparts* magazine in June 1967 and immediately picked up by the mainstream press, the muckraking revealed CIA support for an "astounding variety" of US citizen groups, writes the historian Hugh Wilford, including "university professors, journalists, aid workers, missionaries, civil rights activists, even a group of wealthy women known as the Committee of Correspondence, all had belonged to the CIA's covert network of front operations."[23] Blindsided by the episode, the Johnson administration responded by prohibiting all covert financial assistance for US educational institutions and private voluntary organizations. The decision fit the mood on Capitol Hill. Although Florida Democrat Dante Fascell attempted to replace covert funding of overseas private-sector groups with a publicly funded "Institute of International Affairs," amid the fallout from the scandal the proposal was stillborn.[24]

Support for democratic institutions abroad declined still further as a US policy priority during the presidencies of Richard M. Nixon and Gerald R. Ford. In the Nixon administration's strategic pursuit of détente, there was no place for the promotion of democracy; as the administration worked to establish areas of cooperation with the Soviets, the "Nixon Doctrine" aimed to lower the cost of global containment by deepening ties with authoritarian allies in the developing world. "U.S. style democracy won't work here," Nixon speciously claimed during a tour of South America in 1967. "I wish it would."[25] Détente's relaxation of Cold War tension rarely extended to the developing world—as the administration's covert efforts to destabilize Chile, resulting in the brutal 1973 military overthrow of democratically elected socialist president Salvador Allende, made starkly evident.

Yet beneath the realpolitik of the Nixon-Ford years, support for US democracy promotion was slowly stirring inside the Washington Beltway. From his position as chairman of the House International Relations Subcommittee on International Organizations and Movements, Donald M. Fraser (D-MN) became increasingly interested in democracy promotion over the course of the 1970s. A pioneer in the effort to institutionalize human rights in US foreign policy, Fraser corresponded widely with politicians and human rights advocates overseas. In 1974, for example, he wrote to some seventy-five foreign lawmakers in an effort to create an "informal network of parliamentarians for human rights."[26] By the end of the decade, the Minnesota lawmaker had gained an awareness and appreciation for political development efforts abroad, particularly the Federal Republic of Germany's *Stiftungen*—foundations associated with West Germany's four major political parties: the Social Democrats (Friedrich Ebert Stiftung), the Christian Democrats (Conrad Adenauer Stiftung), the Free Democrats (Friedrich Naumann Stiftung), and the Christian Socialists (Hans Seidel Stiftung). With an annual budget from the Bundestag that would reach $150 million in the early 1980s, the foundations offered scholarships for up-and-coming foreign leaders in political training programs in Germany and project-based initiatives abroad. In an early effort to emulate the German model, Fraser and Fascell in 1978 sponsored legislation to establish an "Institute on Human Rights and Freedoms."[27]

The bill failed. But Fraser and Fascell had tapped into rising interest on the part of American political leaders in political development efforts overseas. On one level, the US commitment to Basket III of the Helsinki Accords stimulated interest in a bipartisan mechanism for monitoring rights violations in the Soviet Union. On another level, a growing awareness in Washington of the West German *Stiftungen* and their contribution to the nascent democratization processes in Spain and Portugal led US political leaders to echo Fraser and Fascell's call for a US equivalent. In 1979, political consultant and fundraiser George Agree created the American Political Foundation (APF), a nongovernmental group aimed at sparking bipartisan dialogue between like-minded political activists in the United States and overseas. With members including political heavy hitters such as US trade representative William E. Brock III, Democratic National Finance Council chairman Charles T. Manatt, and international vice president of the US Chamber of Commerce Michael A. Samuels, the APF initiated a series of meetings between 1981 and 1982 to explore the possibility of a democracy promotion "quango"—a British-inspired acronym for "quasi-autonomous nongovernment organization."[28] Drawing on the work of political development theorist William A. Douglas, whose 1972 study *Developing Democracy* emerged as an influential blueprint, Brock, Manatt, and Republican National Committee chairman Richard Richards on the eve of Reagan's Westminster address sent the president a letter on behalf of APF, recommending a detailed bipartisan study to determine "how the United States can help build democratic values and institutions in other nations."[29]

The missive's timing was impeccable. In announcing the democracy initiative at Westminster, Reagan noted the example of West Germany before favorably mentioning the APF study. "I look forward to receiving their recommendations" the president asserted, "and to working with these institutions and the Congress in the common task of strengthening democracy throughout the world."[30] More concretely, the White House subsequently allocated the APF $300,000 from the foreign aid budget to conduct the study.[31]

In the weeks after Westminster, the Reagan administration moved slowly to integrate democracy promotion into US foreign policy. At a cabinet-level meeting in August 1982 to sketch the organizational structure of the program, White House officials jostled over whether the initiative should have a covert component run out of the NSC's back office, or even be handed over to the spooks at Langley. The following January, the administration issued National Security Decision Directive (NSDD) 77, mandating the creation of an international political committee "responsible for planning, coordinating and implementing international political activities in support of United States policies and interests relative to national security." Significantly, such activities included "aid, training and organizational support for foreign governments and private groups to encourage the growth of democratic political institutions and practices," and the following month the administration submitted a $65 million "Project Democracy" funding request to Congress for forty-four democracy assistance projects funded through the United States Information Agency (USIA).[32]

While the White House democracy initiative was taking shape, the APF study gained support from across the political spectrum. The interim report, directed by Georgetown University historian Allen Weinstein and released in

April 1983, framed US support for democracy overseas as embodying both idealist and realist concerns: on the one hand, Weinstein argued, the initiative tapped into the wellspring of US values; on the other, the project would add a dose of political stability to US economic development projects abroad and strengthen the hand of friendly reformers.[33] "Bipartisan American support for the Christian Democratic and Social Democratic reformers in Latin America, for example," the report maintained, "has been based on a realization that if such parties lead genuine movements for social change, anti-democratic communist and other revolutionary groups cannot seize the leadership and banner of reform."[34]

Significantly, in addition to drawing support from US political leaders on both sides of the aisle, the democracy initiative garnered support from business and labor leaders. In early 1983, the Chamber of Commerce threw its weight behind the proposal. The "business-democracy linkage should be self-evident, especially to Americans," the Chamber of Commerce's Samuels confidently asserted in a draft memo. "The fact that no nation has ever succeeded in creating a free society based on governmental ownership of all business activity," Samuels added, "should lead us to reject the notion that political freedom can endure without economic freedom."[35] Sounding a similar theme, a May 1983 private-sector task force assigned to assess the relationship between business and democracy promotion expansively concluded that "the history of the post World War II period demonstrates that business involvement is an essential precondition for establishing a pluralist democracy."[36]

The democracy program also found support among anticommunist labor leaders. In a thinly veiled reference to the Carter administration's human rights policy, American Federation of Labor and Congress of Industrial Organizations (AFL-CIO) president Lane Kirkland argued in congressional testimony that although the United States had pressured human rights abusing regimes, "we have largely ignored the other side of the coin."[37] For its part, since the early Cold War the AFL-CIO had extended significant support to anticommunist labor organizations abroad.[38] In the early 1980s, the organization had shifted its attention to Poland, raising nearly $250,000 in private donations by November 1981 for the newly formed Self-Governing Trade Union "Solidarity" (Niezależny Samorządny Związek Zawodowy "Solidarność"), an autonomous national labor union created by the Gdańsk Accords following a hard-won victory by striking workers.[39] Kirkland was by no means a Reagan supporter, but he found common ground with the fortieth president in opposing Poland's communist regime. "Well, at last we have something we can agree on," Reagan amiably told Kirkland in an Oval Office meeting following the government crackdown on Solidarity in December 1981.[40] More broadly, Kirkland's vision of a US human rights policy that would build on the efforts of the AFL-CIO was not incompatible with Reagan's democracy initiative. "There is a policy on human rights that makes sense," he told members of Congress. "It is to help those trade union, party and native entrepreneurs struggling to set up democratic institutional guarantors of human rights in ways that they themselves choose."[41]

As Kirkland's testimony made clear, the democracy initiative appealed to a cross section of cold warriors who wanted the United States to escape the national malaise of the post-Vietnam era and play to the United States' strengths in the confrontation with the communist world. "Americans should stop being embarrassed about sharing our political know-how—money, mimeo machines and political action plans—with leaders and parties and institutions in beleaguered democracies;" argued William Safire in his weekly *New York Times* column. "More than that, we should carry the banner of political consciousness-raising to third-world and even Communist countries."[42] Neoconservatives were also supportive. "Conservatives might refuse to support labor unions abroad and liberals might balk at promoting free enterprise in a state-run economy," the political activist and commentator Ben J. Wattenberg reflected shortly after Reagan's Westminster address, and "we also shouldn't be supporting any phony Marxist revolutionaries who chant democratic code-words or for that matter tin-pot, proto-fascist generals who think democracy means only being anti-communist." Nonetheless, he concluded, "We cannot preach armed revolution in the communist countries, but we can fan the sparks of freedom there and elsewhere. Let's give this one a careful and sympathetic look."[43]

With support from influential members of Congress, representatives from business and labor, and cold warriors, the democracy initiative came to fruition in late 1983. After a prolonged and rancorous debate, lawmakers on Capitol Hill legislated seed money for the NED, a bipartisan, nonprofit, private organization that would be annually funded by US government appropriations. The NED would disburse its funding to four affiliate institutes: a Republican and a Democratic Institute for International Affairs, the Free Trade Institute, and the Center for Private Enterprise, which would, in turn, channel assistance to democracy initiatives abroad.[44] Although the Congress had rejected the initial White House Project Democracy, the Reagan administration supported the NED with gusto. The NED was a program "with a vision and a noble purpose," Reagan declared at the endowment's inaugural ceremony. "It's such a worthwhile, important initiative" the president added, "that I'm tempted to ask: Why hasn't it been done before?"[45]

Why did the Reagan administration embrace democracy promotion? First, the initiative served as shorthand for the Reagan administration's select emphasis on political and civil rights. "Democracy, after all, is a form of government which is based on the freely given consent of the governed," noted the introduction to the State Department's *Country Reports on Human Rights Practices for 1983*. "But consent can only be freely given if the means for the free expression of consent, or of dissent, exist; such means include freedom of speech, freedom of press, freedom of assembly and association, an independent judiciary, and free elections." Accordingly, respect for human rights, the report concluded, "is built into the very foundations of the democratic form of government."[46] Significantly, such statements were not merely public relations boilerplate but a reflection of the administration's vision of human rights and international relations. As Elliott Abrams asserted in a letter to Freedom House executive director Leonard Sussman, "Democratic institutions . . . are the only guarantee of human rights over the long run."[47]

As such, the emphasis on democracy fit nicely with the Reagan administration's hard-line approach to East-West relations. According to the country report's introduction, the United States' democratic constitution protected diversity, pluralism, and minority rights; in the USSR, by contrast, "minority rights have been systematically, even brutally, eroded." More controversially, the report echoed Kirkpatrick's 1979 essay "Dictatorships and Double Standards," emphasizing that "while non-Communist dictatorships are capable, to varying degrees, of evolving into democracies, Communist dictatorships are singularly resistant to democratization."[48] Promoting human rights thus required a robust commitment to the global containment of communism, even if it meant supporting right-wing dictators. "Preventing Communist dictatorships from establishing themselves," the report maintained, "ought to be an especially high priority of any realistic and serious human rights policy."[49] Democracy promotion, in other words, served to legitimate the Reagan Doctrine's call to roll back perceived communist gains in the developing world. And by consistently framing US-style democracy as a nonideological manifestation of popular will, the White House could claim the political center in a century of aberrant political ideologies. As Reagan asserted at the NED inauguration, in a world "beset by '-isms' . . . it suddenly dawned on me that we, with this system that so apparently works and is successful, have just assumed that the people would look at it and see that it was the way to go. And then I realized, but all those -isms, they also are missionaries for their cause, and they're out worldwide trying to sell it. And I just decided that this nation, with its heritage of Yankee traders, we ought to do a little selling of the principles of democracy."[50] Secretary of state George P. Shultz played a particularly important role in fusing the Reagan administration's strident anticommunism with the liberal internationalist appeal of democracy promotion. Testifying on Capitol Hill in February 1983, Shultz championed democracy promotion as a strategy to protect US national security interests while remaining tied to the United States' moral underpinnings. "If we are to achieve the kind of world we all hope to see—with peace, freedom and economic progress—democracy has to continue to expand. Democracy is a vital, even revolutionary force. It exists as an expression of the basic human drive for freedom," Shultz averred.[51] When congressional lawmakers expressed concern that the democracy promotion initiative could backfire, adversely affecting US foreign relations, Shultz responded expansively, "Don't be nervous about democracy, about holding that torch up there."[52]

The Reagan administration's democracy promotion project also attempted to align the United States with processes of democratization that were already underway in the developing world, while deploying US leverage to safeguard political and economic interests. Beginning in 1979, when the Ecuadoran military handed over the reins of political power after more than a dozen years of military rule, a wave of democratization swept across Latin America, ousting dictators and military juntas over the course of the 1980s from Guatemala City to Montevideo. In the mid-1970s, the region could boast only five democratically elected governments; by 1986, democratic transitions in Argentina (1983), Bolivia (1982), Brazil (1985), El Salvador (1980), Guatemala (1986), Honduras (1981), Peru (1980), and Uruguay (1985) had increased the number of Latin American democracies to fourteen, and nearly 90 percent of the hemisphere's four hundred million inhabitants could claim to be living in an electoral system.

At the outset of the decade, the Reagan administration's overriding emphasis on supporting right-wing authoritarians left the White House poorly positioned to receive newly installed regional democrats. Argentina was a case in point. Turning a blind eye to overwhelming evidence that the military junta had kidnapped, tortured, and murdered thousands of its own citizens since the 1976 coup d'état, the Reagan administration had embraced the ruling generals in Buenos Aires as Cold War allies—right up until the disastrous attack on the British-held Malvinas Islands precipitated their ignominious return to the barracks. The newly elected president, Raúl Alfonsín, who faced the unenviable task of leading the debt-ridden nation into a post-dictatorship future, criticized the Reagan administration's willingness to ignore state-sanctioned violence in the interest of anticommunism. "When Carter was President, I felt obliged to go to the US Embassy for the July 4th party and pay my respects," Alfonsín told reporters shortly after winning Argentina's 1983 presidential election. "Those were the only years I have ever gone. I did so to pay my respects because of his human-rights policy."[53]

With democratization processes sending military regimes packing across the hemisphere, the Reagan administration's embrace of democracy promotion was an attempt to adjust US diplomatic rigging to changing political headwinds. "Today, all who cherish human rights and individual freedom salute the people of the Americas for their great achievements," Reagan declared on International Human Rights Day on December 10, 1984. "And we pledge to our neighbors the continued support and assistance of the United States as they transform our entire hemisphere into a haven for democracy, peace, and human rights."[54] But if the US response to Latin American democratization was, at least initially, primarily reactive, Reagan officials quickly shifted gears. In a world that seemed to be moving inexorably in the direction of democracy, US policymakers were quick to claim the mantle of global leadership and to emphasize a US commitment to promoting human rights toward both the communist world and repressive anticommunist regimes such as Chile and South Africa. "From our beginning, regard for human rights and the steady expansion of human freedom have defined the American experience," Reagan asserted in his Human Rights Day address. "And they remain today, the real, moral core of our foreign policy."[55]

In practice, however, the United States offered little in the way of concrete assistance to the hemisphere's fledgling democracies. "Although the Reagan administration presented its policy toward the newly emerging democratic governments of South America as a policy of democracy promotion," writes the political scientist Thomas Carothers, "the only identifiable prodemocracy element of the policy was verbal support."[56] More troubling was the administration's unwillingness to press military regimes on human rights issues. In Uruguay, for example, "despite the fact that torture and political imprisonment remained pervasive in the country, the military hoped surface improvements such as the release of prisoners would be enough to quell U.S. criticism," argues the historian Debbie Sharnak, "and indeed Reagan was willing to take them largely at face value and see glacial movement toward democratic elections as signs of goodwill."[57]

If claiming to lead the democratic tide was both a bow to political reality and an effort to link hemispheric developments to deep-seated US ideals, the Reagan administration also recognized the role democracy promotion could play in advancing neoliberal economic policies. From the outset, Reagan officials understood a free market economy protecting the interests of corporate capitalism as an essential ingredient for a functioning democracy. As Reagan declared in 1987, "The democratic and free-market revolutions are really the same revolution."[58] De-emphasizing questions of social and economic inequality, and emphasizing a direct relationship between market logic and democratic process, the Reagan administration's free market fundamentalism contributed to the emergence of a neoliberal orthodoxy among the Washington, DC–based institutions that played an outsize role in shaping the international economic landscape—the so-called Washington Consensus, consisting of the International Monetary Fund, the World Bank, and the US Department of the Treasury.

The Latin American debt crisis of 1981–82, provided the Reagan administration with an opportunity to implement neoliberal ideas on an unprecedented scale. In the 1970s, third-world nations—often run by military dictatorships with no civilian oversight—had borrowed hundreds of billions of dollars from London and New York banks flush with "petrodollars" deposited by oil-producing nations enjoying a windfall from rising energy prices. At the outset of the 1980s, an appreciating US dollar combined with a steep hike in US interest rates, dubbed the "Volcker shock" after Federal Reserve chairman Paul Volcker, quickly brought developing nations to their knees. "Since both third-world debt and currency reserves were denominated in American dollars, for every point the U.S. Fed raised its rate, $2.5 billion was added to the interest of outstanding loans; for every 20 percent the dollar appreciated, another 20 percent was added to the balance," the historian Greg Grandin writes. "And as the interest payments on loans increased by over 50 percent between 1980 and 1982, the recession greatly reduced first-world demand for third-world products, with commodity prices falling nearly 30 percent from 1981 to 1982."[59]

Although justifiably concerned that the resulting debt crisis could metastasize into a global financial contagion, US policymakers recognized their ability to use structural adjustment as leverage to elicit wide-ranging economic reforms. In exchange for debt rescheduling, indebted nations were required to undertake rapid structural adjustment policies aimed at fiscal austerity, privatization, and market liberalization. The effects were wrenching: an explosion of financial speculation accompanied by rising inflation, deepening unemployment and cutbacks to social services, and a growing gap between social classes. The period is often referred to as the "lost decade"; by 1990, an incredible 46 percent of the population of Latin America was living in poverty.[60] With a foreign debt of some \$45 billion, Argentina was no exception. "The country . . . is still on the edge of a precipice," Alfonsín complained in mid-1984. "If we accept recessive economic recipes, our democracy itself would be at stake."[61] But for the committed free marketeers in the Reagan administration, these were bumps on the road to a world where trade liberalization, privatization, and deregulation were the order of the day. And with Latin American democrats drowning in debt and the Reagan administration holding the lifeline of structural adjustment, US officials recognized a unique opportunity to construct political and economic consent that would facilitate new forms of US hegemony. "Abandoning America's postwar promise to act as a global stabilizer, Reagan used monetary policy as a club to assert America's national interest on the world stage," Grandin writes, "institutionalizing an international system of financial and speculative capitalism that allowed the United States to maintain its primacy even as its industrial base was eroding."[62]

Finally, in addition to bolstering the Reagan administration in its confrontation with the communist world, aligning the United States behind processes of democratization abroad, and advancing US neoliberal economic goals, the democracy initiative served to shore up support at home. From the outset, White House officials recognized the democracy promotion initiative's utility in confronting the inroads New Politics liberals had made into the heart of the US foreign policy establishment since the late 1960s. The result, the Reagan administration repeatedly argued, had been a US retreat from global commitments, even in the face of rising Soviet adventurism. As Weinstein, who served as a foreign policy adviser to Reagan during the 1980 election campaign, delicately put it, "Post-Vietnam America has been a deeply self-absorbed, fitful, and uncertain place only now awakening from its self-imposed dogmatic slumbers."[63]

The importance of containing New Politics liberals was clearly evident in the selection of Carl Gershman as president of the NED. A liberal hawk serving as the executive director of Social Democrats, USA, Gershman expressed an undisguised disdain for the Carter administration's foreign policy approach. In July 1980, only a few months after Kirkpatrick penned her seminal article "Dictatorships and Double Standards," Gershman had published an even more sustained—and scathing—critique of the Carter administration in the pages of the neoconservative journal *Commentary*. The breakdown of the bipartisan Cold War consensus amid the US defeat in Vietnam, Gershman argued, had left "a paralyzing residuum of division and demoralization." In the early 1970s, a new foreign policy establishment had emerged, focused on transforming the US engagement with the international arena in light of the debacle in Southeast Asia. Rejecting the Cold War shibboleths of previous decades, the new establishment championed "the idea that the containment of communism by the United States was neither possible, necessary, nor even desirable," Gershman asserted. Instead, the Soviet Union was portrayed as a status quo power, détente was seen as both desirable and necessary, and US efforts to prevent the spread of communism were understood to lead "inevitably to protracted conflicts like Vietnam in which the United States sought vainly and at great cost to hold back the march of history."[64]

Carter's victory in the 1976 election, Gershman asserted, signified the ascendance of the new establishment approach to international affairs. The president's Notre Dame address, with its emphasis on moving beyond the "inordinate fear of communism" and the "moral poverty" of the Vietnam War, was, in Gershman's view, a "perfect synthesis of the ideas propounded by the new establishment during the preceding years." In actual contests of power and policy, however, it had failed spectacularly. The new establishment had "devalued the importance of national-security concerns . . . saturating American foreign policy with defeatism masquerading as optimism and 'maturity' and 'restraint,'" Gershman concluded, "cravenly following international political fashion even if this meant denigrating the interests and values of one's own country, and worrying less about Soviet insecurity, in the name of which virtually any Soviet action could be condoned or blamed upon the United States."[65]

Following the 1980 election, Gershman followed the migration of liberal hawks into the Reagan camp. When Reagan appointed Kirkpatrick as the US ambassador to the United Nations, she hired Gershman as chief counselor. "It is a team long on loyalty to Kirkpatrick and sharing her neoconservative views," noted one observer, "but short on experience in international diplomacy."[66] Four years later, Gershman's appointment as head of the NED sent a clear signal: as the centerpiece of the administration's human rights policy, democracy promotion could serve as the lynchpin in Reagan's effort to contain New Politics liberals. As Reagan declared in a 1984 address at Georgetown University, a signal challenge for the United States was to "restore bipartisan consensus in support of U.S. foreign policy." The president continued, "We must restore America's honorable tradition of partisan politics stopping at the water's edge, Republicans and Democrats standing united in patriotism, and speaking with one voice as responsible trustees for peace, democracy, individual liberty, and the rule of law."[67]

It was a point repeatedly emphasized by Reagan officials. After a prolonged period of national suffering in the 1970s, Kirkpatrick argued in early 1984, "first aid has been administered, efforts to restore our health and capacity to believe in ourselves has taken hold." With newfound national confidence, she continued, "at least we are no longer a willing victim, no longer ready to assist in the legitimization of our defeat and disappearance."[68] Secretary of State Shultz followed suit. In an address to State Department employees in April 1985 commemorating the tenth anniversary of the fall of South Vietnam, Shultz cast the US intervention in Southeast Asia in distinctly moral terms. "Whatever mistakes in how the war was fought, whatever one's view of the strategic rationale for our intervention, the *morality* of our effort must now be clear," he declared. The ignominious US withdrawal, Shultz continued, ushered in a grim era in the United States of "introspection, self-doubt, and hesitancy." Bluntly criticizing liberal internationalists' efforts in the 1970s to rein in the power of what Arthur M. Schlesinger Jr. famously described as the "imperial presidency," Shultz continued: "Some Americans tended to think that *American* power was the source of the world's problems, and that the key to peace was to limit *our* actions in the world. So we imposed all sorts of restrictions on ourselves. Vietnam—and Watergate—left a legacy of congressional restrictions on presidential flexibility, now embedded in our legislation. . . . These weakened the ability of the President to act and to conduct foreign policy, and they weakened our country. Thus we pulled back from global leadership." A decade later, Shultz concluded, the isolationism and self-defeatism of the 1970s had dissipated, and the United States was once again assuming its traditional leadership position. "The American people believe in their country and in its role as a force for good," Shultz asserted. "They want to see an effective foreign policy that blocks aggression and advances the cause of freedom and democracy."[69]

If the democracy project was central to mustering domestic support for the US Cold War crusade, Reagan officials also used it to combat the broader influence of the New Left in US society. Teaching in US schools had become "dominated by cultural relativism," Abrams told an audience of US educators at a National Council for the Social Studies conference in November 1983, that is, "the doctrine that there are no absolutes, that one cannot say that one culture or tradition is preferable to another, that the very attempt to discriminate between opposing traditions is a form of 'ethnocentrism,' and that virtue consists only in being 'open' to every 'life style.'" Brandishing a recently published council booklet on human rights, Abrams assailed the organization for describing a basic equivalency between an emphasis on political rights in the

United States and Western Europe and support for economic rights in Eastern Europe. It was a narrative, Abrams bluntly told the audience, that was fundamentally wrong. Citing a State Department report estimating that Soviet premier Joseph Stalin oversaw the killing of between twenty-five million and thirty million people in the Soviet Union's first three and a half decades, Abrams acidly remarked, "To conclude that the Soviet Union and the United States differ in their ideas about freedom . . . and leave it at that, is rather like saying that Hitler and the Jews held different views about the nature of religious freedom."

Rather than cultural relativism, Abrams maintained, American social studies teachers should focus on the exceptionalism that defined their own nation's political system. "The ends which our Founding Fathers chose to pursue, of course, were human rights. The purpose of government, they declared, was to secure these rights. Not, it should be stressed, to promote virtue or piety, privilege or wealth, empire or dominion: only rights." Indeed, Abrams concluded, "there is only one human rights political tradition in the world today, and this is embodied in the political system known as democracy."[70]

By mid-decade, the democracy promotion initiative had emerged as the defining feature of the Reagan administration's human rights policy. An overriding emphasis on democratic institutions, the protection of civil liberties, and the free market infused the State Department's annual *Country Reports on Human Rights Practices*. More significantly, top US policymakers continued to champion the issue. As Reagan eloquently put it in mid-1985, "In the storm-tossed history of our globe, the United States has been a strong and steady rudder, holding the world fast to the course of democratic progress."[71] Similarly, Shultz described the wave of democratization over the previous half-dozen years—particularly Latin America—as a "democratic revolution." In a major policy address in February 1985 at the Commonwealth Club in San Francisco, Shultz declared that "as a matter of fundamental principle, the United States supports human rights and peaceful democratic change throughout the world, including in noncommunist, pro-Western countries." In a clear shift from the Kirkpatrick Doctrine's emphasis on supporting repressive allies, Shultz maintained that democratic institutions were "the best guarantor of stability and peace, as well as of human rights."[72]

The Reagan administration's democracy promotion initiative reached its apogee in early 1986. Having laid the rhetorical groundwork, the White House response to popular unrest in Haiti and the Philippines offered a more concrete expression of US efforts to promote democracy overseas. In February 1986, the Reagan administration withdrew US support from the brutal Haitian president Jean-Claude Duvalier following massive strikes and protests that brought Port-au-Prince to a standstill. With even the Haitian military turning against him, Duvalier fled to France. A few weeks later, as popular unrest in the Philippines intensified following deeply fraudulent elections, Shultz prevailed on a very reluctant President Reagan to withdraw US support from the autocratic Ferdinand Marcos. Bereft of a key source of political legitimacy, Marcos boarded a US Air Force flight to Guam in the early hours of February 25, setting the stage for a democratic transition led by opposition leader Corazon Aquino. The following month, Reagan embraced the "democratic revolution" in a defining address to a joint session of Congress. Lauding the wave of democratization that was sweeping Latin America, Reagan asserted that "the American people believe in human rights and oppose tyranny in whatever form, whether of the left or the right."[73]

The Reagan administration's actions in Haiti and the Philippines sent a shock wave rippling across the Washington Beltway. Once Duvalier and Marcos had stepped down, US "support for authoritarian governments that opposed communism could not be taken for granted," Shultz proudly wrote in his memoirs. "The United States supported people who were themselves standing up for freedom and democracy, whether against communism or against another form of repressive government."[74] Indeed, the administration's actions were lauded in the press. "Whatever comes next in the Philippines and Haiti, dictators are reeling and America is their scourge," the *New York Times* enthused. "Hats off to President Reagan."[75]

Moreover, Reagan's tough stance against Duvalier and Marcos, combined with the president's lofty rhetoric, was taken as a dramatic shift from the administration's rejection of human rights at the outset of the decade as well as from the Kirkpatrick Doctrine's emphasis on supporting repressive right-wing allies. Reagan had undertaken a "turnaround on human rights," an influential article in *Foreign Affairs* asserted, "a 150- if not a 180-degree change."[76] Even stalwart critics of the administration were impressed. "American policy in this instance expressed what we want to believe are the deepest American values," wrote *New York Times* columnist Anthony Lewis following Marcos's departure. "We used our influence on the side of democracy. We made no excuses for dictators. And our means were peaceful: not weapons or covert military intervention but the words of politics and diplomacy."[77]

The administration's melding of the Reagan Doctrine's call to roll back communism with US democracy promotion also won bipartisan support on Capitol Hill from moderates such as Senate Foreign Relations Committee chairman Richard G. Lugar (R–IN) and House Foreign Affairs Committee member Stephen J. Solarz (D–NY). After leading the official US delegation of observers to oversee the Philippine election and stridently denouncing the widespread voter fraud, Lugar emerged as a particularly strong supporter of US democracy promotion. "The strongest suit of American foreign policy is the promotion and protection of democracy abroad," he later wrote. "Democratic countries celebrate human rights, they enhance our security, and they are good trading partners committed to a higher standard of living for all citizens."[78]

Such bipartisanship facilitated significant White House successes. Despite facing tough critics on Capitol Hill, the NED managed to survive annual congressional budgetary battles, and by mid-decade the organization was funding political aid projects across the globe. In 1986, the NED allocated more than $1 million for political aid programming to Africa, $3 million to Asia, $2.5 million to Europe, and $5.5 million to Latin America.[79] From the outset, such efforts were understood as advancing US interests in the Cold War. As NED president Gershman told members of Congress in 1985, "The best bulwark against totalitarianism is democracy."[80] The Polish opposition movement was an NED favorite; after allocating nearly $500,000 to Polish activists in 1984, NED funding nearly doubled in 1985, then doubled again in 1986. The funds covered the cost of a wide range of programs carried out by organizations in Poland, especially Solidarity, as well as exile groups in Western Europe, including dissident publications, plays, theater events, and music performances; a social fund for political prisoners and their families; and "flying universities"— secret lectures and seminars organized in private homes. The point of the lance in the US effort to support anticommunist activists in Eastern Europe, NED funding for Polish opposition groups would reach $3.3 million by 1989.[81]

As US support for the Polish opposition deepened, the democracy promotion initiative also dovetailed with the Reagan Doctrine's call to support anticommunist wars of liberation in the developing world. Despite conflicts, rivalries, and power struggles within the administration that reached, in Kirkpatrick's phrase, "Shakespearean" proportions, there was virtually no disagreement among Reagan officials regarding the necessity of a muscular US response to communist adventurism.[82] Although in his memoirs, for example, Shultz recounted frequent clashes with administration hard-liners over third-world hot spots such as Central America, notably CIA director William J. Casey and national security adviser William P. Clark, the secretary of state did *not* oppose US support for anticommunist militants.[83] As Shultz maintained in an interview many years later, "I wasn't comfortable with some of the things the CIA did, but I was comfortable with the Reagan doctrine."[84]

Indeed, in his 1985 San Francisco address Shultz explicitly tied the democracy promotion initiative to the Reagan Doctrine's emphasis on rolling back communist gains in the developing world. The United States "should support the forces of freedom in communist totalitarian states," Shultz bluntly declared. "We must not succumb to the fashionable thinking that democracy has enemies only on the right, that pressures and sanctions are fine against rightwing dictators but not against leftwing totalitarians." Similarly, the secretary called for strong US support for nations threatened by communism. "So long as communist dictatorships feel free to aid and abet insurgencies in the name of 'socialist internationalism,'" Shultz demanded, "why must democracies, the target of this threat, be inhibited from defending their own interests and the cause of democracy itself?"[85] Casting the defense of democracy in stark terms, the secretary of state depicted anticommunist struggles as a defining feature of the emerging world order.

Congressional lawmakers increasingly supported the administration's efforts to roll back communism. In Afghanistan, US aid to the mujahideen rose from $122 million in 1984 to $250 million in 1985, nearly doubled in 1986, and reached $630 million in 1987.[86] Beginning in 1986, US support to the Afghan rebels included technologically advanced US ground-to-air heat-seeking Stinger missiles.[87] Correspondingly, in the months following Reagan's second inauguration, the Congress repealed the Clark Amendment prohibiting covert operations in Angola, legislated military assistance to noncommunist resistance in Cambodia, and approved nonlethal aid to the Contras.[88] In sum, by mid-1986 the administration's emphasis on democracy promotion, as the core of its human rights policy, had made significant steps toward re-creating the bipartisan Cold War consensus between the executive and legislative branches that had foundered in the late 1960s.

The democracy promotion initiative was particularly important in US policy toward Nicaragua. Eschewing the complexities of the Nicaraguan political landscape in favor of a stark vision of Central America as a battleground in the East-West confrontation, top US policymakers portrayed the Sandinistas as brutal Soviet clients, committed to establishing totalitarianism at home and supporting like-minded revolutionaries abroad. The Sandinistas were a "bad news government," Shultz declared in February 1985. "I see no reason why we should slam the door on people just because they have been taken behind the Iron Curtain."[89] Moreover, the FSLN could not be trusted to fulfill its side of any negotiation with the United States or the international community. Despite US efforts to work with the Sandinistas, Managua had "not been interested in talking seriously and sincerely," Reagan told a group of supporters the following year. "All of a sudden, now their apologists come out and say, 'Oh, it's time to give new talks a chance,'" the president continued. "Well, that sounds just fine and peaceful and nonharmful; but what some people don't seem to understand is that if we delay aid for a few months while we're talking, the Sandinistas will take that time and use it to finish off the contras." For Reagan, negotiations were thus pointless. "That's the Communist strategy—to kill them off," he concluded dramatically. "And when the execution is complete, they'll end the talks."[90]

More to the point, Reagan administration officials repeatedly emphasized that since the Sandinistas were communists, they could not, by definition, be democratic, nor could the FSLN be trusted to fulfill its side of any negotiation with the United States or the international community. "The Sandinistas are communists, therefore, such agreements are lies," Elliot Abrams bluntly asserted. "It is preposterous" he added, "to think we can sign a deal with the Sandinistas to meet our foreign policy concerns and expect it to be kept."[91] Indeed, Reagan's criticism of Managua negotiating in bad faith was, in fact, an apt description of the administration's own strategy; despite repeated assurances that the United States was committed to successive rounds of high-level talks with Nicaragua as well as support for regional diplomatic efforts, in private the Reagan administration viewed such initiatives as purely instrumental—a necessary sop to Congress in the effort to convince congressional moderates to support Contra funding. "If we are just talking about negotiations with Nicaragua, that is so far-fetched to imagine that a communist government like that would make any reasonable deal with us," Reagan told the National Security Planning Group in June 1984, "but if it is to get Congress to support the anti-Sandinistas, then that can be helpful."[92]

The outsize US role in supporting the Contras provided the most clear-cut example of how democracy promotion could be harnessed to advance Cold War goals. Throughout the 1980s, human rights organizations and Central America–focused advocacy groups produced a steady stream of reports detailing Contra attacks on civilians and targets such as cooperative farms, schools, and health centers. "They had already destroyed all that was the cooperative: a coffee drying machine, the two dormitories for the coffee cutters, the electricity generators, seven cows, the plant, the food warehouse," Nicaragua coffee cooperative member Doroteo Tinoco Valdivia told the US lawyer Reed Brody, who collected direct eyewitness testimony of Contra tactics from 145 Nicaraguans in late 1984. After they captured one of the cooperative's members, Tinoco recounted, the Contras "cut his throat, then they cut open his stomach and left his intestines hanging out on the ground like a string." Echoing dozens of reports published over the course of the 1980s, such testimonies, Brody concluded in a grim report published the following year, revealed "a distinct pattern" of Contra abuses.[93]

Reagan officials consistently dismissed such reports as the work of defeatist liberals and Sandinista sympathizers. Instead, the administration repeatedly championed the Contras as Nicaragua's only hope for a democratic future. The Contras, Secretary of State Shultz declared in August 1984, "want only to bring democracy to their people."[94] Reagan repeatedly sounded a similar refrain. In a 1985 radio address, for example, the president began by praising anticommunist liberation struggles. "One of the most inspiring developments of recent years is the move against communism and toward freedom that is sweeping the world. In the Soviet Union and Eastern Europe, we see the dissidents; in Poland, the Solidarity movement. We see freedom fighters in Afghanistan, Ethiopia, Cambodia, and Angola," the president declared. "These brave men and women" he continued, "are fighting to undo the infamous Brezhnev doctrine, which says that once a nation falls into the darkness of Communist tyranny, it can never again see the light of freedom." Underscoring the significance of Nicaragua in Reagan's understanding of the global Cold War, the president then turned his attention to Central America:

> Nowhere do we see this more than in Nicaragua, whose Sandinista government is a Marxist-Leninist clique that broke the hearts of the freedom-loving people of their country by imposing a brutal dictatorship soon after taking control in 1979. Functioning as a satellite of the Soviet Union and Cuba, they moved quickly to suppress internal dissent, clamp down on a free press, persecute the church and labor unions, and betray their pledge to hold free elections. Now they're exporting drugs to poison our youth and linking up with the terrorists of Iran, Libya, the Red Brigades, and the PLO. The Sandinistas aren't democrats, but Communists; not lovers of freedom, but of power; not builders of a peaceful nation, but creators of a fortress Nicaragua that intends to export communism beyond its borders.

By contrast, Reagan concluded, the Contras were "the true heroes of the Nicaraguan struggle—non-Communist, democracy-loving revolutionaries—[who] saw their revolution betrayed and took up arms against the betrayer. . . . We should call them freedom fighters."[95]

In its effort to link the Contras to the broader democracy promotion initiative, the White House proved more than willing to test the boundaries of

US and international law. With strong backing from CIA director Casey, in early 1984 dozens of small mines—secretly built in a garage in northern Virginia—were laid in Nicaragua's three principal harbors. By early April, two Nicaraguan fishing boats had hit mines, as had merchant ships from Panama, the Netherlands, Liberia, and Japan.[96] Almost immediately, the US role in the operation was revealed. When five crew members of the Soviet oil tanker *Lugansk* were injured by a mine on March 20, minister of foreign affairs Andrei Gromyko presented the US Embassy with a formal protest charging the United States with "carrying out a policy of state-endorsed terrorism."[97] Although the State Department quickly dismissed Moscow's criticism, the Reagan administration soon found itself saddled with complaints from key regional players, including Colombia, Mexico, Panama, and Venezuela, as well as principal members of the Western alliance.[98]

More worrying for the administration were infuriated members of Congress. Senator Barry M. Goldwater (R-AZ) captured the tone in a letter to Casey on April 9. "It gets down to one, little, simple phrase: I am pissed off!" An influential member of the Senate Intelligence Committee, Goldwater accused the Reagan administration of giving the mining operation the green light without briefing the committee. "The President has asked us to back his foreign policy. . . . [H]ow can we back his foreign policy when we don't know what the hell he is doing? . . . This is an act violating international law. It is an act of war. For the life of me, I don't see how we are going to explain it."[99] The fact that Casey—well known for both his disdain for Congress and his incoherent mumbling—had mentioned the mining once during a two-hour briefing with the committee on March 8 did little to assuage angry legislators.

More broadly, the mining operation illuminated the contradictions in the melding of the democracy promotion initiative and the Reagan Doctrine. Critics argued that mining Nicaragua's harbors was a violation of the United Nations Charter, the Inter-American Treaty of Reciprocal Assistance (Rio Pact), and the Charter of the Organization of American States, all of which limited the use of force against member states to self-defense. It also called into question the United States' commitment to the principle of freedom of navigation, a defining feature of US foreign policy dating back to the venerable Jay Treaty of 1794 and a core element of liberal internationalism in the twentieth century.[100] The Wilsonianism underpinning Reagan's embrace of democracy promotion, in other words, was hard to square with the Reagan Doctrine's go-it-alone interventionism on behalf of the Contras.

Amid the blowback from the mining operation, on April 6 the Reagan administration notified the United Nations that the United States would not accept the World Court's jurisdiction in disputes affecting Central America for the following two years. The decision was aimed at preempting a suit against the US covert war that the Sandinistas intended to file on April 9. But it was perceived by administration critics as further evidence of Reagan's willingness to follow the "rules-based system" established after 1945 only when it dovetailed with White House objectives. The United States had played a foundational role in the creation of the World Court in 1945 under the Charter of the United Nations, had accepted its jurisdiction the following year, and appeared before the court in subsequent decades nearly a dozen times. Like the sea mines in Nicaraguan harbors, the Reagan team's sudden rejection of the World Court was a stunning repudiation of a pillar of US-led liberal internationalism in the aftermath of the Second World War. "The U.S. action is unprecedented not only because the United States has never before disputed World Court jurisdiction," noted a House of Representatives Democratic Study Group report, "but also because no other nation has ever requested a suspension of jurisdiction before a specific suit was filed."[101]

The sea mines fiasco, and, to a lesser extent, the administration's thumbing its nose at the World Court, temporarily solidified congressional opposition to the Reagan administration's war on Nicaragua. In 1983, the chairman of the House Select Committee on Intelligence, Edward P. Boland (D–MA), had successfully sponsored legislation designed to prevent US aid from being used to overthrow the Nicaraguan government. Following the revelations of the mining operation, by mid-1984 Boland and many of his colleagues were convinced that stronger measures were necessary. In a major setback for the White House, in October 1984, restive legislators passed a second Boland Amendment, which sought to unequivocally curtail all US funding for the Contras: "During fiscal year 1985, no funds available to the Central Intelligence Agency, the Department of Defense, or any other agency or entity of the United States involved in intelligence activities may be obligated or expended for the purpose or which would have the effect of supporting, directly or indirectly, military or paramilitary operations in Nicaragua by any nation, group, organization, movement, or individual."[102] A landmark moment in the debate over Central America, the congressional aid cutoff posed a direct threat to the Reagan administration's ability to wage its proxy war against Nicaragua.

Corresponding with Reagan's support for the Contras as a pillar of the administration's democracy promotion initiative, the White House rejected the Sandinistas' own efforts to foster a democratic political system in Nicaragua. When the FSLN held national elections for president and for ninety-six members of the National Constituent Assembly in November 1984, the Reagan administration responded by denouncing the vote as a fraud—four months before the ballots were cast.[103] The election itself was scrutinized by more than six hundred journalists and four hundred international electoral observers, including delegates from the United States and most Western European nations, as well as Bolivia, Brazil, Czechoslovakia, and Mexico.[104] Despite war-induced press censorship and sporadic harassment of opposition candidates by groups of Sandinista supporters, with a voter turnout of 75 percent the election was generally considered remarkably free and fair. "In not one of the polling stations that I visited did I see any fraud, irregularities or violations of the electoral law," wrote Larry Leaman, an observer working for the US-based NGO Witness for Peace (WFP).[105] Even the US Embassy in Managua, after dispatching seven teams to observe the voting, cabled Washington a series of statements from foreign observers emphasizing the "calmness and tranquility" of the voting process.[106]

The results came as little surprise: FSLN candidate Daniel Ortega Saavedra won the presidency and the Sandinistas won sixty-one seats in the assembly. But despite the FSLN's strong showing, with the remaining seats in the assembly split between half a dozen opposition parties from across the political spectrum, the 1984 election demonstrated a political pluralism that set Nicaragua apart from its neighbors. As one journalist noted, "Any left-wing candidate foolhardy enough to have run in nearby El Salvador's elections would probably have been assassinated."[107]

President Reagan, however, immediately dismissed the results. "I have just one thing to say," the commander in chief told the press on the day of the election. "It's a phony."[108] In fact, it was Reagan, not the Sandinistas, who sabotaged the Nicaraguan election. In the lead-up to voting day, the United States worked closely with the right-wing political opposition, convincing presidential candidate Arturo Cruz to strategically drop out of the race and take advantage of the political opening created by the election season to hold anti-Sandinista rallies. Cruz, who was later revealed to be on the CIA's payroll, played the role of "teaser and pro-abstention propagandist" whose primary function was "denouncing what he claimed were inadequate conditions for a free election."[109] It was a strategy that underscored the US refusal to accept a democratic outcome in Nicaragua unless it forced the Sandinistas from power. As US ambassador to Nicaragua Anthony Quainton recalled in a later interview, "there was no desire to have free elections" because they would have "legitimized Daniel Ortega."[110] Similarly, underscoring the Cold War interventionism at the heart of Reagan's democracy promotion initiative, a

US official in Managua candidly told an election monitoring commission that "the United States is not obliged to apply the same standard of judgment to a country whose government is avowedly hostile to the U.S. as for a country, like El Salvador, where it is not." The Sandinistas, the official concluded, "could bring about a situation in Central America which could pose a threat to U.S. security. That allows us to change our yardstick."[111]

Two days after Nicaraguan ballots were cast, American voters went to the polls for their own presidential election. In one of the biggest landslides in US history, Reagan decisively defeated Democratic candidate Walter Mondale, winning forty-nine states and 525 of 538 electoral votes. Buoyed by the president's renewed mandate, the administration intensified its efforts to use the democracy promotion initiative to drum up support for the Contras. Claiming the moral high ground, Secretary of State Shultz tried to turn the tables on liberals' criticism that rising US intervention in Central American would lead to a Vietnam-style quagmire. "Our goals in Central America *are* like those we had in Vietnam: democracy, economic progress, and security against aggression," Shultz claimed. Like North Vietnamese communists, the Sandinistas, "employ slogans of social reform, nationalism, and democracy to obscure their totalitarian goals." The secretary of state concluded, "Broken promises; communist dictatorship; refugees; [and] widened Soviet influence, this time near our very borders—here is your parallel between Vietnam and Central America."[112]

As congressional support for the democracy promotion initiative swelled following US actions on Haiti and the Philippines, the Reagan administration redoubled its efforts to secure congressional funding for the anti-Sandinista rebels. Offering a scathing appraisal of Sandinista militarization, repression of civil liberties, and interventionism throughout the region, Shultz exhorted the Senate Committee on Foreign Relations to support the president's February 25, 1986, assistance request. "Only a democratic opening in Nicaragua can alter these dim prospects," Shultz warned. "And the resistance is a major element in the present equation that can help create that opening."[113] Cold War hawks quickly jumped on the bandwagon. "The success of the elections in the Philippines points the way for a similar policy in Nicaragua," claimed Senator Lugar in a pro-Contra press release.[114] Neoconservative commentator Norman Podhoretz went a step further. Reagan's tough stand against Duvalier and Marcos had put the ball in liberals' court, Podhoretz asserted. "It is now up to the liberals to demonstrate the good faith of their own devotion to democratic institutions by backing the Administration when it works against nondemocratic regimes of the left—specifically, at the moment, Nicaragua."[115]

The most forceful call for bipartisan support for the democracy promotion initiative, however, came from the president himself. Reagan's embrace of the "democratic revolution" in his March 1986 address to Congress was a powerful paean to Wilsonian internationalism that resonated on both sides of the political aisle. It was also a call to arms emphasizing the imperative of US support for "freedom fighters" struggling against communism across the globe and placing special emphasis on the Nicaraguan Contras. As *New York Times* reporter Bernard Weinraub noted, "Mr. Reagan seemed to be saying the United States would promote ballots for dealing with right-wing regimes, such as Ferdinand E. Marcos's in the Philippines, but bullets for left-wing dictatorships like that in Nicaragua."[116]

The central problem with this formulation, however, was that in the case of Nicaragua, US democracy promotion meant orchestrating a regime change. Reagan came close to admitting as much when asked by a journalist whether the United States sought to "remove" the FSLN from power. "Well, remove in the sense of its present structure, in which it is a Communist totalitarian state, and it is not a government chosen by the people," the president responded.[117] A foreign diplomat in Managua put it differently. Asked what the Sandinistas could do to conciliate Reagan, he responded, "Well, they could shoot themselves."[118] Not surprisingly, this formulation was unacceptable to Sandinista officials. Human rights groups were also deeply uncomfortable with the Reagan administration's use of human rights rhetoric to advance Cold War goals. As the Americas Watch Committee asserted in a 1985 report, "Such a concerted campaign to use human rights in justifying military action is without precedent in US–Latin American relations, and its effect is an unprecedented debasement of the human rights cause."[119]

The unique role of the National Endowment for Democracy further underscored the interventionism underpinning Reagan's democracy promotion agenda. The NED's status as a private entity with public funding allowed it to claim autonomy from the US government. But with the hawkish Carl Gershman at the helm, the endowment tacked closely to Reagan's intervention against the Sandinistas, in effect serving as a channel for nonlethal aid to political opponents of the FSLN. Over the course of 1985 and early 1986, for example, the NED provided the Friends of the Democratic Center in Central America (Prodemca) roughly $400,000 in grants.[120] Founded in 1981 with grants from numerous right-wing foundations, Prodemca had quickly become a magnet for neoconservatives concerned with the threat of communism in Central America. In turn, Prodemca dispersed the NED funds to anti-Sandinista civic organizations such as the opposition newspaper *La Prensa*.[121]

During the same time period, however, Prodemca placed full-page advertisements in the *Washington Post*, the *New York Times*, and the *Washington Times*, encouraging Congress to support Reagan's $100 million aid package to the Contras.

Critics cried foul, arguing that the NED was, in effect, giving Americans' tax dollars to an organization that supported the Contras' terrorist tactics. In their view, Prodemca's claim that the money to pay for the advertisements came from a different bank account than the one used for NED funds missed the broader conflict of interest at stake. Gershman's response was predictable. "Prodemca is a centrist, bipartisan U.S. organization dedicated to promoting democracy in Central America," he asserted in an NED press release. Sidestepping the difficult questions of politics and policy that the incident had brought to light, Gershman dealt platitudes and waited for the dust to settle: "We continue to have every confidence in their commitment to democratic values."[122]

Swept up in the momentum of Reagan's sweeping 1984 election victory and the powerful appeal of the president's call to support democracy abroad, the Congress in 1985 fell into line. In a dramatic reversal of the second Boland Amendment's aid cutoff, in June 1986 the House narrowly passed Reagan's request for $100 million in lethal and nonlethal aid for the Contras, and in August the Senate followed suit. The president signed the bill into law in October.[123] After years of setbacks on Contra aid, White House officials breathed a sigh of relief. "This year many Senators and Congressmen on both sides of the aisle joined us in supporting military assistance to the brave freedom fighters in Nicaragua," Reagan declared in a national radio address the following month. "I believe we're beginning to see the recreation of the fundamental bipartisan consensus on national security issues that guided this nation through much of the postwar era."[124]

The successful passage of the $100 million aid package for the Contras was a defining success in Reagan's embrace of democracy promotion as both the centerpiece of the administration's human rights policy and a pillar of US engagement with the global arena. Reagan's 1982 Westminster address, building on rising support among a bipartisan array of US politicians, labor leaders, and academics, had facilitated the 1983 creation of the NED. By 1986, the NED was developing into the flagship for US-funded training and political aid overseas. Enthusiastically describing the emergence of a "prodemocratic consensus," the endowment's 1987 annual report asserted that supporters on both sides of the political aisle agreed "that democratic governments tend to be friendly to the United States and peaceful in their foreign relations; that they tend more toward political stability and economic prosperity than non-democratic systems; that the growth of democracy serves our national interests; and that to further those interests we should support those who are struggling to establish democratic systems and defend democratic values." The NED, the report expansively concluded, "is a product of this consensus."[125]

More importantly, by mid-decade the interplay between the democracy initiative and the Reagan Doctrine moved to the center of US foreign policy. Reagan's 1986 shift on Haiti and the Philippines, followed by his pledge to oppose dictatorships on both the right and the left, marked a critical development in the administration's two terms in office. Skeptics remained unconvinced. "We've always been attracted to the idea of not only making the world safe for democracy, but making the world a democratic Garden of Eden," Jeane Kirkpatrick asserted in March 1986. "I think it's just not practical as an operational goal."[126] But the ascendance of the democracy initiative marked a shift away from the Kirkpatrick Doctrine's narrow support for right-wing Cold War allies and was lauded by liberals and conservatives alike, while Reagan officials increasingly recognized the initiative's utility in advancing US interests at home and abroad.

Yet, from the outset, Reagan's intervention in Central America was undertaken in the spirit of a human rights policy that defined communism as the ultimate violation and justified US efforts to orchestrate a regime change—to force the FSLN, in other words, "to say 'Uncle,'" as Reagan brashly told reporters. Indeed, in the aftermath of the second Boland Amendment's aid cutoff, it was no coincidence that NSC staffer Oliver L. North referred to his efforts to secretly channel aid to the Contras, including offshore bank accounts, dummy corporations, hired ships and airplanes, and communications infrastructure, as "Project Democracy."[127] Yet, beginning in late 1986, revelations of North's illegal activities—soon known as the Iran-Contra scandal—would threaten to upend the Reagan presidency.

Chapter 5

Tracking the "Indiana Jones of the Right"

Right-Wing Transnational Activism, Public Diplomacy,

and the Reagan Doctrine, 1981-1990

Jack Wheeler was an adventurer. He was twelve years old when president Dwight D. Eisenhower honored him as the youngest Eagle Scout in the history of the Boy Scouts. Two years later, in 1957, he climbed the Matterhorn. At sixteen, he was nearly hit by a Russian cargo ship while swimming naked across the Hellespont—where the Black Sea meets the Aegean—to reenact the Greek myth of Leander visiting his lover, Hero. Enrolling as an anthropology student at the University of California, Los Angeles (UCLA), Wheeler was hardly a typical undergraduate; sporting his UCLA varsity jacket, the seventeen-year-old killed a tiger in South Vietnam known as the "man-eater of Dalat." "I'd wounded him. It was the middle of the night, and I had to go out and try to find him with a flashlight at the end of my rifle," Wheeler recalled many years later. "It was close. I ended up shooting him in the chest."[1] Undeterred, in the summer of 1960 Wheeler lived with a clan of the Amazonian Jívaro, who gave him a shrunken human head as a farewell present.[2]

Over the next two decades, Wheeler's many adventures, as one admiring journalist put it, made "Tarzan a milquetoast."[3] He hiked Kilimanjaro and Fujiyama, met with cannibals in the New Hebrides and Bambuti Pygmies in eastern Congo, entered the *Guinness Book of World Records* for a parachute jump at the North Pole, and retraced Hannibal's passage across the Alps with four elephants. After founding Wheeler Adventures in the early 1970s, Wheeler offered bespoke tours for small groups of wealthy patrons ranging from African safaris to retracing the path of Meriwether Lewis and William Clark across the US Pacific Northwest. "We only get one crack at life," he told a journalist in 1979. "It lasts but the snap of a finger. What a waste, what a damned shame, if you are lowered away, for all eternity, without once having your mortal soul purged with the emetic of high adventure."[4]

Wheeler eventually visited more than 180 countries, filling his La Jolla, California, home with souvenirs from the farthest corners of the globe, from bits of human bone picked off an 800-year-old Mongolian battlefield to shields of New Zealand's Maori tribespeople. Yet Wheeler was more than a mere rough-and-tumble thrill seeker. He was a deeply conservative intellectual—with a bachelor's degree in anthropology from UCLA, a master's in philosophy from the University of Hawaii, and a doctorate in philosophy from the University of Southern California, where he held a brief stint as a lecturer in Aristotelian ethics. In the mid-1960s, Wheeler had been a staunch supporter of Ronald Reagan's bid for California governor; twenty years later, with "the Gipper" in the White House, Wheeler played an important role in popularizing the Reagan Doctrine's call to support third-world guerrilla conflicts against the Soviet Union and its proxies. With an unparalleled ability to meet anticommunist revolutionaries on their home turf—often very inhospitable terrain—and with ties to influential conservatives in Washington and in the private sector, Wheeler blended an adventurer's authenticity with a powerful critique of what he perceived as the deepening fissures in the Soviet empire. Described as an "ideological gangster" in the Soviet newspaper *Izvestia*, Wheeler emerged as a culture hero for hard-line American conservatives.[5] "That's him," an awestruck young conservative beamed in 1986. "The Indiana Jones of the right."[6]

Wheeler was only a bit player in the broader evolution of the Reagan Doctrine. Yet his activities illuminate the emergence of a network of conservatives—including both Reagan administration officials and private-sector individuals and organizations—that coalesced in the mid-1980s around a shared commitment to rolling back Soviet gains abroad while containing the US Left at home. In this process, Central America took center stage. With congressional legislators wielding the power of the purse, White House officials knew it would be no easy task to secure US economic and security assistance for the Salvadoran government and counterrevolutionary forces seeking to destabilize leftist Nicaragua. More broadly, polls consistently indicated that the prospect of a US intervention in Central America enjoyed little support among the American people.[7] "The problem is how I am perceived," Reagan told the National Security Council (NSC) in February 1982. "I was a hawk in Vietnam because I believe if you ask people to die you should give them a chance to win," the president continued. "The best way to prevent war is to get to the problem early. Can I do something without adding to the perception of me as a hawk?"[8]

It was a question that would shape White House policy for the duration of Reagan's two terms in the Oval Office and, in the process, create spaces for nonstate actors—like Wheeler—to influence US foreign policy. Beginning in the late spring of 1983, the administration turned to public diplomacy. The White House Outreach Working Group on Central America initiated an expansive campaign, dispatching speakers across the nation, publishing alarmist reports on developments in Central America, and creating a forum for conservative activists who feared communist expansion in the Western Hemisphere. Correspondingly, the Office of Public Diplomacy for Latin America and the Caribbean (S/LPD)—housed in the Department of State but closely tied to the White House—orchestrated an intense campaign to influence public opinion on Nicaragua and El Salvador. Under the leadership of Otto J. Reich, the S/LPD aggressively confronted media reporting that failed to toe the administration's line and worked to shape ordinary Americans' perception of the region by disseminating hundreds of thousands of pages of pro-administration publications.

Public diplomacy played an important role in pushing Reagan's policies toward Central America. Indeed, top White House officials singled out the S/LPD for its role in securing congressional passage of Contra aid in mid-1986. Yet, as the administration increasingly turned to democracy promotion as the centerpiece of its human rights policy, the public diplomacy campaign illuminated the Reagan team's willingness to use the power of the executive branch to mislead the American people through what one S/LPD official described as a "'White Propaganda' operation." Correspondingly, both Faith Ryan Whittlesey and Reich worked closely with US conservatives in the private sector who channeled millions of dollars into campaigns to discredit US opponents of Reagan's Central America policy and secretly funneled aid to Contra forces. More troubling was top administration officials' willingness to disregard the checks and balances at the heart of US democracy by engaging in a web of illegal operations—later revealed in the Iran-Contra scandal—that aimed at maintain the Contras as a fighting force in the absence of congressional funding. Intertwined with the Reagan administration's democracy promotion initiative, in other words, were deeply undemocratic practices that misled the American people, violated US law, and fueled the conflicts in Central America.

Like his adventuring, Jack Wheeler's conservatism developed at an early age. Shortly after climbing the Matterhorn, Wheeler was shocked by images of Soviet tanks crushing the 1956 Hungarian uprising. "I realized, at 12 years, that the Soviets were just the same as the Nazis," Wheeler recalled in an interview. Five years later, while his high school class watched John F. Kennedy's presidential nomination, Wheeler sat with his back to the television. "I wouldn't watch it," he remembered. "I said he cheated."[9]

By the time he finished his degree at UCLA, Wheeler's conservatism was taking shape. He supported Barry M. Goldwater's quixotic campaign bid in the 1964 presidential election, but it was Ronald Reagan who won Wheeler's political heart. After seeing Reagan address the UCLA student union in 1965, Wheeler asked his father—a well-known Los Angeles television personality—to arrange a meeting. Shortly thereafter, Wheeler and his father met Reagan, who was gearing up for the 1966 California gubernatorial race, at his Pacific Palisades home. As the three discussed politics, Wheeler was hooked; "I've never worked in a campaign, but I believe in what you say, and I would like to help you," he declared. Reagan obliged, appointing Wheeler state chair of Youth for Reagan.[10]

The experience was a formative one. Thrust into an emerging network of young conservatives, Wheeler formed lasting friendships with individuals who would work closely with Reagan during his years as governor in Sacramento and in the White House. And it was Wheeler's fellow Youth for Reagan activists who introduced him to the work of the writer and philosopher Ayn Rand. "It was far and away the single greatest intellectual experience of my life reading *Atlas Shrugged*," Wheeler remembered. "So then I read everything else."[11]

By the late 1960s, Wheeler was a dedicated advocate of the free market and a vehement anticommunist. As a graduate student at the University of Hawaii, Wheeler stood out on a campus roiled by anti–Vietnam War protests. His founding of a new organization, Students for Laissez-Faire, drove "campus liberals completely crazy," he recalled, "which was our intention." Yet in the troubled 1970s, as the Vietnam War ended in defeat, the economy reeled from stagflation, and the Nixon administration plunged into scandal. "After all that I did not want to have anything to do with politics in any way whatsoever," he remembered, instead focusing his energy on philosophy and adventure.[12] "I'm not some mindless person doing death-defying feats," Wheeler told a journalist shortly before crossing the Alps, elephants in tow. "I have a life wish, not a death wish. But, dammit, I just don't want to sell insurance. I want to go to the North Pole."[13]

The death of his wife to cancer in 1981 plunged Wheeler into a period of mourning and extended seclusion. Politics pulled him back to the surface. After trouncing Jimmy Carter in the 1980 election, Reagan had entered the Oval Office intent on pursuing a hard-line approach toward the communist world. Riding the president's coattails were a number of Wheeler's former Youth for Reagan colleagues, including his longtime friend Dana Rohrabacher, a special assistant to the president and a speechwriter.[14] Wheeler wanted a piece of the political action but wondered what a philosopher-adventurer could contribute to the Reagan revolution. "You have to credential yourself," Rohrabacher told him, "make yourself a specialist."[15]

Suddenly, talking with Rohrabacher on the telephone, Wheeler had an epiphany. "I was in my office looking at a map of the world I keep on the wall," Wheeler later recalled. "All of a sudden the map looked different. I told my friend, 'I'm looking at one, two, three, four, five, maybe six Third World countries where there are anti-Soviet guerrilla wars.'" Reflecting on the moment years later, Wheeler underscored the power of the revelation. "It was like a *Gestalt*. I suddenly saw the world differently and that something very important was going on . . . the related parts of a geopolitical phenomenon rejecting Soviet imperialism." Rohrabacher, too, was impressed. "My God, Jackson," he responded, "you're right."[16]

Infused with energy, Wheeler began preparing to visit the revolutionary groups in the third world waging wars of liberation against the Soviet Union and its proxies. Wheeler knew that the Reagan administration was providing covert aid to the Afghan mujahideen and the Nicaraguan Contras. But he believed that administration officials failed to see the full picture. "There had been perusal of the pieces," he asserted, "but nobody had attempted a systematic study of the entire phenomenon of anti-Soviet guerrilla warfare."[17] Accordingly, Wheeler created the Freedom Research Foundation and secured funding from the Reason Foundation, a seven-year-old libertarian think tank in Santa Barbara, California. He spent nearly six months studying contemporary anticommunist revolutionary movements. In the process, Wheeler credentialed himself: "My background, going to all these remote places, getting to know different and remote people, my philosophy background," he told a journalist, "gave me whatever skills I have to get to these various groups, gain their confidence, and be with them without much difficulty."[18]

By June 1983, Wheeler was ready. His six-month itinerary included a handful of the world's most dangerous places: Angola, Mozambique, Nicaragua, and Afghanistan. With all the preparations in place, he flew to Washington, where Rohrabacher had organized a send-off reception at the White House. Then Wheeler embarked on his "Big Safari."[19]

In the same month that Wheeler passed through Washington, a select group of visitors shuffled into room 450 of the Executive Office Building—a stone's throw from the Oval Office—for a special briefing by the White House Outreach Working Group on Central America. In contrast to the exuberance of the building's storied French Second Empire architecture, the mood among the event organizers was grim. Communism, they warned, was on the march: the success of the 1979 Nicaraguan revolution had brought the red tide of totalitarianism to the United States' very doorstep, while revolutionaries in neighboring El Salvador were outfighting government forces at every turn. Yet, in the United States, the legacy of the Vietnam War hung like a funeral shroud over the Central America debate. Most Americans knew next to nothing about the cluster of small, impoverished nations south of the Mexican border. But the prospect of a US military intervention in Central America resurrected memories of body bags shipped home from Southeast Asia, protests from college quads to city commons, and US helicopters frantically lifting off from rooftops in Saigon. Inside the Washington, DC, Beltway, a generation of "New Politics" liberals who had come of age in Vietnam's final fraught chapter rejected the Cold War shibboleths that had guided US foreign policy since the 1940s. The administration faced fierce opposition on Capitol Hill for US economic and security assistance for the Salvadoran government and counterrevolutionary forces seeking to destabilize leftist Nicaragua and broad skepticism among the American people regarding the prospect of a US intervention in Central America.

In response, the Reagan administration had turned to public diplomacy. In January 1983, Reagan signed National Security Decision Directive (NSDD) 77, mandating that the administration "strengthen the organization, planning and coordination of the various aspects of public diplomacy of the United States Government relative to national security."[20] Public diplomacy, the directive continued, "is comprised of those actions of the U.S. government designed to generate support for our national security objectives." Central America quickly emerged as a focal point of the administration's public diplomacy efforts, and in May 1983, Whittlesey, the newly appointed assistant to the president for public liaison, established the White House Outreach Working Group on Central America.

From its inception, the working group understood Reagan's aggressive approach to the Cold War as operating both at home and abroad. The Reagan administration's Central America policy required a "two-track effort" of "equal intensity and seriousness," a 1983 working group memorandum declared, involving both US overt and covert assistance to halt "Soviet/Cuban efforts in Central America" and, in the United States, mobilizing public opinion in support of the White House. In this struggle, the working group could expect no quarter from New Politics liberals and their more radical New Left bedfellows. "The tragedy of Vietnam is gone, but the anti-war cadres and their anti-capitalism allies still exist as formidable foes to any moves to stop the 'march of socialism,'" the memo asserted, casting opponents of a US intervention in Central America as communist-sympathizing fifth columnists. "And at this hour they are cocked and ready to take the high ground of public opinion the instant they even think the Administration may move."[21]

In the face of such implacable opposition, the working group's memo proposed a strategic and tactical blueprint for mobilizing public opinion. Strategically, the White House needed to deliver a powerful one-two punch to the heart and gut of the American people. The rationale for a US intervention in Central America "must appeal to the American sense of humanity, compassion, and indignation at unspeakable cruelties," the memo advised, while also tapping into "American instincts for self-protection from clearly perceived economic (loss of jobs), political (loss of freedom), and/or military (loss of battle) threats from foreign powers." At the same time, the administration should tap into "emotions [that are] are essentially subliminal" by "downplay[ing] pure ideology such as 'war against communism'; we are talking about bullies and crooks who take from the honest, working people the world over."[22]

Tactically, the working group memo envisioned a far-reaching effort to mobilize public opinion on Central America. Underscoring the extent to which White House officials viewed public diplomacy as the domestic side of the Cold War, the document was drafted like a set of battle plans. In phase 1, the administration would create a "speakers strike force" drawn from the upper ranks of the Departments of State and Defense and from the CIA. A dozen influential research and educational institutions would be "mobilized as a command/control system with outreaches to a wide range of other educational institutions that serve significant segments of society, ranging from graduate-level students to high school; business/labor/professional leaders; thought leaders and media." Correspondingly, the administration would cultivate friendly journalists and develop the capacity to orchestrate "proadministration demonstrations."

In phase 2, the administration would unleash a public diplomacy blitzkrieg, touched off by a major statement on Central America from the president himself. Delivered on a Saturday, the message would be timed to catch the media off guard: "Like the military at Pearl Harbor, the media is essentially operating with skeleton, second-string staffs assigned for weekend work; so opportunities for immediate negative responses are muted." Over the following days, top administration officials would rotate through the major television and radio news shows, friendly journalists would publish favorable stories, the Speakers Strike Force would fan out across a dozen US cities for interviews and talk show appearances, and "street theater [would be] brought into play in scenarios designed to support the Administration." Although conceding, in a suggestively tepid manner, that "it is difficult to exercise any real control in the American society, nor is it desirable if one believes in a free and open society," the memo concluded that centralized command and clockwork precision would be essential in gaining "the high ground of public opinion."[23]

The working group failed to orchestrate a public diplomacy offensive on the scale envisioned by the 1983 memo. Yet Whittlesey did succeed in elevating the visibility of the Central America issue. Between May 1983 and April 1984, the working group dispatched speakers to 150 engagements in sixty-eight cities to raise public awareness on the issue and push the administration's hard-line right-wing agenda.[24] As Whittlesey told the Council for National Policy's Board of Governors in a mid-1984 address, "The Sandinista regime in Nicaragua started on its path toward Marxism-Leninism immediately after they came to power in 1979."[25] The group also produced eight editions of a news brief, the *White House Digest*, written in "simple language" accessible to ordinary Americans. The goal, Whittlesey recalled in a later interview, was to generate "material that a group of Young Farmers of America, the Nurses Association or the Gas Association could understand, and [to explain] why this issue is an important issue for them and for the country as a whole."[26] Echoing right-wing alarmism over Central America, the May 9 edition of the digest, for example, declared that "the immediate Soviet objective in Latin America is to enhance the USSR's influence at the expense of the U.S."[27] In addition to domestic distribution, the *White House Digest* was sent to all US diplomatic posts in Central America as well as the Voice of America international radio broadcast program.[28]

The working group also reacted vigorously to critics of US interventionism in Central America. In February 1984, for example, a working group staffer responded to correspondence criticizing the administration's policies from the San Francisco–based Commission on Social Justice with a four-page letter detailing Sandinista ties to Marxism and support for leftist revolutionary movements elsewhere in the region.[29] A few months later, Whittlesey fired off a critical missive to daytime television talk show host Phil Donahue for failing to provide balanced coverage of the Salvadoran conflict, with a carbon copy to Grant Tinker, president of the National Broadcasting Corporation (NBC).[30]

More importantly, the working group organized regular briefings on Central America for domestic interest groups visiting the White House. "Most Americans think (Central America) is somewhere off the coast of Spain," Whittlesey admitted to a journalist in December 1983. "So we really have an uphill struggle in terms of public education generally."[31] In response, the working group facilitated as many as five briefings a day in room 450 of the Old Executive Office Building. As Whittlesey recalled in an interview, "A group would call up, like the Nurses Association, and say they want to come to the White House to talk about health issues. We would say in a very nice way, 'That's fine. We'll talk about health issues for half the time, but the rest of the time we are going to talk about things that we think you should be informed about. It will be an exchange of views. You'll have a chance for questions and answers but we think your membership and your leaders would be interested in these other issues as well.'" Over the course of two years, Whittlesey concluded, the group was able "to educate the leaders of a wide variety of interest groups on the fundamental principles of Reagan policies. It paid tremendous dividends."[32]

In addition to briefing domestic interest groups, the working group also organized weekly briefing sessions for conservative supporters of the Reagan administration's intervention in Central America. With regular attendance by representatives from the NSC, the State Department, the CIA, and the United States Information Agency (USIA), Whittlesey tapped into the priority accorded to Central America by top Reagan administration policymakers to secure high-profile speakers at the sessions, including President Reagan, vice president George H. W. Bush, national security adviser William P. Clark, and UN ambassador Jeane J. Kirkpatrick.[33] NSC staffer Lieutenant Colonel Oliver L. North was the most frequent briefer. With a flair for the dramatic, North incorporated aerial maps of Soviet military airstrips and bases and charts of Soviet military aid to Latin America into a narrative depicting Soviet-style totalitarianism on the march in Central America. "I showed this picture to a man who had lived in a Siberian gulag for 25 years, and he said, 'Where did you get the picture of the gulag?,'" North told listeners on one occasion as a projector beamed an image of concrete buildings on a barren road. "I told him this picture is not from the Soviet Union. It is from Nicaragua," North continued. "He said, 'No, I lived in this gulag, I know the gulag.' I told him, 'My friend, time has passed you by. This is Nicaragua today.'"[34]

Not all attendees at the weekly briefings were impressed. At a June 1983 meeting, the political scientist Howard J. Wiarda observed as NSC staffer Jackie Tillman excitedly introduced a Nicaraguan named Miguel Bolaños as a Sandinista intelligence official who had defected to the United States. Bolaños "proceeded to read an anti-Sandinista statement that had clearly been prepared by the White House. It was heavy on alleged Sandinista murders, kidnapping, and corruption, but short on analysis or verifiable evidence," Wiarda recalled. "The meeting turned into a fiasco as it became obvious Bolaños could not read, in either English or Spanish, and so Jackie had to read it for him."[35] At the briefing session a few weeks later, Wiarda watched as a group of Honduran peasants took the stage and White House officials warned of the Cuban threat to Tegucigalpa. "Poor people: they speak no English, have never been outside of Honduras or on an airplane before, and appear in the White House briefing room in their sombreros and work clothes," Wiarda confided to his journal. "We're given a glimpse of these Rousseauian 'noble savages' as though their lifestyle is what we're fighting for in Central America. Whose crazy idea is this?"[36]

If skeptics like Wiarda found little of value in the working group briefings, the sessions nonetheless played a foundational role in the domestic side of the Reagan administration's Cold War strategy. Unlike the sessions tailored for uncommitted or uninformed interest groups, the signal importance the Reagan administration placed on containing the US Left was distinctly evident in the briefing sessions geared toward conservative supporters. "On such afternoons the enemy was manifold, and often within," wrote Joan Didion, one of the few journalists to report on the briefings. "The 'Red Empire' was of course the enemy," Didion continued. Yet "'Christian communists' were also the enemy. 'Guilt-ridden masochistic liberals' were the enemy, and 'the radical chic crowd that always roots for the other side,' the 'Beverly Hills liberals with their virulent hatred of America.'"[37] The US media, in particular, was seen as embodying liberals' defeatism. The briefers repeatedly emphasized, Didion noted, that the United States was forced to deal through surrogates in Central America in large part owing to the liberal bias of the media, which fueled public opposition to a direct US intervention.

In response, the working group facilitated the creation of a network of right-wing actors advocating an aggressive US response to perceived communist inroads in Central America. By mid-1983, the group had briefed nearly three dozen conservative organizations, including regionally focused foreign policy groups such as the Council for Inter-American Security, religious organizations like Jerry Falwell's Moral Majority, and powerful conservative mobilizers such as the Richard A. Viguerie Company.[38] These nonstate actors subsequently utilized their own resources and networks to advocate on behalf of anticommunism in Central America. As Whittlesey noted to former secretary of state Henry Kissinger following his own speaking session at the Wednesday briefings, "Organizations briefed through the programs of the Working Group have, in turn, generated newsletters, editorials, newspaper advertisements, op-ed pieces, television talk shows, radio shows and direct mail pieces which have reached millions of Americans with messages of support for the President's Central American policy."[39]

At this moment of rapidly expanding state and nonstate right-wing organizing, Wheeler returned in November 1983 from his six-month foray into the badlands of anticommunist revolutionary struggle. He had spent five weeks in rebel-held territory in Angola with the União Nacional para a Independência Total de Angola (National Union for the Total Independence of Angola [UNITA]), and crossed fifty-two hundred kilometers of "the most torturous bush tracks imaginable" in the back of a Soviet-made truck. It was, he wrote, "a very intense experience, emotionally and physically exhausting." Yet UNITA's struggle against the Cuban-backed ruling regime, Wheeler believed, was "deadly serious," and the charismatic leader Jonas Savimbi "will do whatever it takes to secure the freedom and prosperity of his country."[40] Similarly, in Afghanistan, Wheeler had met mujahideen commanders desperate for modern weapons and Afghan children crippled by Soviet bombs.[41] And in Nicaragua, he had spent a month hiking with Contra guerrillas through the mud of Central American rainforests, "straight up the side of one forested mountain, straight down the other, avoiding anything remotely resembling a trail or path, over and over—and over—again." Exhausted and "far more dehydrated than I had ever been in, say Timbuktu," Wheeler was nonetheless exhilarated by the Contras' resolve. "Far from being reactionary 'Somocistas,'" he wrote, "the Contras seemed to me to represent a genuine peasant rebellion against a totalitarian regime."[42]

Flying straight from Central America to Washington, Wheeler presented his findings in a special meeting at the Executive Office Building, organized by Rohrabacher, to an audience of CIA, NSC, and White House officials. Wheeler was blunt: "There really is a world wide rebellion going on inside the Soviet Empire. We should support it," he declared. "We should have a program of support for the whole phenomenon of anti-Soviet liberation movements, and our goal should be to break apart the Soviet Empire, to attack its structure."[43] Over the following months, he kept up the momentum, publishing an initial series of articles in *Reason* magazine on his experiences in Angola, Afghanistan, and Nicaragua and, as he continued to explore anticommunist wars of liberation, additional pieces on Cambodia and Mozambique.[44]

Wheeler's message hit Washington at just the right moment. In the White House, Whittlesey's Outreach Working Group on Central America had begun to solidify a network linking cold warriors in the administration with conservatives in the private sector. Correspondingly, in the face of congressional opposition to US funding for the Contras, North was expanding covert support that relied increasingly on private donors. And at Foggy Bottom, secretary of state George P. Shultz embraced a human rights policy emphasizing US democracy promotion and the free market—and defining communism as the ultimate human rights violation.

In this fluid political environment, Wheeler's recommendations for inflicting pain on the Soviet Union—at a relatively low cost to the United States—combined with the authenticity of his travels in guerrilla territory, hit conservatives like a sledgehammer. Although it was not until 1985 that the columnist Charles Krauthammer coined the term "Reagan Doctrine," Wheeler's emphasis on supporting "freedom fighters" abroad contributed to a growing consensus among conservatives that the United States should support anticommunist wars of national liberation. "Jack was the one who brought it all together," one White House official told the *Washington Post*. "He took random struggles and crystallized the concept that they were all part of the same historical movement."[45] As his influence increased, Wheeler developed a close friendship with Oliver North, briefed Jeane Kirkpatrick and CIA director William J. Casey, testified before numerous congressional committees, and presented his ideas to conservative think tanks such as the Cato Institute.[46] Correspondingly, Wheeler influenced conservatives outside the Washington Beltway. His foundation built a mailing list of thirty thousand names and began publishing a monthly newsletter titled *Freedom Fighter*.[47] Keeping up his credibility, he returned to Afghanistan twice more, joining a contingent of mujahideen in an attack on a Soviet command post. "Amidst all the explosions, the collapsing walls, the choking dust, we all were doubled over with laughter, tears streaming down our faces," he wrote in *Reason* in mid-1985. "It was the farthest thing from being terrified. Just like a sky-dive, when you're in the middle of it—no fear at all, just exhilaration."[48]

By mid-decade, Wheeler's activism had accelerated the growth of a wide-ranging conservative network that included Reagan administration officials and private-sector conservatives. In forums like the White House Outreach Working Group on Central America and on the pages of conservative publications like *Reason*, Wheeler pounded home the message that the Soviet Union was cracking at the seams.[49] The "guerrilla wars being waged now in eight Soviet colonies on three continents represent a geopolitical phenomenon of immense historical significance," Wheeler wrote in 1985. "Just as the Third World rejected Western colonialism in the 1950s and '60s, so it is rejecting Soviet colonialism in the 1980s. And it is using the Soviet strategy of armed guerrilla resistance—'wars of liberation'—to do so."[50] In the process, Wheeler played an important role in popularizing the Reagan Doctrine and ringing terms like "freedom fighters" to describe the Contras and the mujahideen. As conservative political activist Paul Weyrich told a reporter, "Wheeler, with his adventurous activity and his slides, which are gripping, really captured the imagination of a lot of people. The conservative movement is sometimes fractured by other kinds of issues. But the Reagan Doctrine unites it across the board."[51]

As the right-wing mobilized around the Reagan Doctrine, in Washington, the Office of Public Diplomacy for Latin America and the Caribbean emerged as a tireless advocate for the Reagan administration's policies in the hemisphere. In early 1983, Reagan's authorization of NSDD 77 had led to the creation of the Special Planning Group to oversee public diplomacy. In turn, on June 21 the Special Planning Group created the S/LPD within the Department of State and mandated that the State Department provide office space, staff, logistical support, and an operating budget. Reflecting White House dissatisfaction with the State Department's Public Affairs Bureau—ordinarily tasked with public diplomacy initiatives—the S/LPD was authorized to draw personnel from the State Department, the Defense Department, the United States Agency for International Development (USAID), and the USIA. Interagency cooperation with the new office, National Security Adviser Clark pointedly noted, was essential. "I would like to underscore once again that there is no higher public diplomacy priority on the president's mind."[52]

Indeed, the rising emphasis on public diplomacy corresponded with the Reagan administration's deepening commitment to supporting the Salvadoran government against a leftist insurgency and funneling US covert aid to the Contras. By 1983, millions of dollars in US assistance was flowing to San Salvador and the Contras had grown to a force of seven thousand and were attacking civilian and military targets across northern Nicaragua. The Reagan administration faced opposition, however, on Capitol Hill and among an increasingly vocal array of civil society groups, including solidarity organizations, church groups, and human rights advocates. Concerned with reports of rampant state-sanctioned violence in El Salvador, congressional lawmakers enacted a certification process making US military and economic aid to San Salvador contingent on human rights improvements. Correspondingly, the successful passage of the first Boland Amendment in December 1982 prohibited the Department of Defense or the CIA from attempting to overthrow the Nicaraguan government with US funds, a restriction that would be strengthened to prohibit all lethal aid to the Contras by a second Boland Amendment in June 1984.[53] Significantly, congressional concerns over Central America reflected widespread public skepticism regarding US intervention in the region. In an April 1983 *Los Angeles Times* poll, for example, only 33 percent of respondents asserted that US involvement in El Salvador was vital to US national defense, while only 10 percent supported CIA support for the Contras.[54]

These developments fueled the Reagan administration's concern that the White House was losing the battle for Americans' support on Central America. "I was informed when the office was created that the President, Vice President, and others were, to say the least, very upset with the inability of the Executive Branch to publicly communicate with the American people what the USG was doing in Central America," the director of the S/LPD, Reich, later recalled.[55] Indeed, in the spring and summer of 1983, top Reagan administration officials were deeply concerned that the American people and their elected officials on Capitol Hill failed to perceive the critical importance of Central America for US national security. It was essential, Shultz had informed Reagan in May 1983, that the United States "help the American people understand the Soviet-Cuban-Nicaraguan threat to the whole region. And we have to obtain the support of the Congress."[56] Two months later, national security adviser Robert C. McFarlane sounded a similar theme in a hasty memo for an upcoming status report. "I want the President to know that: 1. We are losing. 2. A principal reason we are losing is too little resources. (In short, the war effort is suffering a slow death of a thousand cuts[.]) BUT 3. The American people have no sense of why we are losing[.] ([T]hey do not know about the cuts and their effect.) 4. We will continue to lose until we establish political accountability in this country."[57] Reagan concurred. A few days later, the president identified a "deteriorating security situation" in Central America and asserted that "there is a persistent lack of public understanding of our interests, objectives, the threat, and our policies for dealing with Central American problems." In response, Reagan ordered the creation of a presidential commission to develop bipartisan support for the administration's Central America policy as well as a revitalized "public affairs / legislative action plan."[58]

Reich needed no encouragement from the president. Reich's father was a Jewish Austrian who had escaped the Nazi Anschluss in 1938 by hiking the Alps into Switzerland. He fought briefly with the French Foreign Legion in North Africa before the fall of Paris, finally taking refuge in Cuba in 1942. Reich's mother was Cuban, and he was raised in a deeply antifascist and anticommunist Cuban household. Reich was fourteen years old when the 1959 Cuban revolution swept Fulgencio Batista from power, and, the following year, his family joined the exodus of Cubans fleeing the revolutionary regime to the United States. The multigenerational refugee experience was defining for Reich's intellectual maturation. "As soon as I was old enough to ask questions I wanted to know how and why my father ended up in Cuba. Why was there a Second World War? Why did my grandparents get killed by people called Nazis and who were these people? So I started studying history and politics and political science and also economics." By the early 1980s, Reich epitomized the hard-line anticommunism of the US-based Cuban exile community, intensified by a tour of duty in the US Army at the Panama Canal Zone in the late 1960s, lobbying on Capitol Hill in the 1970s for the Council of the Americas (a Latin America–focused trade association), and a brief stint working on development projects with USAID in El Salvador at the beginning of the Reagan administration.[59]

Tapped as director of the S/LPD, Reich shared the Reagan administration's concerns that the US people and their elected representatives failed to grasp the root of the problem in Central America. "The spring and summer of 1983, it must be remembered, was a very difficult period for our Central American policy," Reich noted a few years later. "Daily news stories presented a distorted picture of Central American realities and of U.S. policy. Editorial opinion was overwhelmingly opposed to U.S. policy. Public opinion polls indicated that clear majorities of Americans did not know even the basis of what was occurring in the region and therefore they did not support U.S. involvement, much less increased involvement." As a result, Reich concluded, congressional legislators were "unwilling to provide the resources to allow the policy to work properly."[60]

Reich hit the ground running. Starting with a staff of two, he had secured by January 1986 twenty-one full-time positions for the S/LPD and an annual budget of over $1 million.[61] With close ties to the White House, including both North at the NSC and Whittlesey's working group, Reich's office quickly emerged as the point of the lance for the domestic side of the Reagan administration's containment strategy. The communist threat in Central America, an internal S/LPD memo asserted, "involves simultaneous action in three arenas: the Central American region; the international—where the purpose is to isolate and fragment the target governments through propaganda and political action to keep them from receiving any outside economic or military support; and, the U.S. domestic arena where the purpose is to delegitimate the target governments and bring about a cutoff of all U.S. assistance."[62] The S/LPD's public diplomacy mission, in other words, was a struggle for *US* hearts and minds—a defining battleground in the global Cold War.

In particular, Reich shared the Reagan administration's belief that the liberal bias of the US media was hamstringing the administration's Central America policy. There was "hysteria" in the press that the Reagan administration was leading the United States into another Vietnam, Reich recalled in a later interview—a supposition that was "absolutely false." Editors routinely "distorted the facts," silencing journalists who supported White House policies toward Central America. "I know reporters who, although they opposed the Reagan policy, quit their jobs," Reich asserted, "because they would go down to Central America, see that the Administration was telling the truth, file stories that were killed by their editors back here because the editors were watching CBS News or reading the *New York Times*, and had a different idea and thought the reporters had been coopted by the Reagan Administration."[63] Other reporters were victims of an extensive and sophisticated communist propaganda campaign. "Many of our press are being played like a violin by the Sandinistas," Reich told the *Los Angeles Times* in December 1983.[64]

In response, the S/LPD engaged in an intense campaign to shape US perceptions on Central America. S/LPD officers appeared on national network television and radio news programs, and Reich made a point of confronting media outlets that ran stories that criticized the White House or sympathized with the leftist forces in Central America. After *CBS Evening News* featured a two-part documentary on El Salvador titled *Behind Rebel Lines*, in April 1984, for example, Reich spent nearly an hour reviewing the film with the program's diplomatic correspondent, followed by a two-hour meeting with the network's Washington bureau chief. "It is a very slow and arduous effort to try to show to the networks that they are not illustrating to the American people an accurate picture of what is happening in Central America," Secretary of State Shultz wrote approvingly to Reagan after detailing Reich's efforts. "We are attempting to build the kinds of relationships with the news media that will enable us to dispel the disinformation and misinformation which has been so prevalent in coverage while at the same time aggressively expressing our policy objectives."[65]

Correspondingly, S/LPD officers fanned out across the US heartland. With help from the State Department's Public Affairs Bureau, between October 1983 and November 1984, the S/LPD arranged 1,570 speaking engagements and radio, television, and editorial board interviews in more than one thousand US cities.[66] Meetings with newspaper editorial staff, recalled career Foreign Service Officer John A. Bushnell, could be "explosive." On assignment with the Public Affairs Bureau shortly before Reich took the reins at the S/LPD, Bushnell met with dozens of editorial teams of small- and medium-size newspapers in fifteen states over a nine-month period in 1982 and 1983. Bushnell quickly recognized a pattern: as with other new issues, the subject of Central America was typically assigned to junior editors. In turn, as they researched the issue, junior editors received far more informational material from groups opposed to US intervention in the region than they did favorable material from the State Department. The result was a pattern of editorials across the country that downplayed the importance of Central America for US national security, Bushnell recalled, prompting him to develop an argumentative strategy that played on the anticommunism of senior editors. "Generally one or more senior editors would agree with me and point out that the paper's editorial policy was solidly anti-communist. Soon the junior editors would be defending themselves from questioning by senior editors. . . . In many cases editorials would appear fairly soon after my visit which were favorable to US policy while not excusing human rights violations by all sides."[67]

Back in Washington, S/LPD staffers began producing an avalanche of publications supporting the administration's policies. With extensive interagency support—including from the National Security Agency, the CIA, the FBI, the Defense Department's Defense Intelligence Agency and the US Southern Command, the State Department's Bureau of Intelligence and Research, and the USIA—the S/LPD "broke new ground," Reich later asserted, in accelerating declassification of US government information on Central America and "by obtaining unclassified information which corroborated classified information which could not be declassified because of the source or method of acquisition."[68] By 1986, the office had provided more than two thousand background briefings to newspaper, television, and magazine reporters on breaking news in Central America; moreover, on several occasions, Reich noted, the S/LPD "'killed' erroneous news stories" by providing news outlets with information about developing events.[69]

Yet the S/LPD's prolific publication efforts went beyond the media. In Reich's effort to shape public opinion, he set out to harness government resources to inject the Reagan administration's message into the bloodstream of US society. By 1986, the S/LPD had developed a mailing list of over thirty-three hundred names, including individuals and organizations involved in the media, education, business, and foreign affairs and, in government, key Reagan administration officials and Foreign Service Officers and ambassadors posted in Latin America and Western Europe.[70] Correspondingly, drawing on government resources, the S/LPD produced at least thirty-nine resource books, booklets, pamphlets, and white papers between 1983 and 1986.[71] These materials were disseminated widely. One mailing in 1985 of three booklets on Central America, for example, reached 1,600 university libraries, 520 political science and international relations departments, 162 area studies faculties, 130 foreign affairs organizations, 122 editorial writers, and 107 religious organizations.[72] A few months later, the S/LPD published a 600-page book, *Grenada Documents: An Overview and Selection*; a 45-page booklet, *The Soviet-Cuban Connection in Central America and the Caribbean*; a 40-page booklet, *The Sandinista Military Build-Up*; a 31-page booklet, *Broken Promises: Sandinista Repression of Human Rights in Nicaragua*; and a 23-page pamphlet, *Misconceptions about U.S. Policy toward Nicaragua*. Some fifteen hundred copies of *each* of the publications were produced and distributed in the United States and to US diplomatic posts in Latin America and Western Europe.[73]

As the S/LPD's efforts to shape the media message shifted into high gear, Jack Wheeler was hard at work drumming up private-sector support for anticommunist guerrilla forces in the third world. In June 1985, Wheeler organized the Democratic International—a right-wing response to the communist Tricontinental—in Jamba, Angola, the provisional capital of Jonas Savimbi's UNITA. Sponsored by Lewis Lehrman, a wealthy conservative director of the political lobby Citizens for America, the gathering brought together representatives from guerrilla groups in Laos, Afghanistan, and Nicaragua.[74] It was a "historic meeting," Wheeler wrote shortly afterward. "The emergence of armed democratic insurgencies throughout the Soviet Empire signifies the end of expansion of Soviet imperialism and the start of its contraction."[75] The Reagan administration agreed. Although the White House prudently decided against sending an official representative to the meeting, the president personally sent Lehrman a letter emphasizing that "their goals are our goals."[76]

If Wheeler continued to play an important role in drumming up US conservatives' support for anticommunist guerrilla movements, his activities by the mid-1980s were being overshadowed by a right-wing movement in full mobilization.[77] In September 1985, Wheeler rubbed elbows with representatives from anticommunist insurgent groups in Afghanistan, Angola, Cambodia, Ethiopia, Laos, Nicaragua, and Vietnam at the annual conference of the World Anti-Communist League in Dallas, Texas—a "Freedom Fighters Ball and Banquet" organized by retired US Army general John K. Singlaub.[78] More importantly, Singlaub was working closely with North to raise millions of dollars from overseas donors for military assistance to the Contras and tens of millions of dollars for nonmilitary assistance from wealthy US conservatives, such as Texas oil baroness Ellen Garwood and Colorado beer magnate Joseph Coors.[79] "God in his mysterious way has put Gen. Singlaub in communism's way," Garwood told reporters at the gathering, "and the general is saying, 'They shall not pass.'"[80]

Private-sector conservatives also accelerated efforts to drum up public support for the Reagan administration's intervention in Central America. In particular, in 1985 the National Endowment for the Preservation of Liberty (NEPL), a nonprofit foundation created by the American Conservative Trust, spent more than $3 million on a public information campaign supporting Reagan's position on Nicaragua.[81] NEPL's activities continued the following year, with television advertisements and documentaries, speaking tours, and media interviews that NEPL president Carl R. "Spitz" Channell estimated reached 62.5 million Americans.[82]

Right-wing mobilization dovetailed with the tireless efforts of the S/LPD to change the tenor of the debate in the United States regarding the Reagan administration's policies toward Central America. "What the President accurately described in 1983 as 'a steady drumbeat of criticism' against our policy," Otto Reich asserted shortly after leaving the S/LPD in 1986, "was suddenly confronted by another 'drumbeat,' one in favor of the President, which relentlessly presented information or challenged inaccuracies and sent a signal: if you are going to question the veracity or accuracy of the Administration you will be confronted with a barrage of contrary but verifiable facts. Attacking the President was no longer cost-free."[83] Indeed, top White House officials recognized the importance of the S/LPD in securing congressional passage of Contra aid in mid-1986—a significant victory for the administration following years of resistance on Capitol Hill. "It is clear we would not have won the House vote without the painstaking deliberative effort undertaken by many people in the government and outside," national security adviser John M. Poindexter noted to CIA director Casey in a memo on public diplomacy and Central America.[84] In recognition of Reich's efforts, Reagan presented the S/LPD with a Meritorious Honor Award, "for exceptionally outstanding service in developing, preparing, and implementing public diplomacy programs in support of United States policy in Central America."[85]

If the S/LPD played an important role in pushing Reagan's policies toward Central America, Reich's aggressive tactics blurred the boundaries between public diplomacy, propaganda, and lobbying. The S/LPD's efforts to shape the media message quickly extended beyond briefing and background material to include soliciting pro-administration letters and opinion editorials for publication in major newspapers and magazines by private-sector individuals. A February 1984 S/LPD memo, for example, identified fourteen themes for op-ed pieces to be written by outside sources, including a piece emphasizing US support for social reform in Central America aimed at "urban, liberal audiences" to be written by an election observer; a piece aimed at media outlets in the Southwest emphasizing the risk of a "tremendous increase in the refugee flow to the U.S." from Central America if communist threat gains were not reversed; and an op-ed to be written by a Jewish author emphasizing that "the communists in Central America are anti-Semitic."[86]

Such efforts evolved into what S/LPD deputy director Jonathan S. Miller described as "the Reich 'White Propaganda' operation." In March 1985, an op-ed piece supportive of the Reagan administration's policies in Central America ran in the *Wall Street Journal* under the byline of John F. Guilmartin Jr., a former lieutenant colonel in the US Air Force and an adjunct professor of history at Rice University. "It is devastating in its analysis of the Nicaraguan arms build-up," Miller wrote in a memo to White House director of communications Patrick J. Buchanan. Although confiding that S/LPD staff "worked extensively on this piece," Miller noted that "officially, this office had no role in its preparation." Similarly, the S/LPD ghostwrote op-ed pieces for the *Washington Post* and the *New York Times* for leading Contra figures to sign.[87] Such fabrications developed into standard operating procedure: as one internal S/LPD memo blandly noted, "When necessary, S/LPD will draft the response and request private sector individuals or key government officials to sign the piece, as appropriate."[88]

Correspondingly, Reich combined efforts with Whittlesey's White House Outreach Working Group to delegitimize opponents of the administration's Central America policies. Attending one of the working group briefings, Wiarda was shocked as a White House official "in charge of 'dirty tricks'" proudly reported her efforts to undermine a rally during the previous weekend organized by opponents of US interventionism in Central America. Thanks to secret White House efforts, she reported:

the pro-Administration rally started a day before the "anti" one so the "pro" one got more publicity. She got pro-Administration, ex–Black Panther Eldridge Cleaver on national television; she used veterans and "captive nations" exiles to offset the left's appeal; she secured five pictures in the *Washington Post* for her rally versus one or two for the opposition; she sent pro-Administration demonstrators with large signs into the anti-Administration rally to disrupt it; she took pictures of the left demonstrators with their pro-Soviet flags and files to turn over to the FBI; and she set up a media event that got lots of coverage of captive nations with pictures and memorabilia.

Listening to the presentation, Wiarda "sat back in wonder" and noted, "I had naively thought dirty tricks died with Nixon!"[89]

The S/LPD employed similar tactics. In the July newsletter of *Accuracy in the Media*, conservative journalist Daniel James asserted that Sandinista defectors to the United States had revealed that the Nicaraguan government engaged in sex trafficking to cultivate favorable news stories in the foreign media. "One of the oldest methods is to see that the bachelors among them are suitably accompanied by trusted Sandinista females," James wrote. A frequent briefer at the White House outreach briefings, James had close ties to the S/LPD.[90] In fact, Reich had supplied much of the background material for the piece, and he subsequently leaked allegations that gay reporters were similarly supplied by the government with pro-Sandinista men. "This thing is sordid," Reich claimed.[91] With no evidence to support such assertions— aimed at journalists with extensive experience in Central America, including the *New York Times*' Stephen Kinzer and the *Washington Post*'s John Lantigua— these efforts were aimed at undermining Americans' faith in the objectivity of the US media.

Reich also tried more direct methods of pressuring media outlets to temper criticism of the Reagan administration's Central America policy. In a meeting with the producers at National Public Radio (NPR) in 1985 after the network ran a report on Contra human rights violations, Reich attacked NPR's journalistic integrity, emphasized that he had "gotten others to change some of their reporters in the field because of a perceived bias," and warned that the S/LPD would be monitoring the network's future stories on Central America. Reich's threat, NPR foreign affairs correspondent Bill Buzenberg later asserted, was "a calculated attempt to intimidate." The gambit was at least a partial success; in a subsequent meeting over a proposed report on the region, Buzenberg recalled his editor asking him "What would Otto Reich think?"[92]

More broadly, the S/LPD's depiction of Sandinista Nicaragua in its bliz-
zard of publications and media interventions was uniformly negative, alarmist, and one-sided. "I saw the regime in Nicaragua as a group of third world,
totalitarian, Marxists. A bunch of opportunists, frankly," Reich recalled in an
interview. "They were typical third world brutal dictators with the added
Marxist/Leninist ideology, which has proven effective only in one thing and
that is in staying in power, in the USSR up until the 1980s," he continued.
"Seventy-five years, however, is a heck of a long time and I didn't want to see
a 75-year dictatorship in all of Central America."[93]

At the S/LPD, Reich constructed an image of the FSLN as a brutal totalitarian state, guided by its Soviet-Cuban backers and dedicated to regional
conquest. In the aftermath of the 1979 revolution, the Sandinistas had killed
thousands of political opponents and held as many as ten thousand political
prisoners, claimed a representative S/LPD report titled *From Revolution to Repression: Human Rights in Nicaragua under the Sandinistas*. "The Sandinistas have
attempted to crush groups that oppose their Marxist-Leninist system, including democratic parties, the private sector, independent labor confederations,
and even the church."[94] Such claims were widely discounted by human rights
groups as politically motivated. As the Americas Watch Committee asserted
in one of the dozens of human rights reports published during the decade,
"Around the core of fact . . . U.S. officials have built an edifice of innuendo
and exaggeration."[95]

Similarly, the S/LPD took the lead in advancing the administration's assertion that the Sandinistas had failed to keep a 1979 promise to the Organization
of American States to hold democratic elections. When the FSLN announced
national elections would be held in November 1984, the State Department
released a report dismissing the process as fundamentally flawed.[96] With more
than six hundred journalists and four hundred international electoral observers
in attendance, the election was widely praised in the international media. In
the United States, however, reporting on FSLN presidential candidate Daniel
Ortega Saavedra's victory at the polls competed with rumors of an impending
delivery of Soviet MIG fighter jets to Nicaragua—a development that would
have dramatically escalated Nicaragua's military capabilities. In fact, there
were no MIGs—it was a baseless claim that originated in the Department of
Defense and was propagated by the S/LPD to direct the US public's attention
away from the successful election. It worked: over the course of seven days, the
S/LPD provided over thirty background briefings on the (non)issue and fielded
over one hundred phone calls from journalists.[97]

Finally, the S/LPD followed Reagan's lead in casting the Contras as democratic underdogs in a desperate struggle against communist totalitarianism. This effort was complicated by the Contras' tactics; seeking to destabilize the Sandinista government, demoralize the Nicaraguan people, and weaken the nation's economy, the Contras regularly attacked "soft targets" such as government-funded agricultural cooperatives, health stations, and schools. By the spring of 1987, the Contras had damaged or destroyed sixty-one hospitals and health centers, and more than 350 educators and health workers had been wounded, kidnapped, or killed.[98] Correspondingly, throughout the 1980s, human rights organizations consistently reported a pattern of Contra violence against civilians, including kidnapping, torture, sexual violence, and murder.[99] As Americas Watch concluded in 1987, "The Nicaraguan government commits sporadic violent abuses and systematically engages in denials of due process in trials involving those accused of aiding the contras and in forcible relocations. . . . On the other hand, the contras systematically engage in violent abuses. Indeed, violations of the laws of war by the contras—as in their attacks on peasant cooperatives—are so prevalent that these may be said to be their principal means of waging war."[100] By 1987, 9,638 civilians had been wounded, kidnapped, or killed and 250,000 Nicaraguans had been displaced.[101]

In the effort to promote the Reagan administration's intervention against Nicaragua, the S/LPD consistently—and falsely—described the Contras as moderate democrats. "The goal of the armed democratic resistance is the same as that of the internal political opposition: to bring about the implementation of genuine democracy," an S/LPD report asserted in January 1986.[102] Reich's office also tried to delegitimize human rights reporting on the Contras' systematic targeting of civilians, making a relativist argument that abuses had been perpetrated by both sides in the conflict. Another S/LPD tactic was to dismiss criticism of the Contras as the work of a far-reaching Sandinista disinformation operation. In response to a widely read human rights fact-finding mission to Nicaragua, for example, the S/LPD asserted that the FSLN "has waged an intensive propaganda campaign, especially in the United States, in which it made false or exaggerated allegations of abuses by the democratic resistance [the Contras]."[103] Finally, the S/LPD's efforts extended to training the Contras in media relations. As a March 1985 S/LPD memo noted, "Two of our contractors . . . made a clandestine trip to the freedom fighter camps along the Nicaraguan/Honduras border (the purpose of this trip was to serve as a pre-advance for many selected journalists to visit the area and get a true flavor of what the freedom fighters are doing; i.e., not baby killing)."[104]

Critics of the Reagan administration's intervention in Central America were deeply troubled by the S/LPD's tactics. The contention that Nicaragua was engaged in a widespread propaganda campaign was "a classic example of the pot calling the kettle black," representative John Conyers Jr. (D–MI) wrote in February 1986. "There is one campaign of disinformation about Nicaragua: it is the one coming from the White House." Noting that the Nicaraguan government was far less repressive than its US-backed neighbors and that 60 percent of the economy remained in private hands, Conyers concluded, "The Administration has provided no credible evidence that this impoverished country of 2.8 million people has presented a security threat to the U.S."[105]

But Reich's hardball tactics were indicative of the administration's determination to support the Contras with or without congressional authorization. As the second Boland Amendment aid restrictions kicked into effect, Reagan directed the NSC to keep the Contras together "body and soul." The result was a massive black operation run out of North's office. North quietly solicited $6.3 million earmarked for the Contras from US conservatives in the private sector—particularly through the support of NEPL—along with $34 million from allies abroad.[106] Correspondingly, in 1985, the NSC began secretly selling missiles to Iran—in direct violation of congressional legislation. In exchange, the administration hoped the Iranians would secure the release of US hostages held by terrorist groups in the region. Adding a further layer of complexity (and illegality) to the operation, North received permission from National Security Adviser Poindexter the following April to divert earnings from the arms-for-hostages deal to the Contras. North subsequently passed more than $3 million to the Contras through a thicket of offshore bank accounts and dummy corporations.[107]

Beginning in late 1986, amid the heated debate over US policy toward Nicaragua, the Iran-Contra scandal broke like a firestorm. Despite a hasty cover-up that led to the destruction of thousands of classified documents, media scrutiny and congressional investigations over the following months revealed a pattern of White House malfeasance. "Far from being the work of a few mid-level 'rogue operatives,'" writes the historian Malcolm Byrne, "it involved at various stages an array of senior officials including the president and vice president themselves."[108] Fourteen individuals were eventually charged with criminal violations, and although Reagan avoided impeachment, the scandal significantly weakened the president, consuming his attention throughout 1987 and hamstringing executive oversight of US foreign policy.[109]

As the congressional hearings proceeded, few observers connected the scandal with the Reagan administration's human rights policy or the democracy promotion initiative. Yet Iran-Contra illuminated how deeply undemocratic practices could be framed as consonant with the protection of human rights. Defining communism as the ultimate violation of human rights and labeling Nicaragua as a Soviet satellite, the Reagan administration used democracy promotion to justify US efforts to orchestrate a regime change in Managua. At the S/LPD, Reich recognized the utility of articulating the administration's criticism of Nicaragua in the language of human rights, effectively castigating the Sandinistas for denying political rights and civil liberties, and consistently—and falsely—described the Contras as moderate democrats.

Reich's success was short-lived. Sparked by the Iran-Contra scandal, an investigation in September 1987 by the comptroller general determined that the "S/LPD engaged in prohibited, covert propaganda activities designed to influence the media and the public to support the Administration's Latin American policies."[110] Similarly, the majority report of the congressional committees investigating Iran-Contra offered a brief yet highly critical assessment of the S/LPD. Public diplomacy, the report concluded, "turned out to mean public relations-lobbying, all at taxpayers' expense."[111] In his determination to wage the Cold War, Reich apparently saw no irony in engaging in illegal activities to portray the FSLN as violating human rights. Neither did North, who referred to his expansive web of black operations in Central America as "Project Democracy."[112]

If Iran-Contra revealed Reagan administration officials' willingness to break the law, it also created an opening for congressional activism in US policy toward Central America; despite opposition from administration hardliners, Speaker of the House Jim Wright (D-TX) in early August 1987 managed to convince the White House to sign on to a peace plan for Central America. In turn, the Wright-Reagan plan, as it came to be called, accelerated ongoing Central American diplomatic efforts, led by Costa Rican president Oscar Arias. With the successful signing of the Esquipulas Accord on August 7, 1987, the five Central American nations pledged themselves to "democratic pluralism, free elections, and a concerted effort to end internal fighting by seeking a cease-fire with [their] armed opponents, instituting an amnesty for them, and initiating a process of political reconciliation and dialogue."[113]

Despite the Reagan administration's continued efforts to drum up congressional support for Contra funding, Washington's war on Nicaragua was increasingly supplanted by a regional effort to reach a negotiated solution.

Jack Wheeler emerged from the Iran-Contra scandal unscathed. As one observer noted in 1988, Wheeler had carefully cultivated a position as a "second-string player" in North's operation—thus avoiding criminality—"only by dint of his superior intellect."[114] And, as the political firestorm consumed Washington, Wheeler maintained a low profile and kept up his livelihood of shepherding wealthy patrons on remote expeditions. Yet Wheeler remained an outspoken supporter of anticommunist guerrillas throughout the second half of the 1980s and repeatedly predicted—correctly—that the Soviet Union would go "belly up" within five years.[115]

Wheeler had been a mere bit player in the broader evolution of the Reagan Doctrine. But his activities shed light on the network of conservatives—both in the White House and in the private sector—that came together in the mid-1980s around a shared commitment to supporting anticommunist wars of liberation. Wheeler played an important role in that process. Reflecting on the political developments over the previous half decade in a 1988 address at the Heritage Foundation, Wheeler noted, "Five years does not seem like a long time. Yet when I first began speaking to conservative groups five years ago, about remote guerrilla wars in unknown places like Angola and Mozambique and Afghanistan . . . it seems like this was a long time ago that all of this was so unfamiliar. Today, there is no one in this room who does not know who Jonas Savimbi is, who is not a knowledgeable supporter of the freedom fighters."[116]

Chapter 6

"The Grindstone on Which We Sharpen Ourselves"

Solidarity Activism and the US War on Nicaragua, 1981-1990

In the spring of 1969, a US military jeep rumbled past lush rice paddies in South Vietnam's Mekong delta. At the edge of a village it rolled to a halt, and the lone occupant took in his surroundings. Air Force captain S. Brian Willson was newly arrived in South Vietnam and still finding his footing in an ugly war a long way from the quaint little towns of his native upstate New York.

Born on the fourth of July in 1941, the tall, burly Willson embodied the can-do attitude and patriotic spirit that typified US society in the quarter century after the Second World War. The son of an insurance salesman and a stay-at-home mother, Willson grew up in a conservative working-class household in Ashville, New York, a rural hamlet an hour's drive from bustling Erie. He excelled at football and baseball, but it was academic success that set him apart from his peers: after graduating valedictorian from Chautauqua High School in 1959, Willson earned a bachelor's degree in sociology from Eastern Baptist Seminary College. Enrolling in the law degree program at American University, Willson supported Barry M. Goldwater's quixotic presidential bid in 1964 and began studying Russian in anticipation of a career as an FBI agent.[1] "I did everything my country wanted, right from the beginning," Willson remembered many years later. "I was even born on the correct day."[2]

The war in Vietnam, however, would change everything. Drafted into the army in 1966, Willson opted instead to enlist in the air force, where he was assigned as an intelligence officer at Binh Thuy Air Base. As he approached the village in the spring of 1969, Willson was planning to interview residents as part of a routine security assignment.

Suddenly, US military aircraft streaked over Willson's head and pulverized the village with 500-pound bombs and napalm. Stunned, he stepped out of the jeep. The village was burning; "most of the inhabitants," Willson remembered, "had just been murdered or maimed."[3] As he stared at the destruction, an old man stumbled out of the acrid smoke. His eyes met Willson's, and for an instant the two men stared at each other. "I really wanted to go tell him I was sorry, that I loved him, that he was my brother," Willson remembered. Instead, he got into the jeep and drove off in a daze, stopping a few minutes later to stab the palm of his hand with a Swiss Army knife. "I thought I was having a nightmare, and I watched the blood dripping down, hoping to wake up in upstate New York," Willson recalled. "Then I saw a woman carrying buckets on a wooden yoke. And then a water buffalo. I knew I wasn't in upstate New York. I think I was crying and pounding the seat next to me, thinking, 'this is really happening, and I'm all alone.'"[4]

Seventeen years later, in the fall of 1986, Willson joined three other veterans on the steps of the Capitol building in Washington, DC. Announcing the Veterans Fast for Life initiative, the men pledged to go without food until the US government curtailed its support of the Contras' war on Sandinista Nicaragua. Dismissed by detractors as a sensationalist attempt to hold the government hostage, the project, Willson asserted, was "a non-violent, public expression of our outrage at U.S. barbarism in Nicaragua."[5]

For more than a month, the three increasingly emaciated vets appeared daily on the Capitol steps, generating a flurry of media attention and an outpouring of support. "We are deluged with calls from across the country and Europe from people who are organizing solidarity actions, vigils, relay fasts, and prayer services in an effort to stop the war," the activist Jennifer Atlee-Loudon wrote from the makeshift office of Veterans Fast for Life. At the Capitol, solidarity protests swelled, with black-clad activists brandishing white crosses with the names of Nicaraguans killed by the Contras. Back at the office, "We get sacks of mail," Atlee-Loudon continued, and "the phone never stops ringing. People call to thank the vets for what they are doing and to say they are fasting with them. They plead, 'Don't let them die. Tell them we will do all we can for Nicaragua."[6] By the time the veterans ended the fast, Willson had lost thirty-five pounds and was so weak that he could hardly stand at the press conference podium.[7]

All but forgotten in the broader history of US-Nicaraguan relations, Willson's activism nonetheless illuminated a key feature of the struggle to shape

US policy toward the leftist Sandinista government. Following the triumph over the Somoza dictatorship, the Nicaraguan revolution emerged as a key site of transnational solidarity activism in the final phase of the global Cold War. Galvanized by the Sandinista effort to enact a sweeping socioeconomic transformation, activists from across Western Europe, Latin America, and the United States descended on Managua to help shoulder the revolutionary burden. They were joined by thousands of Cubans—reflecting Fidel Castro's outsize influence on the Central American isthmus—and, as US-Nicaraguan tension deepened, delegations from the Soviet Union and its satellite states in Eastern Europe.

The Nicaraguan revolution generated revolutionary imaginaries on the part of solidarity activists, allowing them to map disparate political agendas onto the Sandinista reality. Although these groups were rooted in local networks and communities, as well as distinct national contexts, the transnational Nicaragua solidarity network developed within the context of long-standing struggles of the Left in support of anticolonialism and national liberation, the promotion of socioeconomic justice in the developing world, and opposition to the imperialist impulse of US global Cold War policymaking. The network also reflected, however, new arenas of popular mobilization in the late Cold War, particularly the rise of the human rights movement, processes of democratization, and opposition to neoliberal economic reforms.

For US activists, as the Reagan administration's hostility toward the Sandinistas deepened and the Contra war intensified, Nicaragua took on a unique significance. With the painful memory of the US defeat in the Vietnam War still fresh, a growing network of US activists feared that repeated condemnations of the Sandinistas by Reagan, support for the Contras, and the extensive US military maneuvers in the region would lead to US soldiers fighting and dying on Nicaraguan soil. As the Contra war intensified, the widespread abuses of the Contras against civilian targets elicited a rising chorus of criticism from US-based human rights organizations, churches, and Latin America–focused solidarity groups. By mid-decade, US activism had established a powerful voice in the Central America debate. Hundreds of Americans were living and working in Nicaragua in capacities that ranged from university teaching to reporting Contra atrocities, while thousands visited the embattled nation to see the achievements of the revolution firsthand and engage in solidarity activities such as harvesting coffee. Correspondingly, in the United States a heterogeneous grassroots movement emerged in opposition to the Reagan administration's war on Nicaragua. Across the nation, from Fairbanks, Alaska, to St. Augustine, Florida, activists organized diverse local fundraising and awareness campaigns, as well as concerted efforts to convince congressional lawmakers to cut off US funding for the Contras.

In the process, competing conceptions of human rights and democracy emerged as a flashpoint in the struggle over US policy toward Nicaragua. By mid-decade, Reagan officials had embraced democracy promotion as the centerpiece of the administration's human rights policy, and the administration had taken important steps toward re-creating the bipartisan Cold War consensus that had shattered in the late 1960s amid the divisiveness of the Vietnam War. Yet US solidarity activists embodied a powerful rejection of the White House's democracy promotion initiative, and they played a defining role in growing grassroots opposition to the Reagan administration's war on Nicaragua and in lobbying members of Congress to vote against aid to the Contras. Indeed, on the issue of Central America, the administration was never able to win the support of the majority of the American people, and congressional resistance to Reagan's support for the Contras led the White House to engage in illegal activities that, when revealed in the Iran-Contra scandal, brought the Reagan administration to the brink of ruin.

Solidarity activists countered Reagan's democracy promotion initiative—and the administration's corresponding portrayal of Nicaragua as a communist totalitarian police state—with their own vision of the promise of the Nicaraguan revolution. They frequently embraced the FSLN's lofty ideals of self-determination, participatory democracy, and socioeconomic transformation. "Nicaragua is a sign of what can be done at the local level, with very humble means, to bring about reform," one American asserted. "It's like an ember glowing in the dark, being blown on by people who have big spirits and are willing to sacrifice their own skin to keep this ember glowing."[8] As the Contra war intensified, such visions clashed with the reality of deepening Nicaraguan economic hardship, widespread suffering, and rising disillusionment and, in the United States, deepening divisions within the Left. President Reagan, a US solidarity activist living in Nicaragua asserted at mid-decade, "has become the grindstone on which we sharpen ourselves."[9]

Although Willson emerged as an important figure in the broader US solidarity movement, his activism was a long time coming. During his stint in the air force, although increasingly outspoken against the war in Vietnam, he completed his tour of duty, returning to civilian life with an honorable discharge. He finished law school and was admitted to the District of Columbia Bar in 1973.[10] Over the following decade, Willson worked in a variety of capacities: as a criminologist and a criminal lawyer, on a dairy farm in Upstate

New York, as an aide to a state senator, and as a local political official himself. All things considered, Willson was, as he later put it, "quite normal and successful in the North American sense of things."[11] But the memory of Vietnam hung heavy. "Before the war I wanted to be a successful North American, have a better job, a house, a family. I didn't have any interest after Vietnam. My fundamental belief system got wiped out."[12]

For Willson, as for many Americans, the Reagan administration's escalating intervention in Central America immediately evoked the specter of Vietnam. In the mid-1980s, Willson was directing an outreach center for Vietnam vets, and his understanding of the US conduct of the war in Southeast Asia had crystallized into a damning critique. "As I pondered Vietnam . . . I realized that we had participated in a massive way in the violations of many international laws, including the Hague Convention of 1907, the Geneva Convention of 1949, the Nuremburg Principles of 1946/1950, the United Nations Charter, among others," Willson asserted. He continued: "The common torture, mutilation and murder of prisoners and civilians, the destruction of thousands of huts and villages, coastal and aerial bombardment of civilian targets, defoliation and destruction of crops and massive land areas, the forced transfer of much of the population into 'strategic hamlets,' the use of forbidden gas and chemicals, the seizure and destruction of medical resources, among other behaviors, were all violations of international law and fundamental standards of decency and fair rules."[13] Watching the Reagan administration's undeclared war on Nicaragua unfold, Willson was convinced that it was following the same script. Before joining the Veterans Fast for Life project, Willson visited Nicaragua, toured the war-damaged northern border region, and studied Spanish. It seemed all too familiar. "It just smelled like Vietnam," he remembered.[14] Fasting intensified Willson's commitment to ending US support for the Contras, and he spoke of creating a veterans' peacekeeping force that would shield Nicaraguan civilians from the Contras' atrocities. "As ex–kill warriors, we would like to be peace warriors," he told reporters. "We want to continue the spirit of the fast by putting our lives on the line."[15] All the time, Willson carried with him the painful memory of that spring day in 1969. "Since Central America started heating up, I see that old man all the time. I call him Hue. . . . Sometimes I talk to him, and say, 'Well, Hue, how are we going to wage peace today?'"[16]

By the time Willson began channeling his energies into peace activism, a heterogeneous array of organizations in the United States were actively protesting the Reagan administration's intervention in Central America. As the historian Roger Peace writes, "No single leader or organization directed this decentralized campaign. Instead, there were overlapping networks of religious, leftist, and peace groups—and smaller numbers of labor, veteran, feminist, and civic groups—working on common 'days of action,' educational activities, legislative lobbying, and transnational initiatives."[17] Not surprisingly, groups with a track record of involvement in US–Latin American affairs, such as the North American Congress on Latin America (NACLA), took a lead role in opposing US support for the Contras. Formed by New Left student activists in 1967, NACLA had developed its *Report on the Americas* into a trenchant anti-imperialist critique of US influence in the region.[18] Over the course of the 1980s, NACLA's reporting was a staple for scholars and activists involved in the Central America debate, with articles broadly supportive of the leftist revolutionary movements in the region and deeply opposed to US interventionism.

Similarly, Latin America–focused research and lobby groups that had sprouted in the 1970s turned their attention to Central America in the Reagan era. With close ties to liberals on Capitol Hill, the eight-member Washington Office on Latin America (WOLA) served as a prolific source of information on political developments in Central America—in stark contrast to the Reagan administration's depiction of events—and an influential congressional lobby to curtail US support for the Contras. In a representative 1986 report, for example, WOLA detailed Contra kidnappings of Nicaraguan civilians, attacks on cooperatives, and the use of antitank mines on heavily trafficked roads. "Given the likelihood that the war will increase in scope in the coming months," the report maintained, "it is especially important that U.S. citizens have access to first-hand, accurate information on how this war—financed in large part by U.S. tax dollars—is affecting human life."[19] Meanwhile, at the Council on Hemispheric Affairs (COHA) a dedicated staff of five, supported by a dozen interns, churned out hundreds of press releases on "coffee, too many cigarettes and 15 hours of work a day."[20] Both organizations operated on donations from private foundations, religious organizations, and individual donors.[21]

Latin America–focused organizations such as WOLA and COHA were joined by broad-based groups such as the Coalition for a New Foreign and Military Policy, an umbrella entity comprising fifty national religious, research, and social justice organizations.[22] Engaged in issues ranging from ending the arms race to opposing South African apartheid, the coalition worked to coordinate grassroots activism and political lobbying into a progressive national agenda. As the Reagan administration's pressure on Nicaragua intensified, the coalition mobilized its support base. "Standing between U.S. overt and covert intervention are a body of over 16 separate laws on human rights," a legislative update asserted in August 1981. "These laws, enacted by Congress over the past seven years, are the first line of defense for the American people to a precipitous and dangerous return to a 'Vietnam-style' foreign policy by U.S. policymakers."[23] The following spring, 118 national organizations, ranging from the American Friends Service Committee to the Libertarian Party, had signed the coalition's "Statement in Opposition to Covert Intervention in Nicaragua," accusing the Reagan administration of violating international law and warning of the risk of escalating violence. "Neither the lessons of history," the statement concluded, "nor any interpretation of U.S. international responsibilities can, in any way, justify these actions."[24]

Human rights organizations also entered the fraught debate over US policy toward Central America. Over the course of the 1970s, human rights advocates had established broad grassroots support, organized an influential lobby in Washington, and demonstrated an ability to effectively mobilize on behalf of human rights issues. As US support for the Contras deepened, human rights organizations responded with dozens of reports assessing the human rights situation across the Central American isthmus. Again and again, on-the-ground research and reporting by widely respected organizations such as Amnesty International, the Americas Watch Committee, and the Lawyers Committee for Human Rights rejected the Reagan administration's repeated claims of widespread state-sanctioned violence in Nicaragua. Instead, report after report emphasized that the Sandinista regime in Managua was *not* carrying out systematic disappearances, illegal killings, or torture and, while acknowledging serious limits on civil society freedoms in the context of the Contra war, categorically denied that Nicaragua was a totalitarian state. As Americas Watch asserted in 1985—in its eighth report on Nicaragua since 1982—"We find that the most violent abuses of human rights today are being committed by the contras, and that the Reagan administration's policy of support for the contras is, therefore, a policy clearly inimical to human rights."[25]

Throughout the 1980s, advocacy organizations that had been active in the previous decade—including Latin America–focused organizations, broad-based umbrella groups such as the Coalition for a New Foreign and Military Policy, and human rights organizations—would play a key role in shaping public opinion and lobbying on Capitol Hill. Echoing efforts to curb US assistance to repressive right-wing regimes in the 1970s, these organizations focused on US support for the Contras—whose systematic use of kidnapping, torture, and murder formed a grisly tableau of human rights violations. As the Reagan administration's intervention in Central

America intensified, they were joined by activists from across the United States, who channeled their opposition to the US interventionism into a heterogeneous grassroots movement.

Church-based grassroots activism was particularly important in shaping the debate on Central America. In early November 1983, representatives from the US Christian peace movement gathered for an annual retreat. Located on the Kittatinny Ridge of northeast Pennsylvania overlooking the fall colors of the densely wooded Delaware Valley, the Kirkridge retreat center might have seemed a far cry from the turmoil in Central America. But the discussions—involving delegates from Protestant, Roman Catholic, and evangelical churches—quickly illuminated a common concern over political developments in the circum-Caribbean. Intensifying US pressure on the Sandinistas, expanding US military exercises throughout the region, and the recent US invasion of Grenada, the delegates warned, heralded "the threat of a U.S.-sponsored invasion of Nicaragua." In response, the delegates made a far-reaching "promise of resistance." "We oppose any such invasion," they asserted in a widely disseminated statement. "We will resist with our minds, hearts, and bodies any intervention by the United States, directly or indirectly, in Nicaragua."[26]

In particular, the delegates at Kirkridge endorsed the newly created Witness for Peace (WFP) initiative. Following a thirty-person exploratory visit to Nicaragua in the spring of 1983, and meetings in the summer between more than three dozen leaders from Protestant and Catholic church groups, WFP was formed in October 1983 as a vehicle for faith-based peace activism focused on Central America.[27] The organization was created by US Christians who "believe that U.S. policy toward Nicaragua is simply wrong and is only making the situation there much worse," wrote Jim Wallis, editor of *Sojourners* and chair of the WFP advisory committee. Although most of the project's organizers "have both supportive and critical feelings toward the Nicaraguan government," Wallis continued, "all of us believe that the positive forces in Nicaragua deserve our nurture and support. We are convinced that the hostility of the U.S. government will only strengthen the forces in Nicaragua that tend toward ideological rigidity and military solutions."[28]

In early December 1983, the first WFP short-term delegation arrived in Nicaragua. Ranging from a twenty-three-year-old Mennonite community center teacher to a Presbyterian minister in his late sixties, the fifteen-member delegation was committed to forming a "protective shield" by placing US citizens between the Contras and Nicaraguan civilians.[29] "Our hope is that the Witness for Peace might help save lives," Wallis asserted, and "urge the

U.S. government to re-examine and change its policy toward Nicaragua, provide access to eyewitness reports of the consequences of U.S. policy in the area, and show Nicaraguans that the policies of the Reagan administration do not represent all North Americans."[30]

Witness for Peace tapped into widespread concern among liberal US Christians regarding the US policy toward Nicaragua, and the organization quickly emerged as a leader in grassroots resistance to US interventionism. First, WFP developed the short-term delegations into an extensive program. Within five years, more than three thousand US citizens had visited Nicaragua in 146 two-week WFP delegations. Second, building on the success of the short-term delegations, WFP rapidly organized an infrastructure for activism in the United States. By 1988, WFP had twenty paid staff members in the United States (along with six in Nicaragua) coordinating with eleven self-supporting regional offices. With a nonprofit status exempting it from federal taxes, the WFP had an operating budget of more than $1 million, with 73 percent given by individuals as well as grants from more than three dozen foundations and religious organizations.[31]

Witness for Peace activists in the United States worked to raise popular awareness of the situation in Nicaragua. They spoke at local churches, raised funds, and organized public demonstrations and vigils, such as the 1986 "Campaign of Conscience," which garnered 435,000 signatures. WFP worked to shape the message in the national US media. In March and April 1986, for example, WFP ran advertisements in the *New York Times* and the *Washington Post* calling on Americans to "stop the lies" on Nicaragua.[32] WFP activists were also engaged with local media. As returned short-termer Lillian Adams noted, the editor of her local newspaper "used to be an almost knee-jerk anticommunist, and all there needed to be was the allegation that Nic[aragua] was a communist, Marxist regime, and he was against it." After meeting multiple times with Nicaragua solidarity activists, however, "now he takes a much more thoughtful stand."[33] Similarly, returned short-termer Bob Barnes encouraged activists to write letters on US-Nicaraguan relations to their local newspapers. His own letter, published in Nevada's *Grass Valley Union*, had touched off a back-and-forth discussion that ultimately involved some forty letters and editorials over the course of the year. Noting that the newspaper had some ten thousand regular readers, Barnes concluded, "Who knows who you may hear from and who you may influence? It takes only a stamp, some paper and a few minutes to find out."[34]

Third, in addition to short-term delegations, Witness for Peace also established a long-term team of volunteers who lived for at least one year in

Nicaragua. They joined the hundreds of US citizens who took up residence in revolutionary Nicaragua over the course of the 1980s; in 1984, some seven hundred Americans were estimated to be living in Nicaragua and working in sectors including agriculture, education, and the government. In turn, they mixed with solidarity activists from Latin America and Europeans from both sides of the Iron Curtain.

On one level, the long-termers facilitated the visits of the frequent short-term delegations. "I watched them unwrap Nica[ragua] for themselves," wrote long-termer Anne Whoerle of one twelve-day delegation, "and it was at once gratifying and tiring to see the surprise, the pain, the joy and the fear reverberate through the group . . . on their 12-day tour."[35] On another level, the long-termers developed into an extensive network for reporting Contra abuses. The hundreds of small-scale Contra attacks and the resulting death and destruction rarely made the mainstream news in the United States. "When reporters do cover events, they tend to want to arrive quickly, confront quick sources, suck out the dramatic items, then race back to Managua to file the report," noted a WFP newsletter. "The result is usually a rushed and often inaccurate report."[36] Instead, WFP long-termers were stationed across the country, particularly in the border areas most targeted by the Contras; by the end of 1984, 20 long-termers had taken up residence in Nicaragua, and over WFP's first five years, a total of 146 long-term volunteers lived in more than sixty locations.[37] When an attack occurred, a long-termer would visit the site and follow a reporting procedure, "while at the same time standing with the people and ministering to the deep suffering that accompanies the loss of crops, a home, or a loved one."[38]

The dual role of both reporting Contra abuses and attending to the needs of the victims was a heavy burden for WFP volunteers. "I felt myself being cracked open, split in half: the violent absurdity of seeing a teen-age boy quietly weeping above the crosses, one of them bearing his brother's name," one short-termer wrote after attending a funeral for fourteen Nicaraguans killed by Contras near the town of Achuapa. Similarly, Whoerle recalled struggling to keep her emotions in check at a funeral for three Nicaraguans killed in a Contra attack. "As the three graves filled with dirt, my eyes filled with tears and my jaws clenched with anger," Whoerle wrote. "I had no right to be there sharing their grief, because I could never cry enough to repent for my whole nation, could never begin to atone for the damage we've done even to the families of the three we buried that afternoon."[39]

Witness for Peace long-termers were also challenged by their unique position in the conflict. Writing to WFP supporters in the United States, Whoerle recognized the subjectivities inherent in the WFP endeavor and the struggle to situate her experience within the broader political landscape. "Some of you must be wondering, where is the journalistic objectivity?" she wrote. "How do I know the contra were responsible for this particular catastrophe? Did I talk to any eyewitnesses? What are three deaths, in a world where war is common? Don't we have to defend ourselves against a rumored threat from another superpower?" Whoerle, however, was undeterred. "Well, the journalist is right here," she concluded. "She's learning the humility that results from living in a place where death is a topic of daily conversation, where the roads she travels are lined with the remains of burned trucks and civilian graves. She's learning that reporters, like everyone else, are part of a larger society, and that her particular society is viewed as a cruel monster by a people subjected to its whim."[40]

In Washington, reporting by volunteers like Whoerle facilitated WFP's extensive grassroots organizing and political lobbying. The WFP media office integrated material from the reports into press conferences, a weekly telephone service with a recorded message on Contra attacks, printed monthly news briefs, and a bimonthly newsletter with a mailing list that grew to forty-three thousand.[41] The material also facilitated fundraising; in 1987, WFP mailed more than one million fundraising packets detailing Contra violence toward civilians.[42] Lobbying members on Congress to vote against aid authorization bills for the Contras was an equally important aspect of WFP's advocacy. Facing off against the Reagan administration's concerted efforts to win congressional support, it was a long and grinding struggle and activists savored the occasional success. "We have influenced our Congressman, who was nothing but a pork barrel politician before we went to Nic[aragua] to vote against all contra aid," one WFP supporter wrote in 1986. "He even went to Nic[aragua] in March to see what all the fuss was about and came back saying that what was needed was economic aid for the government. What a step for him!"[43] Such victories, however, were rare. At the tail end of a meeting between a delegation of opponents of Contra aid and Republican senator John Heinz III of Pennsylvania, WFP long-termer Jennifer Atlee-Loudon recalled:

I was the last to speak. The case had been argued fully. There was nothing left to say. I had no lofty credentials with which to introduce myself. "My name is Jennifer Atlee. I work in the war zones of Nicaragua with the people you are killing." I reached into an envelope on my lap and laid some photos out on the glass top of his mahogany desk—slowly, deliberately, one by one—until the desk was covered with tortured, mangled bodies looking up at him.

He stayed in his chair until I laid the last photo down. The last picture was of Paulina, a little four-year-old, with tears running down her face. One little hand is wrapped tightly around her mother's fingers and her other arm is missing—the only vestige is a little round stub tied off at the end like a sausage. She is the victim of a land mine—MADE IN THE USA.

Heinz slammed his chair back, banging into the wall behind him. Although startled, I pursued, "This is it, Senator. This is what you are doing. Their blood is on your hands."

"The contras are an instrument," he snapped at me.

"They are a bloody instrument," I snapped back.

"They are a bloody instrument, but I hate those lying Sandinistas, and they must be stopped!" He was on his feet, shoving the pictures back at me. Paulina fluttered to the floor, landing face up on the thick white carpet. I gathered her back into my envelope with the others. The Senator's aides proceeded to escort us out of the office.[44]

Such lobbying efforts revealed the competing meanings attached to human rights in the fierce domestic debate over the Reagan administration's war on Nicaragua. Dismissing the White House's depiction of the Contras as moderate democrats valiantly struggling against the repressive Sandinistas, US activists spotlighted Contra atrocities, using the counterrevolutionaries' repeated violations of the political and civil rights of Nicaraguan civilians as evidence to convince legislators to curtail US assistance. Their efforts underscored the central position human rights had obtained on the US political landscape in the 1980s, notwithstanding activists' palpable frustration with their limited success. "The next morning," Atlee-Loudon concluded, when Heinz voted for $27 million in aid to the Contras, "he knew exactly what he was doing."[45]

Human rights also played a defining role for Americans who visited Nicaragua on short-term solidarity brigades. Recognizing the importance of solidarity visits in shaping US public opinion as well as the benefits international work brigades could offer Nicaragua, the Sandinista government strongly encouraged such visits. In response, as many as one hundred thousand US *brigadistas* visited Nicaragua over the course of the 1980s.[46] Countering Reagan's denunciation of Nicaragua as a communist totalitarian police state, solidarity activists frequently embraced the FSLN's lofty ideals of self-determination, participatory democracy, and socioeconomic transformation. US activists "could be found in the weekly vigils in front of the U.S. Embassy, armed with banners and posters; conducting fasts in grassroots urban neighborhoods and poor rural zones; building clinics and schools; picking coffee and cotton; delivering manifestos to the media and holding press conferences to denounce their government's policy," one Spanish activist later recalled. "They were like a horde of ants, with their generally light-skinned faces protected from the tropical sun by straw hats or baseball caps."[47]

Central America's close geographic proximity to the United States and cultural and linguistic ties to North America made it accessible for US citizens. By the mid-1980s, an entire infrastructure had grown up around short-term solidarity visits. Americans joined educational tours, organized by US-based organizations such as NACLA, Witness for Peace, or the Nicaraguan government tourist agency Turnica. "When President Ronald Reagan declared himself to be a 'Contra' in March of 1986, I decided to travel to Central America and to study the situation there for myself," noted Stuart Rawlings, who spent two weeks on a tour with a dozen other Americans. "I packed clothes for a tropical climate; and I brought along my guitar, some magic equipment, and a thousand animal balloons for children."[48] Such tours facilitated meetings between US citizens and supporters of the Sandinista political project while also showcasing the Contras' targeting of noncombatants and destruction of schools, clinics, and cooperatives.

In addition to educational tours, Americans visited Nicaragua on short-term work brigades. Many went to Nicaragua to help harvest coffee, which, accounting for roughly one-third of Nicaragua's exports, was a mainstay of the nation's economy. In 1983, facing a severe shortage of harvesters owing to the military mobilization, the Managua-based Nicaraguan Committee for Solidarity solicited international assistance, resulting in an influx of inexperienced yet earnest US volunteers. Coffee-harvesting *brigadistas* working with the Washington, DC–based National Network in Solidarity with the Nicaraguan People, for example, were required to cover the cost of round-trip airfare to Miami; additionally, round-trip airfare from Miami to Managua on Aeronica, the Nicaraguan national airline, cost about $280. Once on the ground in Nicaragua, participants paid a $50 registration fee and exchanged a mandatory $60 into Nicaraguan córdobas, with the cost of food and lodging covered by the government.[49]

Coffee harvesting was only one of many *brigadista* activities. Groups volunteered on state-run cotton, rice, tobacco, and sugarcane farms or engaged in reforestation projects, such as a 1984 group that planted twenty-six thousand trees in a single month.[50] Other *brigadistas* built houses, schools, or medical clinics. "Our government sends bombs; we deliver hammers and nails," a construction brigade declared in 1984. "Our government finances destruction and murder; we have traveled 3,000 miles to help Nicaraguans put their country back together."[51]

Volunteers on work brigades could expect few creature comforts. *Brigadistas* had to quickly adjust to a diet of rice and beans and communal sleeping arrangements. "Visualize sixty-one people sleeping side-by-side on the wood-plank floor," one volunteer recalled, "in four neat rows (two on the men's side and two on the women's side), feet dovetailing and not an inch gone to waste!"[52] Although no immunizations were required for US citizens to visit Nicaragua, work brigades risked food- and waterborne infections and malaria, as well as a range of localized risks, such as severe pain and temporary paralysis of the arm and chest resulting from the sting of an urticating caterpillar that fed on coffee leaves. The work itself was labor-intensive. "The picking does not seem difficult at first, a simple matter of reaching inside the opened pods and removing in one piece the attached ball of cotton," noted one cotton-harvesting *brigadista*. "It soon becomes evident, however, that the cotton bags attached to our waists are not filling at the same rate as those of the Nicaraguans supervising us, and the work seems much more difficult as the heat of the day rises."[53]

Americans participated in cultural brigades as well. Nearly two dozen members of the Artists' Brigade for the New Nicaragua, for example, worked with Nicaraguan muralists and gave musical performances and lessons. Debra Wise, the lone puppeteer in the group, offered a seminar on shadow puppetry and performed with a redheaded hand-and-rod puppet named Tillie. "Her running joke was that she had learned that the Nicaraguan government had given up being a puppet," Wise recalled, "and she had come to Central America to see how she could do the same thing."[54]

Wise's anti-imperialist puppet show illuminated a defining feature of US brigades to Nicaragua: solidarity activists rejected wholesale the Reagan administration's justifications for intervening against the Sandinistas. Some focused on the social and economic gains achieved by the Sandinista revolutionary government. In a fiery missive sent to the US Embassy in Managua, the 1984 construction brigade emphasized that "the Sandinistas have done more for their people in five years than Somoza did in half a century. In place of death squads, torture chambers and unbridled corruption, they have instituted health care, education, and democracy—for all the people."[55]

For others, US brigades to Nicaragua fit into the broader history of the US Left's solidarity with international struggles for social justice. "The Sandinista Revolution in Nicaragua seems to me to be the most profound and positive event to occur in our hemisphere in a quarter-century, and I believe it is in our interest as a people to work for its survival," former anti–Vietnam War activist and writer Jeff Jones asserted in a collection of interviews with *brigadistas*. "In the tradition of the Abraham Lincoln Brigades, of the Mississippi Freedom Summer, and of the Internationalists who fought with Sandino in the 1920s," Jones continued, the brigades to Nicaragua were "our way of reaching for the best in our own nation's history."[56]

Similarly, *brigadistas* drew comparisons between the social and economic achievements of the Sandinista government and Reagan's domestic cuts to social welfare programs. At the same time that the White House was lobbying Congress for tens of millions of dollars in aid to the Contras, "in Black communities across the country, we have been faced with tremendous cutbacks: in health care, day care, education, food stamps, grants to higher education," one *brigadista* asserted. "Our teenagers have the highest unemployment rate in the nation. Our rate of infant mortality has risen to almost twice the rate of white infants since Reagan started cutting social programs."[57]

Solidarity activists carried their fervor into confrontations at the US Embassy in Managua. According to one estimate, solidarity activists protested at the embassy every Thursday for 329 weeks in a row.[58] Visiting groups also met frequently with US Foreign Service Officers posted in Nicaragua. Not surprisingly, such encounters were often rife with tension. In one meeting, after listening to ambassador Anthony Quainton summarize US policy toward Nicaragua, a church group asked the ambassador to stand and join them in a group prayer. Quainton agreed, but to his surprise the group began praying for the overthrow of the Reagan administration. On another occasion, a member of a group from Hollywood bluntly asserted that "he had never heard so many lies in one presentation before," Quainton recalled in a later interview. "He wanted me to know that the next time there were Nuremburg trials, I would be guilty." Pressured by Reagan administration hard-liners on one side and solidarity activists on the other, the "constant drumbeat of moral indignation" Quainton concluded, ". . . was hard to take."[59] When the ambassador refused to meet with one group that protested at the embassy, referring to it as containing "antisocial elements," the members took the title as a badge of honor; a few days later, when the group squared off against residents of a cotton farm in a pickup baseball game, the Nicaraguans sarcastically referred to the matchup as the "'antisocials' versus the 'socialists.'"[60]

Not surprisingly, with only short-term stays in Nicaragua and on visits shaped by the Sandinista government, US *brigadistas* were prone to idealizing the achievements of the revolutionary regime and their own role in it. "Nicaragua is so poor. The people have so little," asserted the journalist Zachary Sklar, who joined a brigade at mid-decade. "But what they have is tremendous: a sense that Nicaragua is their own, that they can make of it what they want, that there is hope, that their views and complaints will be heard and understood. There is a nobility to the struggle, an honoring of all who have contributed, a memory and reverence for those who have died, a willingness to die defending something that you've suffered to win and that will be better for your children." Projecting an idealized revolutionary imaginary onto the complex Nicaraguan political landscape, Sklar concluded that revolutionary Nicaragua was "a society of the future."[61]

Such enthusiasm for the Nicaraguan revolution could come across as political naïveté. After landing at Managua's August C. Sandino Airport on an overcast afternoon in February 1985, for example, one US brigade formed a large circle in the terminal and militantly held their fists in the air while chanting "No pasaràn" (They shall not pass). Watching the scene unfold, an American working as a logistics operator for the television network ABC was unimpressed. "Jeez, why'n hell would anybody want to come here?" he griped. "This place is the dregs." When a journalist embedded with the group informed him that the Americans were en route to pick coffee, "he broke out laughing so hard he had to hold his hand over his mouth."[62] Nicaraguans, too, could be skeptical of solidarity activists, referring to the influx of internationals as "Sandalistas"—a sarcastic amalgam playing on solidarity activists' support for the FSLN and penchant for casual footwear.[63]

US *brigadistas* frequently returned to the United States with a positive impression of the gains Nicaraguans had made since the overthrow of the Somoza dictatorship and a heightened opposition to the Reagan administration's efforts to destabilize the revolutionary government. "This policy is causing needless suffering by the Nicaraguan people," wrote Stuart Rawlings after he completed his educational tour of Nicaragua, "and it is forcing the new Nicaraguan government into an unnecessary bond with the Soviet Union and other 'communist' nations."[64] Indeed, for many short-termers, visiting Nicaragua deepened their commitment to grassroots activism in the United States. As one WFP short-timer remembered, "I came back last July obsessed by Nicaragua."[65]

By the mid-1980s, a short-termer returning from Nicaragua could join one of hundreds of local and regional activist organizations that formed a heterogeneous and loosely connected network in solidarity with Nicaragua. Although the movement was capable of organizing major events, such as Central America Week demonstrations and meetings with elected officials in Washington, DC, its main strength was at the community and regional levels.[66] Indeed, in 1986 Central America Week included seventy-five events in fifty-two cities across twenty-eight states, including press conferences, radio and television appearances, film screenings, teach-ins, prayer services, art exhibitions, theater performances, vigils, fasts, and demonstrations—from a rally against US aid to the Contras in Woodrow Wilson Park in Birmingham, Alabama, to activists bearing crosses with the names of Nicaraguan victims in Seattle's bustling Pike Place Market.[67]

Grassroots solidarity activism focused on Nicaragua was both broad and diverse and sought to create a compelling counterpoint to the Reagan administration's justifications for ratcheting up US pressure on the Sandinistas. In late 1983, for example, the Interreligious Foundation for Community Organization (IFCO) facilitated a statewide campaign in Indiana. Building on a pilot program the previous summer in twenty-five communities in Kansas, an IFCO resource team of nearly two dozen fanned out across Indiana, speaking face-to-face with nearly five thousand people and reaching some seven hundred thousand through news reporting in newspapers, radio, and television.[68] The following year, IFCO oversaw an even bigger campaign in Oregon and Washington, with seventy-one local coordinators facilitating 423 events. With support from numerous local church and secular activist organizations, staffers made personal contact with nearly twelve thousand individuals and reached an estimated two million others via newspapers, radio, or television.[69]

More typical of the solidarity movement were smaller-scale efforts conducted by local organizations focused on community-based activism. Print publications served as an important mechanism to raise awareness and spur readers to action. In March 1985, for example, the St. Louis Inter-Faith Committee on Latin America provided readers with an update on developments in Central America in the *Inter-Faith Witness*, while two thousand miles away the *Council for Human Rights in Latin America Newsletter*, based in Eugene, Oregon, reported on a Nicaraguan National Assembly member's recent address at the University of Oregon.[70] Two months later, the Commission on International Peace and Reconciliation, based in Des Moines, Iowa, enjoined readers of its newsletter to encourage elected officials to oppose the US embargo against Nicaragua, and, in July, the Denver Justice and Peace Committee used the pages of its newsletter the *Mustard Seed* to urge activists to protest the upcoming Young Americans for Freedom conference, where retired general John K.

Singlaub—known for channeling private aid to the Contras—was scheduled to speak.[71]

Offering a counterpoint to the Reagan administration's portrayal of the Sandinistas as Soviet stooges, such publications were crafted by activists working with limited budgets and frequently on a volunteer basis. "This is our first issue. We confess we feel proud of it," the editors of *Nicaraguan Perspectives* wrote in July 1981. "Behind it there are many hours of discussion and hard work."[72] Similarly, seeking volunteers, the editors of a Sonoma, California, newsletter made no bones about the nature of the position: "long hours, hard work, no pay . . . no experience necessary, we'll train you."[73]

In addition to print media, solidarity activists organized events to raise awareness of US policy toward Central America, fundraise for solidarity activism, and encourage elected officials to oppose the Reagan administration's interventionism. For organizations involved in a variety of social justice activities, Nicaragua-focused events could fit into a broader slate of programming, such as the August 1986 Richmond Human Rights Coalition's calendar of events, which included a Marxism study group meeting, a vigil to support a nuclear test ban, and a yard sale to help fund a Virginia-based Nicaragua work brigade.[74] The threat of a US invasion in Central America, however, made Nicaragua a focal point for many activists, who channeled their energies into hundreds of local and regional events. In July 1985, for example, the Denver Justice and Peace Committee announced "Let Nicaragua Live!," a commemoration of the sixth anniversary of the revolutionary triumph, featuring "food, drink, crafts, information, theater, dance, music, poetry, auction, and raffle."[75] Similarly, a 1985 demonstration in Santa Rosa, California, involved a march from the courthouse to a federal building, where a handful of civil disobedience activists engaged in a sit-in at an army recruiting office. Outside, onlookers were treated to a show of political street theater: "Two 'newscasters' [read] the news while a 10' tall puppet of Reagan reacted from behind a long, low screen. Occasionally a woman would pop up from behind the screen with signs, paper missiles, etc., and illustrate the speaker's words. Finally, a 10' tall, sad-looking Third World woman puppet joined Reagan and the performance came to an end."[76]

US activists' efforts were an important feature shaping the political debates around Central America. Yet the Central America movement experienced significant challenges. Activists faced an uphill battle; given the power and resources of the executive branch, activists' confrontation with Reagan was, from the outset, a lopsided one. Moreover, public ignorance bedeviled solidarity activists. A 1983 poll revealed that only a quarter of Americans were aware that the Reagan administration was supporting El Salvador; three years later, roughly one-third of individuals polled knew that the administration was backing the Contras.[77] For activists, such shocking ignorance could be enervating. Central America specialists participating in IFCO's 1983 awareness-raising project, for example, were "visibly shaken by the ignorance and stereotypes they ran into," noted an IFCO follow-up report. "Some of them reasoned 'if newspaper reporters did not know the simplest facts about Central America, how could the U.S. public know?' and '. . . if U.S. citizens blindly believe what Reagan says without knowing the truth, what hope is there for popular U.S. support for peace and justice between Central America and U.S. America?'"[78]

Correspondingly, the decentralized nature of the solidarity movement impeded a coordinated strategy. Local organizations at times competed with one another for funds and new members. Without national leadership, the movement struggled to project a clear message in the US media. Similarly, the multiplicity of newsletters produced at the grass roots by local organizations did not fill the need for a single, unifying publication that, as Roger Peace writes, "would arguably have given activists a stronger sense of movement identity, increased public recognition . . . and furthered educational outreach."[79]

Nonetheless, solidarity activism was crucial in raising popular awareness, lobbying elected officials, and fundraising. "Active lobbying by church and human rights groups and constituent letter-writing campaigns provided administration critics a sense that they had a cushion of support to oppose the president," writes the political scientist Cynthia J. Arnson. "These domestic pressures reinforced members' willingness to oppose policy, often servicing as a justification for such opposition."[80] Moreover, throughout the 1980s, a majority of Americans opposed a US military intervention in the region. The tens of thousands of signatories to the pledge of resistance, nationwide protest events such as Central America Week, and myriad local-level awareness-raising events, fundraisers, and lobbying efforts made it harder for the Reagan administration to leverage US power against Nicaragua.

Finally, for the FSLN, with no end in sight for the Contra war and the Nicaraguan economy pushed to the breaking point, transnational solidarity offered a glimmer of hope. Sandinista officials understood the signal importance of US solidarity activism in raising popular awareness and lobbying elected officials and, especially after the Reagan administration imposed the 1985 embargo, in donating material aid to Nicaragua. Indeed, in response to the FSLN's appeals for assistance, Nicaragua received some $5 million annually in material aid from solidarity organizations abroad.[81] When Ben Linder—a US citizen living and working in northern Nicaragua—was killed by Contras in April 1987, Daniel Ortega Saavedra himself delivered the eulogy after leading the funeral procession in Matagalpa. Linder, an engineer working on a hydro-electric power project, had come to Nicaragua "filled with dreams born of his conviction that the ethical values of the U.S. people are much more important than the illegal policy of the U.S. government," Ortega declared. "He demon-strated that the U.S. people are noble, and that the U.S. people abhor the murder of Nicaraguan children, women, youths, and peasants. The people of Lincoln are opposed to slavery; they are opposed to terrorism; and they are firm defenders of peace among peoples." In a reference to Ernest Hemingway's classic novel of the Spanish Civil War, Ortega plaintively asked, "For whom does the bell toll here in Nicaragua?," before listing eight international activists who had been killed by the Contras. Ortega ended with Linder, whose "song of love, peace, and hope is intensified by his sacrifice."[82]

When he learned of the death of Linder, the Vietnam veteran-turned-peace activist S. Brian Willson escalated his efforts to bring US support for the Contras to a halt. In April 1987, Willson led the Veterans Peace Action Team on a protest march across Contra-contested northern Nicaragua. Vow-ing to blame the Reagan administration if they were harmed by Contras, the group of some seventy unarmed Americans had walked seventy-three miles after six weeks, from the valley city of Jinotega north to rugged Wiwilí on the banks of the Río Coco.[83] "The acts of terror against innocent civilians is deliberate and intentional; it is conceived, organized and carried out by the United States government and its proxies and paid for by the tax dollars of United States citizens," the team declared in a subsequent statement sent to Reagan and all members of Congress. "It relies on terror and fear and eco-nomic deprivation to accomplish its immoral and illegal ends. Our hands are all stained by the blood of the war's innocent victims. You, we and the North American people have much to answer and atone for."[84]

Willson returned to Nicaragua with a second Veterans Peace Action Team in June. The team's destination was the embattled village of El Cedro, which had endured three Contra attacks that had destroyed many of the buildings and left twenty-five residents dead. After dedicating a reconstructed health post to Linder, who was killed about fifteen kilometers away, Willson spoke of a long-term project that would build houses, coffee processing plants, and education facilities.[85]

Willson's experiences in Nicaragua intensified his commitment to nonviolent activism. Back in the United States, he refused to pay taxes to the federal government. "As a citizen of a nation that kills, and prepares for the killing of human beings throughout the world in violation of our Supreme as well as International law," Willson wrote the Internal Revenue Service, "I am obligated to not only cease my own participation directly or as an accessory to these crimes, but also to do everything reasonable in my power to stop these violations of my country from continuing."[86]

In the summer of 1987, Willson turned his attention to the Concord Naval Weapons Station (CNWS), a 13,000-acre military storage facility northeast of San Francisco. With evidence that shipments of US military aid to Central America originated at the CNWS, Willson joined a number of local organizations, including the Franciscan Affinity Group, the San Francisco office of the American Friends Service Committee, and the Bay Area Pledge of Resistance, in planning a summer-long series of demonstrations at the train tracks used to transport munitions to cargo ships. Beginning on June 10, 1987, protesters held daily vigils and blocked vehicles in a coordinated protest dubbed the "Nuremberg Actions."[87] "We decided to invoke the Nuremberg Principles which imposes a duty upon all citizens, whether civilian or military or other government employee, to uphold the law," Willson later affirmed. Accordingly, "the citizen has a duty to make known the violations of law committed by his or her government and do everything reasonable to stop those violations from continuing—even when ordered otherwise by a superior. We desired to uphold the law."[88]

In the late summer, Willson decided to escalate the protest by initiating a forty-day fast on train tracks used by munitions trains from the CNWS. Timed to correspond with the anniversary of the 1986 Veterans Fast for Life initiative, the fast would provide time to "to atone for our collective complicity in death policies," Willson wrote, "and to envision resistance actions in response to those policies."[89] Willson described the project in detail in written correspondence with local and state law enforcement officers and elected officials.[90] He also informed the commander of the CNWS, Captain Lonnie Cagle. "I want you to know in advance of this plan," Willson wrote to Cagle on August 21. "If not incarcerated, deceased, or otherwise disabled, I am committed, as the spirit moves me, to be physically on the tracks for part of each of the 40 days." The fast, Willson concluded, was a way "to put our bodies on the line to save lives of other people who are worth no less than us."[91] Amid the daily protests and preparations for the fast, Willson found time to celebrate, marrying Holley Rauen, a midwife and fellow peace activist. The two had met in Nicaragua a few months earlier.

On September 1, 1987, surrounded by some two dozen protesters, Willson knelt on the tracks to begin the fast. At 12:01 p.m., a munitions train approached, the driver blowing the horn. It was moving slowly but did not stop. The protesters scattered, but Willson remained on the tracks, eyes fixed on the engine until the moment of impact.

The incident at the Concord Naval Weapons Station incensed solidarity activists. But Willson was swimming against the tide. By the mid-1980s, the Reagan administration's embrace of democracy promotion as the centerpiece of its human rights policy had changed the political calculus in the United States. Reagan's shift toward pro-US dictatorships in the Philippines and Haiti in 1986, combined with top US policymakers' repeated emphasis on promoting democracy as a core US foreign policy goal, was crucial in winning the support of moderates on Capitol Hill. The democracy promotion initiative was especially important for US policy toward Nicaragua. After repeatedly rejecting the White House's funding packages for the Contras, the Congress in 1986 passed $100 million in aid. Top Reagan administration officials played a key role in securing the necessary votes. "In 1979, Nicaraguan democrats and their sympathizers throughout the world believed that the end of the Somoza regime marked a new beginning for Nicaragua," secretary of state George P. Shultz asserted in one widely disseminated 1986 speech. "Nicaraguans learned very quickly, however, that instead of democracy, they had fallen prey to what the Sandinistas say is 'revolution by vanguard' and what the rest of us know is communist totalitarianism."[92] Reagan's personal involvement in the issue was particularly effective. "When a president gets to the point that he can pinpoint 20 people and work face to face with them, he's hard to stop," Speaker of the House Thomas P. "Tip" O'Neil (D-MA) reportedly pointed out after the vote.[93]

But the success was more broadly indicative of the changed political calculus in Washington as the gravitational pull of the democracy initiative refashioned a new Cold War consensus. The power of the democracy project was evident in the widening divisions among American liberals. At the outset of the decade, the defection of liberal Cold War hawks such as Jeane J. Kirkpatrick and Carl Gershman to the Reagan camp had rippled through the US center-left. Tapped to lead the National Endowment for Democracy (NED), Gershman oversaw funds to opposition forces in Nicaragua including the newspaper *La Prensa* and the Nicaraguan labor group the Confederación de

Unificación Sindical.[94] Correspondingly, by mid-decade, Democrats like AFL-CIO president Lane Kirkland had thrown their support behind the democracy initiative. While Kirkland was focused primarily on Eastern Europe, his support for Reagan's democracy project was felt by US solidarity activists focused on Nicaragua as well. Revealing the split in the US center-left, Kirkland, for example, in 1987 openly opposed labor union participation in a national march against US intervention in Central America.[95]

By mid-decade, with the democracy initiative gaining steam and conditions in Nicaragua deteriorating, more and more moderate liberals were following the neoconservatives' footsteps. The well-known liberal political scientist Robert S. Leiken's February 1984 *New Republic* essay "Nicaragua's Untold Stories" offered a damning critique of Sandinista commandants living in luxury while the majority of the population suffered the combined effects of economic hardship and military mobilization.[96] Leiken's sharp criticism of the FSLN came as a shock to liberals inside the Washington Beltway; underscoring Leiken's impact, the liberal stalwart Edward Kennedy (D-MA) read the article into the *Congressional Record*.[97]

Meanwhile, political operators with a track record of supporting Democrats, such as Bernard Aronson, a former adviser to Walter Mondale, and Bruce P. Cameron, a longtime lobbyist for Americans for Democratic Action, increasingly played an important role in reframing the Nicaragua issue as an issue of the Sandinista rejection of democracy and refusal to grant civil liberties, facilitating the Reagan administration's efforts to secure congressional funding.[98] Nicaragua, Cameron concluded, "seemed to be at the end of a long chain of death dealing that began in Moscow and traveled through Havana to Managua."[99] Such criticism of the Sandinistas was increasingly echoed in mainstream media outlets, which, in turn, were used to advance Reagan's foreign policy agenda. "I do not think either political party wants to be blamed for the communization of Central America," representative Jack Kemp (R-NY) told members of Congress. Citing the *New Republic*'s criticism of Managua in the lead-up to the congressional vote on the $100 million in aid to the Contras, Kemp insightfully asserted, "Rather it appears that we are rapidly developing a bipartisan consensus on the idea of expanding democratic opportunities of the Nicaraguan people while protecting the security of the western hemisphere."[100]

Even within the US Left, the Reagan administration's democracy initiative sowed discord. To be sure, opposition to the US intervention in Central America cut across the US Left, papering over rifts on issues such as Sandinista domestic and foreign policy and fueling conspiracy theories on the right of communist fifth columnists.[101] But the Left risked romanticizing the Sandinista political project while rejecting *any* criticism of Managua by Reagan officials as patent lies. Given Reagan's interventionism and the pattern of misinformation propagated by the White House, such a response was understandable; nonetheless, the result lent the discussion of Central America an illiberal tenor. Attendees at a 1982 Latin American Studies Association plenary meeting on Nicaragua, for example, were so hostile to deputy assistant secretary of state for inter-American affairs James Cheek that the association's shaken president, Harvard professor Jorge I. Domínguez, described it as "grossly unprofessional" and an "expression of naked intolerance."[102] Similarly, in the lead-up to the 1984 Nicaraguan election, George Black, editor of NACLA's *Report on the Americas*, published a *New York Times* op-ed that criticized Reagan's war on Nicaragua *and* Sandinista hard-liners. In response, NACLA received so many angry letters from Sandinista supporters in the United States that the organization's staff hastily dispatched a statement disassociating itself from the op-ed; Black, too, published a backpedaling explanation.[103]

Reflecting on the episode involving Black, the journalist Michael Massing questioned the US Left's support for the Sandinistas. Despite FSLN limits on civil liberties, "too often . . . [the U.S. Left] has adopted a reflexive stance, seeing all events inside Nicaragua through the prism of U.S. aggression," Massing suggested in *The Nation* in April 1985. Although emphasizing the signal importance of resisting the Reagan administration's pressure on Nicaragua, Massing concluded, "In the end, however, such a one-note approach provides a narrow basis for analysis."[104] A subsequent roundtable on Massing's piece revealed the significant divisions within the US Left. Given Reagan's pressure on Managua, argued Princeton law professor Peter Falk, the Left could not, in good conscience, criticize the Sandinistas. "Surely it would be odd behavior for someone to write in an influential Sri Lankan newspaper about the failings of Tamil culture at a time when the Tamils are being threatened with a massacre," Falk wrote. "Or for a dedicated German socialist in the 1930s to write in a respected mainstream Berlin newspaper about the duplicitous role of Jewish banking houses."[105] Others called for a balance between opposing the White House and keeping an eye on Sandinista repression. For the historian William Appleman Williams, however, such an approach missed a fundamental problem. Williams, whose seminal 1959 work *The Tragedy of American Diplomacy* had laid the foundation for a generation of revisionist scholarship critical of US Cold War policy, rejected interventionism on both sides of the political spectrum. The US Left was unable "to break free of the classic US myth of judging and saving the world," Williams wrote. "Lefties want to save the world in the image of the United States just as desperately as do the neolib-erals, the neoconservatives, and the cowboys in the sky." The best way for the US Left to help political developments overseas, Williams concluded, was by "giving them a chance to make their own mistakes, and then allowing them to try to correct them."[106] Such debates illuminated the rifts within the US Left, as well as the deeper divide between US moderates and leftists. More broadly, as the Reagan administration's democracy initiative offered a compelling blue-print for foreign policy, the divisions that had developed in the Democratic Party in the late 1960s continued to impede a forward-looking liberal-left alliance.[107]

Over the course of the 1980s, solidarity activists worked assiduously to raise awareness of the situation in Central America and to pressure elected officials to oppose the Reagan administration's undeclared war on Nicaragua. Tens of thousands of US *brigadistas* visited Nicaragua and hundreds took up residence in the embattled nation. But the Reagan administration's embrace of democ-racy promotion as the centerpiece of its human rights policy changed the po-litical landscape in the United States. Contemporary observers recognized that the administration was narrowly reframing human rights around democracy promotion, the free market, and anticommunism. And like the human rights policy as a whole, the democracy initiative dismissed social and economic rights claims. "Time and again in recent years, the Administration has sought to promote democracy by urging little more than the mere holding of elec-tions," Human Rights Watch and the Lawyers Committee for Human Rights maintained in a 1987 report. "The Administration has proceeded as if popular sovereignty could be achieved through no more than the simple, periodic act of voting." Such a narrow understanding of democracy, the report concluded, "fails to address the root causes of many human rights abuses."[108] Yet, by mid-decade, Reagan's reconstitution of the bipartisan Cold War consensus around the concept of democracy promotion deepened divisions among liberals and illuminated the lack of a cohesive strategy within the US Left. Correspond-ingly, the worsening economic situation in Nicaragua, the FSLN's reliance on Soviet support, and Sandinista constraints on civil liberties increasingly eclipsed the revolution's social and economic promises.

Yet as protests such as the "Nuremberg Actions" at the CNWS made clear, solidarity activists remained committed throughout the decade to resisting the Reagan administration's undeclared war on Nicaragua. For Willson, crushed by a CNWS munitions train, the cost was high. Willson suffered a fractured skull, brain damage, and nineteen broken bones. In an eight-hour operation, doctors amputated both of his legs below the knees.[109] Underscoring the close ties between the solidarity activist community and the FSLN, Ortega immediately sent a message thanking Willson for his sacrifice, and less than a week after the accident Nicaraguan First Lady Rosario Murillo personally visited the hospitalized activist.[110] "We have feelings of solidarity, love and sympathy for Brian, his wife, Holley, his friends, his relatives and all those who share the ideal of peace," Murillo told reporters before visiting the protest site, where Willson's blood still stained the train tracks.[111]

Willson himself was undeterred. "I've joined the legion of kids in Nicaragua without legs," he told reporters.[112] At the eye of the storm of indignation expressed by solidarity activists, Willson remained steadfast in his pacifism. "Despite your anger & outrage at what has happened, I ask you to express your opposition to this violence here on the tracks & in Central America nonviolently," he wrote. "We must confront violence with nonviolence. We all have to put our lives on the line for peace & justice—it does not have to be in front of a train."[113] It was a remarkable message of hope amid the grim destruction of the US intervention against Nicaragua and Willson's own sacrifice. And on September 2, only one day after the accident, protesters swarmed the tracks; remarkably, every munitions train for the next twenty-eight months was blocked.[114] Yet, as Willson could attest, changing the world came with a cost. "If we want peace, we can have it," he concluded, "but we are going to have to pay for it."[115]

Chapter 7

From the Cold War to the End of History

US Democracy Promotion, Interventionism,

and Unipolarity, 1987-1990

At the close of the 1980s, the Cold War ended. As popular uprisings across Eastern Europe threatened to catapult captive nations out of the Soviet orbit, in Moscow a new generation of Soviet leadership refused to dispatch Red Army troops in support of sclerotic client regimes. Instead, promising political openness and economic reform, the charismatic premier Mikhail Gorbachev did the incredible: in a matter of months the Soviet Union relinquished its empire, the fruit of its hard-won victory in the Second World War and the principal cause of the four decades of Cold War that followed. With policymakers and pundits across the globe struggling to keep up with the pace of transformative events, by the end of 1989 the Iron Curtain was a relic of a bygone age. "Nearly a century and a half ago, Marx and Engels declared that Europe was being haunted by the specter of communism," wrote Czech historian Vilém Prečan the following year. "Today, however, communist Europe finds itself haunted by the specter of democracy."[1]

If the momentous events of 1989 marked a vindication of the US containment strategy, formulated in the late 1940s and implemented over the course of nine presidential administrations, by the end of Ronald Reagan's second term human rights had become increasingly institutionalized in the US foreign policymaking process. After initially rejecting human rights as a liberal internationalist boondoggle, the Reagan administration by late 1989 had responded to criticism on Capitol Hill and from NGOs by embracing a narrowly defined approach to human rights focusing on political rights and civil liberties. Promoting democracy, in particular, emerged as a defining feature of the administration's foreign policy framework, and by mid-decade a new bipartisan consensus was forged, fusing the Reagan Doctrine's support for anticommunist militants with the rhetoric of advancing democracy abroad. The illegalities of the Iran-Contra scandal, however, underscored the risks of pursuing democracy promotion in the interest of Cold War goals.

Yet the rising visibility of the Reagan administration's human rights policy also had another effect: increased institutionalization of human rights as a US policy priority in the vast bureaucratic machinery of foreign policy formulation and implementation. From Foreign Service Officers in distant embassies tasked with generating congressionally mandated annual human rights reports to the president's own justifications for US actions in the international arena, over the course of the 1980s human rights became increasingly accepted as a legitimate US foreign policy goal. By the time Reagan left office, recalled career diplomat George Lister, human rights had been "injected into the State Department's bloodstream."[2] Even the administration's critics were forced to concede the point. As the executive director of Human Rights Watch Aryeh Neier admitted in 1987, "The administration today solidly accepts the principle that it is the responsibility of the United States to promote human rights worldwide. That was not the view in 1981."[3] The newfound centrality of the US brand of human rights talk was further evident following the 1988 presidential election. From the outset, the George H. W. Bush administration presented human rights promotion as an incontrovertible US foreign policy objective embedded in the best of American moral traditions.

As the denouement in US-Nicaraguan Cold War relations made clear, however, the interventionism that had defined Reagan's approach to democracy promotion remained a potent element in Bush's foreign policy. Underscoring the power of the democracy initiative, secretary of state James A. Baker III adeptly shifted the focus inside the Washington Beltway from the Contras to the 1990 Nicaraguan election. Portraying the Sandinistas as a retrograde totalitarian regime in a vibrant age of democratization, the White House won bipartisan support in its effort to maintain the Contra threat and US economic pressure as well as provide an infusion of funds for the electoral opposition.

If 1989 was, for many, the annus mirabilis, for Nicaraguans the late 1980s were a time of hardship and spent illusions. Following the 1979 revolution, the FSLN had sought to provide a new model of democracy for third-world nations seeking to break free from the legacies of colonialism and underdevelopment. A decade later, with annual inflation surpassing 30,000 percent and the Contra war claiming tens of thousands of lives, the social and economic promises of the revolution receded into memory. Under Gorbachev's watch, the Soviet Union became increasingly less willing to bankroll Nicaragua, and at the tail end of the 1980s deep state spending cuts coupled with government mismanagement fueled domestic opposition. Watching the situation unfold, the brilliant Uruguayan writer Eduardo Galeano lamented Nicaragua's lost idealism. "The pitiless, ever-growing siege and blockade are not taking place because democracy does not exist in Nicaragua, but so that it never will. They are not taking place because a dictatorship exists in Nicaragua, but so that one may yet again," he wrote. "They are not taking place because Nicaragua is a satellite, a sad pawn on the chessboard of the great powers, but so that it may be one again."[4]

Throughout 1987, the Iran-Contra affair hung like a shadow over the White House. Reagan avoided impeachment, but as the scandal rippled through the top echelons of the administration, executive oversight of US foreign policy faltered. "The Iran-Contra affair disrupted the efficient functioning of the foreign policy network," one top CIA analyst later observed, "because the key players in it were all fighting for their lives in a major scandal."[5] In particular, as former NSC staffer Jack F. Matlock Jr. writes, Iran-Contra arrested developments in US-Soviet relations, "delay[ing] decisions that could have produced treaties on strategic and conventional arms in 1988."[6]

Ironically, however, despite upending the Reagan presidency, Iran-Contra also helped clear the path for the most important foreign policy achievements of the administration's two terms in office. Resignations by top-level hardliners created opportunities to reshape the administration's policymaking process and foreign policy agenda. As the scandal roiled the White House in late 1986, national security adviser John M. Poindexter was replaced by Frank C. Carlucci III, an experienced foreign affairs hand who had joined the diplomatic corps in the late 1950s and risen from embassy postings in sub-Saharan Africa and South America to high-profile appointments in the Nixon, Ford, Carter, and Reagan administrations.[7] Carlucci not only eliminated Lieutenant Colonel Oliver L. North's office but fired some 65 percent of the NSC staff. When the vice president warned that Reagan was concerned that Carlucci was going too far, the new national security adviser was undeterred, confidently firing off a handwritten note that read simply, "Don't worry, Mr. President, this will come out all right."[8] The following year, Carlucci was shifted to the Pentagon to replace secretary of defense Caspar Weinberger, while his low-profile deputy, Colin Powell, was elevated to coordinate the NSC. In turn, Powell worked closely with the well-respected former

Tennessee senator Howard H. Baker Jr., who replaced chief of staff Donald Regan—another casualty of Iran-Contra—in February 1987.[9]

In an administration known for high-stakes intrigues and lax oversight by the president, the personnel changes introduced a much-needed dose of organizational structure. Seeking to avoid a repetition of the Iran-Contra fiasco, Baker and Powell tightened the reins, mandating in early 1988 that "no Administration official should provide assistance or encouragement of any kind to private individuals or third parties raising funds" on behalf of the Contras. "We believe that any such assistance or encouragement, no matter how well intentioned, would be misunderstood, misinterpreted, and, therefore, counterproductive," they concluded.[10] Underscoring the message that the days of North's off-the-books escapades were over, the memo was quickly released to the press.[11] The changes also facilitated greater cooperation among the president's top advisers. After years of bureaucratic battles with hard-liners like Weinberger, secretary of state George P. Shultz found common ground with Carlucci and Powell in late 1987 and 1988. "All three were pragmatic men and experienced government servants," one analyst noted, "who were able to put the national interest ahead of their egos and who had a firm grip on reality."[12]

The reorientation facilitated the administration's most significant foreign policy achievements. With support and guidance from Matlock, a pragmatic Soviet specialist and the former US ambassador in Moscow, Shultz doggedly pushed for a policy of engagement with the Kremlin on arms control, bilateral issues, regional concerns, and human rights. In a series of summits beginning with a 1985 meeting at Geneva, Reagan and Soviet premier Gorbachev established a working relationship that facilitated the tough negotiations leading to the 1987 signing of the Intermediate-Range Nuclear Forces Treaty. More importantly, the decrease in tension between the United States and the Soviet Union gave Gorbachev breathing room as he pursued a wide-ranging domestic reform agenda focused on restructuring the USSR's moribund economy (perestroika) and stimulating greater political transparency and social openness (glasnost). By late 1988, Gorbachev was moving beyond the Cold War's ideological confrontation. In an address to the United Nations in December, the Soviet leader announced a massive unilateral military reduction that would entail cashiering half a million Red Army soldiers and mothballing ten thousand tanks, eighty-five hundred artillery pieces, and nearly a thousand combat aircraft.[13] "He sounded as if he saw us as partners making a better world," Reagan enthused in his diary after meeting with Gorbachev following the address.[14] Two months later, the last Soviet troops would cross the Friendship

Bridge spanning the Amu River, ending the USSR's bloody decade-long military intervention in Afghanistan.[15]

While US–Soviet relations thawed, human rights became increasingly institutionalized in the US foreign policymaking process. To be sure, Iran-Contra revealed a dangerous slippage between lofty ideals and raw Cold War interventionism. But if the illegalities of the scandal captured the spotlight in late 1986 and 1987, they overshadowed a deeper process of human rights institutionalization. A decade earlier, as 1970s congressional human rights activism reached its zenith, an amendment to sections 116(d) and 502B(b) of the Foreign Assistance Act of 1961 required the State Department to submit annual country reports on human rights. Widely perceived as the brainchild of "bleeding heart" liberals and fiercely resisted by the Ford administration, the requirement initially confronted a mix of antipathy and confusion among the diplomatic corps.[16] "You can imagine how difficult it was in the beginning," recalled Lister, who worked on human rights issues at Foggy Bottom during the Carter and Reagan administrations. "There was bureaucratic inexperience. There was also bureaucratic resistance. Some said human rights are fine, but they have nothing to do with foreign affairs. There was a lack of information and reference material, etc."[17]

Yet the annual country reports requirement, combined with the congressionally mandated creation of the Bureau of Human Rights and Humanitarian Affairs, forced the issue of human rights into the State Department's bureaucratic machinery. Tasked with drafting the reports, US embassies responded by creating a new position: the "human rights officer." As a result, hundreds of Foreign Service Officers across the globe dutifully set about gathering information on human rights, which, particularly in countries with a poor record, often led them to establish contacts among NGOs and activists. The accumulation of information—especially from nontraditional sources—led to new insight, and in addition to drafting the annual country reports, human rights officers began regularly reporting on political developments through the prism of human rights; as cables dispatched to Washington from US embassies on human rights issues snowballed, the issue gained legitimacy in the State Department as a US foreign policy concern. "I soon discovered this work is like pushups—the more you do, the more you can do," Lister recalled.[18]

To be sure, liberals and conservatives battled fiercely over the role human rights should play in US foreign policy during the Carter administration, and the Reagan team initially sought to shuffle the issue to the backburner in the initial months of Reagan's presidency. But the integration of human rights reporting into the flow of information crisscrossing the State Department and the slow accretion of human rights concerns as a factor in foreign policy decisions continued apace. "Human rights reporting became routine," wrote Richard Schifter, who represented the United States in the United Nations Commission on Human Rights from 1981 to 1986 and then as assistant secretary of state for human rights and humanitarian affairs from 1986 to 1992. "The arrival in Washington of a gradually swelling stream of messages about human rights violations in various parts of the world in turn made the regional bureaus of the State Department increasingly aware of these problems and caused them to effect appropriate United States reactions."[19]

The Reagan administration's about-face on the issue of human rights beginning in late 1981 further contributed to the process of institutionalization. Unlike the outspoken former civil rights activist Patricia Derian, who spent four years as Jimmy Carter's Human Rights Bureau chief in continual turf wars, Elliott Abrams, who took the helm of the bureau in November 1981, elicited far greater cooperation from the department's geographic bureaus by emphasizing "quiet diplomacy" with human rights violating regimes rather than public shaming.[20] Particularly at the outset of the decade, liberal internationalists rightly castigated the administration for turning a blind eye to abusive right-wing allies; they drew inspiration from Derian's successful efforts to free the imprisoned Argentine journalist Jacobo Timerman, who after his release told the Senate Foreign Relations Committee, "A silent diplomacy is silence; a quiet diplomacy is surrender."[21] But Abrams did make human rights palatable for government officials who had looked askance at Derian's activism. Correspondingly, by mid-decade, the bipartisan appeal of the Reagan administration's democracy promotion initiative further contributed to the institutionalization of human rights as a legitimate US foreign policy concern.

The rising visibility of human rights was evident in US-Soviet relations. Beginning in 1984, eliciting human rights improvements in the USSR was designated one of four overarching US strategic goals. As relations warmed between Reagan and Gorbachev, top US officials consistently raised human rights concerns with their Soviet counterparts, particularly regarding political prisoners and Soviet citizens seeking exit visas. US pressure, combined with the openings for human rights advocacy created by the 1975 Helsinki Final Act and the meetings of the Conference on Security and Cooperation in Europe (CSCE), contributed to a striking reorientation of Soviet policy.[22] Under Gorbachev, Schifter later wrote, top Soviet officials increasingly came to

"share our concerns about their country's totalitarian system and favored liberalization for the sake of their own people and not just to accommodate the
United States."[23]

If the US emphasis on human rights in its policy toward the communist
world fit easily within the containment framework, defining US policy toward
developing nations posed a more complex challenge. Not surprisingly, given
the administration's initial embrace of right-wing authoritarian regimes, the
White House response to a wave of democratic transitions, particularly in
South America, was largely reactive. Nonetheless, the Reagan administration's
rising support for newly elected civilian leaders was a significant about-face,
underscoring an important transition in US foreign policy: in a region where
US officials had frequently viewed military leaders as more stable Cold War
allies than their civilian counterparts, beginning in the mid-1980s US officials
lauded the stability of democracy. Reagan was a particularly outspoken advocate of the wave of democracy sweeping the hemisphere, repeatedly sounding
the theme in public pronouncements. "In looking back over these 6 ½ years, . . .
I cannot help but reflect on the most dramatic change to my own eyes: the exciting new prospects for the democratic cause," the president told listeners in a
mid-1987 address. He continued:

> A feeling of energy and hope prevails. Statism has lost the intellectuals, and
> everywhere one turns, nations and people are seeking the fulfillment of their
> age-old aspirations for self-government and self-determination. . . .
>
> Yes, we may, then, live at the moment Churchill once anticipated: a mo-
> ment when the world would have a chance to redeem the opportunity it
> missed four decades ago—a chance for the "broad sunlit uplands" of free-
> dom, a chance to end the terrible agony of the 20th century and the twin
> threats of nuclear war and totalitarian ideology, a chance, above all, to see
> humanity live and prosper under that form of government that Churchill
> called the worst form of government except, as he said, for all the others:
> democracy.

"This is the opportunity before us," Reagan expansively concluded. "It's one
we must seize now for ourselves and future generations."[24]

Significantly, US support for democratization processes was not limited to
presidential boilerplate. Over the course of the decade, US officials developed
new methods to assist developing nations overcome the logistical challenges
of national elections. The US-backed government of El Salvador served as a
defining test case: as part of the effort to drain popular support for leftist

revolutionaries, between 1982 and 1984, the United States spent at least $12 million to modernize the Salvadoran electoral system. Working closely with the Central Elections Commission in San Salvador, US officials focused on "technical assistance, technology transfer, and election administration," writes the historian Evan D. McCormick, in a project that eventually introduced "new balloting procedures, created El Salvador's first comprehensive, digitized national electoral registry, and instituted new means of fraud prevention."[25] Such efforts contributed to the development of a US democracy assistance tool kit that could be tailored to local conditions across the developing world and facilitated working relationships between various US stakeholders in the democracy promotion agenda, including Foreign Service Officers, United States Agency for International Development (USAID) officials, the National Endowment for Democracy (NED), and private contractors.

Corresponding with the rising significance of democracy promotion for US government officials, by the end of the 1980s the NED had consolidated its position as the flagship US democracy assistance foundation. In 1987, the NED was operating on an annual budget of nearly $20 million and funding projects in fifty countries in Africa, Asia, Europe, and Latin America.[26] It was a heady moment in the organization's short history. "When historians look back upon the 1980s, they are likely to conclude that the most significant global trend of the decade was the resurgence of democracy," NED president Carl Gershman presciently maintained in the organization's 1987 annual report. During the 1980s, Gershman continued, a "new pro-democratic consensus" had taken hold in the United States. The NED, he concluded, "is a product of that consensus."[27]

Taken as a whole, the Reagan administration's embrace of democracy promotion as the centerpiece of its human rights policy marked a defining shift in US Cold War foreign policy. Yet there were distinct characteristics of the US human rights policy and, in particular, the US democracy promotion initiative. First, the Reagan administration emphasized the procedural aspects of electoral democracy. In the eyes of US officials, democratization primarily entailed elections; more expansive definitions of political rights and civil liberties, whether political pluralism, freedom of the press, or simply an end to state-sanctioned political violence, were often given short shrift.[28] "Once an 'election' took place in a favored nation, even if flawed," argued Jerome J. Shestack, who had served as Carter's representative to the UN Commission on Human Rights, "the [Reagan] Administration downplayed abuses committed by military forces still controlling the now 'free' government."[29]

Second, as with US policy toward the communist world, US democracy promotion toward developing nations mapped onto the Cold War containment strategy. "Today the goals of our foreign policy are the same as they have been for the last four decades," Reagan declared in a mid-1987 radio address. "We stand against totalitarianism, particularly imperialistic expansionist totalitarianism. We are for democracy and human rights, and we're for a worldwide prosperity that only free economies can give and the pursuit of human happiness that only political freedom allows."[30] Accordingly, as military leaders vacated presidential palaces across the region, for US policymakers allowing an opening for leftists to take power—whether by revolution or reform—was never in the cards. While lauding the wave of democratization sweeping the hemisphere, American officials sought to replace dictatorial US clients with elected moderates who would fall in line with US interests. "The United States wanted stable viable 'democratic' regimes that could pre-empt more radical change by incorporating broad popular forces in electoral participation, yet guarantee continuity with the anti-communist and anti-reformist traditions of their military predecessors," the political scientists Barry Gills, Joel Rocamora, and Richard Wilson wrote in an influential early assessment. The Reagan administration worked to empower pro-capitalist political elites while retaining close ties to conservative military establishments, Gills, Rocamora, and Wilson continued, an approach they described as "low intensity democracy": "a halfway house between previous 'unstable' representative democratic systems in the Third World and the moribund and counterproductive military dictatorships of the 1960s and 1970s which had often been established and maintained with U.S. support."[31]

Third, US democracy promotion was striated with neoliberalism. "Two great winds are sweeping across Latin America: the wind of free enterprise and the wind of democracy," Reagan confidently told members of the Council of the Americas in May 1987. "They are warm and nurturing winds that carry with them the gentle rains of hope for Latin America's future." In a region that had suffered "the disaster of state-controlled and -dominated economies," the president continued, "in both small and large steps, nations are beginning on the difficult path away from statism and toward freer economies."[32] Praising like-minded intellectuals, such as Peruvian economist Hernando de Soto, Reagan officials repeatedly emphasized the nexus between political freedoms and the free market.[33] The administration's free market fundamentalism fueled the development of a neoliberal orthodoxy among the Washington, DC–based financial institutions—the so-called Washington Consensus, consisting of the

International Monetary Fund, the World Bank, and the US Department of the Treasury. Correspondingly, US officials dismissed out of hand the contention that real democracy flowed from social and economic rights. As Schifter bluntly asserted at the end of the decade, "I remain skeptical about the idea that food, jobs, housing, medical care and the many other relevant economic and social questions belong on the human rights agenda."[34]

Shackled with debt, leaders in the developing world found little solace in the Reagan administration's emphasis on the interrelated freedoms of democracy and the market. Indeed, despite gaining formal political representation, the standard of living for millions of Latin Americans during the "lost decade" of the 1980s declined significantly, resulting in labor unrest and rising disenchantment with democracy. As Mexican politician and academic Jorge G. Castañeda writes:

> In 1980, 136 million Latin Americans, or 41 percent of the continent's population, lived in poverty; by 1986 the figure had grown to 170 million individuals, or 43 percent; toward the end of the decade it was estimated at the horrifying figure of anywhere between 203 and 270 million. Unemployment and underemployment had reached 80 million, representing 44 percent of the labor force. The real minimum wage for the entire region fell 13 percent between 1980 and 1987, but this aggregate figure masks profound differences between countries. In Mexico, Brazil, and Chile, the drop was 43 percent. The decline in median real wages was almost as drastic: 23 percent in Mexico, in Uruguay nearly 30 percent, Peru 62 percent by 1991.[35]

Amid the crisis, Latin American democrats, economists, and human rights activists recognized that the Reagan administration's support for neoliberal economic reforms significantly impeded the expansion of Latin American policies aimed at promoting social welfare and economic justice. In a 1988 meeting among South American heads of state, for example, there was general agreement that meeting debt servicing demands was deepening inequality, accelerating instability, and eroding popular support for democracy. Having paid $160 billion over the previous six years to service a $420 billion foreign debt, none of the leaders mentioned the US role in supporting democracy.[36] Reflecting on the paltry US assistance to fledgling civilian governments in Latin America, the political scientist Thomas Carothers dubbed the Reagan administration's approach, "democracy by applause."[37] Some human rights advocates went a step further. "Mass deprivation of economic justice in some three-quarters of the nations of the world creates international tension and undercuts stability. The long-term interests of the developed states require redress of the economic deprivation of the poor states," Shestack maintained in 1989. "The Reagan Administration's failure to address economic and social rights either in its own or multilateral initiatives was a serious deficiency in its human rights record."[38]

The evolution of US policy toward Chilean dictator Augusto Pinochet underscored both the rising significance and the narrow framing of human rights and democracy promotion in US foreign policy during the 1980s. By the late 1970s, US-Chilean relations had reached their nadir, a result of the visibility of the Pinochet dictatorship's abuses and the sustained efforts of human rights advocates, the Carter administration's emphasis on human rights, and congressional outrage at the brazen 1976 assassination in Washington, DC, of former Chilean ambassador Orlando Letelier and his colleague Ronni Moffitt—a US citizen—by the Chilean secret police.[39] The Reagan administration had entered office determined to reset relations with Pinochet. After a series of high-level US officials had made goodwill trips to Santiago, including UN ambassador Jeane J. Kirkpatrick, by late summer 1981 "the legacy of suspicion about U.S. intentions and doubt about U.S. leadership," the US Embassy reported, "has largely been swept away."[40]

But by mid-decade, the Reagan administration was moving in fits and starts toward a policy of sustained pressure on Pinochet to oversee a democratic transition. The most important impetus for the shift was rising popular opposition in Chile to the military dictatorship. In the aftermath of the 1973 military coup, with guidance from free market advocates at the University of Chicago—known as the "Chicago Boys"—Pinochet turned Chile into a laboratory for neoliberal economics, privatizing the banking sector, deregulating finance, selling off hundreds of state-owned firms, liberalizing investment rules to favor multinationals, eviscerating labor laws, and privatizing health care and the public pension fund.[41] A wrenching economic crisis in 1982, however, revealed the risks of wholesale deregulation, privatization, and liberalization. As the Chilean banking industry teetered on the brink of collapse and the country edged toward defaulting on its foreign debt, thousands slipped into the ranks of the extreme poor. Popular protest against the dictatorship surged. In response, Pinochet unleashed the military, quashing massive demonstrations in 1983 and 1984 and intermittently imposing a state of siege. Yet government brutality added to Chilean instability by sparking a wave of retaliatory left-wing violence.[42]

The Reagan administration viewed deepening political polarization in Chile with rising concern. As domestic unrest intensified, the overarching US fear was that the dictatorship's repression would push moderate Chileans into the arms of the radical Left. "If Pinochet remains intransigent and blocks the needed transition, the country will become increasingly polarized," Shultz informed Reagan in September 1985. "This policy will only benefit the Communists. We will continue to seek cooperation, dialogue and compromise, but there is a growing tension between our national interest in an orderly and peaceful process and Pinochet's apparent desire to hang on indefinitely."[43] Correspondingly, the wave of democracy sweeping the region left Pinochet— with his goose-stepping soldiers in Nazi-style helmets—increasingly isolated.[44] Along with other dictatorships in the region, Chile was "the odd man out" in an increasingly democratic hemisphere, Shultz publicly warned in March 1986, although he hastened to add that "the Cuba-Nicaragua pattern, being totalitarian in its nature, is by far the worst of this group."[45]

Significantly, the rising US emphasis on Chilean democratization was *not* a repudiation of Pinochet's overthrow of Salvador Allende or the dictatorship's far-reaching neoliberal economic policies. To the contrary, Shultz, who had been closely connected to the Chicago Boys' economic policy prescriptions for Chile as a professor at the University of Chicago Business School, considered Chile's economic program "outstanding." Despite a drop in copper prices, the Chilean government had "managed to put into effect the best economic policies you can find anywhere," Shultz asserted at an NSC meeting in November 1986. Reagan agreed. Pinochet had "saved his country" from communism, the president maintained, adding a moment later that it was "a great achievement." Reluctant to break with the Chilean dictator, Reagan wondered "if there was some way we could appear as not being opposed to him, to indicate that we respect what he has accomplished, yet say we want to help Chile for Chile's sake." When the president floated the idea of inviting Pinochet for a state visit, the secretary of state was quick to object. "No way," Shultz responded. "This man has blood all over his hands. He has done monstrous things." But a few minutes later, both men were again praising Pinochet's economic policies, which Reagan described as "amazing." Shultz concurred. "They stand on Adam Smith," he concluded approvingly. "They inherited an economy guided by the idea of protection of industry, import substitution, high tariffs. They brought those tariffs right down. They said if you can't compete, try something else."[46]

Despite top Reagan officials' tacit approval of Pinochet's overthrow of the democratically elected Allende administration and the dictatorship's neoliberal economic policies, they feared that domestic unrest in the face of government repression would destabilize the South American nation. As the US democracy promotion initiative gathered momentum in Reagan's second term in office and Shultz increasingly wrestled the upper hand from administration hard-liners, supporting a democratic transition in Chile—while safeguarding US economic interests—gained traction as a US policy priority. Focusing on the clause in the 1980 Chilean constitution mandating a national plebiscite in 1988 to determine whether Pinochet would remain in power for an additional eight years, the State Department's stated policy by late 1986 was to "bring pressure on Pinochet to cooperate in a peaceful democratic transition and to strengthen the democratic center as an alternative, while weakening the Communists."[47]

The policy translated into significant—if halting—steps to demonstrate US opposition to Chilean government repression and support for a return to democracy. Shultz charged the new ambassador to Chile, Harry G. Barnes Jr., with a clear mandate to build bridges with the Chilean moderates. As one Chilean opposition member told a US Embassy official in March 1988, Barnes "has underscored the U.S. commitment to a democratic transition and to free, fair elections while stressing that the U.S. will in no way interfere with the results of the voting for it."[48] Correspondingly, Abrams—who shifted from the Human Rights Bureau to become assistant secretary of state for inter-American affairs in 1985—utilized George Lister, a Latin America expert, to cultivate relations with moderate Chilean politicians and anti-Pinochet human rights advocates in Washington.[49]

US efforts to promote a democratic transition in Chile intensified in late 1987. The United States sent clear signals of support for a democratic transition at the United Nations and the World Bank and removed Chile from preferential trade programs.[50] The Reagan administration also oversaw a rapid increase in US democracy assistance earmarked for Chile. In fiscal year 1987, the NED disbursed more than half a million dollars in Chile to fund voter education campaigns, the publication of books and pamphlets, educational programs run by trade unions, and workshops on polling and political campaigning strategies.[51] The following year, underscoring the bipartisan appeal of US democracy promotion, senator Tom Harkin successfully passed legislation providing an addition $1 million to the NED for Chile—in addition to the regular appropriation of $600,000—for voter registration and civic education programs in the months leading up to the October plebiscite.[52] USAID also provided $1.285 million to a nonpartisan Chilean organization for voter registration.[53] While maintaining the facade of political neutrality, US funding was clearly aimed at supporting the coalition of opposition parties campaigning for a "no" vote against a continuation of the dictatorship. As one

USAID official maintained, "We've helped register millions of voters and we consider each one of those a vote against Pinochet."[54]

With polls showing the "no" vote in the lead, in the final days leading up to the October 5 plebiscite intelligence reports indicated that the dictatorship would refuse to accept a victory for the "NO" campaign. US officials quickly responded by reiterating support for free and fair voting. "A message went directly to Pinochet," Abrams later wrote. "We sent instructions to the CIA station chief to deliver an extremely tough message to his intelligence contacts at the top levels of the regime. Ranking U.S. military officers said the same thing to top Chilean generals. We asked the British, who had excellent ties with the Chilean military, to do the same, and they energetically did."[55] In the end, Chileans voted decisively against a continuation of the dictatorship. Unable to suppress his defeat—44 percent to 53 percent of the votes—Pinochet reluctantly stepped down, paving the way for national elections the following year.

The victory of the "no" vote in the Chilean plebiscite was heralded in the United States as a milestone for the democracy promotion agenda. Most US policymakers' accounts—like subsequent scholarly discussions—recognized that although the United States played an important part in Chile's return to democracy, it was a secondary role in a process that was thoroughly Chilean.[56] Nonetheless, US officials perceived the US role in the plebiscite as a defining success. The United States, Barnes cabled the State Department, "emerged from the plebiscite as a champion of democracy."[57] In Washington, top Reagan officials agreed, framing the plebiscite as a referendum on democracy, not Pinochet's neoliberal reforms. "The economic policies of free and open markets developed by the 'Chicago Boys' had brought to Chile the healthiest economy in Latin America," Shultz wrote approvingly in his memoirs. "This experience with freedom in the marketplace fanned the desire for freedom in the political arena."[58]

More broadly, as the Reagan administration neared the end of its term in office, top officials lauded the signal role the United States had played over the course of the decade in democratization abroad. The Reagan administration, Colin Powell asserted, "championed that democratic trend and that recognition of the power of economic freedom."[59] Abrams sounded a similar theme. "In 1980, no one predicted that President Reagan's Latin policy would be an extraordinary success. Nor did anyone predict that his Administration would come to be a more effective advocate and supporter of democracy in the region than any of its predecessors," Abrams wrote in a *New York Times* op-ed shortly before the plebiscite. "Yet the key ingredients were there: strong belief in individual freedom in all parts of life, and a willingness to use America's influence in this region as throughout the world." As a result, Abrams expansively concluded, "those ingredients have combined to associate our country with the greatest expansion of democracy in Latin history."[60]

If the United States' policy toward Chile revealed both the rising significance of democracy promotion as a US policy priority in the 1980s and the Reagan administration's narrow framing of both democracy and human rights, the denouement in US-Nicaraguan Cold War relations illuminated an increasingly sophisticated relationship between US democracy promotion and interventionism. Facing fallout from the Iran-Contra scandal and unable to head off regional support for the peace plan proposed by Costa Rican president Oscar Arias, the Reagan administration's efforts to drum up congressional support in its final years in office for continued US military assistance to the Contras were largely stillborn. But George H. W. Bush's victory in the 1988 presidential election heralded a new chapter in the US intervention against the Sandinistas. With the 1990 Nicaraguan presidential election looming on the horizon, the Bush administration reset relations with the Congress and, taking a lesson from the US role in the Chilean plebiscite, dramatically increased US democracy assistance to the Nicaraguan opposition.

In the aftermath of Iran-Contra, top Reagan officials kept up a steady drumbeat of criticism directed toward Managua and remained steadfast in its commitment to the Contras. But despite Reagan officials' saber rattling, in the late 1980s Americans had little appetite for supporting the Contras. Throughout the decade, a slim majority of the public had opposed US aid to the Contras; although polls narrowed following Oliver North's bravura performance on Capitol Hill during the Iran-Contra hearings, by the spring of 1988 a *Washington Post–ABC News* poll found that a majority of Americans opposed Contra aid by a margin of 55 percent to 40 percent.[61]

Indeed, despite the Reagan administration's efforts to cast the Contras as noble freedom fighters, many Americans perceived Contras and Sandinistas alike in equally negative terms. The words "Central America" brought to mind "poverty, uneducated people, and conflict," Democratic Party pollster Stanley Greenberg reported after completing a focus group research project in September 1987. "I just have this overwhelming feeling of negative, just 'ooh,'" one woman told Greenberg. "Sort of like living here at the ghetto in New York or Chicago—all the bad things that happen." Asked to describe a hypothetical Contra or Sandinista, focus group participants depicted them in identically negative terms: "'unshaven,' 'scruffy, bearded'; he was 'sweaty,' 'dirty,' 'dark dirty'; he was 'Spanish-looking, Mexican type clothing, uncultivated, sandals,' 'dark complexion'; he looked like 'Pancho Villa,' a 'bandoleer of ammo,' 'wearing fatigues,' 'militaristic,' 'trigger-happy, scared.'" The only difference, one individual asserted, was that the Contra "is more of a failure."[62] Such responses, replete with inaccurate stereotypes, illuminated the challenge the Reagan administration faced in securing aid to the Contras.

In Washington, public opposition, combined with the halting steps toward regional peace negotiations, influenced congressional legislators deeply divided on the issue of Contra support. In September 1987, Reagan's request for $270 million in US aid to the Contras for an eighteen-month period elicited sharp criticism from Congress members who argued that it was a blatant attempt to undermine the Arias peace plan.[63] Although the Congress approved an interim package of "humanitarian" aid, when the aid debate resurfaced in January 1988 the White House backtracked in the face of determined public opposition—scaling back its request to $36.25 million, with only $3.6 million earmarked as military aid.[64] Nonetheless, the House narrowly defeated the request the following month, leaving the Contras bereft of official US funding. With less than one year left in office, it was a signal defeat for the Reagan administration. "Throughout the region," writes the historian William M. LeoGrande, "people interpreted the House vote as the death knell for the contras."[65]

Indeed, after nearly a decade at war with the United States, the Sandinistas would outlast the Reagan administration. Yet, with as many as fifteen thousand Contras operating along both the Honduran and Costa Rican borders, the human and material cost of the Contra war was immense, accelerating serious economic problems and exacerbating political and social tensions within the embattled nation. First, the conflict strengthened the hand of Sandinista hard-liners. Nicaragua remained almost continuously in a state of emergency, leading Amnesty International to report in 1986 that the government had curbed civil rights and liberties including "freedom of expression, freedom of movement, freedom of association, habeas corpus and the rights to strike and hold public meetings and demonstrations," as well as deteriorating conditions for political prisoners.[66]

Fueling Nicaraguan disillusionment was the government's imposition of Patriotic Military Service, a national military conscription. Beginning in late 1983, all men from seventeen to twenty-four years old were required to serve two years in the regular armed forces.[67] As the war intensified, between 1980 and 1981 Nicaragua's military force increased from 15,000 to 40,000 soldiers. The combined military services and reserves reached 119,000 soldiers in 1985 and would remain at more than 10 percent of the population in the second half of the decade.[68] Yet, from its inception, thousands of Nicaraguans openly opposed the draft. Demonstrations, protest marches, and confrontations with FSLN military recruiters flared in cities and towns throughout the nation.[69] Middle-class families fled the country to protect their sons, while draft-age males from the working and peasant classes escaped to neighboring Honduras or Costa Rica or went into hiding in the local community. Although Nicaragua remained far less repressive than neighboring El Salvador or Guatemala, in the superheated atmosphere of the Contra war such developments boded poorly for the FSLN's ability to retain support at home and abroad.

Second, as the war intensified, Sandinista efforts to manage the economy sparked domestic opposition. By mid-decade, private business owners' foot-dragging and the fear of nationalizations had brought private investment to a virtual halt and some 60 percent of managers and professional workers had moved abroad since 1979.[70] For their part, small producers chafed at official government price-fixing on basic food items, which frequently forced them to sell at or below cost. Predictably, they responded by dramatically limiting production, hoarding, or risking hefty fines and even jail time by selling on the black market.[71] Since an estimated 93 percent of basic food items in Nicaragua were produced by smallholders, the result was serious shortages; by mid-decade, production of corn and beans—staples of the Nicaraguan diet— had dropped 50 percent.[72] At the same time, heavy inflation pushed consumer goods beyond the financial reach of many rural families; the price of a shirt increased 140 times between 1978 and 1984, while the official price of grain increased only seven times.[73]

Correspondingly, the FSLN's vision of a transformed system of agricultural production through state-run farms proved inefficient and contributed to rising disaffection in the countryside. Agricultural cooperatives were intended to dramatically improve the rural standard of living as well as increase crop production. From the outset, however, state-run farms were plagued by inefficient administration, capital investment shortages, mismanaged use of land and resources, labor discipline problems, inefficient mechanisms for supply and distribution, and, in particular, a lack of market incentives.[74] As a result, peasant disaffection with Sandinista agricultural policy created strong counterrevolutionary support in rural border areas and swelled the ranks of the Contra forces. "They wanted a change for the better in their lives, land, schools, clinics, good prices for their crops, but they did not accept the attack on their traditions, their way of life, and their beliefs," vice president Sergio Ramírez reflected many years later. According to Ramírez, the FSLN's refusal to redistribute land among the peasantry played a fundamental role in pushing the peasants into the arms of the counterrevolutionary forces. "Poor or not, the collective proposal clashed with their worldview."[75]

The cost of the Contra war also forced Nicaragua to turn to the Soviet bloc for aid. Between 1981 and 1989, the Soviet bloc provided Nicaragua with 140,000 metric tons of military equipment worth some $2.7 billion.[76] In May 1985, only a week after the US Congress voted against $14 million in aid to the Contras, Daniel Ortega Saavedra arrived in Moscow to meet with Soviet officials. Perceived by congressional Democrats and Republicans alike as an intentional slap in the face, Ortega's motivation in reality was economic. "The trip to Moscow basically responded to Nicaragua's vital need for oil in view of the fact that Mexico is no longer able to continue meeting the demands or forms of payments proposed by Nicaragua," a subsequent FSLN press release admitted.[77] The Soviets responded favorably, increasing their contributions from 70 percent of Nicaraguan oil needs to nearly 100 percent. The Nicaraguan economy survived, but just barely. "It is becoming a beggar economy," one foreign diplomat confided. Ortega "is begging from country to country."[78]

Ultimately the cost of the Contra war, combined with Sandinista mismanagement, brought the Nicaraguan economy to its knees. By mid-decade, 40 percent of the national budget was allocated to defense, and Nicaragua faced a punishing trade deficit of $500 million and foreign debt that accounted for more than 20 percent of GDP.[79] The relative value of Nicaraguan currency was plummeting; by 1987 inflation exceeded 1,000 percent and the córdoba dropped to 30,000 to $1 on the black market, exacerbating shortages of corn, beans, rice, eggs, potatoes, and cooking oil; meat, noted a US government report, "has become a thing of the past for virtually all lower income families."[80] "You can't survive on the salaries set by the government if you are a worker," a foreign diplomat noted. "Most people live by bartering goods on the black market or having two jobs."[81] In fact, in Managua many residents were struggling to meet basic needs by working *three* jobs.[82]

The human and material cost of the war dramatically curtailed the social and economic promises that had guided the Sandinista government in the early post-Somoza era. In 1984 alone, the Contras killed 113 teachers, kidnapped 187 others, and destroyed 19 schools, forcing the Sandinista government to close 840 adult-education collectives and 354 schools in war zones, while the financial crisis led government officials to pare down education programs across the country.[83] By the end of the decade, the number of teachers killed by Contras had risen to 300, but it was low wages that forced a quarter of all teachers to leave their classrooms; 60 percent of those who remained had no formal training.[84] Similarly, in the face of Contra attacks and strained state finances, dozens of health centers were destroyed or shuttered. The results were predictable: infectious diseases such as malaria increased and rising numbers of children died of preventable illnesses.[85]

The unfulfilled promises of the revolution were painfully evident in Managua. Over the course of the 1980s, the city staggered under an influx of tens of thousands of migrants fleeing war zones or grinding poverty. By the end of the decade, half the houses were estimated to be overcrowded and almost 10 percent of the city's 1.15 million inhabitants were squatting in makeshift shantytowns that had sprouted across the capital, entirely lacking city services except what could be pirated by enterprising residents. Even established neighborhoods experienced the strain of inadequate government resources. Managua's waste disposal system, for example, was so overwhelmed that less than half of the garbage was regularly collected—leaving the equivalent of two football fields waist-deep in trash rotting in the city's streets every week.[86]

If the challenges of daily life in Managua revealed the hard road Nicaraguans had traveled from the heady days of the early post-Somoza triumph, the Sandinista government's reluctant decision to impose harsh austerity measures effectively ended the FSLN's bid to serve as a model of social justice. With the economy collapsing under the weight of hyperinflation and unsustainable deficit spending, in February 1988 the FSLN fired eight thousand government workers, cut government spending by 10 percent, and introduced market reforms to replace the system of subsidies. A second round of austerity measures was introduced in June. "There was a consensus that we didn't have any alternative to the adjustment," recalled Alejandro Martínez Cuenca, then serving in the Ministry of Planning. Critics charged that the reforms were a homegrown neoliberalism—an austerity program along the lines of the harsh prescriptions of the International Monetary Fund but without the benefits of any external assistance. But the government's options were limited. "It wasn't a program we designed in order to impose our economic doctrine; instead, it was a practical response to unsustainable macroeconomic imbalances, an economic blockade, and a lack of outside resources."[87]

Then, in October 1988, Hurricane Joan swept across the southern Caribbean and hit Nicaragua with an incredible ferocity. In addition to killing more than one hundred people and leaving one-tenth of the population homeless, the storm washed away the FSLN's efforts to stabilize the economy. Prices doubled monthly between November 1988 and January 1989, creating an annual inflation for 1988 of 36,000 percent. The government responded in February with another brutal round of austerity measures, cutting state spending by 44 percent and firing thirty-five thousand civil servants. Correspondingly, in what was dubbed "Nicastroika," a raft of state-owned properties were sold to the private sector and subsidies for state-owned firms were eliminated.[88]

The austerity measures worked: inflation rates had dropped to the single digits by summer 1989 and exports increased. But the cost was extraordinarily high. In 1988, the government admitted that the average worker's wage covered less than half the minimum "market basket" necessary for a family; other studies estimated that it covered as little as 7 percent. By all counts, it was not enough—Nicaraguans were drinking half as much milk, for example, as they had in 1980. By 1990, an incredible 80 percent of Nicaraguans were living in poverty.[89] For many Nicaraguans struggling to survive, the lesson was clear. "We fought a revolution, and we struggled to build a society that would be free to progress, and where it would all go to the workers and peasants. We are not progressing, we are regressing. And poor people are poorer today than they were before," one working-class Sandinista supporter told the anthropologist Roger N. Lancaster. "Why? I suppose it's obvious: because the Sandinistas have crossed the United States. And now we know what the United States can do to a country without even sending in troops. You ask me what's the solution? We have to make peace with the United States. There's no other way that I can see."[90]

FSLN officials concurred. In early 1988, the Sandinistas agreed to most of the Contras' demands in an agreement signed at the border town of Sapoá, including a general amnesty for all Contras and former members of Anastasio Somoza Debayle's National Guard. The following February, the FSLN offered sweeping concessions to opposition political parties, agreed to advance the date of national elections from November to February 1990, and invited international observers to scrutinize the election.[91] Such efforts reflected a clear-eyed strategy to bring US aggression to a halt. As Ramírez recalled, "We saw the elections as the best way to achieve a stable situation that would finally allow us to start rebuilding the country. We thought that the signs of discontent, the increasing resistance to military service and the economic disaster, were temporary situations that would be remedied, specifically, by the end of the war."[92]

As war-torn and impoverished Nicaragua stumbled toward the ten-year anniversary of the overthrow of the Somoza dictatorship, in Washington at the outset of 1989 the mood was buoyant. With widespread democratization proceeding apace in Latin America, along with elections in the Philippines, progress in South Korea, and liberalization trends in Eastern Europe, US policymakers increasingly perceived, in the words of the political sociologist Larry J. Diamond, "a kind of global Zeitgeist for democracy."[93] Carl Gershman took a similar view. "Today we live during a period of democratic optimism," the NED president declared in an address at Georgetown University in December 1988. The process of democratization, Gershman averred, "seems inexorable," especially in the developing world, "where the disillusionment with revolutionary movements and statist systems has given democracy a new attractiveness." In an age of global democratic ferment, "it should be possible to acknowledge and reaffirm the interrelationship between democracy and human rights, Gershman confidently concluded. "It should also be possible to embrace a new understanding of the way in which efforts to advance democracy and to protect human rights reinforce and strengthen each other."[94]

The incoming Bush administration echoed the optimism inside the Washington Beltway around global democratization. "Great nations of the world are moving toward democracy through the door to freedom," Bush declared in his January 1989 inaugural address. "Men and women of the world move toward free markets through the door to prosperity. The people of the world agitate for free expression and free thought through the door to the moral and intellectual satisfactions that only liberty allows." As onlookers enjoyed one of the warmest inaugural days on record, Bush continued, "We know what works: Freedom works. We know what's right: Freedom is right. We know how to secure a more just and prosperous life for man on Earth: through free markets, free speech, free elections, and the exercise of free will unhampered by the state."[95] Significantly, the forty-first president's emphasis on democracy was more than mere rhetorical boilerplate. At Bush's first cabinet meeting, secretary of state James A. Baker III identified the "democratic revolution," particularly in Latin America, at the top of a list of significant developments occurring in the world, followed, not surprisingly, by the spread of the free-enterprise system abroad.[96]

The emphasis on democracy and the free market served as the cornerstone for the Bush administration's human rights policy. Underscoring the process of institutionalization that had occurred over the course of the decade, the Bush administration from the outset identified human rights promotion as a core US foreign policy objective. Human rights, Baker asserted during his confirmation hearings on Capitol Hill, "is one of the very basic foundations of our foreign policy, and for that matter, our national security policy." Playing to the issue's bipartisan appeal, Baker added, "I don't think that we should distinguish in our human-rights standards in applications between situations where human rights are violated on the left or situations where human rights are violated on the right. I think our standards ought to be straight and we ought to play it down the middle." Reflecting on the shift since Alexander M. Haig Jr.'s memorable 1981 assertion that countering terrorism would take precedence over promoting human rights, Aryeh Neier, of Human Rights Watch, noted, "Today, it is unthinkable that . . . Baker would propose replacing a concern for human rights with a concern for any other cause."[97]

A low-profile operator and a close friend to the president, Baker moved into the seventh floor of the State Department with a record of hard work and a pragmatic approach to policy issues. "I'm more interested in the game than in philosophy," he once confided. After running a tight ship as White House chief of staff in Reagan's first administration, the Houston native—known for wearing business suits and cowboy boots—served as secretary of the Treasury for three and a half years, then turned his attention to running Bush's 1988 presidential campaign. In the process he established a reputation as an expert tactician. "'Genius' is too strong a word," parsed the *New Yorker*, "but even by Washington's exacting standards Baker's political gift is seen on all sides as remarkable."[98]

Surveying the political landscape in Washington, the new administration recognized the imperative of establishing a working relationship with Congress. Both Bush and Baker had experienced firsthand the fierce battles over the direction of US foreign policy between liberal internationalists on Capitol Hill and the Reagan White House. "As we discussed foreign policy plans during the transition," Baker recalled in his memoirs, "the President made it clear that he wanted to move away from the politics of confrontation between the legislative and executive branches that had characterized much of the diplomatic debate in the previous eight years."[99] Baker wholeheartedly agreed. "I think two main elements are necessary for the success of your foreign policy: (1) bipartisanship, and (2) continued American leadership," he told Bush in a January 23 cabinet meeting.[100]

But in the effort to secure congressional support, the US intervention in Central America loomed ominously. Central America was the "one huge stumbling block" on the path to bipartisanship, Baker recalled. Underscoring the signal importance of the region in shaping US foreign policy in the late Cold War, Baker viscerally described Central America as a "bleeding sore"; Nicaragua, he asserted, was "our country's Vietnam of the 1980s."[101]

Meetings with members of Congress reinforced the Bush team's perception that US policy toward Nicaragua was the principle roadblock to establishing solid executive-legislative relations. The debate over Contra aid "was like a food fight that had gone on for years," Baker recalled. "It had degenerated into raw confrontation, with no quarter given or asked."[102] Indeed, over the course of Reagan's two terms in office, the battle lines between Contra supporters and opponents had solidified. Between 1983 and 1988, more than two-thirds of the members in the House of Representatives had perfect voting records for or against Contra aid. Less than 30 percent had changed sides even once, leaving only a handful willing to consider voting across party lines.[103] Although Baker supported the Contras, the evidence was clear: Central America "was first and foremost a domestic political issue," he recalled. "Any hopes for a diplomatic solution, much less achieving a bipartisan foreign policy, were doomed unless Central America was removed from its domestic political context."[104] Top Bush officials concurred. The Reagan administration "had made a serious mistake in this constant confrontation with the Congress," recalled national security adviser Brent Scowcroft. "It was not producing results, it was embittering everything, and nothing was getting done." Like Baker, Scowcroft recommended breaking with Reagan's adversarial approach. "I thought we ought to change that. I thought we ought to go up and try to co-op the Congress."[105]

With support from the president, Baker began a sustained effort to shift the terms of the debate over US policy toward Nicaragua from Contra aid to democracy promotion. Focusing on the Sandinista government's pledge in the Esquipulas agreement to hold national elections in February 1990, Baker proposed making a free and fair election sine qua non for a cessation of US hostility toward Managua. The United States would provide humanitarian aid to the Contras, maintaining them as a fighting force to deter Sandinista backsliding. Correspondingly, the United States would work to incentivize the Sandinistas to follow through on the democratic reforms mandated by Esquipulas—and let the Nicaraguan people decide the fate of their nation at the ballot box. The administration's position was a significant departure from the Reagan administration's dismissal of the 1984 Nicaraguan election as a "sham" and marked a savvy recognition of the bipartisan support for democracy promotion on Capitol Hill. "I believed the American people would support a policy that refocused on the debate on democratic principles," Baker later wrote. "In simple terms, the Democrats couldn't very well oppose a policy that endorsed elections—and neither could the most ardent contra supporters."[106] In a further effort to extend the olive branch to congressional Democrats, the Bush administration nominated Bernard Aronson—an unusual liberal Democrat who supported Contra aid—to succeed Abrams as assistant secretary of state for inter-American affairs.[107]

Baker waded into the discussions with members of Congress as if he were conducting diplomatic negotiations with a foreign power. Beginning in early March, the secretary of state touched off what would develop into more than forty hours of talks with House members over the course of more than three weeks. To skeptical Republicans, Baker emphasized his own conservative credentials. "I support military aid to the contras, too," he told archconservative senator Jessie Helms (R-NC). "There's just one problem. You can't get the votes for it and I can't get the votes for it. Even Ronald Reagan couldn't get the votes for it. But we *can* get the votes for this."[108] Similarly, in meetings with Democrats, Baker was blunt. "Look, I'd actually prefer military aid to the contras," he told senator Chris Dodd (D-CT). "But we realize that's not in the cards, so I'm not even going to ask for it. This is not a scheme or a trick. We want to try diplomacy, but it won't work without the leverage of a unified approach."[109] To members of both parties, Baker emphasized bipartisanship. "We have a chance to heal the bitterest foreign policy fight of the last 10 years," he told George J. Mitchell (D-MN). "What the President and I are trying to do is what Democrats in Congress called on the United States to do when they voted down military aid: support the Central American peace process."[110]

After considerable wrangling, Baker's plan bore fruit. At a White House ceremony on March 24, Bush signed into law $50 million in nonmilitary aid to the Contras—$4.5 million per month until the 1990 election—in exchange for a tacit agreement that the White House would support a democratic transition rather than a Contra-led regime change.[111] Underscoring the administration's willingness to forge a bipartisan policy, the White House acceded to congressional Democrats' demand to make Contra funding contingent on a review at the end of 1989, which, one reporter put it, seemed "to amount to a veto authority over the new approach on Nicaragua." But the administration played down the apparent infringement on executive power. "This is a unique circumstance," one Bush official asserted. "The lack of congressional support has caused the policy to fail. The only way to put together a successful policy was to agree with the Hill. It doesn't mean we're going to negotiate on everything."[112]

If the Bush administration's bipartisan accord on Central America was widely understood as a departure from the interventionism of the Reagan era, US policy in the months leading up to the 1990 Nicaraguan elections nonetheless illuminated the power of democracy promotion as a mechanism to advance US interests abroad. From the outset, the Bush administration used US leverage to keep the pressure on the Nicaraguan economy. The White House reportedly pressured the World Bank and the Inter-American Development bank not to join a June 1989 meeting in Stockholm to discuss aid to Nicaragua and pressed Western European nations to tie economic support to democratization.[113]

Correspondingly, the Bush administration worked to convince the Soviet Union to curb Soviet bloc and Cuban military and economic assistance to Nicaragua in the months leading up to the election. As the Bush team entered the White House, Soviet premier Mikhail Gorbachev struggled to advance an expanding reform agenda. "I lead a strange country. I am trying to take my people in a direction they do not understand and many do not want to go," Gorbachev candidly confided to Henry Kissinger in a private meeting in mid-January 1989. "When I became General Secretary I thought that by now perestroika would be completed. Instead the economic reform has only just begun." In order to reform the Soviet system, Gorbachev concluded pointedly, "I need a long period of peace."[114]

Bush officials recognized that Gorbachev's domestic travails presented an opportunity to make headway on Central America. Yet they also viewed Gorbachev's "new thinking" with skepticism in light of continued Soviet support of client states in the developing world. "Interestingly enough, one of the places that led to a sense of caution on my part, and on the President's part, about whether the Cold War was over was our discussion with the Soviet Union about places like Central America," recalled Scowcroft. "There, we detected absolutely no change from the Cold War." With the exception of winding down the Soviet intervention in Afghanistan, Scowcroft asserted, "out in the periphery, out where the rubber was meeting the road . . . the Soviet Union was doing the same old thing."[115] Indeed, between March 1988 and early 1989, Nicaragua had received $400 million worth of military assistance from the Soviets—some fifteen thousand metric tons of vehicles, small arms, ammunition, and spare parts.[116] Central America, Scowcroft concluded, "became a kind of barometer of how much the Soviets really seemed to be acting on their fine words."[117]

Accordingly, in the spring of 1989 the Bush administration viewed curtailing Soviet assistance to Nicaragua as both critical to securing regional peace and as a test case for Gorbachev to follow through on his conciliatory rhetoric.[118] "Together we must send a clear message to others outside this hemisphere: This is not a dumping ground for their arms or their failed ideologies," Bush told a group of Latin America experts in late March at the Carter Presidential Center in Atlanta. "We are looking for signs of new thinking. The Soviet Union now has an opportunity to demonstrate it in Central America."[119] Gorbachev complied, assuring Bush in an exchange of letters that the USSR would no longer supply weapons to the Sandinistas, a message he reiterated to Baker in a subsequent meeting in Moscow.[120]

Nonetheless, Nicaragua remained a defining issue in US–Soviet relations. According to the president's briefing book for Bush's summit meeting with Gorbachev off the Malta coast in December 1989, the "top U.S. issue is Central America."[121] The summit, held over the course of three stormy days less than a month after the fall of the Berlin Wall, is rightly remembered as heralding the peaceful end to the Cold War's superpower confrontation. The Soviet Union, Gorbachev memorably declared, would become "part and parcel of the world economic system."[122] Yet, regarding US policy toward the Sandinistas, Bush and Gorbachev butted heads. "We see how you perceive the situation in Latin America. But it is not quite clear to us what you want from Nicaragua," Gorbachev asserted. "There is political pluralism in that country, and there are more parties there than in the United States. And the Sandinistas—what kind of Marxists are they?! This is laughable." The roots of the problem, the Soviet premier continued, "are economic and social issues. Why does the U.S. fail to see them?" If the United States was concerned about political power in the Central American nation, Gorbachev advised, the 1990 elections would be the solution. "Let the United Nations monitor them," he concluded. "Frankly speaking, it is not our business. Let this process go where it will."[123]

If Gorbachev was willing to spar with Bush over Nicaragua, the Soviets nonetheless fell in line with US policy. In the lead-up to the 1990 election, Soviet military assistance to Nicaragua ground to a halt. Economic aid, too, was slashed. In the interest of peace, the Soviet Union would "renounce power tactics and persistently seek a balance of interests," foreign minister Eduard Shevardnadze told a Spanish reporter shortly after Malta. In Central America, he continued, "it is impossible to overestimate . . . the adherence of Nicaraguan leaders to the idea of free, honest elections under international control."[124] Behind closed doors, the Kremlin took a realistic approach. "Democratization in Nicaragua is one of the main conditions for the continuation of the process of peaceful settlement of the Central American conflict, which has introduced complicating elements into Soviet-American relations," noted a protocol approved by the Communist Party Central Committee shortly before Nicaraguans went to the polls. Underscoring the dramatic shift in Soviet foreign policy over the previous decade, the protocol advocated "ever more pragmatic, de-ideologized" relations with Nicaragua.[125]

As Western European and Soviet bloc aid to Nicaragua dwindled, the Bush administration's maintenance of US economic pressure on Nicaragua in the lead-up to the election served as an unmistakable reminder to Nicaraguan voters of US opposition to the incumbent regime. Only a week after the bipartisan accord, Bush extended trade sanctions on the Sandinista government on the grounds that "the actions and policies of the government of Nicaragua continue to pose an unusual and extraordinary threat to the national security and foreign policy of the United States."[126] The message was clear: as a senior Bush administration official warned shortly before election day, "If they want 30,000% inflation, they can do that." But, the official continued, "if I were sitting down there in their shoes, I'd want those economic sanctions off; I wouldn't want them tightened. And there are some things that we can do to tighten them."[127] Secretary of State Baker was equally candid. "We have the Sandinistas in an economic chokehold," he told members of Congress in September 1989.[128]

Corresponding with US economic pressure on Managua, the Bush administration weaponized the US democracy promotion infrastructure against the Sandinistas. This marked a significant divergence from the Reagan administration's policy in the lead-up to 1984 Nicaraguan election. Whereas the Reagan administration had dismissed the balloting as a "sham" and, in an attempt to deny the election legitimacy, had reportedly encouraged the US-backed candidate Arturo Cruz to withdraw from the race, the Bush administration in anticipation of the 1990 election set out to marshal US resources to secure a regime change. In mid-1989, the United States played a key role in bringing together fourteen Nicaraguan mini-parties into a political coalition to challenge the FSLN at the ballot box. With parties spanning the political spectrum from the far Right to the far Left, the Unión Nacional Opositora (National Opposition Union, [UNO]) coalition was held together by little more than a shared aim of unseating the FSLN and the prospect of US funding. From the outset, US support for UNO presidential candidate Violeta Barrios de Chamorro was unmistakable. The widow of Pedro Joaquín Chamorro, whose assassination in early 1978 had galvanized opponents of the Somoza dictatorship, Violeta Chamorro had briefly served on the five-member Junta for National Reconstruction after the 1979 revolutionary triumph. In 1980, however, Chamorro resigned from the junta and spent the remainder of the decade as one of the most outspoken opponents of the FSLN, using the opposition newspaper *La Prensa*—which was heavily censored by the government—as a sounding board for criticizing the Sandinistas. After Chamorro was selected as the UNO presidential candidate, she was quickly invited to the White House for a photo op with Bush, who pointedly promised to "assist in Nicaragua's reconstruction," if UNO won the election, including ending the US trade embargo.[129]

Correspondingly, the Bush administration set out to convince congressional legislators to allocate funds for UNO's election campaign. After dropping the possibility of covert aid to UNO in the face of resistance from Democrats on Capitol Hill, the Bush administration turned to overt assistance channeled through the National Endowment for Democracy. It was a calculated decision. By focusing on the need to strengthen the procedural aspects of the Nicaraguan electoral process, the White House articulated US policy toward Nicaragua in politically neutral terms that lowered the volume on anti-Sandinista rhetoric, sidestepped the Contras, and embedded support for UNO in the context of US democracy promotion activities over the previous decade. "We must now give NED the funds to undertake another, immediate infusion of support for the democratic process—including election monitoring, voter registration, get-out-the-vote efforts, communication support and building party infrastructures—all of which is consistent with what the NED has previously done in Chile, Poland, Panama, the Philippines and other countries," Secretary Baker wrote to Speaker of the House Thomas S. Foley (D-WA). "These funds would not be used for political campaigning."[130] Seeking to capitalize on the bipartisan appeal of shepherding democratic transitions abroad, Baker concluded, "This is a rare chance for us to support democratization in a totalitarian society."[131]

Such statements bore little connection to reality. On the one hand, Nicaragua was hardly totalitarian; the FSLN victory in the 1984 election had been heavily scrutinized by international observers and was generally considered the most free and fair in Nicaragua's history. On the other hand, the administration's antipathy toward the Sandinistas was thinly veiled. "All of us would like to continue lethal contra aid," Baker told a group of Republican senators in October 1989. "At this time, however, we don't have the bipartisan consensus we need for a viable, long term program. Our fight—Nicaragua's fight—is today through the ballot box."[132] Where military aid to the Contras had failed, in other words, political aid—ostensibly neutral but ultimately benefiting UNO—would serve US interests.

Moreover, US policy blurred the lines between covert and overt funding. The CIA was already reportedly providing $10 million to $12 million annually in political aid to Nicaraguan civic opposition groups. In the lead-up to the 1990 election, Langley allocated an additional $6 million to assist UNO through training programs and anti-Sandinista print media and radio broadcasts—with agents running operations in Costa Rica to sidestep the White House promise to Congress not to provide covert aid to opposition groups in Nicaragua.[133]

Nonetheless, the Bush administration's emphasis on democracy promotion in Nicaragua won support on Capitol Hill. In addition to a $3.9 million appropriation to the NED earmarked for Nicaragua in fiscal year 1989, in October 1989 the Congress legislated a special NED allocation of $7.7 million for fiscal year 1990. It was a dramatic increase compared to the $1.9 million that the NED had received in total for Nicaragua programs over the previous four years.[134] At the White House signing ceremony, Bush reiterated the administration's embrace of the democracy initiative. "This legislation represents another step forward in our efforts to promote democracy in countries that have been deprived of political and economic freedom," the president declared. "Around the world, the tide of democracy is advancing, as more and more authoritarian and totalitarian regimes realize that human progress is inseparable from principles of liberty."[135]

Like the Bush administration, the NED claimed political neutrality. The organization's charter prohibited direct financial support of candidates for public office; rather than explicitly supporting UNO, the 1990 special allocation was tailored to "promote the long-term development of political parties in Nicaragua and to provide civic and voter education aimed at encouraging participation and instilling confidence in the electoral process."[136] But NED officials did little to hide their views. In the second half of the 1980s, NED funds had served as a lifeline for *La Prensa* and NED director Carl Gershman had established strong ties with Violeta Chamorro.[137] In May 1989, the NED director warmly invited Chamorro to a democratic conference in Washington, DC, themed the "Democratic Revolution" and invited her to address members of the House of Representatives in a luncheon session. "Your selfless devotion to democratic values and your courage, generosity, humility and indomitable will embody the spirit of the Nicaragua people and the finest hopes for your country," he enthused in a letter to Chamorro in early April 1989.[138] The 1990 election, Gershman publicly declared, was "not only an election, but also a plebiscite on 10 years of Sandinista rule."[139] Similarly, shortly before Nicaraguans went to the polls, an NED press release elided the decadelong US effort to destabilize the Sandinista government; the election, the organization declared, was "an historic opportunity to break Nicaragua's cycle of repression, violence and economic decline and open the way toward a new period of democracy and development."[140]

As the Bush administration's use of the NED shifted the focus in Washington to political aid, Contra forces continued to operate inside Nicaraguan territory. During negotiations with Congress, Baker had repeatedly emphasized the Bush administration's willingness to move beyond Reagan's die-hard support for the Contras. "We are not interested in supporting people who are engaged in cross-border raids, laying of anti-personnel mines and that sort of thing," Baker told the House Appropriations Committee.[141] Moreover, in the effort to secure NED funding, the White House struck a conciliatory tone. "If it's a fair election, I guess we'd have to deal with them," Baker told members of Congress in September.[142]

In Nicaragua, however, Contra operations continued. According to the government, in nineteen months of cease-fire, Contras had killed 736 soldiers and civilians and wounded 1,150 others.[143] The Department of Defense admitted in late 1989 that roughly four thousand Contras were operating inside Nicaragua and that the United States was supplying them with $150,000–$200,000 a month in cash.[144] In October, a bus in northern Nicaragua hit a US-made Claymore land mine set by Contra forces, killing eighteen reservists.[145] When the FSLN responded by suspending the cease-fire, the Bush administration successfully framed the resumption of hostilities as "a pretext to end the electoral process, which has broad international support and legitimacy," as a State Department official told reporters.[146] A few days later, when Bush and Ortega both attended a diplomatic gathering in Costa Rica, Bush derided the Nicaraguan president as an "animal at a garden party" and dismissively told reporters, "We didn't come here to have a contretemps with this little man showing up in his military uniform at a democracy meeting."[147] With the spotlight in Washington fixed on the 1990 elections, such criticism succeeded in obscuring the aggression of the US-backed Contras; indeed, both the House and the Senate passed resolutions condemning Ortega for canceling the cease-fire.[148]

Meanwhile, in the war-torn border regions of Nicaragua, the Contras served as unofficial members of the UNO coalition. In the months leading up to the election, reports accumulated of marauding detachments of militants warning locals not to vote for the FSLN. "Their top message is: 'Vote for the UNO or the war will continue," noted the *Los Angeles Times*.[149] It was hardly an abstract threat; in January 1990, in one of many all-but-forgotten incidents, more than a dozen Contras arrived at the Jinotega farm of Nicaraguan peasant Humberto Jirón. The message was simple: if you vote for the FSLN, they told him, we will kill you.[150]

In the dry, dusty heat of late February 1990, the Nicaraguan people decisively rejected incumbent president Daniel Ortega and the FSLN in favor of US-supported opposition candidate Violeta Chamorro. It was generally regarded as the most heavily scrutinized election in history; between two thousand and three thousand observers descended on Managua from seventeen countries, including representatives from the United Nations and the Organization of American States, as well as European and Latin American parliamentary delegations. Nonstate actors abounded as well, especially from the United States, including observer groups from the International Human Rights Law Group, Freedom House, Hemisphere Initiatives, and the Latin American Studies Association. The UN mission had begun in August 1989 and included nationwide monitoring of the voter registration process and compliance with electoral regulations. The majority of observer groups focused on election day itself, visiting more than half the 4,394 polling stations, and watched the vote counting at 600.[151]

Confident of an FSLN victory, the Sandinistas embraced the international attention. "It is preferable to be invaded by observers to an electoral process in which we have nothing to hide than to confront an invasion of U.S. troops with all its consequences," Ortega observed.[152] Indeed, on voting day—February 26, 1990—international observers found few irregularities. Yet the final tally revealed Nicaraguans' exhaustion with the Contra war, concern with the economic situation, and frustration with the revolutionary government. With 86 percent of eligible voters casting ballots, the UNO coalition won the presidency by a 14 point majority (55% to 41%) and gained a majority in the National Assembly (fifty-one seats to the FSLN's thirty-nine), as well as in most urban municipal elections.[153]

The election results shocked Sandinistas and Chamorro supporters alike. Preelection polling had predicted a decisive FSLN victory, and in the immediate aftermath, wrote the journalist Alma Guillermoprieto, the nation "came to a complete halt while the stunned people of Nicaragua contemplated the magnitude of what they had done, and tried to imagine the unimaginable consequences of their act."[154] To their credit, FSLN leaders respected the result; as the election results trickled in, Ortega and other top FSLN officials met in a tense midnight meeting with former president Jimmy Carter, who had arrived in Managua shortly before the voting as the head of a high-profile election observer team. Emphasizing the Sandinistas' achievements, Carter played the role of an impartial advocate of democracy, encouraging Ortega to respect the will of the electorate. "In my opinion, the FSLN can come out as heroes, having triumphed in a revolution against an oppressive dictator, survived a war against an enemy that was financed abroad, and at the end of ten years, brought democracy."[155] At six o'clock the following morning, an exhausted Ortega conceded defeat. Nicaraguans, he solemnly declared, could take pride "in contributing, in this unjust world divided between the powerful and the weak, a little dignity, a little democracy, a little social justice, from this small territory in Central America."[156]

To be sure, Nicaraguan voters bore the ultimate responsibility for Chamorro's victory. The significance of US financial support in shaping the election's outcome was debatable; due to bureaucratic delays in both the United States and Nicaragua, much of funding arrived only a few weeks before election day.[157] Yet the extent of US involvement over the course of the 1980s in supporting the Contras, pressuring the Nicaraguan economy, and, in the months leading up to the 1990 election, shepherding the fragile opposition coalition underscored the power of the democracy promotion initiative in advancing US political goals. The election, pointedly noted the report of the Latin American Studies Association's observer team, "represented a 'free and fair' electoral process within a climate of United States–generated military and economic pressure." The Bush administration's shift from lethal aid to the Contras to political aid to UNO, the report concluded, "suggests that U.S. foreign policy has shifted its modalities but not its fundamental intentions toward Latin America."[158] Similarly, in an influential analysis shortly after the election, the sociologist William I. Robinson argued that the "claim that the United States was 'not taking sides' when one side had been the target of ten years of U.S. warfare and the other was the creature of U.S. intervention would have been a comical assertion had U.S. officials not made it repeatedly during the electoral process, each time with a straight face."[159] Nicaraguan vice president Sergio Ramírez concurred. "The war itself would prove to be the great electoral adversary," he later recalled, "and we could not defeat it with its absences, its separations, its misery, its death, and the inability to imagine its end for people who suffered under its fatal weight."[160]

In Washington, UNO's victory was seen as a triumph of democracy. "Any friend of democracy can take heart in the fact that Violeta Chamorro won the election," George Bush declared on February 27. "And the election process, by all accounts free and fair, is a credit to the people of Nicaragua, who chose to determine their . . . nation's future at the ballot box. And that is a victory for democracy."[161] Underscoring US support for UNO, Bush quickly lifted the five-year-old trade sanctions against Nicaragua and moved to restore Nicaragua's sugar quota on the US market, eligibility for preferential treatment under the Caribbean Basin Initiative and Generalized System of Preferences, and access to the Export-Import Bank and the Overseas Private Investment Corporation. Bush further requested a shipment of $21 million in food aid to Nicaragua and $300 million in emergency aid from Department of Defense funds.[162] At a summit meeting with Central American presidents the following June, Secretary of State Baker shared Bush's enthusiasm. It was "a historic meeting," Baker asserted. "This is the first Summit when all of your nations have been led by democratically elected leaders." The region could now spend "more time on devel[opment]," Baker noted in a handwritten addendum to the typed address, "than WAR."[163]

More broadly, the FSLN's defeat was viewed by many in Washington as a fitting encore to the dramatic and largely peaceful end of the Cold War in late 1989. In the heady months following the fall of the Iron Curtain, Ronald Reagan's 1982 declaration at Westminster that "day by day democracy is proving itself to be a not-at-all-fragile flower" appeared prescient, even prophetic. "It is long past time to realize that our active intervention *is* appreciated when it is on the side of democracy, just as our support for dictatorships is long remembered," Elliott Abrams asserted in an op-ed less than twenty-four hours after Ortega conceded defeat. Reiterating a common conservative critique, Abrams argued that "the American liberal view since Vietnam has held that U.S. intervention is almost always morally wrong and politically harmful, a reflection of the many flaws that plague our society. This fundamentally negative view of our society was projected onto the people of other nations, who were said to want above all 'to be left alone' by the United States—unless, of course, they were struggling with a right-wing dictatorship." Chamorro's victory, Abrams concluded, "not only liberates Nicaragua from oppression; it also should liberate us from the myths that so often dominate our foreign policy. In their triumph over the Sandinistas, the people of Nicaragua have reminded us that American intervention is welcome when we join the struggle for freedom."[164]

Similarly, conservative columnist George F. Will cast the Nicaraguan election as the final step in a US intellectual and political journey decades in the making. "The pilgrimage is over. The long march of the West's 'progressive' intellectuals has come to a bedraggled end in Nicaragua, a peasant nation about as far, socially, as a nation can get from the conditions where the revolt against modernity was supposed to take root," Will opined. With Marxism discredited across the globe, he added, "the reputations of many people and the interpretations of many events are undergoing revision. The U.S. effort in Vietnam looks more worthwhile in light of the subsequent blood baths and waves of boat people. They discredit those who, in their zeal to see America defeated, professed to see humanitarianism on the other side."[165]

As conservative US pundits and policymakers celebrated the FSLN's defeat, for Nicaraguans, the Cold War was finally over. Yet hopes that the UNO victory would usher in a period of peace and prosperity quickly turned to rising disillusionment and frustration in the early years of the 1990s as power struggles between the FSLN, UNO, and former Contra groups roiled the Nicaraguan political landscape. By 1993, more than half of Nicaraguans indicated that they had no faith in *any* political party and 85 percent expressed disinterest in the ongoing political battles.[166] Correspondingly, Chamorro's neoliberal economic policies exacerbated working-class precarity. Rapid privatization and market liberalization benefited an expanding business elite—at the expense of the majority of the population. Unemployment would double between 1990 and 1995, reaching ten times the level of 1984.[167] "Supermarkets have sprung up all over Managua with well-stocked shelves of primarily imported foodstuffs," noted the political scientist Gary Prevost. "However, the price of goods is comparable to North American standards and is, therefore, out of reach of ordinary Nicaraguans."[168]

Throughout his term in office, Bush maintained close ties to the Chamorro administration. In April 1991, Chamorro was warmly received at the White House by the president and First Lady Barbara Bush. Chamorro's "blend of resolve and compassion," Bush asserted, "inspires a nation to become the best it can be."[169] As singer Johnny Mathis sang in the background, Chamorro was feted at a state dinner where Washington Beltway insiders like Gershman rubbed elbows with pro-administration movie stars. It was a striking coda to Nicaragua's revolutionary era; as the White House guests dined on poached salmon and champagne aspic, caviar sauce, paillettes parmesan, potato croquettes, jardiniere of vegetables, and chateaubriand with béarnaise sauce, 40 percent of Nicaraguans had descended to extreme poverty, and, in the months since the 1990 election, more than thirteen hundred children had died of diarrhea and measles.[170]

The Reagan Imprint: Democracy Promotion in US Foreign Relations after the Cold War

In the summer of 1989, a young political scientist named Francis Fuku-yama published a short article in the *National Interest*, a minor academic journal with a circulation of six thousand. Drawing from the ideas of German philosopher G. W. F. Hegel, Fukuyama argued that with the defeat of totalitarianism—the triumph against Nazism at mid-century followed by the fall of communism at the century's end—liberalism stood unchallenged astride the globe. "What we may be witnessing is not just the end of the Cold War, or the passing of a particular period of postwar history," Fukuyama boldly proclaimed, "but the end of history as such: that is, the end point of mankind's ideological evolution and the universalization of Western liberal democracy as the final form of human government."[1]

Fukuyama's provocative argument, expansively titled "The End of History?" appeared in print at a propitious moment—an interstitial space in the dramatic ending of the Cold War. Six months earlier, Mikhail Gorbachev had announced a sweeping unilateral military reduction at the United Nations; six months later, the Soviet empire in Eastern Europe was disappearing. In the interval, "The End of History?" propelled Fukuyama—a little-known Soviet policy analyst—to a kind of intellectual stardom as the article crossed over into the mainstream press, stimulated a vibrant debate in academic and policymaking circles, and was quickly translated for consumption abroad. Not surprisingly, "The End of History?" made a particularly big splash in Washington, DC. The summer issue of the *National Interest*, one newsstand reported, was "outselling everything, even the pornography."[2]

If the Hegelian overtones of "The End of History?" drew both praise and scorn in heavy doses, Fukuyama's emphasis on the triumph of liberal democracy illuminated a defining development of the 1980s: the emergence of democracy promotion as a central tenet of US foreign policy. Two decades earlier, the Cold War consensus among American policymakers had lain in tatters. The Democratic Party was fractured amid the debate over the US intervention in Vietnam, with liberal cold warriors increasingly overshadowed by "New Politics liberals" who rejected the logic of the Cold War. As liberal internationalists criticized the Nixon White House for supporting repressive right-wing allies, cold warriors on both sides of the aisle attacked Nixon for pursuing détente with Moscow. A decade before Fukuyama published "The End of History?," influential Cold War liberals—soon to be known as neoconservatives—were deeply disillusioned with Carter's emphasis on noninterventionism, multilateralism, and human rights. Migrating to the Reagan camp, they played an outsize role in shaping US foreign policy following Reagan's landslide victory over Carter in the 1980 election.

In the following decade, the Reagan administration's embrace of democracy promotion as the centerpiece of the US human rights policy had far-reaching effects. First, the administration effectively used democracy promotion to refashion a bipartisan foreign policy consensus. Second, during the 1980s, human rights were increasingly institutionalized in the formulation and implementation of US foreign policy. Narrowly framed as civil rights and political liberties—and excluding social and economic rights—human rights became increasingly embedded as a US policy priority across the vast foreign policy bureaucracy. The results were remarkable, if at times unpredictable: at the same time that human rights talk shaped US pressure on the Soviet bloc and its allies, it also contributed to decreased US support for right-wing dictatorships, such as the Philippines, Chile, and South Korea. Combined with political aid from the National Endowment for Democracy (NED), democracy promotion by the end of the decade had evolved into a singular form of US interventionism underpinning broader US strategic goals.

Third, the FSLN's 1990 electoral defeat underscored the importance of the Reagan administration's democracy initiative in the failure of the broader third-world project. In the 1970s, the Non-Aligned Nations Movement (NAM) had developed into a vocal bloc advocating third-world solidarity. In a decade defined by the US defeat in Vietnam, Watergate, and an economy stumbling under the burden of stagflation, third-world nationalists' denunciations of inequality between rich and poor nations and embrace of statist, anti-Western approaches to development appeared to threaten the very foundations of the US hegemonic project.

Over the course of the 1980s, however, the Reagan administration's aggressive deployment of US financial leverage pressured third-world states to accede to the structural adjustment demands of the Washington Consensus. The US war on Nicaragua, in particular, made starkly evident the cost of resisting US hegemony. Combined with rising disillusionment with socialism in an era of perestroika, the US position at the end of the decade had changed dramatically. "By the outset of the post–Cold War era, globalization and the Washington Consensus were sweeping forward in the Third World, as well as in many of America's former Second-World adversaries. Political liberalization was continuing the awesome advance that would increase the number of electoral democracies worldwide from less than 40 in the early 1970s to roughly 120 by the turn of the millennium," enthuses the historian Hal Brands. "Nearly around the globe, it seemed, the liberal practices of free trade, free markets, and free political institutions were on the rise, and alternative models—whether economic or political—were embattled or in some cases essentially defeated."[3]

Fourth, democracy promotion remained a cornerstone of US foreign policy in the early post–Cold War era. Searching for a grand strategy that could replace containment, a process dubbed the "Kennan sweepstakes," the Bill Clinton administration predictably turned to "democratic enlargement," and quietly changed the name of the State Department Bureau of Human Rights and Humanitarian Affairs to the Bureau for Democracy, Human Rights, and Labor.[4] Supporting "market democracies," assistant to the president for national security affairs Tony Lake asserted in September 1993, was both rooted in US ideals and pragmatically forward-looking. "As we fought aggressors and contained communism, our engagement abroad was animated both by calculations of power and by this belief: to the extent democracy and market economics hold sway in other nations, our own nation will be more secure, prosperous and influential, while the broader world will be more humane and peaceful."[5] Clinton concurred. "Ultimately, the best strategy to ensure our security and to build a durable peace is to support the advance of democracy elsewhere," Clinton declared in his 1994 State of the Union address. Sounding distinctly Reaganesque, the president continued, "Democracies don't attack each other, they make better trading partners and partners in diplomacy."[6]

The Clinton administration's embrace of democracy promotion both reflected and contributed to the broader development of a distinct epistemic community focused on democracy promotion. The NED continued to serve as a hub connecting organizations and individuals involved in democracy promotion, an expanding network of think tanks and academics, funding organizations, and NGOs.[7] In late 1990, the NED created the *Journal of Democracy*, edited by the political sociologist Larry J. Diamond and the NED's former director of program Marc F. Plattner, to "unify what is becoming a worldwide democratic movement."[8] In this process, Diamond—among a rising number of scholars and practitioners in the 1990s to champion democratic peace theory—perceived an exceptional role for the United States. "If the United States stays the course of this struggle, as it did in the Cold War, it can create a different world: a community of states under law, a global democratic civilization," Diamond asserted in *Foreign Policy* in 1992. "If it retreats from the challenge and watches the world descend anew into fascism, bigotry, and strife, there could be decades of needless danger and suffering before the democratic moment arrives again."[9] US policymakers agreed; funding for democracy promotion increased from $100 million in 1990 to $700 million in 2000.[10]

To be sure, the Clinton administration's commitment to democracy promotion—and human rights—was distinctly limited. In May 1994, as the Rwandan genocide entered its seventh week and the death toll neared four hundred thousand, Clinton took the opportunity to emphasize the importance of US national interest in foreign policy. "Whether we get involved in any of the world's ethnic conflicts," he intoned in a commencement address at the US Naval Academy, "in the end must depend on the cumulative weight of the American interests at stake."[11] More broadly, in a decade of blossoming human rights activism by international organizations and NGOs, the United States engaged in a long-standing pattern of exceptionalism. As the political scientist Michael Ignatieff writes, "First, the United States signs on to international human rights and humanitarian law conventions and treaties and then exempts itself from their provisions by explicit reservation, nonratification, or noncompliance. Second, the United States maintains double standards: judging itself and its friends by more permissive criteria than it does its enemies. Third, the United States denies jurisdiction to human rights law within its own domestic law, insisting on the self-contained authority of its own domestic rights tradition." Such exceptionalism, Ignatieff concludes, is distinctly American. "No other democratic state engages in all three of these practices to the same extent," he writes, "and none combines these practices with claims to global leadership in the field of human rights."[12]

If the Clinton administration's narrow framing of human rights marked a striking continuity with the Reagan-Bush era, the use of human rights to undergird US interventionism—particularly evident in US policy toward

Nicaragua in the 1980s—resurfaced in the US response to the September 11, 2001, terror attacks. After serving as an important rationale for the George W. Bush administration's 2003 US invasion of Iraq, democracy promotion moved to center stage after the United States failed to locate Iraqi weapons of mass destruction. Describing the United States as "a nation with a mission," Bush framed US foreign policy in sweeping Wilsonian language that became known as the administration's Freedom Agenda. "It is the policy of the United States to seek and support the growth of democratic movements and institutions in every nation and culture," the president asserted during his second inaugural address, "with the ultimate goal of ending tyranny in our world."[13] Bush's words illuminated democracy promotion's durability as an appealing framework for US foreign policy. Indeed, underscoring the long-term significance of the Reagan administration's refashioning of the bipartisan foreign policy consensus, Bush's Freedom Agenda appealed to both neoconservatives and many liberals who perceived a benevolent role for US power in the face of tyranny abroad.[14]

But the enormous human and material cost of the US intervention in the Middle East belied the president's lofty rhetoric. Between 2003 and 2019, 7,014 US soldiers serving in Iraq and Afghanistan were killed; conservative estimates placed the total number of direct war deaths at 465,000. The destabilization of the region in the aftermath of the US invasion—from the rise of the Islamic State in Iraq and Syria, or ISIS, to the expanding influence of Iran—would have a far-reaching geopolitical impact.[15] The US image abroad suffered also irreparable damage as the Bush administration's aggressive effort to apprehend perceived terrorists in the aftermath of September 11 metastasized into a massive and dysfunctional system in which tens of thousands of detainees festered in US-run prisons in Iraq; Afghanistan; Guantánamo Bay, Cuba; and an archipelago of "black sites" where torture—euphemistically described by Bush officials as "harsh interrogation"—was the norm.[16] At home and abroad, the appeal of US democracy promotion as a foreign policy priority plummeted. "The foreign policies of Presidents Ronald Reagan, George H. W. Bush, and Bill Clinton all combined in various proportions an emphasis on democracy with substantial realist elements," noted the political scientist Thomas Carothers in 2007. "Yet to the extent the Bush approach to democracy promotion is distinctive, its distinguishing features—the centrality of military intervention, the focus on the Middle East, and the tie-in with the war on terrorism—have all been highly problematic."[17] As a result, US democracy promotion, Carothers lamented, needed to be "decontaminated" to remove the "negative taint" of Bush's foreign policy adventurism.[18]

By the end of the second Bush administration, it thus seemed that Fukuyama's "End of History?" thesis had been at best premature. Mired in wars
in Afghanistan and Iraq and confronting a major financial crisis, president
Barack Obama faced a resurgent Russia and an increasingly ambitious China.
Correspondingly, charismatic political leaders across the globe were tapping
into widespread voter resentment toward the perceived ill effects of globalization, unchecked immigration, and the loss of tradition, propelling fragile
democracies such as Turkey and Hungary toward authoritarianism—a trend
democracy experts described as "backsliding." As Donald J. Trump's narrow
victory in the 2016 presidential election made clear, right-wing populism also
appealed to millions of voters in the United States. "What went wrong?,"
Diamond wrote in the pages of *Foreign Affairs* in 2019. The answer, he concluded, lay close to home. "In short, democracy lost its leading proponent,"
he asserted. "Disastrous U.S. interventions in the Middle East soured Americans on the idea of democracy promotion, and a combination of fears about
democratic decline in their own country and economic problems encouraged
them to turn inward."[19]

Yet such calls for the United States to reconsecrate the mission of democracy promotion overlooked the interventionism that had underpinned the
project in its foundational stages. The Reagan administration's use of democracy promotion—and, more broadly, the US human rights policy—to advance Cold War goals had set in motion a process that would culminate in US
tanks rolling through the streets of Bagdad. Moreover, the legacy of the Reagan administration's understanding of the free market as a defining human
right and a key element in a functioning democracy had limited appeal for
millions of people who felt left behind in a world increasingly defined by
deep US-led globalization. In the late twentieth century, democracy promotion had emerged as a signal feature of US foreign relations. "Freedom is now
on the offensive," Reagan confidently asserted in 1987. "We turned a corner
in 1981, and if we have courage and are realistic in our approach to world affairs, freedom will not only survive, it will triumph."[20] Whether democracy
promotion would continue to shape the United States' engagement with the
world in the twenty-first century remained to be seen.

Notes

Introduction

1. Ronald Reagan, "Freedom, Regional Security, and Global Peace," address to Congress, March 14, 1986, The American Presidency Project, University of California, Santa Barbara, https://www.presidency.ucsb.edu/node/258530 (hereafter APP).

2. Reagan, "Freedom, Regional Security, and Global Peace."

3. Reagan, "Freedom, Regional Security, and Global Peace."

4. For lack of a better alternative, "American" refers to people from the United States.

5. Minutes, NSC meeting, February 6, 1981, in *Foreign Relations of the United States, 1981–1988*, by United States Department of State, Bureau of Public Affairs (Washington, DC: Government Printing Office, 2016), 3:39 (hereafter *FRUS, 1981–1988*).

6. "Excerpts from State Department Memorandum on Human Rights," *New York Times*, November 5, 1981, A10 (hereafter *NYT*).

7. Ronald Reagan, address to the British Parliament, London, June 8, 1982, transcript, Miller Center of Public Affairs, University of Virginia, Charlottesville, VA, https://miller center.org/the-presidency/presidential-speeches/june-8-1982-address-british-parliament (hereafter MCPA).

8. Tamar Jacoby, "The Reagan Turnaround on Human Rights," *Foreign Affairs* 64, no. 5 (Summer 1986): 1067.

9. Charles William Maynes, "Reagan and the American Resolve: A U.S. Policy for Intervention Everywhere," *Los Angeles Times*, February 9, 1986, G1 (hereafter *LAT*).

10. Walter LaFeber, *Inevitable Revolutions: The United States in Central America* (New York: W. W. Norton, 1993), 9.

11. Alma Guillermoprieto, *The Heart That Bleeds: Latin America Now* (New York: Vintage Books, 1995), 25.

12. NSC meeting minutes, February 11, 1981, Executive Secretariat: Meeting Files, box 1, folder: NSC 00002, Ronald Reagan Library, Simi Valley, CA (hereafter RRL).

13. The term "Reagan Doctrine" was originally coined by neoconservative columnist Charles Krauthammer. See Charles Krauthammer, "Essay: The Reagan Doctrine," *Time*, April 1, 1985.

14. See, for example, Samuel Moyn, *The Last Utopia: Human Rights in History* (Cambridge, MA: Belknap Press of Harvard University Press, 2010); Stefan-Ludwig Hoffmann, ed., *Human Rights in the Twentieth Century* (New York: Cambridge University Press, 2010); Akira Iriye, Petra Goedde, and William I. Hitchcock, eds., *The Human Rights Revolution: An International History* (New York: Oxford University Press, 2012); William Michael Schmidli, *The Fate of Freedom Elsewhere: Human Rights and U.S. Cold War Policy toward Argentina* (Ithaca, NY: Cornell University Press, 2013); Barbara J. Keys, *Reclaiming American Virtue: The Human Rights Revolution of the 1970s* (Cambridge, MA: Harvard University Press, 2014); Jan Eckel and Samuel Moyn, eds., *The Breakthrough: Human Rights in the 1970s* (Philadelphia: University of Pennsylvania Press, 2015); Joe Renouard, *Human Rights in American Foreign Policy: From the 1960s to the Soviet Collapse* (Philadelphia: University of Pennsylvania Press, 2015); Mark Philip Bradley, *The World Reimagined: Americans and Human Rights in the Twentieth Century* (New York: Cambridge University Press, 2016); Sarah B. Snyder, *From Selma to Moscow: How Human Rights Activists Transformed U.S. Foreign Policy* (New York: Columbia University Press, 2018).

15. See, for example, Melvyn P. Leffler, *For the Soul of Mankind: The United States, the Soviet Union, and the Cold War* (New York: Hill and Wang, 2007); James Graham Wilson, *The Triumph of Improvisation: Gorbachev's Adaptability, Reagan's Engagement, and the End of the Cold War* (Ithaca, NY: Cornell University Press, 2015); Hal Brands, *Making the Unipolar Moment: U.S. Foreign Policy and the Rise of the Post–Cold War Order* (Ithaca, NY: Cornell University Press, 2016); Bradley Lynn Coleman and Kyle Longley, eds., *Reagan and the World: Leadership and National Security, 1981–1989* (Lexington: University Press of Kentucky, 2017); Simon Miles, *Engaging the Evil Empire: Washington, Moscow, and the Beginning of the End of the Cold War* (Ithaca, NY: Cornell University Press, 2020); Jonathan Hunt and Simon Miles, eds., *The Reagan Moment: America and the World in the 1980s* (Ithaca, NY: Cornell University Press, 2021). On human rights and US foreign relations in the 1980s, in addition to the sources cited elsewhere in this chapter, see Sarah B. Snyder, *Human Rights Activism and the End of the Cold War: A Transnational History of the Helsinki Network* (New York: Cambridge University Press, 2011); Theresa Keeley, *Reagan's Gun-Toting Nuns: The Catholic Conflict over Cold War Human Rights Policy in Central America* (Ithaca, NY: Cornell University Press, 2020); Rasmus Sinding Søndergaard, *Reagan, Congress, and Human Rights: Contesting Morality in US Foreign Policy* (Cambridge: Cambridge University Press, 2020).

16. Daniel Bessner and Jennifer M. Miller, "Foreign Encounters and U.S. Democracy," *Diplomatic History* 45, no. 1 (January 2021): 23. On democracy as a leitmotif of US foreign policy, see G. John Ikenberry, *Liberal Leviathan: The Origins, Crisis, and Transformation of the American World Order* (Princeton, NJ: Princeton University Press, 2011); Tony Smith, *America's Mission: The United States and the Worldwide Struggle for Democracy in the Twentieth Century*, expanded ed. (Princeton, NJ: Princeton University Press, 2012).

17. On US democracy promotion in the 1980s, see Robert Pee, *Democracy Promotion, National Security and Strategy: Foreign Policy under the Reagan Administration* (New York: Routledge, 2015); Brands, *Making the Unipolar Moment*, 199–71; Evan D. McCormick, "Breaking with Statism? U.S. Democracy Promotion in Latin America, 1984–1988," *Diplomatic History* 42, no. 5 (November 2018): 745–71; Robert Pee and William Michael Schmidli, eds., *The Reagan Administration, the Cold War, and the Transition to Democracy Promotion* (Cham, Switzerland: Palgrave Macmillan, 2019).

18. See, for example, Larry J. Diamond, *Developing Democracy: Toward Consolidation* (Baltimore: Johns Hopkins University Press, 1999); Thomas Carothers, *Critical Mission: Essays on Democracy Promotion* (Washington, DC: Carnegie Endowment for International Peace, 2004).

19. See William I. Robinson, *Promoting Polyarchy: Globalization, US Intervention, and Hegemony* (New York: Cambridge University Press, 1996); Milja Kurki, *Democratic Futures: Revisioning Democracy Promotion* (Abingdon: Routledge, 2013); Wendy Brown, *Undoing the Demos: Neoliberalism's Stealth Revolution* (New York: Zone Books, 2015).

20. Scholarship on US–Central American relations during the 1980s continues to be defined by early studies produced in the 1990s and early 2000s by individuals who served in the Carter or Reagan administrations or as activists opposed to the US intervention. Early studies of US–Central American relations include Cynthia J. Arnson, *Crossroads: Congress, the President, and Central America, 1976–1993* (University Park: Pennsylvania State University Press, 1993); John H. Coatsworth, *Central America and the United States: The Clients and the Colossus* (New York: Twayne, 1994); Robert Kagan, *A Twilight Struggle: American Power in Nicaragua, 1977–1990* (New York: Free Press, 1996); William M. LeoGrande, *Our Own Backyard: The United States in Central America, 1977–1992* (Chapel Hill: University of North Carolina Press, 1998); Robert A. Pastor, *Not Condemned to Repetition: The United States and Nicaragua* (Boulder, CO: Westview Press, 2002); LaFeber, *Inevitable Revolutions.* Later studies include Greg Grandin, *Empire's Workshop: Latin America and the Roots of U.S. Imperialism* (New York: Metropolitan Books, 2005); Malcolm Byrne, *Iran-Contra: Reagan's Scandal and the Unchecked Abuse of Presidential Power* (Lawrence: University Press of Kansas, 2014); Philip W. Travis, *Reagan's War on Terrorism in Nicaragua: The Outlaw State* (Lanham, MD: Lexington Books, 2016). Studies of the Sandinista era include Matilde Zimmermann, *Sandinista: Carlos Fonseca and the Nicaraguan Revolution* (Durham, NC: Duke University Press, 2000); William Michael Schmidli, "'The Most Sophisticated Intervention We Have Seen': The Carter Administration and the Nicaraguan Crisis, 1978–1979," *Diplomacy & Statecraft* 23, no. 1 (2012): 66–86; Gerardo Sánchez Nateras, "The Sandinista Revolution and the Limits of the Cold War in Latin America: The Dilemma of Non-intervention during the Nicaraguan Crisis, 1977–78," *Cold War History* 18, no. 2 (2018): 111–29; Mateo Cayetano Jarquín, "Red Christmases: The Sandinistas, Indigenous Rebellion, and the Origins of the Nicaraguan Civil War, 1981–82," *Cold War History* 18, no. 1 (2018): 91–107; Eline van Ommen, "Sandinistas Go Global: Nicaragua and Western Europe, 1977–1990" (PhD diss., London School of Economics and Political Science, 2019).

21. Although a rising number of scholars have turned their attention to the modern conservative movement, relatively little has been written on US right-wing nonstate actors' Cold War activism in the 1980s. See Martin Durham and Margaret Power, eds., *New Perspectives on the Transnational Right* (New York: Palgrave Macmillan, 2011); Kyle Burke, *Revolutionaries for the Right: Anticommunist Internationalism and Paramilitary Warfare in the Cold War* (Chapel Hill: University of North Carolina Press, 2018); Kathleen Belew, *Bring the War Home: The White Power Movement and Paramilitary America* (Cambridge, MA: Harvard University Press, 2018), 77–102.

22. On US left-wing activism toward Central America, in addition to the sources listed above, see Van Gosse, "'The North American Front': Central American Solidarity in the Reagan Era," in *Reshaping the US Left: Popular Struggles in the 1980s,* ed. Mike Davis and Michael Sprinkler (London: Verso, 1988), 11–50; Christian Smith, *Resisting Reagan: The U.S. Central America Peace Movement* (Chicago: University of Chicago Press, 1996); Bradford Martin, *The Other Eighties: A Secret History of America in the Age of Reagan* (New York: Hill and Wang, 2011); Roger Peace, *A Call to Conscience: The Anti–Contra War Campaign* (Amherst: University of Massachusetts Press, 2012); Héctor Perla Jr., "Heirs of Sandino: The Nicaraguan Revolution and the U.S.-Nicaragua Solidarity Movement," *Latin American Perspectives* 36, no. 6, (November 2009): 80–100; Molly Todd, "'We Were Part of the Revolutionary Movement There': Wisconsin Peace Progressives and Solidarity with El Salvador in the Reagan Era," *Journal of Civil and Human Rights* 3, no. 1 (Spring/Summer 2017): 1–56.

1. Competing Visions

1. Richard V. Allen, interview with Stephen F. Knott, May 28, 2002, Oral History Program, MCPA.

2. Allen, interview.

3. Allen, interview.

4. Allen, interview.

5. Leffler, *For the Soul of Mankind*, 238.

6. On reestablishing relations with China, see, for example, Jeremi Suri, "From Isolation to Engagement: American Foreign Policy and the Opening to China, 1969–1972," in *Foreign Policy Breakthroughs: Cases in Successful Diplomacy*, ed. Robert Hutchings and Jeremi Suri (New York: Oxford University Press, 2015), 101–20; Campbell Craig and Fredrik Logevall, *America's Cold War: The Politics of Insecurity* (Cambridge, MA: Harvard University Press, 2009), 264–68.

7. Jussi Hanhimäki, "An Elusive Grand Design," in *Nixon in the World: American Foreign Relations, 1969–1977*, ed. Fredrik Logevall and Andrew Preston (New York: Oxford University Press, 2008), 37.

8. "Basic Principles of Relations between the United States of America and the Union of Soviet Socialist Republics," May 29, 1972, in *Foreign Relations of the United States, 1969–1976*, by United States Department of State, Bureau of Public Affairs (Washington, DC: Government Printing Office, 2003), 1:389–90 (hereafter *FRUS, 1969–1976*).

9. See Marilyn B. Young, *The Vietnam Wars, 1945–1990* (New York: HarperPerennial, 1991), 240.

10. George C. Herring, *America's Longest War: The United States and Vietnam, 1950–1975*, 4th ed. (New York: McGraw-Hill, 2003), 319–20.

11. Richard M. Nixon, "Address to the Nation Announcing an Agreement on Ending the War in Vietnam," January 23, 1973, transcript, MCPA, https://millercenter.org/the-presidency/presidential-speeches/january-23-1973-address-nation-announcing-agreement-ending-war.

12. Clair Apodaca, *Understanding U.S. Human Rights Policy: A Paradoxical Legacy* (New York: Routledge, 2006), 31–32; Arnson, *Crossroads*, 9.

13. Representative Richard Ottinger (D-NY), quoted in Robert David Johnson, *Congress and the Cold War* (New York: Cambridge University Press, 2006), 205.

14. Bradley, *World Reimagined*, 137.

15. On the relationship between human rights and neoliberalism, see Samuel Moyn, *Not Enough: Human Rights in an Unequal World* (Cambridge, MA: Belknap Press of Harvard University Press, 2018), 173–211.

16. Kenneth Cmiel, "The Emergence of Human Rights Politics in the United States," *Journal of American History* 86, no. 3 (1999): 1249.

17. Bradley, *World Reimagined*, 220.

18. Bradley, *World Reimagined*, 201.

19. On the rise of nonstate human rights advocacy in the 1970s, see Bradley, *World Reimagined*, 128–226; Keys, *Reclaiming American Virtue*, 178–213; Schmidli, *Fate of Freedom Elsewhere*, 56–82.

20. Cmiel, "Emergence of Human Rights Politics," 1235; Umberto Tulli, "'Whose Rights Are Human Rights?': The Ambiguous Emergence of Human Rights and the Demise of Kissingerism," *Cold War History* 12, no. 4 (2012): 579.

21. See Congressional Research Service (hereafter CRS), *Human Rights and U.S. Foreign Assistance: Experiences and Issues in Policy Implementation (1977–1978)*, prepared for the US Senate

Committee on Foreign Relations, 96th Cong., 1st Sess., November 1979, Committee Print (Washington, DC: Government Printing Office, 1979). See also Barbara J. Keys, "Anti-torture Politics: Amnesty International, the Greek Junta, and the Origins of the Human Rights 'Boom' in the United States," in *The Human Rights Revolution: An International History*, ed. Akira Iriye, Petra Goedde, and William I. Hitchcock (New York: Oxford University Press, 2012), 201–21; James N. Green, "Clerics, Exiles, and Academics: Opposition to the Brazilian Military Dictatorship in the United States," *Latin American Politics and Society* 45, no. 1 (December 2008): 88–117.

22. An estimated fifteen hundred Chileans were killed in the first month and a half following the coup, and untold thousands were tortured. On US policy toward Chile during the Allende presidency, see Peter Kornbluh, *The Pinochet File: A Declassified Dossier on Atrocity and Accountability* (New York: New Press, 2003). On human rights advocacy focused on Chile, see Jan Eckel, "'Under a Magnifying Glass': The International Human Rights Campaign against Chile in the Seventies," in *Human Rights in the Twentieth Century*, ed. Stefan-Ludwig Hoffmann (New York: Cambridge University Press, 2010), 321–41; Patrick William Kelly, *Sovereign Emergencies: Latin America and the Making of Global Human Rights Politics* (Cambridge: Cambridge University Press, 2018).

23. On Fraser and congressional human rights activism, see Apodaca, *Understanding U.S. Human Rights Policy*, 33–43; Barbara J. Keys, "Congress, Kissinger, and the Origins of Human Rights Diplomacy," *Diplomatic History* 34, no. 5 (November 2010): 823–51; Sarah B. Snyder, "'A Call for U.S. Leadership': Congressional Activism on Human Rights," *Diplomatic History* 37, no. 2 (2013): 372–97.

24. The McGovern reforms mandated that a representative proportion of women, young people, and racial minorities be included on every state delegation to the national convention. Additionally, the power to select delegates was transferred from closed sessions among party elites to open democratic processes. Jeffrey Bloodworth, *Losing the Center: The Decline of American Liberalism, 1968–1992* (Lexington: University Press of Kentucky, 2013), 139–40. See also Jules Witcover, *Party of the People: A History of the Democrats* (New York: Random House, 2003), 573–76.

25. Ben J. Wattenberg, *Fighting Words: A Tale of How Liberals Created Neo-conservatism* (New York: Thomas Dunne Books, 2008), 137.

26. On the 1972 election, see Bloodworth, *Losing the Center*, 139–44; Robert Gordon Kaufman, *Henry M. Jackson: A Life in Politics* (Seattle: University of Washington Press, 2000), 235–41; John Micklethwait and Adrian Wooldridge, *The Right Nation: Conservative Power in America* (New York: Penguin Books, 2004), 66–68.

27. Wattenberg, *Fighting Words*, 142.

28. Arthur M. Schlesinger Jr., "Human Rights and the American Tradition," *Foreign Affairs* 57, no. 3 (1978): 512.

29. John Lewis Gaddis, *George F. Kennan: An American Life* (New York: Penguin Books, 2012), 622.

30. Daniel J. Sargent, *A Superpower Transformed: The Remaking of American Foreign Relations in the 1970s* (New York: Oxford University Press, 2015), 204–14; Keys, *Reclaiming American Virtue*, 103–26.

31. Kissinger served as assistant to the president for national security affairs from Nixon's inauguration in 1969 until November 1975 and as secretary of state from September 1973 until Carter assumed the presidency in January 1977.

32. Tulli, "'Whose Rights Are Human Rights?,'" 576.

33. "Basic Principles of Relations," 389–90.

34. Richard M. Nixon and Henry Kissinger, telephone conversation, May 17, 1972, transcript, in *FRUS, 1969–1976*, 14:922.

35. Julian E. Zelizer, *Arsenal of Democracy: The Politics of National Security—from World War II to the War on Terrorism* (New York: Basic Books, 2012), 257.

36. Schmidli, *Fate of Freedom Elsewhere*, 67. See also Keys, "Origins of Human Rights Diplomacy," 835–36.

37. Arnson, *Crossroads*, 9–10; Stephen B. Cohen, "Conditioning U.S. Security Assistance on Human Rights Practices," *Journal of International Law* 76 (1982): 254.

38. Congressional correspondence, Donald M. Fraser to Robert S. Ingersoll, March 14, 1975, box 149.G.9.7B, folder: "Human Rights 1975 [2]"; Donald M. Fraser to Henry Kissinger, box 149.G.13.7B, folder: "Human Rights"; and Donald M. Fraser to Henry Kissinger, box 149.G.9.7B, folder: "Human Rights, 1975 [1]," Donald M. Fraser Papers, 1951–1995, Minnesota Historical Society, St. Paul, MN (hereafter FP).

39. Jussi Hanhimäki, *The Flawed Architect: Henry Kissinger and American Foreign Policy* (New York: Oxford University Press, 2004), 429.

40. Snyder, *Human Rights Activism*, 32. On the Helsinki Accords, see also Sargent, *Superpower Transformed*, 214–20.

41. Kaufman, *Henry M. Jackson*, 293.

42. Sarah B. Snyder, "'Jerry, Don't Go': Domestic Opposition to the 1975 Helsinki Final Act," *Journal of American Studies* 44, no. 1 (February 2010): 76.

43. Editorial note, in *FRUS, 1969–1976*, 39:922.

44. Jeremi Suri, *Henry Kissinger and the American Century* (Cambridge, MA: Belknap Press of Harvard University Press, 2007), 244.

45. Keys, *Reclaiming American Virtue*, 221.

46. James Mann, *Rise of the Vulcans: The History of Bush's War Cabinet* (New York: Viking, 2001).

47. See Piero Gleijeses, *Conflicting Missions: Havana, Washington, and Africa, 1959–1976* (Chapel Hill: University of North Carolina Press, 2002).

48. Zelizer, *Arsenal of Democracy*, 263.

49. Robert D. Schulzinger, "Détente in the Nixon-Ford Years, 1969–1976," in *The Cambridge History of the Cold War*, ed. Melvyn P. Leffler and Odd Arne Westad (New York: Cambridge University Press, 2010), 2:391.

50. Hanhimäki, *Flawed Architect*, 438.

51. Lewis Gould, *Grand Old Party: A History of the Republicans* (New York: Random House, 2003), 407.

52. Lou Cannon, *President Reagan: The Role of a Lifetime* (New York: PublicAffairs, 2000), 68.

53. Leffler, *For the Soul of Mankind*, 344. See also H. W. Brands, *Reagan: The Life* (New York. Doubleday, 2015), 66–71.

54. Kim Phillips-Fein, "'If Business and the Country Will Be Run Right': The Business Challenge to the Liberal Consensus, 1945–1964," *International Labor and Working-Class History* 72 (Fall 2007): 192–215.

55. The discussion of Reagan's political trajectory in the 1950s and 1960s is drawn from John Ehrman, *The Eighties: America in the Age of Reagan* (New Haven, CT: Yale University Press, 2006), 13–14; David Farber, *The Rise and Fall of Modern American Conservatism: A Short History* (Princeton, NJ: Princeton University Press, 2010), 159–83; Leffler, *For the Soul of Mankind*, 344–45; Jonathan Schoenwald, *A Time for Choosing: The Rise of Modern American Conservatism* (New York: Oxford University Press, 2001), 190–98.

56. James Mann, *The Rebellion of Ronald Reagan: A History of the End of the Cold War* (New York: Viking, 2009), 21.

57. Brands, *Reagan*, 203. See also Sean Wilentz, *The Age of Reagan: A History, 1974–2008* (New York: HarperCollins, 2009), 66–67.

58. Republican Party Platform of 1976, APP, https://www.presidency.ucsb.edu/docu ments/republican-party-platform-1976.

59. See the presidential campaign debate transcripts in Sidney Kraus, *The Great Debates: Carter vs. Ford, 1976* (Bloomington: Indiana University Press, 1979).

60. Jimmy Carter, "Relation between the World's Democracies," address to the Foreign Policy Association, New York, NY, June 23, 1976, in *Foreign Relations of the United States, 1977–1980*, by United States Department of State, Bureau of Public Affairs (Washington, DC: Government Printing Office, 2014), 1:28 (hereafter *FRUS, 1977–1980*).

61. See Keys, *Reclaiming American Virtue*, 230.

62. Bill Adler, *The Wit and Wisdom of Jimmy Carter* (Secaucus, NJ: Citadel Press, 1977), 113.

63. Jimmy Carter, address to the Chicago Council on Foreign Relations, Chicago, IL, March 15, 1976, in *FRUS, 1977–1980*, 1:22.

64. See Schmidli, *Fate of Freedom Elsewhere*, 90–91.

65. Joshua Muravchik, *The Uncertain Crusade: Jimmy Carter and the Dilemmas of Human Rights Policy* (Lanham, MD: Hamilton Press, 1986), 2.

66. Muravchik, *Uncertain Crusade*, 2. See also Keys, *Reclaiming American Virtue*, 234–35.

67. Douglas Brinkley, *Gerald R. Ford: The 38th President, 1974–1977*, The American Presidents (New York: Times Books, 2007), 142–43.

68. Schlesinger, "Human Rights and the American Tradition," 515.

69. Jimmy Carter, University of Notre Dame commencement address, Notre Dame, IN, May 22, 1977, transcript, MCPA, https://millercenter.org/the-presidency/presidential-speeches /may-22-1977-university-notre-dame-commencement.

70. Jimmy Carter, inaugural address, January 20, 1977, transcript, MCPA, https://miller center.org/the-presidency/presidential-speeches/january-20-1977-inaugural-address; Carter, Notre Dame commencement address.

71. Carter, Notre Dame commencement address. See also Debbie Sharnak, "Sovereignty and Human Rights: Re-examining Carter's Foreign Policy towards the Third World," *Diplomacy & Statecraft* 25, no. 2 (2014): 303–30; Sargent, *Superpower Transformed*, 229–60.

72. Aaron David Miller, *The Much Too Promised Land: America's Elusive Search for Arab-Israeli Peace* (New York: Bantam Books, 2008), 174–90.

73. Gaddis Smith, *Morality, Reason, and Power: American Diplomacy in the Carter Years* (New York: Hill and Wang, 1986), 113. See also Robert A. Strong, *Working in the World: Jimmy Carter and the Making of American Foreign Policy* (Baton Rouge: Louisiana State University Press, 2002), 153–82.

74. Memorandum, Lincoln Bloomfield to Roger Molander, subject: "The NSC and Human Rights Policy," July 3, 1980, in *FRUS, 1977–1980*, 2:628.

75. Douglas Brinkley, "Bernath Lecture: The Rising Stock of Jimmy Carter: The 'Hands On' Legacy of Our Thirty-Ninth President," *Diplomatic History* 20, no. 4 (1996): 521.

76. On the Carter administration's human rights policy toward Latin America, see Kathryn Sikkink, *Mixed Signals: U.S. Human Rights Policy and Latin America* (Ithaca, NY: Cornell University Press, 2004), 122–47; Lars Schoultz, *Human Rights and United States Policy toward Latin America* (Princeton, NJ: Princeton University Press, 1981); Schmidli, *Fate of Freedom Elsewhere*; Vanessa Walker, *Principles in Power: Latin America and the Politics of U.S. Human Rights Diplomacy* (Ithaca, NY: Cornell University Press, 2020).

77. Ernest Conine, "The New World Disorder Takes Its Toll," *NYT*, January 29, 1980, C5. See also John Dumbrell, *The Carter Presidency: A Re-evaluation* (Manchester: Manchester University

Press, 1993); David F. Schmitz and Vanessa Walker, "Jimmy Carter and the Foreign Policy of Human Rights: The Development of a Post–Cold War Foreign Policy," *Diplomatic History* 28, no. 1 (2004): 113–43.

78. See Jimmy Carter, state dinner toast, December 31, 1977, APP, https://www.presidency .ucsb.edu/documents/tehran-iran-toasts-the-president-and-the-shah-state-dinner.

79. Fund for New Priorities in America, *U.S. Policy on Human Rights in Latin America (Southern Cone): A Congressional Conference on Capitol Hill* (New York: Fund for New Priorities in America, 1978), 77. See also Brad Simpson, "'The First Right': The Carter Administration, Indonesia, and the Transnational Human Rights Politics of the 1970s," in *The Human Rights Revolution: An International History*, ed. Akira Iriye, Petra Goedde, and William I. Hitchcock (New York: Oxford University Press, 2012), 179–200; Kenton Clymer, "Jimmy Carter, Human Rights, and Cambodia," *Diplomatic History* 27, no. 2 (April 2003): 245–78.

80. Wattenberg, *Fighting Words*, 166.

81. Muravchik, *Uncertain Crusade*, 8–9.

82. Justin Vaïsse, *Neoconservatism: The Biography of a Movement* (Cambridge, MA: Belknap Press of Harvard University Press, 2011), 128.

83. Kaufman, *Henry M. Jackson*, 352.

84. Editorial note, in *FRUS, 1977–1980*, 1:86.

85. See Raymond Garthoff, *Détente and Confrontation: American-Soviet Relations from Nixon to Reagan* (Washington, DC: Brookings Institution, 1994), 569–73; Snyder, *Human Rights Activism*, 92–96.

86. Coalition for a Democratic Majority, "Unilateral Restraint: The Experiment That Failed," June 22, 1978, box 8, file: "Coalition for a Democratic Majority," Council for Inter-American Security Records, Hoover Institution Archives, Stanford University, Palo Alto, CA (hereafter HIA).

87. Ronald Reagan, "United States Foreign Policy and World Realities," address to the Foreign Policy Association, New York, NY, June 9, 1977, reprinted in *A Time for Choosing: The Speeches of Ronald Reagan, 1961–1982* (Chicago: Regnery Gateway, 1983), 205–6.

88. Ronald Reagan, "Vietnam II," November 30, 1976, reprinted in *Reagan, in His Own Hand: The Writings of Ronald Reagan That Reveal His Revolutionary Vision for America*, ed. Kiron K. Skinner, Annelise Anderson, and Martin Anderson (New York: Free Press, 2001), 135. Reagan gave over one thousand radio addresses between January 1975 and October 1979, which were broadcast by 286 stations. Combined with his biweekly newspaper columns, Reagan estimated that twenty million Americans were exposed to his ideas each week. Reagan, *Reagan, in His Own Hand*, 86

89. Richard Cohen, "Principles," *Washington Post*, May 25, 1982, C1 (hereafter *WP*).

90. Ronald Reagan, "Chile," radio broadcast, July 27, 1979, reprinted in *Reagan, in His Own Hand*, 142–43.

91. Allen Smith, "Leadership, Orientation, and Rhetorical Vision: Jimmy Carter, the 'New Right,' and the Panama Canal," *Presidential Studies Quarterly* 16, no. 2 (Spring 1986): 318. See also Natasha Zaretsky, "Restraint or Retreat? The Debate over the Panama Canal Treaties and U.S. Nationalism after Vietnam," *Diplomatic History* 35, no. 3 (June 2011): 535–62; Dominic Sandbrook, *Mad as Hell: The Crisis of the 1970s and the Rise of the Populist Right* (New York: Anchor Books, 2012), 338–39.

92. Ronald Reagan, "Panama," August 15, 1977, reprinted in *Reagan, in His Own Hand*, 199.

93. Odd Arne Westad, *The Global Cold War: Third World Interventions and the Making of Our Times* (Cambridge: Cambridge University Press, 2005), 279.

94. Jimmy Carter, State of the Union address, January 23, 1980, APP, https://www .presidency.ucsb.edu/documents/the-state-the-union-address-delivered-before-joint-session -the-congress.

95. Garthoff, *Détente and Confrontation*, 952–53.

96. "Common Sense and the Common Danger: Policy Statement of the Committee on the Present Danger," November 11, 1976, reprinted in *Alerting America: The Papers of the Committee on the Present Danger*, ed. Charles Tyroler (Washington, DC: Pergamon-Brassey's, 1984), 3.

97. See, for example, CPD, "What Is the Soviet Union Up To?," April 4, 1977; and "Is America Becoming Number 2? Current Trends in the U.S.-Soviet Military Balance," October 1978, reprinted in Tyroler, *Alerting America*, 3–15, 39–93, respectively.

98. CPD, "The 1980 Crisis and What We Should Do about It," January 22, 1980, reprinted in Tyroler, *Alerting America*, 177.

99. Allen, interview.

100. "Statement by Ronald Reagan," January 31, 1980, box 30, folder: "RR: Selected Foreign Policy and Defense Statements," Richard V. Allen Papers (hereafter RVAP), HIA.

101. Ronald Reagan, "Peace and Security in the 1980s," address to the Chicago Council on Foreign Relations, Chicago, IL, March 17, 1980, box 30, folder: "Chicago Council on Foreign Relations," RVAP, HIA.

102. Ronald Reagan, untitled campaign statement, April 30, 1980, box 30, folder: "RR: Selected Foreign Policy and Defense Statements," RVAP, HIA.

103. Steven Roberts, "Reagan, in Chicago Speech, Urges Big Increases in Military Spending," *NYT*, March 18, 1980, B8.

104. Ronald Reagan, address at the Republican National Convention, Detroit, MI, July 17, 1980, transcript, MCPA, https://millercenter.org/the-presidency/presidential-speeches/july-17-1980-republican-national-convention.

105. Jeane J. Kirkpatrick, "Dictatorships and Double Standards," *Commentary*, November 1979, 38.

106. Kirkpatrick, "Dictatorships and Double Standards," 44–45.

107. Jeane J. Kirkpatrick, interview transcript from *The Cold War*, produced by CNN, 1998, reprinted at National Security Archive, George Washington University, Washington, DC, (hereafter NSA), http://nsarchive.gwu.edu/coldwar/interviews/episode-19/kirkpatrick1.html.

108. Wattenberg, *Fighting Words*, 166. Underscoring the issue's triviality for Wattenberg, other accounts indicate that Carter discussed US efforts to promote human rights in Uruguay, not Ecuador. See Vaïsse, *Neoconservatism*, 134; Keys, *Reclaiming American Virtue*, 256.

109. Tony Dolan, "Foreign Policy: Andy Young Affair," undated, box 27, folder: "Campaign and Transition Files—Tony Dolan," RVAP, HIA.

110. James Conaway, "The Ambassador from *Commentary* Magazine," *WP*, November 1, 1981.

111. Allen, interview; italics in the original.

112. CDM members who joined the CPD included Richard E. Pipes, Midge Decter, Norman Podhoretz, Leon Keyserling, Max Kampelman, Richard Schifter, and John P. Roche. See Jerry W. Sanders, *Peddlers of Crisis: The Committee on the Present Danger and the Politics of Containment* (Cambridge, MA: South End Press, 1983), 150.

113. Conaway, "Ambassador from *Commentary* Magazine."

114. Richard V. Allen, "Ronald Reagan: An Extraordinary Man in Extraordinary Times," in *The Fall of the Berlin Wall: Reassessing the Causes and Consequences of the End of the Cold War*, ed. Peter Schweizer (Stanford, CA: Hoover Institution Press, 2000), 54.

115. William E. Pemberton, *Exit with Honor: The Life and Presidency of Ronald Reagan* (Armonk, NY: M. E. Sharpe, 1997), 89.

116. Scott Kaufman, *Plans Unraveled: The Foreign Policy of the Carter Administration* (De Kalb: Northern Illinois University Press, 2008), 117.

117. Reagan won 50.8 percent of the popular vote; Carter won 41 percent. Independent John Anderson claimed 6.6 percent.

118. Sandbrook, *Mad as Hell*, 397.

119. Kaufman, *Henry M. Jackson*, 372.

120. Jeane J. Kirkpatrick, address before the Veterans of Foreign Wars, Washington, DC, March 5, 1984, box 36, folder 10: "Miscellaneous Materials," Allen Weinstein Papers (hereafter AWP), HIA.

2. "A Hostile Takeover"

1. Ronald Reagan, "First Press Conference," January 29, 1981, transcript, MCPA, https://millercenter.org/the-presidency/presidential-speeches/january-29-1981-first-press-conference.

2. Douglas Kneeland, "A Summary of Reagan's Positions on the Major Issues of This Year's Campaign," *NYT*, July 16, 1980, A14.

3. Karen Elliott House, "Reagan's World: Republican Policies Stress Arms Buildup, a Firm Line to Soviets," *Wall Street Journal*, June 3, 1980, 1 (hereafter *WSJ*).

4. Leffler, *For the Soul of Mankind*, 347.

5. Robert M. Gates, *From the Shadows: The Ultimate Insider's Story of Five Presidents and How They Won the Cold War* (New York: Simon & Schuster, 1996), 190–91.

6. Morris Morley and Chris McGillion, *Reagan and Pinochet: The Struggle over U.S. Policy toward Chile* (New York: Cambridge University Press, 2015), 26.

7. Gates, *From the Shadows*, 192.

8. Don Oberdorfer, "Haig Calls Terrorism Top Priority: Human Rights Goals Demoted as Concern of Foreign Policy," *WP*, January 29, 1981, A1.

9. Minutes, NSC meeting, February 6, 1981, in *FRUS, 1981–1988*, 3:39.

10. Vernon Walters, quoted in James Naughtie, "Walters Favors Tact, Privacy in Promoting Rights," *WP*, July 14, 1981, A4.

11. "Wrong Turns on Human Rights," *NYT*, February 6, 1981, A2; John M. Goshko, "Delayed Rights Report Faults Seoul Regime," *WP*, February 10, 1981, A5.

12. Charles Mohr, "Human Rights Choice Abhors Scolding as U.S. Tool," *NYT*, February 13, 1981, 2.

13. John M. Goshko, "Ultraconservative May Get Human Rights Post at State," *WP*, February 5, 1981, A3.

14. Wilson, *Triumph of Improvisation*, 10.

15. Cannon, *President Reagan*, 162.

16. Michael Schaller, *Reckoning with Reagan: America and Its President in the 1980s* (New York: Oxford University Press, 1994), 52–53; Brands, *Making the Unipolar Moment*, 177; Gil Troy, "Reagan's 100-Day Revolution," in *Living in the Eighties*, ed. Gil Troy and Vincent J. Cannato (New York: Oxford University Press, 2009), 19–20.

17. Brands, *Making the Unipolar Moment*, 37.

18. Caspar Weinberger, remarks to the United Press International Luncheon of the American Newspaper Publishers Association Meeting, Chicago, IL, May 5, 1981, box 46, folder: "White House Files—Weinberger, Caspar, 1981," RVAP, HIA.

19. Leffler, *For the Soul of Mankind*, 346; Craig and Logevall, *America's Cold War*, 313.

20. Pipes, quoted in Beth A. Fischer, *The Myth of Triumphalism: Rethinking President Reagan's Cold War Legacy* (Lexington: University Press of Kentucky, 2019), 16; on the administration's

backtracking, see William Dyess, press statement, March 18, 1981, box 46, folder: "White House Files—Pipes, Richard E., 1981," RVAP, HIA.

21. Bernard Gwertzman, "Haig Cites 'Hit List' For Soviet Control of Central America," *NYT*, A1.

22. Cannon, *President Reagan*, 164.

23. Jeane J. Kirkpatrick, address before the Veterans of Foreign Wars, Washington, DC, March 5, 1984, box 36, folder 10: "Miscellaneous Materials," AWP, HIA.

24. Jeane J. Kirkpatrick, interview with Ann Miller Morin, May 28, 1987, Foreign Affairs Oral History Program of the Association for Diplomatic Studies and Training, Arlington, VA (hereafter ADST).

25. Bernard D. Nossiter, "New Team at U.N.: Common Roots and Philosophies," *NYT*, March 3, 1981, A2.

26. Tim Weiner, "Jeane Kirkpatrick, Reagan's Forceful Envoy, Dies," *NYT*, December 9, 2006.

27. James Conaway, "Jeane Kirkpatrick: the Ambassador from Commentary Magazine," *WP*, November 1, 1981.

28. Conaway, "Jeane Kirkpatrick."

29. David Binder, "Evron Kirkpatrick, 83, Director of Political Science Association," *NYT*, May 9, 1995.

30. The dissertation was subsequently published as Jeane J. Kirkpatrick, *Leader and Vanguard in Mass Society: A Study of Peronist Argentina* (Cambridge, MA: MIT Press, 1971).

31. Conaway, "Jeane Kirkpatrick."

32. Dorothy Rabinowitz, "Reagan's 'Heroine' at the U.N.," *New York Magazine*, July 20, 1981.

33. Jeane J. Kirkpatrick, address to the Franklin County Republican Finance Committee, Columbus, OH, April 3, 1981, box 1, Joseph Shattan Papers (hereafter SP), HIA.

34. Peter Collier, *Political Woman: The Big Little Life of Jeane Kirkpatrick* (New York: Encounter Books, 2012), 79–80.

35. Collier, *Political Woman*, 64.

36. Collier, *Political Woman*, 84.

37. Jeane J. Kirkpatrick, quoted in Conaway, "Jeane Kirkpatrick."

38. Weiner, "Jeane Kirkpatrick."

39. Conaway, "Jeane Kirkpatrick."

40. Conaway, "Jeane Kirkpatrick."

41. Kirkpatrick, address to the Franklin County Republican Finance Committee.

42. Rabinowitz, "Reagan's 'Heroine' at the U.N."

43. "Overhaul U.S. Policy on Human Rights?," *U.S. News and World Report*, March 2, 1981, 50.

44. Jeane J. Kirkpatrick, address to the Council on Foreign Relations, New York, NY, March 10, 1981, box 1, SP, HIA.

45. Jeane J. Kirkpatrick, speech before the Conservative Political Action Conference, Washington, DC, March 21, 1981, box 27, folder: "White House Files—Kirkpatrick, Amb. Jeane, 1981," RVAP, HIA.

46. "Overhaul U.S. Policy on Human Rights?"; italics added.

47. On the use of US military equipment transfers and counterinsurgency training programs to cultivate ties with anticommunist authoritarians, see Schmidli, *Fate of Freedom Elsewhere*, 1–28.

48. Arthur M. Schlesinger Jr., *A Thousand Days: John F. Kennedy in the White House* (Boston: Houghton Mifflin, 1965), 769.

49. Kirkpatrick, Conservative Political Action Conference speech.

50. Ronald Reagan, remarks at the Second Annual Reagan Administration Executive Forum, January 20, 1983, *PPP*, 19 Weekly Comp. Pres. Doc. 81.

51. Vita Bite, "Human Rights and U.S. Foreign Policy," CRS, January 20, 1983, box 11, Latin American Strategic Studies Institute Records (hereafter LASSIR), HIA; Juan de Onis, "U.S. Improving Ties to Latin Rightists," *NYT*, March 8, 1981, 4.

52. Grandin, *Empire's Workshop*, 90.

53. Inter-American Commission on Human Rights, *Report on the Situation of Human Rights in the Republic of Guatemala* (Washington, DC: Organization of American States, 1981).

54. Jefferson Morley, "Rights and Reagan," *Foreign Service Journal* 59, no. 3 (March 1982): 23.

55. See Caleb Rossiter, "Human Rights: The Carter Record, the Reagan Reaction," *International Policy Report*, September 1984, 14–15.

56. John M. Goshko, "Administration Reiterates Aim of Scuttling Carter Rights Policies," *WP*, July 10, 1981, A12.

57. "Amnesty Group Sees Rights Deterioration in Four Latin Nations," *WP*, July 24, 1981, A10.

58. John M. Goshko, "Policy Change on Loans Called Illegal," *WP*, July 15, 1981, A14.

59. Edward Schumacher, "Latins Get Taste of Kirkpatrick Style," *NYT*, August 5, 1981, A3.

60. John Dinges, "Kirkpatrick Trip Upsets Opposition in Chile," *WP*, August 13, 1981, A35.

61. Department of State (DoS) cable, Santiago 923, US Embassy (George W. Landau) to DoS, August 10, 1981, subject: "Ambassador Kirkpatrick's Visit to Santiago: Overview," Digital National Security Archive, ID: CL02364 (hereafter DNSA).

62. George F. Jones, interview with Charles Stuart Kennedy, August 6, 1996, ADST.

63. Dinges, "Kirkpatrick Trip Upsets Opposition."

64. Kirkpatrick, Conservative Political Action Conference speech.

65. Schmidli, "'Sophisticated Intervention,'" 70.

66. DoS cable, Managua 000001, US Embassy (Mauricio Solaún) to DoS, subject: "Nicaraguan Atmospherics," April 27 1979, DNSA, ID: NI00698.

67. Jeane J. Kirkpatrick, "U.S. Security & Latin America," *Commentary* 71, no. 1 (January 1981): 36–37; italics in the original.

68. Kirkpatrick, "U.S. Security & Latin America."

69. Raymond Bonner, "The Diplomat Who Wouldn't Lie," *Politico*, April 23, 2015.

70. Stephen G. Rabe, *The Killing Zone: The United States Wages Cold War in Latin America* (New York: Oxford University Press, 2011), 156; Raymond Bonner, "The Agony of El Salvador," *NYT*, February 22, 1981, SM7.

71. Aldo A. Lauria-Santiago, "The Culture and Politics of State Terror and Repression in El Salvador," in *When States Kill: Latin America, the U.S., and Technologies of Terror*, ed. Cecilia Menjívar and Néstor Rodríguez (Austin: University of Texas Press, 2009), 89.

72. Lauria-Santiago, "State Terror and Repression," 92.

73. Loren Jenkins, "Salvador: From Conquistadores to Comunistas, Why the Killing Will Never End," *WP*, August 16, 1981, 11.

74. Arnson, *Crossroads*, 51.

75. Kirkpatrick, Conservative Political Action Conference speech. In asserting that revolutions occur in periods of relative improvement, Kirkpatrick explicitly drew on the work of the historian Crane Brinton. See Crane Brinton, *The Anatomy of Revolution*, rev. and expanded ed. (1938; New York: Vintage Books, 1965).

76. Kirkpatrick, Conservative Political Action Conference speech.

77. Alexander M. Haig Jr., *Caveat: Realism, Reagan, and Foreign Policy* (New York: Macmillan, 1984), 30.

78. Pastor, *Not Condemned to Repetition*, 190.

79. NSC meeting minutes, February 6, 1981, Executive Secretariat: Meeting Files, box 1, folder: NSC 00001, RRL.

80. NSC meeting minutes, February 6, 1981.

81. NSC meeting minutes, February 6, 1981.

82. DoS, Bureau of Public Affairs, "Communist Interference in El Salvador," February 23, 1981, Special Report No. 80, DNSA, ID: ES01388.

83. LeoGrande, *Our Own Backyard*, 89. See also Arnson, *Crossroads*, 57.

84. LeoGrande, *Our Own Backyard*, 89.

85. NSC meeting minutes, February 18, 1981, Executive Secretariat: Meeting Files, box 1, folder: NSC 00003, RRL.

86. DoS cable, Managua 00095 (Pezzullo to Haig), January 9, 1981, subject: "Meeting with [Tomás] Borge," DNSA, ID: NI01248; DoS cable, Managua 00103 (Pezzullo to Haig), January 9, 1981, subject: "Conversation with Junta Member Sergio Ramírez," DNSA, ID: NI01250; DoS cable, Managua 0440 (Pezzullo to Haig), January 29, 1981, subject: "Meeting with GRN [Government of Nicaragua] Officials," DNSA, ID: CO00972; DoS cable, Managua 0455 (Pezzullo to Haig), January 30, 1981, subject: "Salvadoran Issue," DNSA, ID: CO00974.

87. Lawrence A. Pezzullo, interview with Arthur R. Day, February 24, 1989, ADST.

88. NSC meeting minutes, February 11, 1981, Executive Secretariat: Meeting Files, box 1, folder: NSC 00002, RRL.

89. CIA, National Intelligence Daily, March 2, 1981, Central Intelligence Agency Records Search Tool (CREST), ID: CIA-RDP83T00296R000100030003-5.

90. DoS cable, Managua 00432 (Pezzullo to Haig), January 28, 1981, subject: "FSLN Stirs War Psychosis," DNSA, ID: NI1264.

91. DoS cable, Managua 0758 (Pezzullo to Haig), February 14[?], 1981, included in White House memorandum, Richard V. Allen to Ronald Reagan, February 16, 1981, subject: "Nicaragua," Executive Secretariat: NSC, Country Files, Nicaragua, box 32, folder: "Nicaragua 1/20/81–12/31/82," RRL.

92. White House memorandum, Richard V. Allen to Ronald Reagan, January 30, 1981, subject: "Cable from U.S. Ambassador to Nicaragua, Lawrence A. Pezzullo: Conversation with Junta Member Arturo Cruz," Executive Secretariat: NSC, Country Files, Nicaragua, box 32, folder: "Nicaragua, 1/20/81–12/31/82," RRL.

93. DoS cable, Managua 0780 (Pezzullo to Haig), February 17, 1981, subject: "Meeting with Daniel Ortega," Executive Secretariat: NSC, Country Files, Nicaragua, box 32, folder: "Nicaragua, 1/20/81–12/31/82," RRL.

94. DoS memorandum, Alexander M. Haig Jr. to Ronald Reagan, March 18, 1982, subject: "Determination on Nicaraguan Support for Violence," Executive Secretariat: Meeting Files, box 1, folder: NSC 00003, RRL. On stepped-up surveillance, see John A. Bushnell, interview with John Harter, December 19, 1997, ADST.

95. DoS cable, Managua 0440 (Pezzullo to Haig), January 29, 1981; Pezzullo, interview.

96. DoS cable, State 030214 (Haig to US Embassy Honduras), February 5, 1981, subject: "Memorandum of Secretary Haig's Conversation with Honduran Foreign Minister Elvir," DNSA, ID: NI01266.

97. NSC meeting minutes, February 11, 1981.

98. Pezzullo, interview.

99. NSC meeting minutes, February 18, 1981.

100. DoS cable, BA 1312 (Walters to Haig), February 25, 1981, subject: "My Talk with President Videla," DNSA, ID: AR02377; DoS cable, BA 1311 (Walters to Haig), February 25, 1981, subject: "My Talk with President Videla," DNSA; DoS cable, Santiago 1136 (Walters to Haig), February 26, 1981, DNSA; DoS cable, BA 1335 (Walters to Haig), February 26, 1981, DNSA. Walters subsequently visited Chile and received a promise of support in the El Salvador situation from Pinochet. DoS secret cable, Santiago, US Embassy (Walters) to secretary of state (Haig), subject: "Chile / El Salvador," February 27, 1981, DNSA, ID: CL02359.

101. DoS cable, Santiago 1135 (Walters to Haig), February 26, 1981, subject: "Argentina / El Salvador," DNSA, ID: AR02381.

102. "Presidential Finding on Covert Operations in Central America," secret, March 9, 1981, DNSA, ID: NI01287.

103. LeoGrande, *Our Own Backyard*, 115; Ariel C. Armony, *Argentina, the United States, and the Anti-Communist Crusade in Central America, 1977–1984* (Athens: Ohio University Center for International Studies, 1997); Peter Kornbluh, *Nicaragua, the Price of Intervention: Reagan's War against the Sandinistas* (Washington, DC: Institute for Policy Studies, 1987), 19–20.

104. Oswald Johnston, "U.S., Unconvinced of Salvador Arms Halt, Ends Aid to Nicaragua," *LAT*, April 2, 1981, B7.

105. DoS memorandum, Haig to Reagan, March 18, 1982.

106. NSC memorandum, Roger Fontaine to Richard V. Allen, March 16, 1981, subject: "Your Request for Implications of Aid Cut-Off to Nicaragua," Executive Secretariat: NSC, Country Files, Nicaragua, box 32, folder: "Nicaragua, 1/20/81–12/31/82," RRL.

107. On the significance of LaFever's failed confirmation bid, see Sarah B. Snyder, "The Defeat of Ernest Lefever's Nomination: Keeping Human Rights on the United States Foreign Policy Agenda," in *Challenging US Foreign Policy: America and the World in the Long Twentieth Century*, ed. Bevan Sewell and Scott Lucas (New York: Palgrave Macmillan, 2011), 136–61.

108. "Excerpts from State Department Memo on Human Rights," *NYT*, November 5, 1981, A10.

109. "Excerpts from State Department Memo on Human Rights."

110. On Reagan's approving the memo, see "Reagan Rights Policy Confirmed," *NYT*, November 9, 1981, A4.

111. "Nomination of Elliott Abrams to Be an Assistant Secretary of State," October 30, 1981, *PPP*, 1981, 1004.

112. "Biography of Elliott Abrams," December 27, 1984, box 319, folder: "Abrams," William J. Casey Papers, 1928–1996, HIA. On Jackson and human rights, see Keys, *Reclaiming American Virtue*, 103–26; Kaufman, *Henry M. Jackson*, 287–300; Vaïsse, *Neoconservatism*, 111–22.

113. Don Oberdorfer, "Panel Approves Abrams, Sees 'Commitment' to Human Rights," *WP*, November 18, 1981, A3.

114. Oberdorfer, "Panel Approves Abrams."

115. Judith Miller, "A Neoconservative for Human Rights Post," *NYT*, October 31, 1981, 7; "Senate Panel Backs Abrams for Post on Human Rights," *NYT*, November 18, 1981, A3.

116. *WP*, For the Record, June 4, 1981, A18.

117. Joseph Shattan, "Economic 'Rights' under Communism," undated [1981?], box 2, SP, HIA.

118. *WP*, For the Record.

119. Vita Bite, "Human Rights in U.S. Foreign Relations: Six Key Questions in the Continuing Policy Debate," CRS, December 10, 1981, box 11, LASSIR, HIA; Elliott Abrams, quoted in Charles Maechling Jr., "Human Rights Dehumanized," *Foreign Policy*, no. 52 (Autumn 1983): 124.

120. Elliott Abrams, address to the Education and Research Institute, Washington, DC, August 2, 1983, box 14, SP, HIA.

121. Kirkpatrick, Conservative Political Action Conference speech.

122. DoS cable, Washington 146816 DoS (Haig) to US Embassy Managua, June 5, 1981, subject: "Press Guidance on WP Tanks for Nicaragua Story," DNSA, ID: NI01338.

123. NSC memorandum, William L. Stearman and Roger Fontaine to Richard V. Allen, June 8, 1981, subject: "Military Build-Up in Nicaragua," Executive Secretariat: NSC, Country Files, Nicaragua, box 32, folder: "Nicaragua, 1/20/81–12/31/82," RRL.

124. Memorandum, Richard V. Allen to Ronald Reagan, June 6, 1981, subject: "Nicaraguan Militarization Update," DNSA, ID: CO01028.

125. Roy Gutman, *Banana Diplomacy: The Making of American Policy in Nicaragua, 1981–1987* (New York: Simon & Schuster, 1988), 67.

126. Pezzullo, interview.

127. CIA, National Intelligence Estimate, subject: "Insurgency and Instability in Central America," September 4, 1981, DNSA: CO01054.

128. Joseph E. Persico, *Casey: The Lives and Secrets of William J. Casey: From the OSS to the CIA* (New York: Viking, 1990), 273. See also, Armony, *Anti-Communist Crusade in Central America*.

129. LeoGrande, *Our Own Backyard*, 117–18. See also Edgar Chamorro and Jefferson Morley, "Confessions of a 'Contra,'" *New Republic*, August 5, 1985.

130. Pezzullo, interview.

131. Anthony Quainton, interview with Charles Stuart Kennedy, November 6, 1997, ADST.

132. NSC meeting minutes, November 10, 1981, DNSA, ID: CO01086.

133. NSC meeting minutes, November 10, 1981.

134. NSC meeting minutes, November 10, 1981.

135. Kornbluh, *Nicaragua, the Price of Intervention*, 22–23; LeoGrande, *Our Own Backyard*, 146.

136. "Haig, Meese, Weinberger Warn of Nicaragua Action," *LAT*, November 23, 1981, A5.

137. Gerald Seib, "Haig Calls Nicaragua Rule Totalitarian, Refuses to Rule Out Intervention by U.S.," *WSJ*, November 13, 1981, 2.

138. Duane R. Clarridge, *A Spy for All Seasons: My Life in the CIA*, with Digby Diehl (New York: Scribner, 1997), 197.

139. See Troy, "Reagan's 100-Day Revolution."

140. On the PATCO strike, see Joseph A. McCartin, *Collision Course: Ronald Reagan, the Air Traffic Controllers, and the Strike That Changed America* (New York: Oxford University Press, 2013).

141. Cannon, *President Reagan*, 91.

142. Craig and Logevall, *America's Cold War*, 315.

143. LeoGrande, *Our Own Backyard*, 89.

144. "The Silent War against Nicaragua: Strategy of Terror," *Envío* (Managua, Nicaragua), no. 18 (December 1982), https://www.envio.org.ni/articulo/3383, accessed November 19, 2021.

145. Elliott Abrams, quoted in Hauke Hartmann, "U.S. Human Rights Policy under Carter and Reagan, 1977–1981," *Human Rights Quarterly* 23, no. 2 (May 2001): 424.

146. White House memorandum of conversation, March 17, 1981, subject: "Summary of the President's Meeting with Argentine President-Designate General Roberto O. Viola," Executive Secretariat: NSC, Subject File, box 13, folder: "Memorandum of Conversation, President Reagan, March 9–19, 1981," RRL.

147. Bite, "Human Rights in U.S. Foreign Relations."

148. Andrea Oñate, "The Red Affair: FMLN-Cuban Relations during the Salvadoran Civil War, 1981–92," *Cold War History* 11, no. 2 (May 2011): 134.

149. Jonathan Kwitney, "Apparent Errors Cloud U.S. White Paper on Reds in El Salvador," *WSJ*, June 8, 1981.

150. Robert G. Kaiser, "White Paper on El Salvador Is Faulty," *WP*, June 9, 1981, A1.

151. Bonner, "Agony of El Salvador," SM7.

152. Aryeh Neier, "Tropic of Fire," *Mother Jones*, January 1982, 44.

153. The massacre itself was not unique. Describing the Atlacatl Battalion's actions in the broader military operation, the Commission on the Truth for El Salvador later reported that "in all instances, troops acted in the same way: they killed anyone they came across, men, women and children, and then set fire to the houses." United Nations Security Council, *From Madness to Hope: The 12-Year War in El Salvador: Report of the Commission on the Truth for El Salvador* (New York: United Nations Security Council, 1993), accessed at https://www.usip.org/sites/default/files/file/ElSalvador-Report.pdf.

154. Mark Danner, *The Massacre at El Mozote: A Parable of the Cold War* (New York: Vintage Books, 1994), 127.

3. "Is This Not Respect for Human, Economic, and Social Rights?"

1. Salman Rushdie, *The Jaguar Smile: A Nicaraguan Journey* (New York: Random House, 1987), 23.

2. Daniel Ortega Saavedra, address to the Thirty-Eighth General Assembly of the United Nations, September 27, 1983; published as Daniel Ortega Saavedra, "Address to the United Nations General Assembly," *Contemporary Marxism*, no. 8 (Spring 1984): 104.

3. Harvey Williams, "The Social Programs," in *Revolution and Counterrevolution in Nicaragua*, ed. Thomas W. Walker (Boulder, CO: Westview Press, 1991), 190–93.

4. Ortega, "Address to the United Nations General Assembly," 104.

5. Arnson, *Crossroads*, ix.

6. Harry W. Shlaudeman, interview with William E. Knight, May 24, 1993, ADST.

7. Jaime Wheelock, interview by Marta Harnecker, in "Jaime Wheelock Román on the Nicaraguan Revolution," Center for the Study of American Militarism, 1984, accessed in El Instituto de Historia de Nicaragua y Centroamérica, Universidad Centroamericana, Managua, Nicaragua (hereafter IHNCA).

8. CIA report, January 1981, subject: "Nicaragua: Slow Rebuilding of a Shattered Economy," DNSA, ID: NI01246; LaFeber, *Inevitable Revolutions*, 162–66; Rabe, *Killing Zone*, 155–56.

9. FSLN fact sheet, "Five Years of Transformations in Education, Health and Housing," 1984, box 2, folder: "General Subject Area: 1984," Nicaragua Subject Collection (hereafter NiSC), HIA.

10. See George Black, *Triumph of the People: The Sandinista Revolution in Nicaragua* (London: Zed Press, 1982), 58–62.

11. Stephen Kinzer, *Blood of Brothers: Life and War in Nicaragua* (New York: Putnam, 1991), 15.

12. Rushdie, *Jaguar Smile*, 7.

13. LaFeber, *Inevitable Revolutions*, 228.

14. CIA report, September 6, 1978, subject: "Nicaragua: The Sandinista Guerrillas and Their International Links," DNSA, ID: NI00208; Black, *Triumph of the People*, 126–29; Donald C. Hodges, *Intellectual Foundations of the Nicaraguan Revolution* (Austin: University of Texas Press, 1986), 248–49; Thomas W. Walker, *Nicaragua: Living in the Shadow of the Eagle*, 4th ed. (Boulder, CO: Westview Press, 2011), 36–37.

15. Xavier Argüello, "The Bitter Cost of Experience: Alfonso Robelo," reprinted in *The Nirex Collection: Nicaraguan Revolution Extracts*, ed. Porfirio R. Solórzano (Austin, TX: Litex, 1993), 2:224.

16. Warren Hoge, "Nicaraguan City, Shattered in War, Faces Harsh Peace," *NYT*, August 3, 1979, A3.

17. Alan Riding, "Reporter's Notebook: Somoza Fights on as Aides Worry," *NYT*, June 28, 1979, A2. See also John A. Booth, *The End and the Beginning: The Nicaraguan Revolution*, 2nd ed. (Boulder, CO: Westview Press, 1985), 177.

18. The *Historic Program* idealistically outlined the FSLN's revolutionary goals, including pluralism, a mixed economy, and a nonaligned foreign policy. Primarily written by lifelong Nicaraguan revolutionary Carlos Fonseca, and adopted by the members of the FSLN in San José, Costa Rica, in 1969, it was reprinted numerous times during the decade of FSLN rule. Frente Sandinista de Liberación Nacional (FSLN), *Programa Histórico del FSLN* (Managua: Departamento de Propaganda y Educación Politica del FSLN, 1984).

19. Zimmermann, *Sandinista*, 215.

20. Thomas W. Walker, "The Armed Forces," in *Revolution and Counterrevolution in Nicaragua*, ed. Thomas W. Walker (Boulder, CO: Westview Press, 1991), 79.

21. DoS cable, Managua 02086, US Embassy (Pezzullo) to DoS, May 8, 1981, subject: "[Excised] Nicaragua," DNSA, ID: NI01325.

22. Alan Riding, "Reporter's Notebook: Managua Relaxes," *NYT*, July 23, 1979, A3.

23. International Bank for Reconstruction and Development (IBRD) report, February 16, 1982, subject: "Country Program Paper: Nicaragua," DNSA, ID: NI01446; FSLN fact sheet, "The Nicaraguan Economy after Five Years of Revolution," 1984, box 2, folder: "General Subject Area: 1984," NiSC, HIA; LaFeber, *Inevitable Revolutions*, 238; Booth, *End and the Beginning*, 170; Thomas W. Walker, *Nicaragua: The Land of Sandino* (Boulder, CO: Westview Press, 1981), 78.

24. DoS cable, Managua 3332, US Embassy (Thomas J. O'Donnell) to secretary of state, July 25, 1979, subject: "The GRN Confronts a Shattered Economy: Some Impressions of the First Days," DNSA, ID: NI00998.

25. The directorate consisted of Bayardo Arce, Tomás Borge, and Henry Ruiz (originally members of the Prolonged Popular War faction); Luis Carrión, Carlos Núñez Tellez, and Jaime Wheelock (Proletarian Tendency); and Daniel Ortega Saavedra, Humberto Ortega Saavedra, and Víctor Tirado López (Insurrectional Faction, also known as the Third Way). The Ministry of the Interior went to Borge, Humberto Ortega took the Ministry of Defense, Ruiz was given the Ministry of Planning, and Wheelock was assigned the Ministry of Agriculture and Rural Development. See Walker, *Nicaragua: The Land of Sandino*, 40–41, 156–57.

26. Regis Debray, "Nicaragua: Radical 'Moderation,'" *Contemporary Marxism*, no. 1 (Spring 1980): 10.

27. LaFeber, *Inevitable Revolutions*, 81.

28. Anastasio Somoza García (1896–1956) ruled Nicaragua until his assassination. He was succeeded by his two sons, Luis Somoza Debayle (1922–1967) and Anastasio Somoza Debayle (1925–1980). The former died in office of a heart attack; the latter was overthrown in 1979 and then assassinated while in exile in Paraguay. On US interventionism in Nicaragua in the early twentieth century, see Michel Gobat, *Confronting the American Dream: Nicaragua under U.S. Imperial Rule* (Durham, NC: Duke University Press, 2005); Alan McPherson, *The Invaded: How Latin Americans and Their Allies Fought and Ended U.S. Occupations* (New York: Oxford University Press, 2014).

29. Peter Winn, *Americas: The Changing Face of Latin America and the Caribbean*, 3rd ed. (Berkeley: University of California Press, 2006), 544.

30. Anthony Lake, *Somoza Falling* (Boston: Houghton Mifflin, 1989), 9.

31. "The Dilemmas Confronting the Sandinista Revolution: Three Years after the Victory," *Envío*, no. 13 (July 1982), https://www.envio.org.ni/articulo/3367, accessed November 19, 2021.

32. LaFeber, *Inevitable Revolutions*, 165. See also Leslie Gill, *The School of the Americas: Military Training and Political Violence in the Americas* (Durham, NC: Duke University Press, 2004).

33. Kinzer, *Blood of Brothers*, 119.

34. Sergio Ramírez, address to the Conference on Central America, sponsored by the Sandinista Association of Cultural Workers, 1983; published as Sergio Ramírez, "The Unfinished Revolution and Nicaragua Today," *Contemporary Marxism*, no. 8 (Spring 1984): 214.

35. "Memorandum of Todor Zhivkov—Fidel Castro Conversation, Havana," April 9, 1979, History and Public Policy Program Digital Archive, accessed at Cold War International History Project (hereafter CWIHP), Woodrow Wilson Center for International Scholars, Washington, DC (hereafter WWC), http://digitalarchive.wilsoncenter.org/document/111071; Kinzer, *Blood of Brothers*, 67.

36. Pezzullo, interview.

37. Sergio Ramírez, *Adiós Muchachos: A Memoir of the Sandinista Revolution* (Durham, NC: Duke University Press, 2011), 78.

38. On post-conflict assistance, see K. Cheasty Anderson, "Doctors within Borders: Cuban Medical Diplomacy to Sandinista Nicaragua, 1979–1990," in *Beyond the Eagle's Shadow: New Histories of Latin America's Cold War*, ed. Virginia Garrard-Burnett, Mark Atwood Lawrence, and Julio E. Moreno (Albuquerque: University of New Mexico Press, 2013), 200–225.

39. CIA background paper, February 10, 1982, subject: "National Security Council on Caribbean Basin," DNSA, ID: CO01131; "Transcript of Meeting between US Secretary of State Alexander M. Haig, Jr., and Cuban Vice Premier Carlos Rafael Rodriguez, Mexico City," November 23, 1981, History and Public Policy Program Digital Archive, CWIHP, WWC, http://digitalarchive.wilsoncenter.org/document/111221.

40. Ramírez, *Adiós Muchachos*, 78.

41. Humberto Ortega a compañeros del Estado Mayor del Frente Norte "Carlos Fonseca Amador," 7 enero 1979, colección: partidos político, fondo: FSLN, folder: 0049, IHNCA, author's translation.

42. "Analysis de la coyuntura y tareas de la Revolución Popular Sandinista," in *Sandinistas: Key Documents / Documentos Claves*, ed. Dennis Gilbert and David Block (Ithaca, NY: Cornell University Latin American Studies Program, 1990), 20–21, author's translation.

43. Ramírez, *Adiós Muchachos*, 74.

44. Argüello, "Bitter Cost of Experience," 224.

45. Pastor, *Not Condemned to Repetition*, 116.

46. Department of Defense (DoD) report, May 27, 1983, subject: "Background Paper: Central America," DNSA, ID: CO01307.

47. See Humberto Ortega Saavedra, "Discurso del Ministro de Defensa, Comandante en Jefe del E.P.S. y Jefe de las Milicias Sandinistas Humberto Ortega S. en la clausura de la Reunión de Especialistas," reprinted in Gilbert and Block, *Sandinistas: Key Documents*, 292–313. For the Sandinista cover-up, see DoS cable, Managua 04501, US Embassy (Roger Gamble) to secretary of state, October 13, 1981, subject: "GRN Minister of Defense Ortega Outlines Radical Goals for Sandinista Army," DNSA, ID: NI01393.

48. On Fonseca's influence, see Zimmermann, *Sandinista*.

49. Ramírez, *Adiós Muchachos*, 76.

50. IBRD report, February 16, 1982.

51. "Some Aspects of Nicaragua's Economy," *Envío*, no. 5 (October 1981), https://www.envio.org.ni/articulo/3117, accessed November 19, 2021.

52. FSLN fact sheet, "Five Years of Transformations."

53. FSLN fact sheet, "Five Years of Transformations."

54. "Some Aspects of Nicaragua's Economy." On the literacy campaign, see also Andrew J. Kirkendall, *Paulo Freire and the Cold War Politics of Literacy* (Chapel Hill: University of North Carolina Press, 2010), 118–52.

55. Harry Nelson, "Sandinistas Revolutionize Health Care in Nicaragua," *LAT*, August 25, 1983, C1.

56. "Nicaragua: Three Years of Achievements," *Envío*, no. 13 (July 1982), https://www.envio.org.ni/articulo/3368, accessed November 19, 2021.

57. "Some Aspects of Nicaragua's Economy."

58. FSLN fact sheet, "Five Years of Transformations."

59. "Nicaragua: Three Years of Achievements."

60. CIA report, January 1981.

61. DoS cable, DoS 201360, secretary of state (Haig) to US Embassy, July 30, 1981, subject: "Assessment of Nicaraguan Situation," DNSA, ID: NI01364.

62. "Some Aspects of Nicaragua's Economy."

63. FSLN, *Programa Histórico del FSLN*, 21–22, author's translation.

64. FSLN fact sheet, "Nicaraguan Economy."

65. "Nicaragua: Three Years of Achievements."

66. FSLN fact sheet, "Nicaraguan Economy." See also Katherine Hoyt, *The Many Faces of Sandinista Democracy* (Athens: Ohio University Center for International Studies, 1997), 108; Bruce E. Wright, *Theory in the Practice of the Nicaraguan Revolution* (Athens: Ohio University Center for International Studies, 1995), 191; Laura J. Enríquez, *Agrarian Reform and Class Consciousness in Nicaragua* (Gainesville: University Press of Florida, 1997), 33.

67. Tomás Borge, address at the Second Anniversary of the Sandinista Revolution, July 1981; reproduced in *Sandinistas Speak: Speeches, Writings, and Interviews with Leaders of Nicaragua's Revolution*, by Tomás Borge et al. (New York: Pathfinder Press, 1982), 133.

68. Wheelock, interview. See also "Dilemmas Confronting the Sandinista Revolution."

69. Steve Frazier, "Political Standoff Stymies Nicaragua," *WSJ*, January 8, 1981, 23.

70. "Nicaragua: Three Years of Achievements." See also Dennis Gilbert, *Sandinistas: The Party and the Revolution* (New York: Wiley-Blackwell, 1991), 64–65; Luis Hector Serra, "The Grass-Roots Organizations," in *Revolution and Counterrevolution in Nicaragua*, ed. Thomas W. Walker (Boulder, CO: Westview Press, 1991), 49–75.

71. Tomás Borge, quoted in Tony Ryan, "'Generous in Victory': A Conversation about Human Rights in Nicaragua," *Nicaraguan Perspectives*, no. 6 (Summer 1983), reprinted in Solórzano, *Nirex Collection*, 8:710.

72. Argüello, "Bitter Cost of Experience," 224.

73. Gilbert, *Sandinistas*, 110–11.

74. Americas Watch Committee, "Nicaragua: A Human Rights Chronology, July 1979 to July 1989," July 1989, accessed in IHNCA; DoS cable, DoS 201360, secretary of state (Haig) to US Embassy Honduras, July 30, 1981.

75. "Dilemmas Confronting the Sandinista Revolution."

76. Ramírez, "Unfinished Revolution and Nicaragua Today," 215.

77. "Sandinismo no es democratismo," *Barricada*, March 14, 1980, italics added; reprinted in Gilbert and Block, *Sandinistas: Key Documents*, 112–13.

78. "Excerpts from Speech by Comandante Tomás Borge," *Envío*, no. 8 (January 1982), https://www.envio.org.ni/articulo/3268, accessed November 19, 2021.

79. Ramírez, "Unfinished Revolution and Nicaragua Today," 214.

80. Pezzullo, interview; see also Juan O. Tamayo, "Sandinistas Attract a Who's Who of Terrorists," *Miami Herald*, March 3, 1985.

81. See US Foreign Broadcast Information Service memorandum, March 9, 1982, subject: "Statements by Nicaraguan Leaders on Support for Insurgency in Central America," DNSA, ID: NI01459.

82. NSC meeting minutes, February 11, 1981, Executive Secretariat: Meeting Files, box 1, folder: NSC 00002, RRL.

83. Ramírez, *Adiós Muchachos*, 99.

84. Wheelock, interview; italics added.

85. Ramírez, "Unfinished Revolution and Nicaragua Today," 211.

86. Sargent, *Superpower Transformed*, 176–77.

87. "Nicaragua's Foreign Policy: Ten Years of Principles and Practice," *Envío*, no. 97 (August 1989), https://www.envio.org.ni/articulo/2731, accessed November 19, 2021.

88. "La reunión histórica mas trascendental de Centroamérica," *Soberanía* (Managua), no. 8 (January 1983), reprinted in Solórzano, *Nirex Collection*, 4:789.

89. Communiqué of the Special Ministerial Meeting of the Coordinating Bureau of the Non-Aligned Movement on Latin America and the Caribbean, January 10–14, 1983, reprinted in Solórzano, *Nirex Collection*, 4:795.

90. At NAM's subsequent seventh summit conference in New Delhi in early 1983, Nicaragua was elected as one of the movement's twenty vice presidencies as well as president of the economic commission. "Latin American Consensus in New Delhi," *Barricada Internacional*, March 14, 1983, reprinted in Solórzano, *Nirex Collection*, 4:815.

91. Yuri Pavlov, interview transcript from *The Cold War*, produced by CNN, 1998, reprinted at NSA, https://nsarchive2.gwu.edu/coldwar/interviews/episode-18/pavlov1.html.

92. DoS, Bureau of Intelligence and Research report, June 24, 1981, subject: "Developing Soviet-Nicaraguan Relations," DNSA, ID: NI01346.

93. "Analysis de la coyuntura y tareas de la Revolución Popular Sandinista," 12.

94. DoS cable, Managua 02815, US Embassy (Pezzullo) to DoS, June 27, 1981, subject: "Meeting with EPS Chief of Staff, Joaquin Cuadra," DNSA, ID: NI01347.

95. Wheelock, interview.

96. James P. Wooten, "The Nicaraguan Military Buildup: Implications for U.S. Interest in Central America," nonclassified report, CRS, December 18, 1985, Library of Congress, Washington, DC (hereafter LC), DNSA, ID: NI02639. In 1981, Reagan's NSC circulated higher estimates of Nicaraguan military strength, estimating 20,000–25,000 regular forces and 35,000–50,000 militia members. NSC memorandum, William L. Stearman and Roger Fontaine to Richard V. Allen,

June 8, 1981, subject: "Military Build-Up in Nicaragua," Executive Secretariat: NSC, Country Files, Nicaragua, box 32, folder: "Nicaragua, 1/20/81–12/31/82," RRL.

97. CIA memorandum, September 14, 1983, subject: "Nicaragua: Accelerating Military Assistance," DNSA, ID: CO01337; DoS and DoD, unclassified report, May 1985, subject: "The Sandinista Military Build-Up," DNSA, ID: NI02459; Klaus Storkmann, "East German Military Aid to the Sandinista Government of Nicaragua," *Journal of Cold War Studies* 16, no. 2 (Spring 2014): 59.

98. Stephen Kinzer, "The Beleaguered Revolution," *NYT*, August 28, 1983, SM22.

99. IBRD report, February 16, 1982.

100. DoS cable, Managua 2798, US Embassy (Pezzullo) to DoS, June 30, 1981, subject: "COSEP Refutes Ortega," DNSA, ID: CO01033.

101. "Additional Comments by Xabier Gorostiaga," *Envío*, no. 5 (October 1981), https://www.envio.org.ni/articulo/3119, accessed November 19, 2021.

102. "Additional Comments by Xabier Gorostiaga."

103. IBRD report, February 16, 1982.

104. CRS, "Nicaragua: Conditions and U.S. Interests," November 19, 1981, DNSA, ID: NI01409; DoS cable, DoS 201360, secretary of state (Haig) to US Embassy, July 30, 1981; "Additional Comments by Xabier Gorostiaga."

105. DoS cable, Managua 2971, US Embassy (Quainton) to DoS, June 30, 1982, subject: "Nicaraguan Agrarian Reform: The Slow Pace of Redistribution," DNSA, ID: NI01533.

106. DoS cable, Managua 02086, US Embassy (Pezzullo) to DoS, May 8, 1981.

107. DoS cable, Managua 02086, US Embassy (Pezzullo) to DoS, May 8, 1981.

108. In January 1982, Clark replaced Richard V. Allen as national security adviser. He held the position until November 1983, when he replaced James G. Watt as secretary of the Interior.

109. NSC meeting minutes, February 10, 1982, subject: "The Caribbean Basin," DNSA, ID: CO01132; emphasis in the original.

110. CIA background paper, February 10, 1982.

111. CIA background paper, February 10, 1982.

112. NSC meeting minutes, February 10, 1982; italics added.

113. NSC meeting minutes, February 10, 1982.

114. Clarridge, *Spy for All Seasons*, 197.

115. Don Oberdorfer and Patrick E. Tyler, "U.S.-Backed Nicaraguan Rebel Army Swells to 7,000 Men," *WP*, May 8, 1983, A1.

116. DoS cable, US Embassy Nicaragua (Quainton) to DoS, March 16, 1982, subject: "GRN Proclaims State of Emergency," DNSA, ID: NI01468; Stanley Meisler, "Nicaragua Lacking in Revolutionary Fervor," *LAT*, March 22, 1982, 11.

117. Tomás Borge, address at the Permanent Conference of Political Parties of Latin America, Managua, February 1982, reproduced in *Nicaraguan Perspectives*, no. 4 (Summer 1982): 11.

118. Defense Intelligence Agency, weekly intelligence summary, July 16, 1982, DNSA, ID: NI01547.

119. DoS cable, Managua 4943, US Embassy (Quainton) to DoS, October 10, 1982, subject: "Assessment of Recent Counterrevolutionary Activity," DNSA, ID: NI01610.

120. Dos cable, Managua 4943, US Embassy (Quainton) to DoS, October 10, 1982.

121. CIA report, March 22, 1982, subject: "Nicaraguan Military Buildup," DNSA, ID: NI01474; DoS and DoD, unclassified report, May 1985.

122. Shultz replaced Haig as secretary of state in July 1982. DoS cable, Managua 5441, US Embassy (Gamble) to DoS, November 23, 1982, subject: "Junta Coordinator Reiterates Nicaragua's Policy on Arms Acquisition," DNSA, ID: NI01616.

123. LaFeber, *Inevitable Revolutions*, 296.

124. David Treadwell, "The Times Poll: Public Opposes U.S. Role in El Salvador," *LAT*, April 12, 1983, A11.

125. Regarding the use of the term "freedom fighters," see, for example, Ronald Reagan, question-and-answer session with reporters, May 4, 1983, *PPP*, 19 Weekly Comp. Pres. Doc. 643.

126. George Skelton and Don Shannon, "Reagan Denies Effort to Topple Nicaragua Junta," *LAT*, April 15, 1983, B1.

127. Jean J. Kirkpatrick, "Communism in Central America," *WP*, April 7, 1983, D8.

128. Don Oberdorfer, "Shultz Says Nicaragua Aims at 'All of Central America,'" *WP*, April 16, 1983, A18.

129. Ronald Reagan, address before a joint session of Congress, April 27, 1983, *PPP*, 19 Weekly Comp. Pres. Doc. 608.

130. Memorandum, William J. Casey to Ronald Reagan, June 25, 1983, DNSA, ID: CO01313.

131. Memorandum, Robert C. McFarlane to Oliver L. North, July 7, 1983, subject: "Central American Paper for NSC Meeting," DNSA, ID: CO01321.

132. Memorandum, Ronald Reagan to George P. Shultz, Caspar Weinberger, William J. Casey, and John W. Vessey Jr., July 12, 1983, subject: "Central America," DNSA, ID: IC00133.

133. Kim Rogal, "Reagan's Gunboat Diplomacy," *Newsweek*, August 1, 1983, 14.

134. John Brecher, "A Secret War for Nicaragua," *Newsweek*, November 8, 1982.

135. CIA intelligence memorandum, secret, July 26, 1983, subject: "Nicaragua: Costs of the Insurgency," DNSA, ID: CO01327.

136. Reed Brody, *Contra Terror in Nicaragua: Report of a Fact-Finding Mission: September 1984–January 1985* (Boston: South End Press, 1985), 22.

137. Dirección General de Divulgación y Prensa, "Conspiración de la C.I.A. en Nicaragua," Managua, June 1983, IHNCA. Following the plot's exposure, Nicaragua expelled three US Embassy officials, one of whom was accused of paying Moncada $5,000 to give D'Escoto the wine. The State Department retaliated by closing all six Nicaraguan consulates in the United States and expelling twenty-one Nicaraguan diplomats. William D. Montalbano, "U.S. Envoy Gets a Cool Welcome in Nicaragua," *LAT*, June 11, 1983, A1.

138. Tomás Borge, "Conferencia de prensa sobre 'Manual de operaciones de la CIA,'" October 1984, IHNCA; Amnesty International, *Nicaragua: The Human Rights Record* (London: Amnesty International, March 1986), 34–36.

139. "Food Supply: Nicaragua's Daily Challenge," *Envío*, no. 27 (September 1983) https://www.envio.org.ni/articulo/3534, accessed November 19, 2021; Kenneth Freed, "Sandinistas Direct Bulk of Economy," *LAT*, August 17, 1983, 10.

140. William D. Montalbano, "Leaders Hang On as Revolution Loses Romance," *LAT*, July 10, 1983, A1.

141. Don A. Schanche and Dial Torgerson, "Pope Jeered, Harassed in Nicaragua," *LAT*, March 5, 1983.

142. DoS cable, Managua 2609, US Embassy (Quainton) to DoS, June 14, 1983, subject: "Agrarian Reforms New Focus: The Armed Cooperative," DNSA, ID: NI01725.

143. DoS cable, Managua 3153, US Embassy (Quainton) to DoS, July 19, 1983, subject: "The Sandinista Revolution after Four Years," DNSA, ID: NI01769.

144. Ramírez, "Unfinished Revolution and Nicaragua Today," 215.

145. Tomás Borge, "The U.S. and Nicaragua," *WP*, July 31, 1983, D8.

146. Carlos Núñez Tellez, interview with Robert McCartney, September 1983, published as "Preparing for Elections: An Interview with Comandante Carlos Núñez Tellez," *Contemporary Marxism*, no. 8 (Spring 1984), 188–89.

147. Borge, "U.S. and Nicaragua."

148. The culturally distinct ethnic minorities on Nicaragua's Caribbean coast include English-speaking Afro-Caribbean Creoles (of mixed African, European, and Amerindian ancestry) and the Mískito, Sumu, Rama, and Garífono Amerindian populations. Andrew A. Reding, "Governmental Institutions," in *Revolution and Counterrevolution in Nicaragua*, ed. Thomas W. Walker (Boulder, CO: Westview Press, 1991), 32–33. See also James Jenkins, "The Indian Wing: Nicaraguan Indians, Native American Activists, and U.S. Foreign Policy, 1979–1990," in *Beyond the Eagle's Shadow: New Histories of Latin America's Cold War*, ed. Virginia Garrard-Burnett, Mark Atwood Lawrence, and Julio E. Moreno (Albuquerque: University of New Mexico Press, 2013), 175–99.

149. DoS cable, Managua 04605, US Embassy Managua (Quainton) to DoS, October 14, 1983, subject: "Assessment of Recent Fighting and Shift in Contra Strategy," DNSA, ID: NI01857.

150. Joel Brinkley, "Nicaraguan Army: 'War Machine' or Defender of a Besieged Nation?," *NYT*, March 30, 1985, 1.

151. DoS and DoD, unclassified report, May 1985.

152. Wooten, "Nicaraguan Military Buildup"; Walker, "Armed Forces," 86.

153. DoS cable, Managua 04240, US Embassy Managua (Quainton) to DoS, September 27, 1983, subject: "Wrap-Up on Law of Patriotic Service," DNSA, ID: NI01832.

154. Ortega, "Address to the United Nations General Assembly," 104.

155. DoS cable, Managua 3962, US Embassy Managua (Quainton) to DoS, September 9, 1983, subject: "Contras Bomb Corinto," DNSA, ID: NI01812; DoS cable, Managua 04459, US Embassy Managua (Quainton) to DoS, October 6, 1983, subject: "Anti-Sandinista Guerrillas Destroy East Coast Fuel Dump," DNSA, ID: NI01847; DoS cable, Managua 04594, US Embassy Managua (Quainton) to DoS, October 14, 1983, subject: "Port Corinto Fire Extinguished," DNSA, ID: NI01856; David Rogers and David Ignatius, "The Contra Fight," *WSJ*, March 6, 1985, 1; DoS cable, Managua 04607, US Embassy Managua (Quainton) to DoS, October 14, 1983, subject: "Daniel Ortega Decries Alleged CIA Covert Operations and Announces New Measures," DNSA, ID: NI01858.

156. Rogal, "Reagan's Gunboat Diplomacy," 14.

157. Howard J. Wiarda, *Conservative Brain Trust: The Rise, Fall, and Rise Again of the American Enterprise Institute* (Lanham, MD: Lexington Books, 2009), 113.

158. Quainton, interview.

159. Jack Nelson, "Reagan Says Base Was for Terrorism," *LAT*, October 28, 1983, 1.

160. Stephen Zunes, "The U.S. Invasion of Grenada," *Foreign Policy in Focus*, October 2003, https://www.globalpolicy.org/component/content/article/155-history/25966.html; Tad Szulc, "Grenada: Applying a 'Reagan Doctrine' Doctrine: Reagan Relies on Force," *LAT*, October 30, 1983, D1.

161. Doyle McManus, "Nicaragua: Nation Gets Set for War," *LAT*, September 10, 1983, A1; DoS cable, Managua 05369, US Embassy Managua (Quainton) to DoS, November 19, 1983, subject: "GRN Launches Civil Defense Campaign," DNSA, ID: NI01887.

162. Stephen Kinzer, "Sandinistas Are Drilling to Fight the 'Yankees,'" *NYT*, November 19, 1983, 8.

163. See, for example, Brecher, "Secret War for Nicaragua."

164. Quainton, interview.

165. DoS cable, Managua 5821, US Embassy (Quainton) to DoS, December 14, 1983, DNSA, ID: CO01371.

166. Langhorne A. Motley, interview with Charles Stuart Kennedy, March 7, 1991, ADST.

167. Montalbano, "Leaders Hang On."

168. "The Counterrevolutionaries: What Kind of Freedom Fighters Are They?," *Envío*, no. 29 (November 1983) https://www.envio.org.ni/articulo/3539, accessed November 19, 2021.

4. "Global Revolution"

1. Ronald Reagan, address to the British Parliament, London, June 8, 1982, transcript, MCPA, https://millercenter.org/the-presidency/presidential-speeches/june-8-1982-address-british-parliament.

2. Ronald Reagan, remarks to the members of the Delegations to the Western Hemisphere Legislative Leaders Forum, January 24, 1985, *PPP*, 21 Weekly Comp. Pres. Doc. 77.

3. Jeane J. Kirkpatrick, statement before the Subcommittee on Western Hemisphere Affairs, Senate Foreign Relations Committee, March 1, 1982, box 2, SP, HIA.

4. Ronald Reagan, quoted in Richard Schifter, "Building Firm Foundations: The Institutionalization of United States Human Rights Policy in the Reagan Years," *Harvard Law Review* 2 (Spring 1989): 9.

5. Morton Kondracke, "Speech, Speech! Author, Author!," *New Republic*, July 5, 1982.

6. Tony Dolan, address to the House of Lords Defense Committee, in "Biography of Elliott Abrams," July 20, 1983, box 323, folder: "Dolan," Casey Papers, HIA.

7. Kondracke, "Speech, Speech! Author, Author!"

8. Reagan, address to the British Parliament, June 8, 1982.

9. Cannon, *President Reagan*, 142.

10. Clifford P. Hackett, "Endowing Democracy: An Idea That Came and Went," *Commonweal*, October 7, 1983, 522.

11. Lloyd E. Ambrosius, *Wilsonianism: Woodrow Wilson and His Legacy in American Foreign Relations* (New York: Palgrave Macmillan, 2002); Thomas J. Knock, *To End All Wars: Woodrow Wilson and the Quest for a New World Order* (New York: Oxford University Press, 1992); Smith, *America's Mission*; John A. Thompson, *Woodrow Wilson: Profiles in Power* (New York: Longman, 2002).

12. Michael H. Hunt, *The American Ascendancy: How the United States Gained and Wielded Global Dominance* (Chapel Hill: University of North Carolina Press, 2009).

13. Ikenberry, *Liberal Leviathan*.

14. Martin H. Folly, "Harry S. Truman," in *US Foreign Policy and Democracy Promotion: From Theodore Roosevelt to Barack Obama*, ed. Michael Cox, Timothy J. Lynch, and Nicolas Bouchet (New York: Routledge, 2013), 96.

15. Jennifer M. Miller, *Cold War Democracy: The United States and Japan* (Cambridge, MA: Harvard University Press, 2019), 3.

16. Hugh Wilford, *The Mighty Wurlitzer: How the CIA Played America* (Cambridge, MA: Harvard University Press, 2009); Kaeten Mistry, "The Case for Political Warfare: Strategy Organization and US Involvement in the 1948 Italian Election," *Cold War History* 6, no. 3 (August 2006): 301–29.

17. Leslie Bethell and Ian Roxborough, *Latin America between the Second World War and the Cold War, 1944–1948* (New York: Cambridge University Press, 1997); Grandin, *Empire's Workshop*.

18. Nick Cullather, *Secret History: The CIA's Classified Account of Its Operations in Guatemala, 1952–1954* (Stanford, CA: Stanford University Press, 2006); Piero Gleijeses, *Shattered Hope: The Guatemalan Revolution and the United States, 1944–1954* (Princeton, NJ: Princeton University Press, 1991); James A. Bill, *The Eagle and the Lion: The Tragedy of American-Iranian Relations* (New Haven, CT: Yale University Press, 1989); Stephen Kinzer, *All the Shah's Men: An American Coup and the Roots of Middle East Terror* (Hoboken, NJ: Wiley, 2004).

19. Lars Schoultz, *Beneath the United States: A History of U.S. Policy toward Latin America* (Cambridge, MA: Harvard University Press, 1998).

20. David F. Schmitz, *Thank God They're on Our Side: The United States and Right-Wing Dictatorships, 1921–1965* (Durham, NC: University of North Carolina Press, 1999); Jessica M. Chapman, *Cauldron of Resistance: Ngo Dinh Diem, the United States, and 1950s Southern Vietnam* (Ithaca, NY: Cornell University Press, 2013); Seth Jacobs, *America's Miracle Man in Vietnam: Ngo Dinh Diem, Religion, Race, and U.S. Intervention in Southeast Asia, 1950–1957* (Durham, NC: Duke University Press, 2005).

21. Douglas Little, *American Orientalism: The United States and the Middle East since 1945* (Chapel Hill: University of North Carolina Press, 2008); Salim Yaqub, *Containing Arab Nationalism: The Eisenhower Doctrine and the Middle East* (Chapel Hill: University of North Carolina Press, 2004).

22. Stephen G. Rabe, *The Most Dangerous Area in the World: John F. Kennedy Confronts Communist Revolution in Latin America* (Chapel Hill: University of North Carolina Press, 1999), 148.

23. Wilford, *Mighty Wurlitzer*, 4.

24. Democracy Program, "The Commitment to Democracy: A Bipartisan Approach," interim report, draft copy, April 18, 1983, box 2, folder 41: "Report: Interim, 1983," National Endowment for Democracy Records (hereafter NEDR), LC.

25. Schmidli, *Fate of Freedom Elsewhere*, 43.

26. Official correspondence, Donald M. Fraser to B. M. Snedden (opposition leader, Australian Parliament), July 10, 1974, box 4, folder: "Human Rights" (149.G.13.7B), FP.

27. Democracy Program, "Commitment to Democracy."

28. Hackett, "Endowing Democracy," 522; "A Quango for Democracy?" *NYT*, June 6, 1982; Democracy Program, "Commitment to Democracy."

29. William A. Douglas, *Developing Democracy* (Washington, DC: Heldref Publications, 1972). See also William A. Douglas, "Helping Democracy Abroad: A U.S. Program," *Freedom at Issue*, no. 68 (September/October 1982): 15–19. Quotation from American Political Foundation, "New Bipartisan Democracy Initiative Launched," press release, November 10, 1982, box 1, folder 15: "American Political Foundation Project 1982," NEDR, LC.

30. Reagan, address to the British Parliament, June 8, 1982.

31. Hackett, "Endowing Democracy," 522.

32. White House, National Security Decision Directive 77, January 14, 1983, "Management of Public Diplomacy Relative to National Security," RRL, https://www.reaganlibrary.gov/public/archives/reference/scanned-nsdds/nsdd77.pdf.

33. The executive director of the *Washington Quarterly* and a member of the *Washington Post* editorial board, Weinstein had coordinated the Ad Hoc Citizens Committee for the Madrid-Helsinki Review Meeting beginning in 1980. Although registered as a Democrat, Weinstein served as a foreign policy adviser to Reagan during the 1980 presidential campaign. "Allen Weinstein: Brief Biography," box 27, folder 5: "The Democracy Program Bulletins, 1983," AWP, HIA.

34. Democracy Program, "Commitment to Democracy."

35. Michael A. Samuels, "The Role of Business in Political-Economic Development Abroad," draft address, July 25, 1983, box 27, folder 1: "The Democracy Program Correspondence, 1983," AWP, HIA.

36. "Report of the Business Programs Task Force to the Democracy Program," May 31, 1983, box 1, folder: "Business Program Task Force 1983," NEDR, LC.

37. Lane Kirkland, statement before the Subcommittee on International Operations of the House Foreign Affairs Committee, April 19, 1983, box 26, folder 10: "The Democracy Program, Clippings and Correspondence, 1983," AWP, HIA.

38. Wilford, *Mighty Wurlitzer*, 51–69.

39. Gregory F. Domber, "The Autonomy of Solidarity," in *The Reagan Administration, the Cold War, and the Transition to Democracy Promotion*, ed. Robert Pee and William Michael Schmidli (Cham, Switzerland: Palgrave Macmillan, 2019), 116–18.

40. Lane Kirkland, interview with James F. Shea and Don R. Kienzle, November 13, 1996, ADST.

41. Kirkland, statement before the Subcommittee on International Operations of the House Foreign Affairs Committee, April 19, 1983. Along with Brock, Manatt, Fascell, Samuels, and Agree, Kirkland served as a board member of the APF. Thomas Carothers, *In the Name of Democracy: U.S. Policy toward Latin America in the Reagan Years* (Berkeley: University of California Press, 1993), 203.

42. William Safire, "Organizing the 'World PAC,'" *NYT*, August 19, 1982.

43. Ben J. Wattenberg, "Spectrum," June 21, 1982, CBS Radio Network, transcript, box 1, folder 15: "American Political Foundation Project 1982," NEDR, LC.

44. Carothers, *In the Name of Democracy*, 203–5.

45. Ronald Reagan, remarks at a White House ceremony inaugurating the National Endowment for Democracy, December 16, 1983, *PPP*, 19 Weekly Comp. Pres. Doc. 1702.

46. Department of State, Bureau of Public Affairs, "1983 Human Rights Report," [excerpt from *Country Reports on Human Rights Practices for 1983*] (Washington, DC: Government Printing Office, February 1984), 2.

47. Official correspondence, Elliott Abrams to Leonard Sussman, April 28, 1983, box 37, folder 8: "Abrams, Elliott, 1981–1986," Freedom House Records, 1933–2014 (hereafter FHR), Public Policy Papers, Department of Rare Books and Special Collections, Princeton University Library, Princeton, NJ (hereafter PU).

48. Department of State, Bureau of Public Affairs, "1983 Human Rights Report," 4. See also Jeane J. Kirkpatrick, "Dictatorships and Double Standards," *Commentary*, November 1979, 38.

49. Department of State, Bureau of Public Affairs, "1983 Human Rights Report," 4.

50. Reagan, remarks at a White House ceremony inaugurating the National Endowment for Democracy.

51. George P. Shultz, statement before the Subcommittee on International Operations, Committee on Foreign Affairs, House of Representatives, February 23, 1983, box 28, folder 7: "The Democracy Program Report, Statements, & Transcripts, 1983," AWP, HIA.

52. Don Oberdorfer, "Lawmakers Voice Skepticism on U.S. 'Project Democracy,'" *WP*, February 24, 1983, A1.

53. Kenneth Freed, "Alfonsín's Victory in Argentina Tests U.S. Role in the Americas," *LAT*, November 6, 1983, F2.

54. Ronald Reagan, remarks at a ceremony for the signing of Proclamation 5287, December 10, 1984, *PPP*, 20 Weekly Comp. Pres. Doc. 1891.

55. Reagan, remarks at a ceremony for the signing of Proclamation 5287.

56. Carothers, *In the Name of Democracy*, 133.

57. Debbie Sharnak, "Reagan and the Waning Years of Uruguay's Military Rule: Democracy Promotion and the Redefinition of Human Rights," in *The Reagan Administration, the Cold War,*

and the Transition to Democracy Promotion, ed. Robert Pee and William Michael Schmidli (Cham, Switzerland: Palgrave Macmillan, 2019), 206.

58. Brands, *Making the Unipolar Moment*, 179.

59. Grandin, *Empire's Workshop*, 183–84.

60. Duncan Green, *Silent Revolution: The Rise and Crisis of Market Economics in Latin America* (New York: Monthly Review Press, 2003), 85. See also Mike Davis, *Planet of Slums* (New York: Verso, 2006), 151–73; Kurt Gerhard Weyland, "Neoliberalism and Democracy in Latin America: A Mixed Record," *Latin American Politics and Society* 46, no. 1 (Spring 2004): 135–57; Joseph E. Stiglitz, *Globalization and Its Discontents* (New York: W. W. Norton, 2003).

61. Edward Schumacher, "Defending Argentina's New Democracy," *NYT*, June 10, 1984, SM26.

62. Grandin, *Empire's Workshop*, 184.

63. Allen Weinstein, "The Democratic Decision-Making Process," address at the Colloquy on the Concept of Democracy, Council of Europe, Strasbourg, March 23, 1983, box 26, folder 10: "The Democracy Program, Clippings and Correspondence, 1983," AWP, HIA.

64. Carl Gershman, "The Rise and Fall of the New Foreign-Policy Establishment," *Commentary*, July 1980, 15, 18.

65. Gershman, "Rise and Fall," 21, 24.

66. Seymour Maxwell Finger, "The Reagan-Kirkpatrick Policies and the United Nations," *Foreign Affairs* 62, no. 2 (Winter 1983): 444.

67. Ronald Reagan, address at the Georgetown University Center for Strategic and International Studies, Washington, DC, April 6, 1984, reproduced in "Excerpts from President Reagan's Speech on Foreign Policy and Congress," *NYT*, April 7, 1984, A6.

68. Jeane J. Kirkpatrick, address at a Hoover Institution dinner, Washington, DC, January 10, 1984, box 36, folder 10: "Miscellaneous Materials," AWP, HIA.

69. George P. Shultz, "The Meaning of Vietnam," address at the Department of State, April 25, 1985 (Washington, DC: Department of State, Bureau of Public Affairs, April 1985), 3. Shultz's emphasis on moving beyond the "Vietnam Syndrome" echoed a common theme among neoconservatives.

70. Elliott Abrams, address to the National Council for the Social Studies conference, San Francisco, November 23, 1983, box 12, SP, HIA.

71. Ronald Reagan, remarks at a Flag Day ceremony, June 14, 1985, *PPP*, 1985 Pub. Paper 797.

72. George P. Shultz, "America and the Struggle for Freedom," address to the Commonwealth Club of California, San Francisco, February 22, 1985 (Washington, DC: Department of State, Bureau of Public Affairs, February 1985), 3.

73. Ronald Reagan, "Freedom, Regional Security, and Global Peace," address to Congress, March 14, 1986, *PPP*, 1986, 386. See also Mattias Fibiger, "The Pivot: Neoconservatives, the Philippines, and the Democracy Agenda," in *The Reagan Administration, the Cold War, and the Transition to Democracy Promotion*, ed. Robert Pee and William Michael Schmidli (Cham, Switzerland: Palgrave Macmillan, 2019), 209–30.

74. George P. Shultz, *Turmoil and Triumph: My Years as Secretary of State* (New York: Scribner's, 1993), 642.

75. "Mr. Reagan Scores for Democracy," *NYT*, February 8, 1986, 26.

76. Tamar Jacoby, "The Reagan Turnaround on Human Rights," *Foreign Affairs* 64, no. 5 (Summer 1986): 1066–86.

77. Anthony Lewis, "Why We Celebrate," *NYT*, February 27, 1986, A23; see also Richard Holbrooke, "Removal of Marcos Was a Triumph for Reagan's 'Ad-Hocism,'" *WP*, March 2,

1986, C1; Philip Geyelin, "Democracy Triumphs—What Went Right?," *LAT*, March 2, 1986, H5; Flora Lewis, "A Welcome Reversal," *NYT*, March 16 1986; Jacoby, "The Reagan Turnaround on Human Rights."

78. Richard G. Lugar, *Letters to the Next President* (New York: Simon & Schuster, 1988), 27. See also Stephen J. Solarz, "When to Intervene," *Foreign Policy* 63 (Summer 1986): 20–39; Stephen J. Solarz, interview with Charles Stuart Kennedy, November 18, 1996, ADST.

79. Robert Pee, "The Rise of Political Aid: The National Endowment for Democracy and the Reagan Administration's Cold War Strategy," in *The Reagan Administration, the Cold War, and the Transition to Democracy Promotion*, ed. Robert Pee and William Michael Schmidli (Cham, Switzerland: Palgrave Macmillan, 2019), 68.

80. Carl Gershman, statement to the Subcommittee on International Operations, House Foreign Affairs Committee, March 12, 1985, box 6, folder: "National Endowment for Democracy, 1984–1985," RRL.

81. Domber, "Autonomy of Solidarity," 123–25.

82. Jeane J. Kirkpatrick, quoted in Cannon, *President Reagan*, 324–25.

83. Shultz, *Turmoil and Triumph*, 285–322.

84. George P. Shultz, interview with Stephen Knott, Marc Selverstone, and James Sterling Young, December 18, 2002, Oral History Program, MCPA.

85. Shultz, "America and the Struggle for Freedom."

86. Alan J. Kuperman, "The Stinger Missile and U.S. Intervention in Afghanistan," *Political Science Quarterly* 114, no. 2 (Summer 1999): 228.

87. Kuperman, "U.S. Intervention in Afghanistan," 246; James M. Scott, *Deciding to Intervene: The Reagan Doctrine and American Foreign Policy* (Durham, NC: Duke University Press, 1996), 58–63; George Crile, *Charlie Wilson's War* (New York: Grove Press, 2003), 422–39.

88. Charles William Maynes, "Reagan and the American Resolve: A U.S. Policy for Intervention Everywhere," *LAT*, February 9, 1986, G1.

89. "Shultz Labels Sandinista Rule as 'Bad News,'" *LAT*, February 19, 1985, A2.

90. Ronald Reagan, "Remarks at a White House Briefing for Private Sector Supporters," March 14, 1986, *PPP*, 1986, 353.

91. Wayne S. Smith, "Finding the Truth in U.S. Policy on Nicaragua," *LAT*, August 25, 1985, G2.

92. National Security Planning Group meeting minutes, secret, June 25, 1984, DNSA, ID: IC00463.

93. Brody, *Contra Terror in Nicaragua*, 21–22.

94. Joanne Omang, "U.S. Latin Policies Working, Shultz Says," *WP*, August 21, 1984, A12.

95. Ronald Reagan, radio address to the nation, "Central America," February 16, 1985, *PPP*, 1985, 186.

96. DoS cable, Managua 01842, US Embassy (Gamble) to secretary of state, April 6, 1984, subject: "Counterrevolutionary Activity Reaches New High in March," DNSA, ID: NI02039.

97. Soviet Embassy in Washington, DC, press release, March 21, 1984, DNSA, ID: NI02018.

98. Oswald Johnston and Robert C. Toth, "Mines Plaguing Nicaraguan Ports," *LAT*, April 8, 1984, A1.

99. Letter, Barry M. Goldwater to William J. Casey, April 9, 1984, DNSA, ID: IC00392.

100. Congressional report, House of Representatives, Democratic Study Group, April 11, 1984, "An Examination of the Reagan Administration's Role in Mining the Harbors of Nica-

ragua and Its Effort to Abrogate the Jurisdiction of the World Court over the Issue," DNSA, ID: NI02055.

101. Congressional report, "Examination of the Reagan Administration's Role."

102. "Boland Amendment II," DNSA, Glossary, Nicaragua Collection.

103. Doyle McManus, "Reagan Sees Nicaraguan Vote as 'Soviet-Style Sham,' Urges Regional Leaders to Cooperate," *LAT*, July 20, 1984, B19. See also DoS, "Resource Book: Sandinista Elections in Nicaragua," 1984, box 1, folder 15, LASSIR, HIA.

104. "Election Draws Many U.S. Observers," *NYT*, November 4, 1984, 21.

105. Larry Leaman, "Observing the Nicaraguan Elections," November 7, 1984, box: "Work in Nicaragua," folder: "Reports from Long Termers—November 1984 Elections," Witness for Peace Records (hereafter WFPR), Swarthmore College Peace Collection, Swarthmore, PA (hereafter SCPC).

106. Dennis Volman, "Nicaragua Campaign Races to Chaotic Finish," *Christian Science Monitor*, November 2, 1984, 7; DoS cable, Managua 06157, US Embassy (Harry E. Bergold) to secretary of state, November 5, 1984, subject: "Nicaraguan Election Observers Comments," DNSA, ID: NI02287.

107. Volman, "Nicaragua Campaign," 7.

108. Roy Gutman, "Nicaraguan Vote a Setback for U.S.," *Newsday*, November 5, 1984, 13.

109. Reding, "Governmental Institutions," 26–27.

110. Quainton, interview.

111. Latin American Studies Association, *The Electoral Process in Nicaragua: Domestic and International Influences: The Report of the Latin American Studies Association Delegation to Observe the Nicaraguan General Election of November 4, 1984* ([Pittsburgh, PA]: Latin American Studies Association, 1984), excerpt reprinted in Peter Rosset and John Vandermeer, eds., *Nicaragua: Unfinished Revolution* (New York: Grove Press, 1986), 107.

112. Shultz, "Meaning of Vietnam," 4.

113. George P. Shultz, "Nicaragua: Will Democracy Prevail?," statement before the Senate Committee on Foreign Relations, February 27, 1986 (Washington, DC: Department of State, Bureau of Public Affairs, March 1986), 8.

114. Richard G. Lugar, press release. March 4, 1986, box 10, folder 4, FHR, PU.

115. Norman Podhoretz, "Liberals Wanted Marcos Out, So Why Not Sandinistas?," *LAT*, March 7, 1986, B5.

116. Bernard Weinraub, "The U.S. and Dictators: Reagan's Vow to Oppose All Despots Offers a Rationale for His Efforts to Aid Contras," *NYT*, March 15, 1986, 1.

117. Ronald Reagan, news conference, February 21, 1985, *PPP*, 1985, 209.

118. Steven Strasser, "Reagan's Gunboat Diplomacy," *Newsweek*, August 1, 1983.

119. Americas Watch Committee, *Human Rights in Nicaragua: Reagan, Rhetoric and Reality* (New York: Americas Watch Committee, 1985), 2.

120. Sidney Blumenthal, "Grantee of U.S. Endowment Funds Sandinista Opponents," *WP*, March 19, 1986, A1.

121. National Endowment for Democracy, *Annual Report 1985*, 11, https://www.ned.org /wp-content/uploads/annualreports/1985-ned-annual-report.pdf.

122. NED press release, March 19, 1986, DNSA, ID: NI02722.

123. On the congressional debate over the $100 million aid request, see Arnson, *Crossroads*; Kagan, *Twilight Struggle*; LeoGrande, *Our Own Backyard*.

124. Ronald Reagan, radio address to the nation, "Bipartisan Consensus in Congress," November 15, 1986, *PPP*, 22 Weekly Comp. Pres. Doc. 1575.

125. National Endowment for Democracy, *Annual Report 1987*, https://www.ned.org/wp-content/uploads/annualreports/1987-ned-annual-report.pdf.

126. Doyle McManus, "Reagan Policy Shifts on Dictators and Democracy," *LAT*, March 6, 1986, B1.

127. Joel Brinkley, "Iran Sales Linked to Wide Program of Covert Policies," *NYT*, February 15, 1987, A1.

5. Tracking the "Indiana Jones of the Right"

1. Jack Wheeler, interview with Karen Reedstrom, *Full Context*, May 1996.

2. Wheeler, interview.

3. Paul Dean, "Crossing the Alps in Hannibal's Footsteps," *LAT*, August 14, 1979, F1.

4. Dean, "Crossing the Alps."

5. Paul Dean, "Adventurer Helps Rebel Group Fight Communist Forces," *LAT*, August 1, 1985, E1.

6. Sidney Blumenthal, "Jack Wheeler's Adventures with the 'Freedom Fighters,'" *WP*, April 16, 1986, D1.

7. See, for example, David Treadwell, "The Times Poll: Public Opposes U.S. Role in El Salvador," *LAT*, April 12, 1983, A11; George Black and Judy Butler, "Constraints and Counterrevolution," *NACLA Report on the Americas* 16, no. 1 (January/February 1982): 38–46.

8. NSC meeting minutes, February 10, 1982, subject: "The Caribbean Basin," DNSA, ID: CO01132.

9. Wheeler, interview.

10. Wheeler, interview.

11. Wheeler, interview.

12. Wheeler, interview.

13. Dean, "Crossing the Alps."

14. Rohrbacher had served as the Los Angeles County high school chairman of Youth for Reagan. "Appointment of Dana Rohrabacher as Special Assistant to the President and Speechwriter," October 16, 1987, APP, https://www.presidency.ucsb.edu/documents/appointment-dana-rohrabacher-special-assistant-the-president-and-speechwriter.

15. Blumenthal, "Adventures with the 'Freedom Fighters.'"

16. Dean, "Adventurer Helps Rebel Group."

17. Dean, "Adventurer Helps Rebel Group."

18. Blumenthal, "Adventures with the 'Freedom Fighters.'"

19. Blumenthal, "Adventures with the 'Freedom Fighters.'"

20. White House, National Security Decision Directive 77, January 14, 1983, "Management of Public Diplomacy Relative to National Security," RRL, https://www.reaganlibrary.gov/public/archives/reference/scanned-nsdds/nsdd77.pdf.

21. Memorandum, White House Outreach Working Group on Central America, undated, Series 3: Subject File, Central America, box 36, file: "Central America: Strategy," Faith Ryan Whittlesey Papers (hereafter FRWP), RRL.

22. Memorandum, White House Outreach Working Group on Central America, undated.

23. Memorandum, White House Outreach Working Group on Central America, undated.

24. Memorandum, Faith Ryan Whittlesey to Ronald Reagan, April 17, 1984, subject: "The Central America Outreach Effort," Series 3: Subject File, Central America, box 33, file: "Central America: Correspondence (05/01/1984–05/14/1984)," FRWP, RRL.

25. Faith Ryan Whittlesey, address to the Council for National Policy Board of Governors, August 17, 1984, Dallas, TX, Series 8: Trips and Events, box 20F, file: "08/17/1984–08/18/1984 Dallas, Texas National Council for Policy," FRWP, RRL.

26. Faith Ryan Whittlesey, interview with Ann Miller Morin, December 7, 1988, ADST.

27. White House Office of Media Relations and Planning, "Soviet Objectives and Intentions in Latin America," *White House Digest*, May 9, 1984, Series 7: Speeches and Article—Reference Material, box 19F, file: "White House Digest 04/25/84," FRWP, RRL.

28. Official letter, Leslie Lenkowsky to Faith Ryan Whittlesey, April 30, 1984, Series 3: Subject File, Central America, box 33, file: "Central America: Correspondence (05/01/1984–05/14/1984)," FRWP, RRL.

29. Letter, White House Office of Public Liaison to Pia Moriarty and Bob Williams, February 29, 1984, Series 3: Subject File, Central America, box 33, file: "Central America: Correspondence (12/02/1983–03/31/1983)," FRWP, RRL.

30. Official correspondence, Faith Ryan Whittlesey to Phil Donahue, July 24, 1984, Series 3: Subject File, Central America, box 33, file: "Central America: Correspondence (07/01/1984–07/31/1984)," FRWP, RRL.

31. Tim Golden, "Reagan Countering Critics of Policies in Central America," *LAT*, December 21, 1983, E1.

32. Whittlesey, interview.

33. Golden, "Reagan Countering Critics."

34. Juan Williams, "White House Pitches Latin Policy to Public," *WP*, September 24, 1983, A5.

35. Wiarda, *Conservative Brain Trust*, 172.

36. Wiarda, *Conservative Brain Trust*, 178.

37. Joan Didion, "Washington in Miami," *New York Review of Books*, July 16, 1987.

38. Memorandum, Faith Ryan Whittlesey to James A. Baker III, June 28, 1983, subject: "Outside Support on Central America," Series 3: Subject File, Central America, box 35, file: "Central America: Outside Support," FRWP, RRL.

39. Official correspondence, Faith Ryan Whittlesey to Henry Kissinger, April 3, 1984, Series 3: Subject File, Central America, box 33, file: "Central America: Correspondence (04/01/1984–04/30/1984)," FRWP, RRL.

40. Jack Wheeler, "Fighting the Soviet Imperialists: UNITA in Angola," *Reason*, April 1, 1984.

41. Jack Wheeler, "Fighting the Soviet Imperialists: The Mujaheddin in Afghanistan," *Reason*, September 1, 1984.

42. Jack Wheeler, "Fighting the Soviet Imperialists: The Contras in Nicaragua," *Reason*, June 1, 1984.

43. Wheeler, interview.

44. Jack Wheeler, "Fighting the Soviet Imperialists: The Khmer in Cambodia," *Reason*, February 1, 1985; Jack Wheeler, "From Rovuma to Maputo: Mozambique's Guerrilla War," *Reason*, December 1, 1985.

45. Blumenthal, "Adventures with the 'Freedom Fighters.'"

46. Eric Bailey, "Adventurer Blazes Political Trail," *LAT*, July 17, 1988, D1.

47. Bailey, "Adventurer Blazes Political Trail."

48. Jack Wheeler, "Fighting the Soviet Imperialists: The New Liberation Movements," *Reason*, June 1, 1985.

49. On Wheeler's participation in the Outreach Working Group meetings, see Didion, "Washington in Miami."

50. Wheeler, "Fighting the Soviet Imperialists: The New Liberation Movements."

51. Blumenthal, "Adventures with the 'Freedom Fighters.'"

52. Memorandum, William P. Clark, July 12, 1983, subject: "Tasking for Central America Public Diplomacy," DNSA, ID: IC00146.

53. LaFeber, *Inevitable Revolutions*, 296, 302.

54. Treadwell, "Times Poll."

55. CRS, "'Public Diplomacy,' 'Project Democracy,' and Contra Aid," ca. August 1987, DNSA, ID: IC04273.

56. Memorandum, George P. Shultz to Ronald Reagan, May 25, 1983, subject: "Managing Our Central America Strategy," DNSA, ID: IC00106.

57. Memorandum, Robert C. McFarlane to Oliver L. North and Alfonso Sapia-Bosch, July 7, 1983, DNSA, ID: CO01321; underlining in the original.

58. Memorandum, Ronald Reagan to George P. Shultz, Caspar Weinberger, William J. Casey, and John W. Vessey Jr., July 12, 1983, subject: "Central America," DNSA, ID: IC00133.

59. Otto J. Reich, interview with Charles Stuart Kennedy, August 30, 1991, ADST.

60. Memorandum, Otto J. Reich to Walter Raymond, March 10, 1986, DNSA, ID: IC02469.

61. Memorandum, Ronald I. Spiers to secretary of state, May 7, 1984, subject: "Status Report on the Department's Involvement in Public Diplomacy," DNSA, ID: IC00423; Memorandum, Elliott Abrams and Otto J. Reich to deputy secretary of state, January 28, 1986, subject: "The Future of the Office of the Coordinator for Public Diplomacy for Latin America and the Caribbean (S/LPD)," DNSA, ID: IC02266.

62. Memorandum, DoS, undated [ca. November 1, 1983], subject: "Central America: Next Steps," DNSA, ID: IC00224.

63. Reich, interview.

64. Tim Golden, "Reagan Countering Critics," E1. See also, Williams, "White House Pitches Latin Policy."

65. George P. Shultz to Ronald Reagan, [April 1984], subject: "News Coverage of Central America," DNSA, ID: IC00397.

66. Memorandum, Otto J. Reich to Wes Egan, February 8, 1985, subject: "Organization of Office of Public Diplomacy for Latin America and the Caribbean (S/LPD)," DNSA, ID: IC00814.

67. Bushnell, interview.

68. CRS, "'Public Diplomacy,' 'Project Democracy,' and Contra Aid"; memorandum, Reich to Egan, February 8, 1985.

69. Memorandum, Reich to Raymond, March 10, 1986; memorandum, Reich to Egan, February 8, 1985.

70. Memorandum, Reich to Egan, February 8, 1985; report, S/LPD, October 1, 1986, subject: "Distribution within the Office of Public Diplomacy for Latin America and the Caribbean," DNSA, ID: IC03499.

71. Department of State memorandum, January 25, 1987, subject: "Office of Public Diplomacy for Latin America and the Caribbean," DNSA, ID: IC04135.

72. Memorandum, Reich to Egan, February 8, 1985.

73. Memorandum, Frank Gardner to George F. Twohie, June 25, 1985, subject: "Current Program of S/LPD," DNSA, ID: IC01255.

74. Jane Hunter, "Tricontranental," *NACLA*, September 25, 2007, https://nacla.org/article/tricontranental.

75. Jack Wheeler, letter to the editor, *LAT*, July 26, 1985, B6.

76. Blumenthal, "Adventures with the 'Freedom Fighters.'"

77. On the mobilization of the right-wing, see Burke, *Revolutionaries for the Right*, 155–96.

78. Peter H. Stone, "Private Groups Step Up Aid to 'Contras,'" *WP*, May 3, 1985, A22.

79. Stone, "Private Groups Step Up Aid."

80. Charles R. Babcock, "Dallas Hosts Anti-Communist League," *WP*, September 17, 1985, A14.

81. White House memorandum, Linda Chavez, January 30, 1986, subject: "Meeting with National Endowment for Preservation of Liberty," DNSA, ID: IC02288.

82. NEPL, press release, February 27, 1986, DNSA, ID: IC02401.

83. Memorandum, Reich to Raymond, March 10, 1986.

84. Memorandum, John M. Poindexter to William J. Casey, August 13, 1986, subject: "Central American Public Diplomacy," DNSA, ID: IC03287.

85. Meritorious Honor Award, ca. June 1986, DNSA, ID: IC02935.

86. Memorandum, February 1[?], 1984, subject: "Themes for Op-Ed Pieces to Be Written by Outside Supporters," DNSA, ID: IC00301.

87. John F. Guilmartin Jr., "Nicaragua Is Armed for Trouble," *WSJ*, March 11, 1985, 28; memorandum, Jonathan S. Miller to Patrick J. Buchanan, March 13, 1985, subject: "'White Propaganda' Operation," DNSA, ID: NI02396.

88. Memorandum, S/LPD, December 17, 1985, subject: "Ninety-Day Plan (12/17/85, Rev. 5)," DNSA, ID: IC02006.

89. Wiarda, *Conservative Brain Trust*, 172.

90. Didion, "Washington in Miami."

91. Sharon Churcher, "Sex and the Sandinistas: An Official Attack on U.S. Reporters?," *New York Intelligencer*, July 29, 1985.

92. William Finnegan, "Castro's Shadow: America's Man in Latin America, and His Obsession," *New Yorker*, October 14, 2002; Jeff Cohen, "The Return of Otto Reich," *Fairness & Accuracy in Reporting*, June 8, 2001, https://fair.org/article/the-return-of-otto-reich/.

93. Reich, interview.

94. Report, S/LPD, March 1986, subject: "From Revolution to Repression: Human Rights in Nicaragua under the Sandinistas," DNSA, ID: NI02683.

95. Americas Watch Committee, *Human Rights in Nicaragua: Reagan, Rhetoric and Reality* (New York: Americas Watch Committee, 1985), 3.

96. DoS, "Resource Book: Sandinista Elections in Nicaragua," 1984, box 1, folder 15, LASSIR, HIA.

97. Memorandum, Reich to Egan, February 8, 1985; Harry Anderson, "The MIGs That Weren't There," *Newsweek*, November 19, 1984, 44; Charles Maechling Jr., "The MIG Hoax: Who's Duping Whom?," *LAT*, November 25, 1984, D5; Roy Gutman, "Nicaraguan Vote a Setback for U.S.," *Newsday*, November 5, 1984, 13; Norman Kempster, "Spy Photos Reveal No MIGs," *LAT*, November 10, 1984, A1.

98. Nicaraguan Mission to the United Nations, fact sheet, "The Costs of the War," April 1987, DNSA, ID: NI02975.

99. See, for example, Americas Watch Committee, *On Human Rights in Nicaragua* (New York: Americas Watch Committee, May 1982); Americas Watch Committee, *Human Rights in Nicaragua: Reagan, Rhetoric and Reality*; Brody, *Contra Terror in Nicaragua*; Washington Office on Latin America (WOLA), *Nicaragua: The Human Tragedy of the War, April–June 1986* (Washington, DC: WOLA, 1986).

100. Americas Watch Committee, *Violations of the Laws of War by Both Sides in Nicaragua in 1987* (New York: Americas Watch Committee, November 1987), 5.

101. Nicaraguan Mission to the United Nations, fact sheet, "The Costs of the War."

102. Office of Public Diplomacy for the United States and the Caribbean, "The Nicaraguan Democratic Resistance," January 1986, box 2, folder: "Nicaragua (1986)," Patrick J. Buchanan Files, RRL.

103. S/LPD, "Human Rights in Nicaragua: A Commentary on the Brody Report," April 17, 1986, box 1, folder: "State Department—Subjects 'Human Rights Abuses,'" LASSIR, HIA.

104. Memorandum, Miller to Buchanan, March 13, 1985.

105. John Conyers Jr., "The Campaign That's Killing the Contra-Aid Bill," *NYT*, March 7, 1986.

106. James Siekmeier, "The Iran-Contra Affair," in *A Companion to Reagan*, ed. Andrew L. Johns (Malden, MA: John Wiley & Sons, 2015), 324.

107. Siekmeier, "Iran-Contra Affair," 329.

108. Byrne, *Iran-Contra*, 3.

109. Siekmeier, "Iran-Contra Affair," 333. On the impact of the scandal on US-Soviet relations, see Jack F. Matlock Jr., *Reagan and Gorbachev: How the Cold War Ended* (New York: Random House, 2004), 321.

110. Official correspondence, comptroller general to Jack Brooks, September 30, 1987, https://www.gao.gov/assets/200/193596.pdf.

111. United States Congress, Select Joint Committee of the House and Senate, *Report of the Congressional Committees Investigating the Iran-Contra Affair*, 100th Cong., 1st Sess., Senate Report 206, House Report 433 (Washington, DC: Government Printing Office, 1987), 34.

112. Joel Brinkley, "Iran Sales Linked to Wide Program of Covert Policies," *NYT*, February 15, 1987, A1.

113. LeoGrande, *Our Own Backyard*, 515.

114. Bailey, "Adventurer Blazes Political Trail."

115. Jack Wheeler, *The Coming Collapse of the Soviet Union*, The Heritage Lectures (Washington, DC: Heritage Foundation, 1988), 1.

116. Wheeler, *Coming Collapse*, 1.

6. "The Grindstone on Which We Sharpen Ourselves"

1. Correspondence, S. Brian Willson to senator Warren Rudman, August 14, 1987, box 14, folder: "Brian Willson," Rita Clark Nicaragua Collection (hereafter RCC), Bucknell University Special Collections, Lewisburg, PA (hereafter BUSC).

2. Stephen G. Bloom, "Fateful Stop in a Political Odyssey," *Philadelphia Inquirer*, September 6, 1987, 27-A.

3. Correspondence, S. Brian Willson to Nathan Kaminsky [Internal Revenue Service], August 13, 1987, subject: "'Collection Information Statement for Individuals' Form," box 14, folder: "Brian Willson," RCC, BUSC.

4. Katy Butler, "A Viet Vet's Haunting Vision," *Philadelphia Inquirer*, January 8, 1987.

5. Official communication, Veterans Fast for Life / Veterans Peace Action Team to Warren Rudman, August 14, 1987, box 14, folder: "Brian Willson," RCC, BUSC.

6. Jennifer Atlee-Loudon, *Red Thread: A Spiritual Journey of Accompaniment, Trauma and Healing* (Washington, DC: EPICA, 2001), 62–63.

7. Bloom, "Fateful Stop."

8. Jim Feltz, interview in *Bearing Witness, Building Bridges: Interviews with North Americans Living and Working in Nicaragua*, ed. Melissa Everett (Philadelphia: New Society Publishers, 1986), 140.

9. Justinian Liebl, interview in Everett, *Bearing Witness, Building Bridges*, 23.

10. Bloom, "Fateful Stop."

11. Official communication, Veterans Fast for Life / Veterans Peace Action Team to Rudman, August 14, 1987.

12. Butler, "Viet Vet's Haunting Vision."

13. S. Brian Willson, "The September 1, 1987 Tragedy at Concord, CA Naval Weapons Station (CNWS): Perspective of the People Invoking the Nuremberg Principles at CNWS," report prepared for hearings by the House Armed Services Subcommittee on Investigations, November 18, 1987, box 14, folder: "Brian Willson," RCC, BUSC.

14. Judson Brown, "Former Fasting Vets Head to Nicaragua," *Daily Hampshire Gazette* (Northampton, MA), December 20, 1986.

15. Kathy Salamon, "U.S. Veterans to Set Up 'Nicaragua Patrol,'" *Register-Pajaronian* (Santa Cruz, CA), December 24, 1986.

16. Butler, "Viet Vet's Haunting Vision."

17. Peace, *Call to Conscience*, 3.

18. See NACLA, "History," https://nacla.org/history, accessed November 18, 2021.

19. WOLA, *Nicaragua*, 1.

20. Barbara Crossette, "Groups Trying to Sway Latin America Policy," *NYT*, November 18, 1981.

21. On the origins of WOLA and COHA, see Schmidli, *Fate of Freedom Elsewhere*; Snyder, *From Selma to Moscow*.

22. The Coalition for a New Foreign and Military Policy was created in 1976 out of the merging of the Coalition on National Priorities and Military Policy (founded in 1969) and the Ad Hoc Coalition for a New Foreign Policy (CNFP). The latter was originally named the Coalition to Stop Funding the War (founded in 1973) but changed its name in 1975. Coalition for a New Foreign Policy Records, 1969–1988, Finding Aid, https://www.swarthmore.edu/library/peace/DG100-150/dg138cnfp.htm (hereafter CNFPR), SCPC.

23. Legislative update, Coalition for a New Foreign and Military Policy, August 27, 1981, box 1, folder: "Coalition Mailings, 1981–1982," CNFPR, SCPC.

24. Official communication, Coalition for a New Foreign and Military Policy to "Dear Senator," May 26, 1982, box 1, folder: "Coalition Mailings, 1981–1982," CNFPR, SCPC.

25. Americas Watch Committee, *Human Rights in Nicaragua: Reagan, Rhetoric and Reality*, 16. As a small sample of the large body of human rights reporting, see, for example, Americas Watch Committee, *On Human Rights in Nicaragua*; Amnesty International, *Nicaragua*; Americas Watch Committee, *Human Rights in Nicaragua 1986* (New York: Americas Watch Committee, February 1987); Americas Watch Committee, *Violations of the Laws of War*; Americas Watch Committee, *Human Rights in Nicaragua, August 1987–August 1988* (New York: Americas Watch Committee, August 1988); Americas Watch Committee, *The Killings in Northern Nicaragua* (New York: Americas Watch Committee, October 1989).

26. "A Promise of Resistance," [originally published in *Sojourners*, December 1983], box 14, folder: "Witness for Peace," RCC, BUSC.

27. WFP, "Annual Report 1987: Retrospective, 1983–1988," box 1, folder: "Annual Report, 1987," WFPR, SCPC.

28. Jim Wallis, "Witness for Peace," [originally published in *Sojourners*, November 1983], box 14, folder: "Witness for Peace," RCC, BUSC.

29. Press release, WFP, undated, subject: "U.S. Christians Launch Witness for Peace in Nicaragua," box 14, folder: "Witness for Peace," RCC, BUSC.

30. Wallis, "Witness for Peace."

31. WFP, "Annual Report 1987."

32. WFP, "Annual Report 1987."

33. Letter, Lillian Adams to WFP members, April 25, 1986, box 2, WFPR, SCPC.

34. Bob Barnes, "Strategy Outlined for Gaining Access to Rural Media," *Witness for Peace Newsletter* 2, no. 5 (November/December 1985): 12.

35. Letter, Anne Whoerle to WFP, June 21, 1986, box 2, WFPR, SCPC.

36. Dan Ouellette and Ron Stief, "WFP Mobile Reporting Team Serves," *Witness for Peace Newsletter* 4, no. 5 (November/December 1987): 8–10.

37. WFP, "Annual Report 1987."

38. Ouellette and Stief, "WFP Mobile Reporting Team Serves."

39. Letter, Anne Whoerle to WFP, June 1, 1986, box 2, WFPR, SCPC.

40. Whoerle to WFP, June 1, 1986.

41. Ouellette and Stief, "WFP Mobile Reporting Team Serves."

42. WFP, "Annual Report 1987."

43. Adams to WFP members, April 25, 1986.

44. Atlee-Loudon, *Red Thread*, 60–61.

45. Atlee-Loudon, *Red Thread*, 61.

46. Peace, *Call to Conscience*, 3.

47. Iosu Perales, "Twenty-Six Years On: Memories of Solidarity," *Envío*, no. 288 (June 2005), https://www.envio.org.ni/articulo/2989, accessed November 19, 2021.

48. Stuart Rawlings, "Nicaragua, Honduras and El Salvador: A Two Month Study of Their People and Politics (April–June, 1986)," October 20, 1986, box 2, folder: "General Subject Area: 1986," NiSC, HIA.

49. "U.S. Volunteers Help Nicaragua with the Harvest," *NYT*, February 16, 1984, A4.

50. "U.S. Volunteers Help Nicaragua"; Jeff Jones, ed., *Brigadista: Harvest and War in Nicaragua* (New York: Praeger, 1986), 97.

51. "Statement by the Construction Brigade," reprinted in Jones, *Brigadista*, 114.

52. Jones, *Brigadista*, 163.

53. Jones, *Brigadista*, 28.

54. Jones, *Brigadista*, 80–81.

55. "Statement by the Construction Brigade," 114.

56. Jones, *Brigadista*, xx.

57. Audrey Seniors, quoted in Jones, *Brigadista*, 133.

58. Larry Rohter, "Sandinistas' Foreign Legion Is Faithful in Defeat," *NYT*, March 13, 1990, 4.

59. Quainton, interview.

60. Jones, *Brigadista*, 45.

61. Zachary Sklar, quoted in Jones, *Brigadista*, 130–31.

62. Neil Henry, "Inside the Revolution: A Reporter's Search for the Spirit of Nicaragua," *WP*, September 29, 1985, SM6.

63. Rohter, "Sandinistas' Foreign Legion."

64. Rawlings, "Nicaragua, Honduras and El Salvador."

65. Adams to WFP members, April 25, 1986.

66. CNFP, "National Campaign for Peace in Central America: The Time for Action Is Now," box 15, folder: "National Campaign for Peace in Central America," CNFPR, SCPC.

67. Inter-Religious Task Force on Central America, "Central America Week," March 1986, box 5, folder: "Central America Week," CNFPR, SCPC.

68. The number of individuals reached through the media was probably higher; The estimate was based on 10 percent of reading, listening, or viewing audiences. Report, Interreligious Foundation for Community Organization (IFCO), "Central American Information Week Conducted in Indiana, November 27–December 6, 1983," box 9, folder: "Indiana Citizen Action on Central America," CNFPR, SCPC.

69. Report, IFCO, "Central American Information Week Conducted in the Pacific Northwest, April 29–May 13, 1984," box 10, folder: "IFCO Report," CNFPR, SCPC.

70. "Nicaragua: Who's the Threat?," *Inter-Faith Witness* [St. Louis Inter-Faith Committee on Latin America], vol. 2, no. 3 (March 1985), box 8, folder: "Nicaragua," CNFPR, SCPC; "Ray Hooker: Autonomy, War and Generosity," *Council for Human Rights in Latin America Newsletter*, March 1985, box 3, folder: "Oregon: Citizen Action on Central America," CNFPR, SCPC.

71. "Concern for Central America," *CIPAR Peaces* [Commission on International Peace and Reconciliation, Des Moines, IA], May 1985, box 3, folder: "Iowa," CNFPR, SCPC; "Campaign to Stop Contra Aid Underway," *Mustard Seed* [Denver Justice and Peace Committee], vol. 6, no. 3 (July 1985), box 2, folder: "Colorado Citizen Action on Central America," CNFPR, SCPC.

72. *Nicaraguan Perspectives* [East Bay Nicaragua Solidarity Committee and Nicaragua Information Center], vol. 1 (July 1981), box 8, folder: "Nicaragua," CNFPR, SCPC.

73. *Nuke Notes / ¡Solidaridad!* [People for Peace in Central America and Sonoma County Direct Action Coalition], April 1985, box 2, folder: "California, Southern: Citizen Action on Central America," CNFPR, SCPC.

74. Richmond Human Rights Coalition, "Calendar of Events," August 1986, box 3, folder: "Virginia: Citizen Action on Central America," CNFPR, SCPC.

75. Flyer, "Let Nicaragua Live!," Denver Justice and Peace Committee, July 1985, box 2, folder: "Colorado Citizen Action on Central America," CNFPR, SCPC.

76. "Dr. Boogie: Peace Maneuvers," *Nuke Notes / ¡Solidaridad!* [People for Peace in Central America and Sonoma County Direct Action Coalition], box 2, folder: "California, Southern: Citizen Action on Central America," CNFPR, SCPC.

77. Arnson, *Crossroads*, 21.

78. Report, IFCO, "Central American Information Week Conducted in Indiana."

79. Peace, *Call to Conscience*, 117.

80. Arnson, *Crossroads*, 21.

81. Peace, *Call to Conscience*, 165.

82. US Foreign Broadcast Information Service, "Ortega Delivers Eulogy," translation, April 30, 1987, DNSA, ID: NI02983.

83. "Americans Protest Contra Aid, Cross Nicaraguan Battle Zone," *San Francisco Examiner*, May 17, 1987; "Marchers Honor Linder," *LAT*, May 19, 1987.

84. Official communication, Veterans Fast for Life / Veterans Peace Action Team to the president, members of the House of Representatives, and members of the Senate, April 4, 1987, box 14, folder: "Brian Willson," RCC, BUSC.

85. Press release, Veterans Fast for Life / Veterans Peace Action Team, June 1987, box 14, folder: "Brian Willson," RCC, BUSC.

86. Willson to Kaminsky, August 13, 1987.

87. Press release, Veterans Peace Action Team, August 25, 1987, box 14, folder: "Brian Willson," RCC, BUSC.

88. Willson, "Tragedy at Concord, CA Naval Weapons Station."

89. Memorandum, S. Brian Willson, subject: "The 1987 Veterans / Citizens Fast for Life and Peace," August 21, 1987, box 14, folder: "Brian Willson," RCC, BUSC.

90. Willson, "Tragedy at Concord, CA Naval Weapons Station."

91. Letter, S. Brian Willson to Lonnie Cagle, August 21, 1987, box 14, folder: "Brian Willson," RCC, BUSC.

92. George P. Shultz, "Nicaragua: Will Democracy Prevail?," statement before the Senate Committee on Foreign Relations, February 27, 1986 (Washington, DC: Department of State, Bureau of Public Affairs, March 1986), 1.

93. Memorandum, Center for Democracy in the Americas, Bruce P. Cameron to Carl R. Channell, July 2, 1986, subject: "Why the President Won on Contra Aid," DNSA, ID: NI03094.

94. National Endowment for Democracy, *Annual Report 1985*, https://www.ned.org/wp-content/uploads/annualreports/1985-ned-annual-report.pdf.

95. Beverly Bickel, Philip Brenner, and William M. LeoGrande, *Challenging the Reagan Doctrine: A Summation of the April 25th Mobilization* (Washington, DC: Foreign Policy Education Fund, October 1987), box 16, folder: "Challenging the Reagan Doctrine," CNFPR, SCPC.

96. Robert S. Leiken, "Nicaragua's Untold Stories," in *Nicaragua: Unfinished Revolution*, ed. Peter Rosset and John Vandermeer (New York: Grove Press, 1986), 23–32; originally published in *New Republic*, February 8, 1984. See also Robert S. Leiken, "The Battle for Nicaragua," *New York Review of Books*, March 13, 1986.

97. Ron Radosh, "Robert S. Leiken: March 19, 1939–June 7, 2017," *PJ Media*, https://pjmedia.com/ronradosh/2017/06/11/robert-s-leiken-march-19-1939-june-7-2017-r-i-p/.

98. Michael Massing, "The Rise and Fall of 'Ollie's Liberals,'" *WP*, June 28, 1987, C1; memorandum, Center for Democracy in the Americas, Cameron to Channell, July 2, 1986.

99. Bruce P. Cameron, *My Life in the Time of the Contras* (Albuquerque: University of New Mexico Press, 2007), 38.

100. Jack Kemp, "The *New Republic* Makes the Case for the Contras," *Congressional Record*, 132, no. 33 (March 18, 1986): E822.

101. See, for example, Joan Frawley, "The Left's Latin American Lobby," Heritage Foundation, October 11, 1984, box 6, LASSIR, HIA.

102. Jorge I. Domínguez, "The President's Corner," *Latin American Studies Association Newsletter* 13, no. 2 (Summer 1982): 3.

103. George Black, "Success Undercut," *NYT*, November 2, 1984; George Black, "Nicaragua: A Letter from the Editor," *NACLA Report on the Americas*, November/December 1984, 3.

104. Michael Massing, "Hard Questions on Nicaragua," *The Nation*, April 6, 1985, 395.

105. Peter Falk, roundtable, "The U.S. Left and Nicaragua," *The Nation*, April 20, 1985, 458.

106. William Appleman Williams, roundtable, "The U.S. Left and Nicaragua," 461.

107. Roundtable, "The U.S. Left and Nicaragua."

108. Human Rights Watch and Lawyers Committee for Human Rights, *The Reagan Administration's Record on Human Rights in 1987* (New York: Human Rights Watch and Lawyers Committee for Human Rights, 1987), 1.

109. Alex Rothenberg, "Activist Recalled for N.E. Efforts," *Boston Globe*, September 3, 1987.

110. "Your sacrifice speaks very loudly of the nobility of the North American people whose great majority are opposed to the use of violence," Ortega wrote. "This demonstrates that your deep love for peace and justice is greater than any adversity that you may encounter in the pursuit of peace." Telegram, Daniel Ortega Saavedra to S. Brian Willson, September 2, 1987, box 14, folder: "Brian Willson," RCC, BUSC.

111. Craig Marine and Don Martinez, "Ortega's Wife Arrives to Visit Maimed Peace Activist," *San Francisco Examiner*, September 5, 1987; "Ortega's Wife Praises Activists," *Philadelphia Inquirer*, September 6, 1987.

112. Timothy McQuay, "Injured War Protester: Fight Will Go On," *USA Today*, September 3, 1987, 3A.

113. Letter, S. Brian Willson, September 4, 1987, box 14, folder: "Brian Willson," RCC, BUSC.

114. Christian G. Appy, *American Reckoning: The Vietnam War and Our National Identity* (New York: Viking, 2015), 282.

115. Letter, S. Brian Willson, September 4, 1987.

7. From the Cold War to the End of History

1. Vilém Prečan, "The Crumbling of the Soviet Bloc: The Democratic Revolution," *Journal of Democracy* 1, no. 1 (Winter 1990): 79.

2. George Lister, "Human Rights: Our World's Best Chance," address at George Washington University, February 5, 1998, box 18, folder 8, George Lister Papers (hereafter LP), Nettie Lee Benson Latin American Collection, University of Texas at Austin (hereafter UTA).

3. Neil A. Lewis, "'Quiet Diplomacy' in a Loud Voice," *NYT*, May 12, 1987, B6.

4. Eduardo Galeano, "A Ballad for Nicaragua—a Pitiful Place, Yet So Desired by the Powerful," *LAT*, February 16, 1988, C7.

5. Douglas MacEachin, quoted in Byrne, *Iran-Contra*, 336.

6. Matlock, *Reagan and Gorbachev*, 321.

7. Robert D. McFadden, "Frank C. Carlucci, Diplomat and Defense Secretary to Reagan, Dies at 87," *NYT*, June 4, 2018.

8. Frank C. Carlucci III, interview with Charles Stuart Kennedy, April 1, 1997, ADST.

9. Gerald M. Boyd, "Regan Replaced by President; Howard Baker Will Head Staff with a Mandate to Reorganize," *NYT*, February 28, 1987, 1.

10. Memorandum, Howard H. Baker Jr. and Colin Powell to White House and NSC Staff, February 10, 1988, subject: "Private Aid to the Nicaraguan Democratic Resistance," box 135, Committee on the Present Danger Records, HIA; emphasis in the original.

11. Bill McAllister, "Reagan: Contra-Aid Fight Not Over," *WP*, February 12, 1988, A30.

12. Terry Deibel, "Reagan's Mixed Legacy," *Foreign Policy*, no. 75 (Summer 1989): 34–35.

13. Leffler, *For the Soul of Mankind*, 421.

14. Ronald Reagan, *The Reagan Diaries*, ed. Douglas Brinkley (New York: Harper, 2007), 675.

15. Artemy Kalinovsky, *A Long Goodbye: The Soviet Withdrawal from Afghanistan* (Cambridge, MA: Harvard University Press, 2011), 174.

16. Keys, "Origins of Human Rights Diplomacy," 840–50.

17. Lister, "Human Rights."

18. Lister, "Human Rights."

19. Schifter, "Building Firm Foundations," 22.

20. Schifter, "Building Firm Foundations," 22–23.

21. Charles Maechling Jr., "Human Rights Dehumanized," *Foreign Policy*, no. 52 (Autumn 1983): 129.

22. See Jack F. Matlock Jr., "U.S. Policy on Human Rights in Relations with the USSR, 1961–91," in *Implementing U.S. Human Rights Policy: Agendas, Policies, and Practices*, ed. Debra Liang-Fenton (Washington, DC: United States Institute of Peace Press, 2004), 245–63; Snyder, *Human Rights Activism*, 174–216; Christian Philip Peterson, "The Reagan Administration's Efforts to Promote Human Rights and Democracy in the Soviet Union," in *The Reagan Administration, the Cold War, and the Transition to Democracy Promotion*, ed. Robert Pee and William Michael Schmidli (Cham, Switzerland: Palgrave Macmillan, 2019), 95–114.

23. Anatoly L. Adamishin and Richard Schifter, *Human Rights, Perestroika, and the End of the Cold War* (Washington, DC: United States Institute of Peace Press, 2009), 132.

24. Ronald Reagan, remarks at a luncheon hosted by the Town Hall of California, August 26, 1987, Los Angeles, *PPP*, 23 Weekly Comp. Pres. Doc. 964.

25. Evan D. McCormick, "US Electoral Assistance to El Salvador and the Culture of Politics, 1982–1984," in *The Reagan Administration, the Cold War, and the Transition to Democracy Promotion*, ed. Robert Pee and William Michael Schmidli (Cham, Switzerland: Palgrave Macmillan, 2019), 164–65.

26. David Lowe, "Idea to Reality: NED at 30," NED: National Endowment Democracy, accessed September 18, 2019, https://www.ned.org/about/history/; National Endowment for Democracy, *Annual Report 1987*.

27. National Endowment for Democracy, *Annual Report 1987*.

28. Sharnak, "Reagan and the Waning Years," 205.

29. Jerome J. Shestack, "An Unsteady Focus: The Vulnerabilities of the Reagan Administration's Human Rights Policy," *Harvard Human Rights Journal* 25, no. 2 (1989): 44.

30. Ronald Reagan, radio address to the nation, "Soviet Union–United States Relations," August 29, 1987, *PPP*, 23 Weekly Comp. Pres. Doc. 975.

31. Barry Gills, Joel Rocamora, and Richard Wilson, eds., *Low Intensity Democracy: Political Power in the New World Order* (Boulder, CO: Pluto Press, 1993), 8.

32. Ronald Reagan, remarks at a White House briefing for the Council of the Americas, May 12, 1987, *PPP*, 23 Weekly Comp. Pres. Doc. 520.

33. See Kate Geoghegan, "Neoliberalism and Democracy Promotion: Hernando de Soto and US Foreign Policy," in *The Reagan Administration, the Cold War, and the Transition to Democracy Promotion*, ed. Robert Pee and William Michael Schmidli (Cham, Switzerland: Palgrave Macmillan, 2019), 137–60.

34. Schifter, "Building Firm Foundations," 16.

35. Jorge G. Castañeda, *Utopia Unarmed: The Latin American Left after the Cold War* (New York: Vintage Books, 1994), 256–57.

36. Alan Riding, "Democracy and Debt: U.S. Policy on Latin America Is Well Received—in Washington," *NYT*, October 30, 1988, E2.

37. Carothers, *In the Name of Democracy*, 132.

38. Shestack, "Unsteady Focus," 44.

39. See Eckel and Moyn, *Breakthrough*; Alan McPherson, "Letelier Diplomacy: Nonstate Actors and U.S.-Chilean Relations," *Diplomatic History* 43, no. 3 (June 2019): 445–68.

40. DoS cable, Santiago 4670, US Embassy (Landau) to DoS, August 10, 1981, subject: "Ambassador Kirkpatrick's Visit to Santiago: Overview," DNSA, ID: CL02364.

41. Grandin, *Empire's Workshop*, 170.

42. Juan de Onis, "Chile under Pinochet: Democracy Still Far Away," *LAT*, November 11, 1983, G2.

43. Secret memorandum, George P. Shultz to Ronald Reagan, ca. September 3, 1985, subject: "U.S. Policy Seeks Peaceful Transition in Chile Based on Broad National Consensus," DNSA, ID: CL02420.

44. "Inauguration of Chile's Pinochet to Be 'Coronation,'" *LAT*, March 10, 1981, A7.

45. Joanne Omang, "Shultz Puts Chile on List of Latin 'Dictatorships,'" *WP*, March 30, 1986, A18.

46. Memorandum of conversation, NSC meeting, November 18, 1986, subject: "Chile," DNSA, ID: CL02477.

47. Secret memorandum, Nicholas N. Platt to John M. Poindexter, November 13, 1986, subject: "Chile: Background Paper for Secretary Shultz's Presentation at NSC Meeting on Chile, Friday, November 14, 11:00 a.m.," DNSA, ID: CL02473.

48. Confidential memorandum of conversation, March 7, 1988, subject: "Opposition's Grassroots Organization for the Plebiscite," DNSA, ID: CL02615.

49. On US contacts with the Chilean opposition, see, for example, memorandum, George Lister to Elliott Abrams, August 21, 1983, subject: "Chile: Socialists/Communists," DNSA, ID: CL02377; memorandum, George Lister to Elliott Abrams, April 3, 1984, subject: "Our Chile Policy," DNSA, ID: CL02382.

50. Lance Compa, "Stop Sending Mixed Signals to Gen. Pinochet," *WP*, January 5, 1988, A19; Harry G. Barnes Jr., "U.S. Human Rights Policies and Chile," in *Implementing U.S. Human Rights Policy: Agendas, Policies, and Practices*, ed. Debra Liang-Fenton (Washington, DC: United States Institute of Peace Press, 2004), 313.

51. Confidential cable, State 049704, DoS (Shultz) to US Embassy Australia; US Embassy Finland, February 18, 1988, subject: "Coordinating Support for Democracy in Chile," DNSA, ID: CL02597.

52. National Endowment for Democracy, *Annual Report 1988*, https://www.ned.org/wp-content/uploads/annualreports/1988-ned-annual-report.pdf.

53. Carothers, *In the Name of Democracy*, 159.

54. Carothers, *In the Name of Democracy*, 159.

55. Elliott Abrams, "'The Gringos Are with Us,'" *Commentary*, April 2013, https://www.commentarymagazine.com/articles/the-gringos-are-with-us/. See also Harry G. Barnes Jr., interview with Charles Stuart Kennedy, April 25, 2001, ADST.

56. On the limits to U.S. influence in the Chilean plebiscite, see, for example, Carothers, *In the Name of Democracy*, 160–62; Kornbluh, *Pinochet File*, 424; Morley and McGillion, *Reagan and Pinochet*, 320. By contrast, in an interview, Schifter maintained that he, Abrams, and Barnes "made it possible for Chile to get rid of Pinochet." Richard Schifter, interview with Charles Stuart Kennedy, September 8, 2003, ADST.

57. Cable, secret, Santiago 7670, US Embassy Chile (Barnes) to secretary of state, October 19, 1988, subject: "Beyond the Plebiscite," DNSA, ID: CL02652.

58. Shultz, *Turmoil and Triumph*, 975.

59. Colin Powell, "Why History Will Honor Mr. Reagan," *NYT*, January 15, 1989, E27.

60. Elliott Abrams, "Latin America in the Time of Reagan," *NYT*, July 27, 1988, A25.

61. Lou Cannon and Tom Kenworthy, "Reagan Again Vows Support for Contras: Most in U.S. Oppose New Aid, Poll Shows," *WP*, March 23, 1988, A23.

62. Stanley Greenberg, "Contras and U.S. Attitudes toward Region," *WSJ*, September 22, 1987, 32.

63. Neil A. Lewis, "New Contra Plan Called a Threat to Latin Accord," *NYT*, September 11, 1987, A1.

64. Tom Kenworthy and Bill McAllister, "White House Seeking to Salvage Aid to Contras," *WP*, February 2, 1988, A1.

65. LeoGrande, *Our Own Backyard*, 532.

66. Amnesty International, *Nicaragua*," 6–7.

67. Walker, "Armed Forces," 88.

68. The military force numbers include both full-time and reserve personnel. James P. Wooten, "The Nicaraguan Military Buildup: Implications for U.S. Interest in Central America," nonclassified report, CRS, December 18, 1985, 4, LC, DNSA, ID: NI02639.

69. Stephen Kinzer, "Military Draft in Nicaragua Is Meeting Wide Resistance," *NYT*, June 26, 1984; Stephen Kinzer, "Nicaragua's Draft Resisters," *San Francisco Chronicle*, January 3, 1985, 16.

70. NSC memorandum, Robert M. Kimmitt, May 18, 1985, subject: "Nicaraguan Sanctions: Sandinista Responsibility for Their Economic Failures," DNSA, ID: NI02479.

71. Rushdie, *Jaguar Smile*.

72. NSC memorandum, Kimmitt, May 18, 1985.

73. Lynn Horton, *Peasants in Arms: War and Peace in the Mountains of Nicaragua, 1979–1994* (Athens: Ohio University Center for International Studies, 1999), 161.

74. Horton, *Peasants in Arms*, 131; Joseph Ricciardi, "Economic Policy," in *Revolution and Counterrevolution in Nicaragua*, ed. Thomas W. Walker (Boulder, CO: Westview Press, 1991), 256; Alejandro Martínez Cuenca, *Sandinista Economics in Practice: An Insider's Critical Reflections* (Boston: South End Press, 1992), 57–58.

75. Ramírez, *Adiós Muchachos*, 162.

76. Soviet bloc military deliveries (in metric tons) between 1980 and 1984 were as follows: 1980: 850; 1981: 900; 1982: 6,700; 1983: 14,000; 1984: 18,000. Statistics from DoS and DoD, unclassified report, May 1985, subject: "The Sandinista Military Build-Up," DNSA, ID: NI02459; DoD, report, ca. February 1989, subject: "Soviet Bloc Military Equipment Supplied to Nicaragua (July 1979–Dec. 1988)," DNSA, ID: NI03145.

77. Pamphlet, "Nicaragua sigue cosechando Solidaridad," 1985, IHNCA.

78. William R. Long, "Bulgarian Meat and Soviet Cars: Nicaragua Looks East to Offset the U.S. Boycott," *LAT*, May 10, 1985, 16.

79. Long, "Bulgarian Meat and Soviet Cars"; NSC memorandum, Kimmitt, May 18, 1985.

80. Stephen Kinzer, "Food Shortages in Nicaragua Take a Serious Turn," *NYT*, July 1, 1986, A2.

81. James LeMoyne, "In Nicaragua, Economy Is Hobbling Sandinistas," *NYT*, December 20, 1987, 20.

82. "There Is Nowhere Else Quite like Managua," *Envío*, no. 91 (February 1989), https://www.envio.org.ni/articulo/2767, accessed November 21, 2021.

83. Nancy Nusser, "The Rollback of the Revolution," *The Nation*, March 30, 1985, 370.

84. Williams, "Social Programs," 203–4.

85. Nusser, "Rollback of the Revolution."

86. "Nowhere Else Quite like Managua."

87. Martínez Cuenca, *Sandinista Economics in Practice*, 74. See also Ricciardi, "Economic Policy," 264.

88. Ricciardi, "Economic Policy," 266.

89. "Harvest of Misery," *Envío*, no. 111 (October 1990), https://www.envio.org.ni/articulo/2639, accessed November 19, 2021; Harry E. Vanden, "Democracy Derailed: The 1990 Elections and After," in *The Undermining of the Sandinista Revolution*, ed. Gary Prevost and Harry E. Vanden (New York: Palgrave Macmillan, 1999), 53, 57.

90. Roger N. Lancaster, *Life Is Hard: Machismo, Danger, and the Intimacy of Power in Nicaragua* (Berkeley: University of California Press, 1992), 186.

91. LeoGrande, *Our Own Backyard*, 537, 556–57.

92. Ramírez, *Adiós Muchachos*, 194.

93. Larry J. Diamond, quoted in George F. Will, "Seed Money for Democracy," *WP*, December 18, 1988, C7.

94. Carl Gershman, address at Georgetown University, December 9, 1988, reproduced in *WP*, December 29, 1988, A22.

95. George H. W. Bush, inaugural address, January 20, 1989, Avalon Project, Yale Law School, https://avalon.law.yale.edu/20th_century/bush.asp.

96. Talking points, cabinet meeting, January 23, 1989, box 108, folder 1: "1989 January," James A. Baker III Papers (hereafter JABP), Seeley G. Mudd Manuscript Library, PU.

97. Aryeh Neier, "Human Rights in the Reagan Era: Acceptance in Principle," *Annals of the American Academy of Political and Social Science* 506 (November 1, 1989): 30–41.

98. John Newhouse, "The Tactician," *New Yorker*, May 7, 1990, 50.

99. James A. Baker III, *The Politics of Diplomacy: Revolution, War and Peace, 1989–1992* (New York: G. P. Putnam's Sons, 1995), 47.

100. Talking points, cabinet meeting, January 23, 1989.

101. Baker, *Politics of Diplomacy*, 47–48.

102. Baker, *Politics of Diplomacy*, 53.

103. LeoGrande, *Our Own Backyard*, 526.

104. Baker, *Politics of Diplomacy*, 50. See also James A. Baker III, interview with Russell Riley, James Sterling, and Robert Strong, March 17, 2011, Oral History Program, MCPA.

105. Brent Scowcroft, interview with Philip Zelikow et al., November 12–13, 1999, Oral History Program, MCPA.

106. Baker, *Politics of Diplomacy*, 54.

107. Clifford Krauss, "An Unlikely Diplomat Seizes the Opportunity to Shape Latin Policy," *NYT*, April 25, 1990, 18.

108. Baker, *Politics of Diplomacy*, 55.

109. Baker, *Politics of Diplomacy*, 6.

110. James A. Baker III, "Talking Points: Call to George Mitchell," March 16, 1989[?], box 108, folder 3: "1989 Mar.," JABP, PU.

111. Arnson, *Crossroads*, 233.

112. David Hoffman, "Is There a Deal-Maker in the White House?," *WP*, March 26, 1989, A10.

113. Doyle McManus, "Baker Urges W. Europe to Pressure Nicaragua," *LAT*, February 14, 1989, 8; Jack Anderson and Dale Van Atta, "U.S. Pressures Nicaragua through Banks," *WP*, June 2, 1989, E5; Mary Speck, "Nicaragua, Putting Clamps on Inflation, Throttles Small Farmers," *WP*, June 5, 1989, A20.

114. Memorandum, Henry Kissinger to George H. W. Bush, subject: "Meeting with Gorbachev—January 17, 1989, 12:00–1:20 p.m.," box 108, folder 1: "1989 January," JABP, PU.

115. Scowcroft, interview.

116. DoD, report, ca. February 1989.

117. Scowcroft, interview.

118. Thomas L. Friedman, "Diplomacy: Baker's Statement on Soviet Aid to Nicaragua May Reflect a Deep and Subtle Pragmatism," *NYT*, April 18, 1989, A20.

119. John M. Goshko and David Hoffman, "Bush Urges Gorbachev to Aid Peace Effort," *WP*, March 31, 1989, A32.

120. Robert S. Greenberger, "U.S. Is Skeptical of Gorbachev Statement on Halt to Arms Supplies for Nicaragua," *WSJ*, May 17, 1989, B3.

121. Briefing Book, "The President's Meetings with Soviet President Gorbachev, December 2–3, 1989, Malta," NSA, https://nsarchive2.gwu.edu/NSAEBB/NSAEBB298/Document%209.pdf.

122. Craig and Logevall, *America's Cold War*, 343.

123. Soviet transcript of the Malta meeting, December 2–3, 1989, NSA, https://nsarchive2.gwu.edu/NSAEBB/NSAEBB298/Document%2010.pdf.

124. Press release, "Shevardnadze's Interview with Spanish News Service," Soviet Embassy, Information Department, December 8, 1989, box 108, folder 12: "1989 Dec.," JABP, PU.

125. "Excerpt from Protocol No. 179 of the Meeting of the Politburo CC CPSU, 'On the Upcoming Elections in Nicaragua,'" February 17, 1990, History and Public Policy Program Digital Archive, CWIHP, WWC, http://digitalarchive.wilsoncenter.org/document/118940.

126. "Bush Extends Sanctions on Nicaragua," *LAT*, April 22, 1989, 8.

127. Norman Kempster, "Way Is Open for Nicaragua to Normalize U.S. Ties, Baker Says," *LAT*, February 2, 1990, A5.

128. "Congressional Meetings on Central America: Draft Talking Points," September 11, 1989, box 108, folder 9: "1989 September," JABP, PU.

129. David Lauter, "Nicaragua's Opposition Candidate at White House," *LAT*, November 9, 1989, A15.

130. Letter, James A. Baker III to Thomas S. Foley, September 20, 1989, DNSA, ID: NI03191.

131. Letter, Baker to Foley, September 20, 1989.

132. James A. Baker III, notes from meeting with Republican leadership, "Talking Points for Senate Republicans," October 17, 1989, box 108, folder 10: "1989 Oct.," JABP, PU.

133. Congressional correspondence, David E. Bonior to "Democratic Colleague," September 22, 1988, DNSA, ID: NI03128; LeoGrande, *Our Own Backyard*, 560.

134. Arnson, *Crossroads*, 235.

135. White House press release, October 20, 1989, box 108, folder 10: "1989 Oct.," JABP, PU.

136. LeoGrande, *Our Own Backyard*, 561. National Endowment for Democracy, *Annual Report 1990*, https://www.ned.org/wp-content/uploads/annualreports/1990-ned-annual-report.pdf. Between 1981 and 1988, the NED had provided civic groups in Nicaragua $1.9 million.

137. On the NED's support for *La Prensa*, see, for example, NED project proposal, ca. 1988, DNSA, ID: NI03051.

138. Letter, Carl Gershman to Violeta Chamorro, October 13, 1988; letter, Carl Gershman to Violetta Chamorro, November 22, 1988; letter, Carl Gershman to Violeta Chamorro, April 3, 1989; letter, Carl Gershman to Violetta Chamorro, May 10, 1989, all located in box 2, folder 21, "Correspondence: Chamorro, Violeta and Cristiana," NEDR, LC.

139. Robert Pear, "U.S. Praises Choice of Nicaragua Opposition," *NYT*, September 4, 1989, 5.

140. NED press release, February 13, 1990, DNSA, ID: NI03229.

141. Doyle McManus, "U.S. Will Warn Contras: No Military Attacks during Diplomatic Efforts," *LAT*, March 15, 1988, 9.

142. Doyle McManus, "U.S. Shifts to Kinder, Gentler Nicaragua Policy," *LAT*, September 18, 1989, 5.

143. David Lauter and Richard Boudreaux, "Bush Blasts Ortega as 'Shameful,'" *LAT*, October 29, 1989, A1.

144. Robert Pear, "Pact in Nicaragua: U.S. Resists Too," *NYT*, November 3, 1989, A8.

145. Richard Boudreaux, "Evidence Links Contras to Raid That Killed 18," *LAT*, November 7, 1989, A1.

146. John M. Goshko, "U.S. Urges Nicaragua to Preserve Electoral Process," *WP*, October 31, 1989, A18.

147. Lauter and Boudreaux, "Bush Blasts Ortega as 'Shameful.'"

148. "Nicaragua Units Attack Contras as Truce Ends," *LAT*, November 2, 1989, P2.

149. Richard Boudreaux, "War Shadows Campaigning in Nicaragua," *LAT*, November 9, 1989, A16.

150. Richard Boudreaux, "Contras' Campaign Tactics Could Boost Sandinistas," *LAT*, February 17, 1990, A1; see also William I. Robinson, *A Faustian Bargain: U.S. Intervention in the Nicaraguan Elections and American Foreign Policy in the Post–Cold War Era* (Boulder, CO: Westview Press, 1992), 138.

151. Lee Hockstader, "Famous, Near-Famous among Observers," *LAT*, February 26, 1990, A9.

152. Marjorie Miller, "World Keeps Watching as Nicaraguan Polls Open," *LAT*, February 25, 1990, A1.

153. Nina M. Serafino, "Nicaraguan Elections and Transition: Issues for U.S. Policy," CRS, March 26, 1990, DNSA, ID: NI03233.

154. Pastor, *Not Condemned to Repetition*, 255; Kagan, *Twilight Struggle*, 705–7; Guillermoprieto, *Heart That Bleeds*, 23.

155. Pastor, *Not Condemned to Repetition*, 262.

156. "Text of the Speech Delivered by the President of Nicaragua," February 26, 1990, Nicaraguan Embassy, Washington, DC, DNSA, ID: NI03230.

157. Latin American Studies Association, *Electoral Democracy under International Pressure: The Report of the Latin American Studies Association Commission to Observe the 1990 Nicaraguan Election* (Pittsburgh: PA: Latin American Studies Association, March 15, 1990), https://lasaweb.org/uploads/reports/electoraldemocracyinternationalpressure.pdf; Kagan, *Twilight Struggle*, 701.

158. Latin American Studies Association, *Electoral Democracy under International Pressure*.

159. Robinson, *Faustian Bargain*, 62.

160. Ramírez, *Adiós Muchachos*, 192.

161. "Bush's Remarks on Nicaragua," *NYT*, February 27, 1990, A13.

162. Serafino, "Nicaraguan Elections and Transition."

163. James A. Baker III, notes from breakfast with Central American presidents, June 18, 1990, Antigua, Guatemala, box 109, folder 2: "1990 June," JABP, PU; emphasis in the original.

164. Elliott Abrams, "Ask Not If, But How, to Aid Liberty," *LAT*, February 27, 1990, B7.

165. George F. Will, "Nicaragua Curtains for the Left," *LAT*, February 28, 1990, B7.

166. Vanden, "Democracy Derailed," 64.

167. Mario Arana, "General Economic Policy," in *Nicaragua without Illusions: Regime Transition and Structural Adjustment in the 1990s*, ed. Thomas W. Walker (Wilmington, DE: SR Books, 1997), 84.

168. Gary Prevost, "The Status of the Sandinista Project," in *The Undermining of the Sandinista Revolution*, ed. Gary Prevost and Harry E. Vanden (New York: Palgrave Macmillan, 1999), 22.

169. Phil McCombs and Donnie Radcliffe, "Chamorro and Chamorro and Chamorro: Warm Fete for Nicaragua's President," *WP*, April 18, 1991, D1.

170. McCombs and Radcliffe, "Chamorro and Chamorro and Chamorro"; "Harvest of Misery"; Prevost, "Status of the Sandinista Project," 23.

Conclusion

1. Francis Fukuyama, "The End of History?," *National Interest*, Summer 1989, 1. Fukuyama quickly expanded the article into a book. Francis Fukuyama, *The End of History and the Last Man* (New York: Free Press, 1992).

2. James Atlas, "What Is Fukuyama Saying? And to Whom Is He Saying It?," *NYT*, October 22, 1989.

3. Brands, *Making the Unipolar Moment*, 339.

4. Hauke Hartmann, "US Policy under Carter and Reagan, 1977-1981" *Human Rights Quarterly*, 23, no. 2 (May 2001): 402.

5. Tony Lake, address at Johns Hopkins University, Washington, DC, September 21, 1993, International Relations, Mount Holyoke College, https://www.mtholyoke.edu/acad/intrel/lakedoc.html.

6. Bill Clinton, State of the Union Address, January 25, 1994, MCPA, https://millercenter.org/the-presidency/presidential-speeches/january-25-1994-state-union-address. On Clinton and democracy promotion, see, Douglas Brinkley, "Democratic Enlargement: The Clinton Doctrine," *Foreign Policy*, no. 106 (Spring 1997): 110–27; John Dumbrell, *Clinton's Foreign Policy: Between the Bushes, 1992–2000* (New York: Routledge, 2009); Nicolas Bouchet, *Democracy Promotion as US Foreign Policy: Bill Clinton and Democratic Enlargement* (New York: Routledge, 2015); Rasmus Sinding Søndergaard, "Bill Clinton's 'Democratic Enlargement' and the Securitisation of Democracy Promotion," *Diplomacy & Statecraft* 26, no. 3 (2015): 534–51; Kate Geoghegan, "A Policy in Tension: The National Endowment for Democracy and the U.S. Response to the Collapse of the Soviet Union," *Diplomatic History* 42, no. 5 (2018): 772–801.

7. On the development democracy promotion networks in the 1990s, see Nicolas Guilhot, *The Democracy Makers: Human Rights and the Politics of Global Order* (New York: Columbia University Press, 2012).

8. Larry J. Diamond and Marc F. Plattner, "Why the 'Journal of Democracy,'" *Journal of Democracy* 1, no. 1 (Winter 1990): 4.

9. Larry J. Diamond, "Promoting Democracy," *Foreign Policy*, no. 87 (Summer, 1992): 46.

10. Pee and Schmidli, *Transition to Democracy Promotion*, 298.

11. Bill Clinton, remarks at the US Naval Academy commencement, Annapolis, Maryland, May 25, 1994, APP, https://www.presidency.ucsb.edu/documents/remarks-the-united-states-naval-academy-commencement-ceremony-annapolis-maryland-0. On Clinton's response to Rwanda, see Philip Gourevitch, *We Wish to Inform You That Tomorrow We Will Be Killed with Our Families: Stories from Rwanda* (New York: Picador, 1999); Samantha Power, *"A Problem from Hell": America and the Age of Genocide* (New York: Harper Perennial, 2002).

12. Michael Ignatieff, "Introduction: American Exceptionalism and Human Rights," in *American Exceptionalism and Human Rights*, ed. Michael Ignatieff (Princeton, NJ: Princeton University Press, 2005), 4. On the United States and human rights in the post–Cold War era, see also Stephen Hopgood, *The Endtimes of Human Rights* (Ithaca, NY: Cornell University Press, 2013).

13. George W. Bush, second inaugural address, January 20, 2005, MCPA, https://millercenter.org/the-presidency/presidential-speeches/january-20-2005-second-inaugural-address-0#dp-expandable-text.

14. See, for example, Maria Ryan, "Bush's 'Useful Idiots': 9/11, the Liberal Hawks and the Cooption of the 'War on Terror,'" *Journal of American Studies* 45, no. 4 (2011): 667–93; Tony Smith, *A Pact with the Devil: Washington's Bid for World Supremacy and the Betrayal of the American Promise* (New York: Routledge, 2007).

15. Neta C. Crawford and Catherine Lutz, "Human Cost of Post-9/11 Wars," Costs of War Research Series (Watson Institute for International and Public Affairs, Brown University, Providence, RI, November 13, 2019), https://watson.brown.edu/costsofwar/files/cow/imce/papers/2019/Direct%20War%20Deaths%20COW%20Estimate%20November%2013%202019%20FINAL.pdf.

16. See Mark Danner, *Spiral: Trapped in the Forever War* (New York: Simon & Schuster, 2016).

17. Thomas Carothers, *U.S. Democracy Promotion during and after Bush* (Washington, DC: Carnegie Endowment for International Peace, 2007), v.

18. Carothers, *U.S. Democracy Promotion*, 33.

19. Larry J. Diamond, "How the Freedom Agenda Fell Apart," *Foreign Affairs*, July/August 2019, 17.

20. Ronald Reagan, remarks to members of the Captive Nations Conference, Washington, D.C., July 24, 1987, *PPP*, 23 Weekly Comp. Pres. Doc. 848.

Bibliography

Oral Histories

Foreign Affairs Oral History Program of the Association for Diplomatic Studies and Training, Arlington, VA (ADST)
Harry G. Barnes Jr., interview with Charles Stuart Kennedy, April 25, 2001
John A. Bushnell, interview with John Harter, December 19, 1997
Frank C. Carlucci III, interview with Charles Stuart Kennedy, April 1, 1997
George F. Jones, interview with Charles Stuart Kennedy, August 6, 1996
Lane Kirkland, interview with James F. Shea and Don R. Kienzle, November 13, 1996
Jeane J. Kirkpatrick, interview with Ann Miller Morin, May 28, 1987
Langhorne A. Motley, interview with Charles Stuart Kennedy, March 7, 1991
Lawrence A. Pezzullo, interview with Arthur R. Day, February 24, 1989
Anthony Quainton, interview with Charles Stuart Kennedy, November 6, 1997
Otto J. Reich, interview with Charles Stuart Kennedy, August 30, 1991
Richard Schifter, interview with Charles Stuart Kennedy, September 8, 2003
Harry W. Shlaudeman, interview with William E. Knight, May 24, 1993
Stephen J. Solarz, interview with Charles Stuart Kennedy, November 18, 1996
Faith Ryan Whittlesey, interview with Ann Miller Morin, December 7, 1988
Oral History Program, Miller Center of Public Affairs, University of Virginia, Charlottesville, VA (MCPA)
Richard V. Allen, interview with Stephen F. Knott, May 28, 2002
James A. Baker III, interview with Russell Riley, James Sterling, and Robert Strong, March 17, 2011
Brent Scowcroft, interview with Philip Zelikow, Ernest May, James H. McCall, and Fareed Zakaria, November 12–13, 1999

George P. Shultz, interview with Stephen Knott, Marc Selverstone, and James Sterling Young, December 18, 2002

Additional

Jeane J. Kirkpatrick, interview transcript from *The Cold War*, produced by CNN, 1998, reprinted at National Security Archive, George Washington University, Washington, DC, http://nsarchive.gwu.edu/coldwar/interviews/episode-19/kirkpatrick1.html.

Yuri Pavlov, interview transcript from *The Cold War*, produced by CNN, 1998, reprinted at National Security Archive, George Washington University, Washington, DC, https://nsarchive2.gwu.edu/coldwar/interviews/episode-18/pavlov1.html.

Jack Wheeler, interview with Karen Reedstrom, *Full Context*, May 1996

Government Documents

Unpublished

Jimmy Carter Library, Atlanta, GA

Gerald R. Ford Library, Ann Arbor, MI

El Instituto de Historia de Nicaragua y Centroamérica, Universidad Centroamericana, Managua, Nicaragua

Ronald Reagan Library, Simi Valley, CA

Published

American Presidency Project. University of California, Santa Barbara.

Central Intelligence Agency Records Search Tool (CREST). Freedom of Information Act Electronic Reading Room.

Cold War International History Project. Woodrow Wilson Center for International Scholars, Washington, DC.

Digital National Security Archive. "Argentina, 1975–1980: The Making of U.S. Human Rights."

——. "Chile and the U.S.: U.S. Policy toward Democracy, Dictatorship, and Human Rights, 1970–1990."

——. "CIA Covert Operations, 1977–2010."

——. "El Salvador: The Making of U.S. Policy, 1977–1984."

——. "The Iran-Contra Affair: The Making of a Scandal, 1983–1988."

——. "Nicaragua: The Making of U.S. Policy, 1978–1990."

Frente Sandinista de Liberación Nacional (FSLN). *Programa Histórico del FSLN*. Managua: Departamento de Propaganda y Educación Politica del FSLN, 1984.

Gilbert, Dennis, and David Block, eds. *Sandinistas: Key Documents/Documentos Claves*. Ithaca, NY: Cornell University Latin American Studies Program, 1990.

National Security Archive. Briefing Book. "The President's Meetings with Soviet President Gorbachev, December 2–3, 1989, Malta." https://nsarchive2.gwu.edu/NSAEBB/NSAEBB298/Document%209.pdf.

Shultz, George P. "America and the Struggle for Freedom." Address to the Commonwealth Club of California, San Francisco, February 22, 1985. Washington, DC: Department of State, Bureau of Public Affairs, February 1985.

———. "The Meaning of Vietnam." Address at the Department of State, April 25, 1985. Washington, DC: Department of State, Bureau of Public Affairs, April 1985.

———. "Nicaragua: Will Democracy Prevail?" Statement before the Senate Committee on Foreign Relations, February 27, 1986. Washington, DC: Department of State, Bureau of Public Affairs, March 1986.

Solórzano, Porfirio R., ed. *The Nirex Collection: Nicaraguan Revolution Extracts.* 10 vols. Austin, TX: Litex, 1993.

United States Congress. Select Joint Committee of the House and Senate. *Report of the Congressional Committees Investigating the Iran-Contra Affair.* 100th Cong., 1st Sess. Senate Report 206. House Report 433. Washington, DC: Government Printing Office, 1987.

United States Department of State, Bureau of Public Affairs. "1983 Human Rights Report." [Excerpt from *Country Reports on Human Rights Practices for 1983.*] Washington, DC: Government Printing Office, February 1984.

———. *Foreign Relations of the United States, 1969–1976.* Vol. 1. Washington, DC: Government Printing Office, 2003.

———. *Foreign Relations of the United States, 1969–1976.* Vol. 14. Washington, DC: Government Printing Office, 2006.

———. *Foreign Relations of the United States, 1969–1976.* Vol. 39. Washington, DC: Government Printing Office, 2007.

———. *Foreign Relations of the United States, 1977–1980.* Vol. 1. Washington, DC: Government Printing Office, 2014.

———. *Foreign Relations of the United States, 1977–1980.* Vol. 2. Washington, DC: Government Printing Office, 2013.

———. *Foreign Relations of the United States, 1981–1988.* Vol. 3. Washington, DC: Government Printing Office, 2016.

United States Office of the Federal Register, National Archives and Records Administration. *Public Papers of the Presidents of the United States.* Washington, DC: Government Printing Office.

Manuscript Collections

Richard V. Allen Papers. Hoover Institution Archives, Stanford University, Palo Alto, CA.

James A. Baker III Papers. Seeley G. Mudd Manuscript Library, Princeton University Library, Princeton, NJ.

Patrick J. Buchanan Files. Ronald Reagan Library, Simi Valley, CA.

William J. Casey Papers, 1928–1996. Hoover Institution Archives, Stanford University, Palo Alto, CA.

Rita Clark Nicaragua Collection. Bucknell University Special Collections, Lewisburg, PA.

Coalition for a New Foreign Policy Records, 1969–1988. Swarthmore College Peace Collection, Swarthmore, PA.

Committee on the Present Danger Records. Hoover Institution Archives, Stanford University, Palo Alto, CA.

Council for Inter-American Security Records. Hoover Institution Archives, Stanford University, Palo Alto, CA.

Donald M. Fraser Papers, 1951–1995. Minnesota Historical Society, St. Paul, MN.

Freedom House Records, 1933–2014. Public Policy Papers, Department of Rare Books and Special Collections, Princeton University Library, Princeton, NJ.

Latin American Strategic Studies Institute Records. Hoover Institution Archives, Stanford University, Palo Alto, CA.

Latin America Working Group. Swarthmore College Peace Collection, Swarthmore, PA.

George Lister Papers. Nettie Lee Benson Latin American Collection, University of Texas at Austin.

National Endowment for Democracy Records. Library of Congress, Washington, DC.

Nicaragua Subject Collection. Hoover Institution Archives, Stanford University, Palo Alto, CA.

Joseph Shattan Papers. Hoover Institution Archives, Stanford University, Palo Alto, CA.

Allen Weinstein Papers. Hoover Institution Archives, Stanford University, Palo Alto, CA.

Faith Ryan Whittlesey Papers. Ronald Reagan Library, Simi Valley, CA.

Witness for Peace Records. Swarthmore College Peace Collection, Swarthmore, PA.

Periodicals

Boston Globe
Christian Science Monitor
Commentary
Commonweal
Contemporary Marxism
Daily Hampshire Gazette (Northampton, MA)
Envío (Managua, Nicaragua)
Fairness & Accuracy in Reporting
Foreign Affairs
Foreign Policy
Foreign Policy in Focus
Foreign Service Journal

Freedom at Issue
Journal of Democracy
Latin American Studies Association Newsletter
Los Angeles Times
Miami Herald
Mother Jones
NACLA Report on the Americas
The Nation
New Republic
New York
New York Intelligencer
New York Review of Books
New York Times
New Yorker
Newsday
Newsweek
Nicaraguan Perspectives
Philadelphia Inquirer
Politico
Reason
Register-Pajaronian (Santa Cruz, CA)
San Francisco Chronicle
San Francisco Examiner
Time
U.S. News and World Report
USA Today
Wall Street Journal
Washington Post
Witness for Peace Newsletter

Memoirs, Reports, and Primary Source Collections

Adler, Bill. *The Wit and Wisdom of Jimmy Carter*. Secaucus, NJ: Citadel Press, 1977.

Americas Watch Committee. *Human Rights in Nicaragua, August 1987–August 1988*. New York: Americas Watch Committee, August 1988.

———. *Human Rights in Nicaragua 1986*. New York: Americas Watch Committee, February 1987.

———. *Human Rights in Nicaragua: Reagan, Rhetoric and Reality*. New York: Americas Watch Committee, July 1985.

———. *The Killings in Northern Nicaragua*. New York: Americas Watch Committee, October 1989.

———. *On Human Rights in Nicaragua*. New York: Americas Watch Committee, May 1982.

———. *Violations of the Laws of War by Both Sides in Nicaragua in 1987*. New York: Americas Watch Committee, November 1987.

Amnesty International. *Nicaragua: The Human Rights Record*. London: Amnesty International, March 1986.

Atlee-Loudon, Jennifer. *Red Thread: A Spiritual Journey of Accompaniment, Trauma and Healing*. Washington, DC: EPICA, 2001.

Baker, James A., III. *The Politics of Diplomacy: Revolution, War and Peace, 1989–1992*. New York: G. P. Putnam's Sons, 1995.

Borge, Tomás, Carlos Fonseca, Daniel Ortega Saavedra, Humberto Ortega Saavedra, and Jaime Wheelock. *Sandinistas Speak: Speeches, Writings, and Interviews with Leaders of Nicaragua's Revolution*. New York: Pathfinder Press, 1982.

Brody, Reed. "Contra Terror in Nicaragua: the Report of a Fact-Finding Mission, September 1984–January 1985." Boston: South End Press, 1985.

Cameron, Bruce P. *My Life in the Time of the Contras*. Albuquerque: University of New Mexico Press, 2007.

Carter, Jimmy. *Keeping Faith: Memoirs of a President*. New York: Bantam Books, 1982.

Clarridge, Duane R. *A Spy for All Seasons: My Life in the CIA*. With Digby Diehl. New York: Scribner, 1997.

Crawford, Neta C., and Catherine Lutz. "Human Cost of Post-9/11 Wars." Costs of War Research Series. Providence, RI: Watson Institute for International and Public Affairs, Brown University, November 13, 2019. https://watson.brown.edu/costsof war/files/cow/imce/papers/2019/Direct%20War%20Deaths%20COW%20Esti mate%20November%2013%202019%20FINAL.pdf.

Eich, Dieter, and Carlos Rincón. *The Contras: Interviews with Anti-Sandinistas*. San Francisco: Synthesis Publications, 1985.

Everett, Melissa, ed. *Bearing Witness, Building Bridges: Interviews with North Americans Living and Working in Nicaragua*. Philadelphia: New Society Publishers, 1986.

Fund for New Priorities in America. *U.S. Policy on Human Rights in Latin America (Southern Cone): A Congressional Conference on Capitol Hill*. New York: Fund for New Priorities in America, 1978.

Gates, Robert M. *From the Shadows: The Ultimate Insider's Story of Five Presidents and How They Won the Cold War*. New York: Simon & Schuster, 1996.

Guillermoprieto, Alma. *The Heart That Bleeds: Latin America Now*. New York: Vintage Books, 1995.

Haig, Alexander M., Jr. *Caveat: Realism, Reagan, and Foreign Policy*. New York: Macmillan, 1984.

Human Rights Watch and the Lawyers Committee for Human Rights. *The Reagan Administration's Record on Human Rights in 1987*. New York: Human Rights Watch and Lawyers Committee for Human Rights, 1987.

Inter-American Commission on Human Rights. *Report on the Situation of Human Rights in the Republic of Guatemala*. Washington, DC: Organization of American States, 1981.

Jones, Jeff, ed. *Brigadista: Harvest and War in Nicaragua*. New York: Praeger, 1986.

Kinzer, Stephen. *All the Shah's Men: An American Coup and the Roots of Middle East Terror*. Hoboken, NJ: Wiley, 2004.

———. *Blood of Brothers: Life and War in Nicaragua*. New York: Putnam, 1991.

Kissinger, Henry. *White House Years*. Boston: Little, Brown, 1979.

———. *Years of Renewal*. New York: Simon & Schuster, 1999.

Kraus, Sidney. *The Great Debates: Carter vs. Ford, 1976*. Bloomington: Indiana University Press, 1979.

Lake, Anthony. *Somoza Falling*. Boston: Houghton Mifflin, 1989.

Latin American Studies Association. *Electoral Democracy under International Pressure: The Report of the Latin American Studies Association Commission to Observe the 1990 Nicaraguan Election*. Pittsburgh, PA: Latin American Studies Association, March 15, 1990. https://lasaweb.org/uploads/reports/electoraldemocracyinternationalpressure.pdf.

Lugar, Richard G. *Letters to the Next President*. New York: Simon & Schuster, 1988.

Martínez Cuenca, Alejandro. *Sandinista Economics in Practice: An Insider's Critical Reflections*. Boston: South End Press, 1992.

Menard-Warwick, Julia, and Peter Menard-Warwick. *Letters Home: A Year in Nicaragua*. Enterprise, OR: Pika Press, 1989.

National Endowment for Democracy. *Annual Report 1985*. https://www.ned.org/wp-content/uploads/annualreports/1985-ned-annual-report.pdf.

———. *Annual Report 1987*. https://www.ned.org/wp-content/uploads/annualreports/1987-ned-annual-report.pdf.

———. *Annual Report 1988*. https://www.ned.org/wp-content/uploads/annualreports/1988-ned-annual-report.pdf.

———. *Annual Report 1990*. https://www.ned.org/wp-content/uploads/annualreports/1990-ned-annual-report.pdf.

Ramírez, Sergio. *Adiós Muchachos: A Memoir of the Sandinista Revolution*. Durham, NC: Duke University Press, 2011.

Reagan, Ronald. *Reagan, in His Own Hand: The Writings of Ronald Reagan That Reveal His Revolutionary Vision for America*. Edited by Kiron K. Skinner, Annelise Anderson, and Martin Anderson. New York: Free Press, 2001.

———. *The Reagan Diaries*. Edited by Douglas Brinkley. New York: Harper, 2007.

———. *A Time for Choosing: The Speeches of Ronald Reagan, 1961–1982*. Chicago: Regnery Gateway, 1983.

Rosset, Peter, and John Vandermeer, eds. *Nicaragua: Unfinished Revolution*. New York: Grove Press, 1986.

Rushdie, Salman. *The Jaguar Smile: A Nicaraguan Journey*. New York: Random House, 1987.

Shultz, George P. *Turmoil and Triumph: My Years as Secretary of State*. New York: Scribner's, 1993.

Tyroler, Charles, II, ed. *Alerting America: The Papers of the Committee on the Present Danger*. Washington, DC: Pergamon-Brassey's, 1984.

United Nations Security Council. *From Madness to Hope: The 12-Year War in El Salvador: Report of the Commission on the Truth for El Salvador*. New York: United Nations

Security Council, 1993. https://www.usip.org/sites/default/files/file/ElSalvador
-Report.pdf.

Washington Office on Latin America (WOLA). *Nicaragua: The Human Tragedy of the War, April–June 1986.* Washington, DC: WOLA, 1986.

Wattenberg, Ben J. *Fighting Words: A Tale of How Liberals Created Neo-conservatism.* New York: Thomas Dunne Books, 2008.

Wheeler, Jack. *The Coming Collapse of the Soviet Union.* The Heritage Lectures. Washington, DC: Heritage Foundation, 1988.

Wiarda, Howard J. *Conservative Brain Trust: The Rise, Fall, and Rise Again of the American Enterprise Institute.* Lanham, MD: Lexington Books, 2009.

Secondary Sources

Adamishin, Anatoly L., and Richard Schifter. *Human Rights, Perestroika, and the End of the Cold War.* Washington, DC: United States Institute of Peace Press, 2009.

Allen, Richard V. "Ronald Reagan: An Extraordinary Man in Extraordinary Times." In *The Fall of the Berlin Wall: Reassessing the Causes and Consequences of the End of the Cold War,* edited by Peter Schweizer, 49–59. Stanford, CA: Hoover Institution Press, 2000.

Ambrosius, Lloyd E. *Wilsonianism: Woodrow Wilson and His Legacy in American Foreign Relations.* New York: Palgrave Macmillan, 2002.

Anderson, K. Cheasty. "Doctors within Borders: Cuban Medical Diplomacy to Sandinista Nicaragua, 1979–1990." In *Beyond the Eagle's Shadow: New Histories of Latin America's Cold War,* edited by Virginia Garrard-Burnett, Mark Atwood Lawrence, and Julio E. Moreno, 200–225. Albuquerque: University of New Mexico Press, 2013.

Apodaca, Clair. *Understanding U.S. Human Rights Policy: A Paradoxical Legacy.* New York: Routledge, 2006.

Appy, Christian G. *American Reckoning: The Vietnam War and Our National Identity.* New York: Viking, 2015.

Arana, Mario. "General Economic Policy." In *Nicaragua without Illusions: Regime Transition and Structural Adjustment in the 1990s,* edited by Thomas W. Walker, 81–96. Wilmington, DE: SR Books, 1997.

Armony, Ariel C. *Argentina, the United States, and the Anti-Communist Crusade in Central America, 1977–1984.* Athens: Ohio University Center for International Studies, 1997.

Arnson, Cynthia J. *Crossroads: Congress, the President, and Central America, 1976–1993.* University Park: Pennsylvania State University Press, 1993.

Barnes, Harry G., Jr. "U.S. Human Rights Policies and Chile." In *Implementing U.S. Human Rights Policy: Agendas, Policies, and Practices,* edited by Debra Liang-Fenton, 299–329. Washington, DC: United States Institute of Peace Press, 2004.

Belew, Kathleen. *Bring the War Home: The White Power Movement and Paramilitary America.* Cambridge, MA: Harvard University Press, 2018.

Bessner, Daniel, and Jennifer M. Miller. "Foreign Encounters and U.S. Democracy." *Diplomatic History* 45, no. 1 (January 2021): 23–27.

Bethell, Leslie, and Ian Roxborough. *Latin America between the Second World War and the Cold War, 1944–1948*. New York: Cambridge University Press, 1997.

Bill, James A. *The Eagle and the Lion: The Tragedy of American-Iranian Relations*. New Haven, CT: Yale University Press, 1989.

Black, George. *Triumph of the People: The Sandinista Revolution in Nicaragua*. London: Zed Press, 1982.

Bloodworth, Jeffrey. *Losing the Center: The Decline of American Liberalism, 1968–1992*. Lexington: University Press of Kentucky, 2013.

Bonner, Raymond. *Waltzing with a Dictator: The Marcoses and the Making of American Foreign Policy*. New York: Vintage Books, 1988.

Booth, John A. *The End and the Beginning: The Nicaraguan Revolution*. 2nd ed. Boulder, CO: Westview Press, 1985.

Borstelmann, Thomas. *The 1970s: A New Global History from Civil Rights to Economic Inequality*. Princeton, NJ: Princeton University Press, 2011.

Bouchet, Nicolas. *Democracy Promotion as US Foreign Policy: Bill Clinton and Democratic Enlargement*. New York: Routledge, 2015.

Bradley, Mark Philip. *The World Reimagined: Americans and Human Rights in the Twentieth Century*. New York: Cambridge University Press, 2016.

Brands, H. W. *Reagan: The Life*. New York: Doubleday, 2015.

Brands, Hal. *Making the Unipolar Moment: U.S. Foreign Policy and the Rise of the Post–Cold War Order*. Ithaca, NY: Cornell University Press, 2016.

Brinkley, Douglas. "Bernath Lecture: The Rising Stock of Jimmy Carter: The 'Hands On' Legacy of Our Thirty-Ninth President." *Diplomatic History* 20, no. 4 (1996): 503–30.

——. "Democratic Enlargement: The Clinton Doctrine." *Foreign Policy*, no. 106 (Spring 1997): 110–27.

——. *Gerald R. Ford: The 38th President, 1974–1977*. The American Presidents. New York: Times Books, 2007.

Brinton, Crane. *The Anatomy of Revolution*. 1938. Rev. and expanded ed. New York: Vintage Books, 1965.

Brody, Reed. *Contra Terror in Nicaragua: Report of a Fact-Finding Mission: September 1984–January 1985*. Boston: South End Press, 1985.

Brown, Wendy. *Undoing the Demos: Neoliberalism's Stealth Revolution*. New York: Zone Books, 2015.

Burke, Kyle. *Revolutionaries for the Right: Anticommunist Internationalism and Paramilitary Warfare in the Cold War*. Chapel Hill: University of North Carolina Press, 2018.

Burke, Roland. *Decolonization and the Evolution of International Human Rights*. Philadelphia: University of Pennsylvania Press, 2010.

Byrne, Malcolm. *Iran-Contra: Reagan's Scandal and the Unchecked Abuse of Presidential Power*. Lawrence: University Press of Kansas, 2014.

Cannon, Lou. *President Reagan: The Role of a Lifetime*. New York: PublicAffairs, 2000.

Carothers, Thomas. *Critical Mission: Essays on Democracy Promotion.* Washington, DC: Carnegie Endowment for International Peace, 2004.

——. *In the Name of Democracy: U.S. Policy toward Latin America in the Reagan Years.* Berkeley: University of California Press, 1993.

——. *U.S. Democracy Promotion during and after Bush.* Washington, DC: Carnegie Endowment for International Peace, 2007.

Castañeda, Jorge G. *Utopia Unarmed: The Latin American Left after the Cold War.* New York: Vintage Books, 1994.

Chapman, Jessica M. *Cauldron of Resistance: Ngo Dinh Diem, the United States, and 1950s Southern Vietnam.* Ithaca, NY: Cornell University Press, 2013.

Clymer, Kenton. "Jimmy Carter, Human Rights, and Cambodia." *Diplomatic History* 27, no. 2 (April 2003): 245–78.

Cmiel, Kenneth. "The Emergence of Human Rights Politics in the United States." *Journal of American History* 86, no. 3 (1999): 1231–50.

——. "The Recent History of Human Rights." *American Historical Review* 1, no. 1 (February 2004): 117–35.

Coatsworth, John H. *Central America and the United States: The Clients and the Colossus.* New York: Twayne, 1994.

Cohen, Stephen B. "Conditioning U.S. Security Assistance on Human Rights Practices." *Journal of International Law* 76 (1982): 246–79.

Coleman, Bradley Lynn, and Kyle Longley, eds. *Reagan and the World: Leadership and National Security, 1981–1989.* Lexington: University Press of Kentucky, 2017.

Collier, Peter. *Political Woman: The Big Little Life of Jeane Kirkpatrick.* New York: Encounter Books, 2012.

Craig, Campbell, and Fredrik Logevall. *America's Cold War: The Politics of Insecurity.* Cambridge, MA: Harvard University Press, 2009.

Crile, George. *Charlie Wilson's War.* New York: Grove Press, 2003.

Cullather, Nick. *Secret History: The CIA's Classified Account of Its Operations in Guatemala, 1952–1954.* Stanford, CA: Stanford University Press, 2006.

Dallek, Robert. *Flawed Giant: Lyndon B. Johnson and His Times, 1961–1973.* New York: Oxford University Press, 1998.

Danner, Mark. *The Massacre at El Mozote: A Parable of the Cold War.* New York: Vintage Books, 1994.

——. *Spiral: Trapped in the Forever War.* New York: Simon & Schuster, 2016.

Davis, Mike. *Planet of Slums.* New York: Verso, 2006.

Diamond, Larry J. *Developing Democracy: Toward Consolidation.* Baltimore: Johns Hopkins University Press, 1999.

Domber, Gregory F. "The Autonomy of Solidarity." In *The Reagan Administration, the Cold War, and the Transition to Democracy Promotion,* edited by Robert Pee and William Michael Schmidli, 115–36. Cham, Switzerland: Palgrave Macmillan, 2019.

Douglas, William A. *Developing Democracy.* Washington, DC: Heldref Publications, 1972.

Dumbrell, John. *The Carter Presidency: A Re-evaluation.* Manchester: Manchester University Press, 1993.

——. *Clinton's Foreign Policy: Between the Bushes, 1992–2000*. New York: Routledge, 2009.

Durham, Martin, and Margaret Power, eds. *New Perspectives on the Transnational Right*. New York: Palgrave Macmillan, 2011.

Eckel, Jan. "'Under a Magnifying Glass': The International Human Rights Campaign against Chile in the Seventies." In *Human Rights in the Twentieth Century*, edited by Stefan-Ludwig Hoffmann, 321–41. New York: Cambridge University Press, 2010.

Eckel, Jan, and Samuel Moyn, eds. *The Breakthrough: Human Rights in the 1970s*. Philadelphia: University of Pennsylvania Press, 2015.

Ehrman, John. *The Eighties: America in the Age of Reagan*. New Haven, CT: Yale University Press, 2006.

Enríquez, Laura J. *Agrarian Reform and Class Consciousness in Nicaragua*. Gainesville: University Press of Florida, 1997.

Farber, David. *The Rise and Fall of Modern American Conservatism: A Short History*. Princeton, NJ: Princeton University Press, 2010.

Fibiger, Mattias. "The Pivot: Neoconservatives, the Philippines, and the Democracy Agenda." In *The Reagan Administration, the Cold War, and the Transition to Democracy Promotion*, edited by Robert Pee and William Michael Schmidli, 209–30. Cham, Switzerland: Palgrave Macmillan, 2019.

Fischer, Beth A. *The Myth of Triumphalism: Rethinking President Reagan's Cold War Legacy*. Lexington: University Press of Kentucky, 2019.

Folly, Martin H. "Harry S. Truman." In *US Foreign Policy and Democracy Promotion: From Theodore Roosevelt to Barack Obama*, edited by Michael Cox, Timothy J. Lynch, and Nicolas Bouchet, 86–101. New York: Routledge, 2013.

Foote, Rosemary. "The Cold War and Human Rights." In *The Cambridge History of the Cold War*, edited by Melvyn P. Leffler and Odd Arne Westad, 3:445–65. New York: Cambridge University Press, 2010.

Fukuyama, Francis. "The End of History?" *National Interest*, Summer 1989, 3–18.

Gaddis, John Lewis. *George F. Kennan: An American Life*. New York: Penguin Books, 2012.

——. *Strategies of Containment: A Critical Appraisal of Postwar American National Security Policy*. Rev. ed. New York: Oxford University Press, 2005.

Garrard-Burnett, Virginia, Mark Atwood Lawrence, and Julio E. Moreno, eds. *Beyond the Eagle's Shadow: New Histories of Latin America's Cold War*. Albuquerque: University of New Mexico Press, 2013.

Garthoff, Raymond. *Détente and Confrontation: American-Soviet Relations from Nixon to Reagan*. Washington, DC: Brookings Institution, 1994.

Gates, Robert M. *From the Shadows: The Ultimate Insider's Story of Five Presidents and How They Won the Cold War*. New York: Simon & Schuster, 1996.

Geoghegan, Kate. "Neoliberalism and Democracy Promotion: Hernando de Soto and US Foreign Policy." In *The Reagan Administration, the Cold War, and the Transition to Democracy Promotion*, edited by Robert Pee and William Michael Schmidli, 137–60. Cham, Switzerland: Palgrave Macmillan, 2019.

——. "A Policy in Tension: The National Endowment for Democracy and the U.S. Response to the Collapse of the Soviet Union." *Diplomatic History* 42, no. 5 (2018): 772–801.

Gilbert, Dennis. *Sandinistas: The Party and the Revolution.* New York: Wiley-Blackwell, 1991.

Gill, Leslie. *The School of the Americas: Military Training and Political Violence in the Americas.* Durham, NC: Duke University Press, 2004.

Gills, Barry, Joel Rocamora, and Richard Wilson, eds. *Low Intensity Democracy: Political Power in the New World Order.* Boulder, CO: Pluto Press, 1993.

Gleijeses, Piero. *Conflicting Missions: Havana, Washington, and Africa, 1959–1976.* Chapel Hill: University of North Carolina Press, 2002.

——. *Shattered Hope: The Guatemalan Revolution and the United States, 1944–1954.* Princeton, NJ: Princeton University Press, 1991.

Gobat, Michel. *Confronting the American Dream: Nicaragua under U.S. Imperial Rule.* Durham, NC: Duke University Press, 2005.

Gosse, Van. "'El Salvador Is Spanish for Vietnam': A New Immigrant Left and the Politics of Solidarity." In *The Immigrant Left in the United States,* edited by Paul Buhle and Dan Georgakas, 302–29. Albany: State University of New York Press, 1996.

——. "'The North American Front': Central American Solidarity in the Reagan Era." In *Reshaping the US Left: Popular Struggles in the 1980s,* edited by Mike Davis and Michael Sprinkler, 11–50. London: Verso, 1988.

——. *Rethinking the New Left: An Interpretative History.* New York: Palgrave Macmillan, 2005.

Gould, Lewis. *Grand Old Party: A History of the Republicans.* New York: Random House, 2003.

Gourevitch, Philip. *We Wish to Inform You That Tomorrow We Will Be Killed with Our Families: Stories from Rwanda.* New York: Picador, 1999.

Grandin, Greg. *Empire's Workshop: Latin America and the Roots of U.S. Imperialism.* New York: Metropolitan Books, 2005.

——. *The Last Colonial Massacre: Latin America in the Cold War.* Chicago: University of Chicago Press, 2004.

Green, Duncan. *Silent Revolution: The Rise and Crisis of Market Economics in Latin America.* New York: Monthly Review Press, 2003.

Green, James N. "Clerics, Exiles, and Academics: Opposition to the Brazilian Military Dictatorship in the United States." *Latin American Politics and Society* 45, no. 1 (December 2008): 88–117.

Guilhot, Nicolas. *The Democracy Makers: Human Rights and the Politics of Global Order.* New York: Columbia University Press, 2012.

Gutman, Roy. *Banana Diplomacy: The Making of American Policy in Nicaragua, 1981–1987.* New York: Simon & Schuster, 1988.

Hanhimäki, Jussi. "An Elusive Grand Design." In *Nixon in the World: American Foreign Relations, 1969–1977,* edited by Fredrik Logevall and Andrew Preston, 25–44. New York: Oxford University Press, 2008.

——. *The Flawed Architect: Henry Kissinger and American Foreign Policy.* New York: Oxford University Press, 2004.

Harmer, Tanya. *Allende's Chile and the Inter-American Cold War.* Chapel Hill: University of North Carolina Press, 2011.

Hartmann, Hauke. "U.S. Human Rights Policy under Carter and Reagan, 1977–1981." *Human Rights Quarterly* 23, no. 2 (May 2001): 402–30.

Herring, George C. *America's Longest War: The United States and Vietnam, 1950–1975.* 4th ed. New York: McGraw-Hill, 2003.

Hodges, Donald C. *Intellectual Foundations of the Nicaraguan Revolution.* Austin: University of Texas Press, 1986.

Hoffmann, Stefan-Ludwig, ed. *Human Rights in the Twentieth Century.* New York: Cambridge University Press, 2010.

Hopgood, Stephen. *The Endtimes of Human Rights.* Ithaca, NY: Cornell University Press, 2013.

Horton, Lynn. *Peasants in Arms: War and Peace in the Mountains of Nicaragua, 1979–1994.* Athens: Ohio University Center for International Studies, 1999.

Hoyt, Katherine. *The Many Faces of Sandinista Democracy.* Athens: Ohio University Center for International Studies, 1997.

Hunt, Jonathan, and Simon Miles, eds. *The Reagan Moment: America and the World in the 1980s.* Ithaca, NY: Cornell University Press, 2021.

Hunt, Michael H. *The American Ascendancy: How the United States Gained and Wielded Global Dominance.* Chapel Hill: University of North Carolina Press, 2009.

Iber, Patrick. *Neither Peace nor Freedom: The Cultural Cold War in Latin America.* Cambridge, MA: Harvard University Press, 2015.

Ignatieff, Michael. "Introduction: American Exceptionalism and Human Rights." In *American Exceptionalism and Human Rights*, edited by Michael Ignatieff, 1–26. Princeton, NJ: Princeton University Press, 2005.

Ikenberry, G. John. *Liberal Leviathan: The Origins, Crisis, and Transformation of the American World Order.* Princeton, NJ: Princeton University Press, 2011.

Iriye, Akira, Petra Goedde, and William I. Hitchcock, eds. *The Human Rights Revolution: An International History.* New York: Oxford University Press, 2012.

Isserman, Maurice, and Michael Kazin. *America Divided: The Civil War of the 1960s.* New York: Oxford University Press, 2000.

Jacobs, Seth. *America's Miracle Man in Vietnam: Ngo Dinh Diem, Religion, Race, and U.S. Intervention in Southeast Asia, 1950–1957.* Durham, NC: Duke University Press, 2005.

Jarquín, Mateo Cayetano. "Red Christmases: The Sandinistas, Indigenous Rebellion, and the Origins of the Nicaraguan Civil War, 1981–82." *Cold War History* 18, no. 1 (2018): 91–107.

Jenkins, James. "The Indian Wing: Nicaraguan Indians, Native American Activists, and U.S. Foreign Policy, 1979–1990." In *Beyond the Eagle's Shadow: New Histories of Latin America's Cold War*, edited by Virginia Garrard-Burnett, Mark Atwood Lawrence, and Julio E. Moreno, 175–99. Albuquerque: University of New Mexico Press, 2013.

Jensen, Steven L. B. *The Making of International Human Rights: The 1960s, Decolonization, and the Reconstruction of Global Values.* New York: Cambridge University Press, 2016.

Johnson, Robert David. *Congress and the Cold War.* New York: Cambridge University Press, 2006.

Joseph, Gilbert M. "Border Crossings and the Remaking of Latin American Cold War Studies." *Cold War History* 19, no. 1 (2019): 141–70.

Joseph, Gilbert M., and Greg Grandin, eds. *A Century of Revolution: Insurgent and Counterinsurgent Violence during Latin America's Long Cold War.* Durham, NC: Duke University Press, 2010.

Joseph, Gilbert M., Catherine C. LeGrand, and Ricardo D. Salvatore, eds. *Close Encounters of Empire: Writing the Cultural History of U.S.–Latin American Relations.* Durham, NC: Duke University Press, 1998.

Joseph, Gilbert M., and Daniela Spenser, eds. *In from the Cold: Latin America's New Encounter with the Cold War.* Durham, NC: Duke University Press, 2008.

Kagan, Robert. *A Twilight Struggle: American Power in Nicaragua, 1977–1990.* New York: Free Press, 1996.

Kalinovsky, Artemy. *A Long Goodbye: The Soviet Withdrawal from Afghanistan.* Cambridge, MA: Harvard University Press, 2011.

Kalman, Laura. *Right Star Rising: A New Politics, 1974–1980.* New York: W. W. Norton, 2010.

Kaufman, Robert Gordon. *Henry M. Jackson: A Life in Politics.* Seattle: University of Washington Press, 2000.

Kaufman, Scott. *Plans Unraveled: The Foreign Policy of the Carter Administration.* De Kalb: Northern Illinois University Press, 2008.

Keeley, Theresa. *Reagan's Gun-Toting Nuns: The Catholic Conflict over Cold War Human Rights Policy in Central America.* Ithaca, NY: Cornell University Press, 2020.

Kelly, Patrick William. *Sovereign Emergencies: Latin America and the Making of Global Human Rights Politics.* Cambridge: Cambridge University Press, 2018.

Keys, Barbara J. "Anti-torture Politics: Amnesty International, the Greek Junta, and the Origins of the Human Rights 'Boom' in the United States." In *The Human Rights Revolution: An International History*, edited by Akira Iriye, Petra Goedde, and William I. Hitchcock, 201–21. New York: Oxford University Press, 2012.

——. "Congress, Kissinger, and the Origins of Human Rights Diplomacy." *Diplomatic History* 34, no. 5 (November 2010): 823–51.

——. *Reclaiming American Virtue: The Human Rights Revolution of the 1970s.* Cambridge, MA: Harvard University Press, 2014.

Kirkendall, Andrew J. *Paulo Freire and the Cold War Politics of Literacy.* Chapel Hill: University of North Carolina Press, 2010.

Kirkpatrick, Jeane J. *Leader and Vanguard in Mass Society: A Study of Peronist Argentina.* Cambridge, MA: MIT Press, 1971.

Knock, Thomas J. *To End All Wars: Woodrow Wilson and the Quest for a New World Order.* New York: Oxford University Press, 1992.

Kornbluh, Peter. *Nicaragua, the Price of Intervention: Reagan's War against the Sandinistas.* Washington, DC: Institute for Policy Studies, 1987.

——. *The Pinochet File: A Declassified Dossier on Atrocity and Accountability*. New York: New Press, 2003.

——. "The U.S. Role in the Counterrevolution." In *Revolution and Counterrevolution in Nicaragua*, edited by Thomas W. Walker, 323–49. Boulder, CO: Westview Press, 1991.

Kuperman, Alan J. "The Stinger Missile and U.S. Intervention in Afghanistan." *Political Science Quarterly* 114, no. 2 (Summer 1999): 219–63.

Kurki, Milja. *Democratic Futures: Revisioning Democracy Promotion*. Abingdon: Routledge, 2013.

LaFeber, Walter. *Inevitable Revolutions: The United States in Central America*. New York: W. W. Norton, 1993.

Lancaster, Roger N. *Life Is Hard: Machismo, Danger, and the Intimacy of Power in Nicaragua*. Berkeley: University of California Press, 1992.

Larkin, Bruce D., ed. *Vital Interests: The Soviet Issue in U.S. Central American Policy*. Boulder, CO: Lynne Rienner, 1988.

Lauria-Santiago, Aldo A. "The Culture and Politics of State Terror and Repression in El Salvador." In *When States Kill: Latin America, the U.S., and Technologies of Terror*, edited by Cecilia Menjívar and Néstor Rodríguez, 85–114. Austin: University of Texas Press, 2009.

Lawrence, Mark Atwood. *The Vietnam War: A Concise International History*. New York: Oxford University Press, 2010.

Leffler, Melvyn P. *For the Soul of Mankind: The United States, the Soviet Union, and the Cold War*. New York: Hill and Wang, 2007.

Leiken, Robert S. "Nicaragua's Untold Stories." In *Nicaragua: Unfinished Revolution*, edited by Peter Rosset and John Vandermeer, 23–32. New York: Grove Press, 1986. Originally published in *New Republic*, February 8, 1984.

LeoGrande, William M. *Our Own Backyard: The United States in Central America, 1977–1992*. Chapel Hill: University of North Carolina Press, 1998.

Little, Douglas. *American Orientalism: The United States and the Middle East since 1945*. Chapel Hill: University of North Carolina Press, 2008.

Logevall, Fredrik. "Domestic Politics." In *Explaining the History of American Foreign Relations*, edited by Frank Costigliola and Michael J. Hogan, 151–67. 3rd. ed. New York: Cambridge University Press, 2016.

MacMillan, Margaret. "Nixon, Kissinger, and the Opening to China." In *Nixon in the World: American Foreign Relations, 1969–1977*, edited by Fredrik Logevall and Andrew Preston, 107–25. New York: Oxford University Press, 2008.

Mann, James. *The Rebellion of Ronald Reagan: A History of the End of the Cold War*. New York: Viking, 2009.

——. *Rise of the Vulcans: The History of Bush's War Cabinet*. New York: Viking, 2001.

Martin, Bradford. *The Other Eighties: A Secret History of America in the Age of Reagan*. New York: Hill and Wang, 2011.

Matlock, Jack F., Jr. *Reagan and Gorbachev: How the Cold War Ended*. New York: Random House, 2004.

——. "U.S. Policy on Human Rights in Relations with the USSR, 1961–91." In *Implementing U.S. Human Rights Policy: Agendas, Policies, and Practices*, edited by Debra Liang-Fenton, 245–63. Washington, DC: United States Institute of Peace Press, 2004.

McCartin, Joseph A. *Collision Course: Ronald Reagan, the Air Traffic Controllers, and the Strike That Changed America*. New York: Oxford University Press, 2013.

McCormick, Evan D. "Breaking with Statism? U.S. Democracy Promotion in Latin America, 1984–1988." *Diplomatic History* 42, no. 5 (November 2018): 745–71.

——. "US Electoral Assistance to El Salvador and the Culture of Politics, 1982–1984." In *The Reagan Administration, the Cold War, and the Transition to Democracy Promotion*, edited by Robert Pee and William Michael Schmidli, 163–88. Cham, Switzerland: Palgrave Macmillan, 2019.

McGirr, Lisa. *Suburban Warriors: The Origins of the New American Right*. Princeton, NJ: Princeton University Press, 2001.

McPherson, Alan. *The Invaded: How Latin Americans and Their Allies Fought and Ended U.S. Occupations*. New York: Oxford University Press, 2014.

——. "Letelier Diplomacy: Nonstate Actors and U.S.-Chilean Relations." *Diplomatic History* 43, no. 3 (June 2019): 445–68.

Micklethwait, John, and Adrian Wooldridge. *The Right Nation: Conservative Power in America*. New York: Penguin Books, 2004.

Miles, Simon. *Engaging the Evil Empire: Washington, Moscow, and the Beginning of the End of the Cold War*. Ithaca, NY: Cornell University Press, 2020.

Miller, Aaron David. *The Much Too Promised Land: America's Elusive Search for Arab-Israeli Peace*. New York: Bantam Books, 2008.

Miller, Jennifer M. *Cold War Democracy: The United States and Japan*. Cambridge, MA: Harvard University Press, 2019.

Miranda, Roger, and William Ratliff. *The Civil War in Nicaragua: Inside the Sandinistas*. New Brunswick, NJ: Transaction, 1993.

Mistry, Kaeten. "The Case for Political Warfare: Strategy Organization and US Involvement in the 1948 Italian Election." *Cold War History* 6, no. 3 (August 2006): 301–29.

Mitchell, Nancy. "The Cold War and Jimmy Carter." In *The Cambridge History of the Cold War*, edited by Melvyn P. Leffler and Odd Arne Westad, 3:66–87. New York: Cambridge University Press, 2010.

Moreton, Bethany. *To Serve God and Wal-Mart: The Making of Christian Free Enterprise*. Cambridge, MA: Harvard University Press, 2010.

Morley, Morris, and Chris McGillion. *Reagan and Pinochet: The Struggle over U.S. Policy toward Chile*. New York: Cambridge University Press, 2015.

——. "Soldiering On: The Reagan Administration and Redemocratisation in Chile, 1983–1986." *Bulletin of Latin American Research* 25, no. 1 (January 2006): 1–22.

Moyn, Samuel. *The Last Utopia: Human Rights in History*. Cambridge, MA: Belknap Press of Harvard University Press, 2010.

——. *Not Enough: Human Rights in an Unequal World*. Cambridge, MA: Belknap Press of Harvard University Press, 2018.

Muravchik, Joshua. *The Uncertain Crusade: Jimmy Carter and the Dilemmas of Human Rights Policy*. Lanham, MD: Hamilton Press, 1986.

Nathans, Benjamin. "Soviet Rights-Talk in the Post-Stalin Era." In *Human Rights in the Twentieth Century*, edited by Stefan-Ludwig Hoffmann, 166–90. New York: Cambridge University Press, 2010.

Neier, Aryeh. "Human Rights in the Reagan Era: Acceptance in Principle." *Annals of the American Academy of Political and Social Science* 506 (November 1, 1989): 30–41.

——. *Taking Liberties: Four Decades in the Struggle for Rights*. New York: PublicAffairs, 2003.

Oñate, Andrea. "The Red Affair: FMLN-Cuban Relations during the Salvadoran Civil War, 1981–92." *Cold War History* 11, no. 2 (May 2011): 133–54.

Pastor, Robert A. *Not Condemned to Repetition: The United States and Nicaragua*. Boulder, CO: Westview Press, 2002.

Peace, Roger. *A Call to Conscience: The Anti–Contra War Campaign*. Amherst: University of Massachusetts Press, 2012.

Pee, Robert. *Democracy Promotion, National Security and Strategy: Foreign Policy under the Reagan Administration*. New York: Routledge, 2015.

——. "The Rise of Political Aid: The National Endowment for Democracy and the Reagan Administration's Cold War Strategy." In *The Reagan Administration, the Cold War, and the Transition to Democracy Promotion*, edited by Robert Pee and William Michael Schmidli, 51–74. Cham, Switzerland: Palgrave Macmillan, 2019.

Pee, Robert, and William Michael Schmidli, eds. *The Reagan Administration, the Cold War, and the Transition to Democracy Promotion*. Cham, Switzerland: Palgrave Macmillan, 2019.

Pemberton, William E. *Exit with Honor: The Life and Presidency of Ronald Reagan*. Armonk, NY: M. E. Sharpe, 1997.

Perla, Héctor, Jr. "Heirs of Sandino: The Nicaraguan Revolution and the U.S.-Nicaragua Solidarity Movement." *Latin American Perspectives* 36, no. 6 (November 2009): 80–100.

——. "Si Nicaragua Venció, El Salvador Vencerá: Central American Agency in the Creation of the U.S.–Central American Peace and Solidarity Movement." *Latin American Research Review* 43, no. 2 (April 2008): 136–58.

Perlstein, Rick. *Before the Storm: Barry Goldwater and the Unmaking of the American Consensus*. New York: Hill and Wang, 2001.

Persico, Joseph E. *Casey: The Lives and Secrets of William J. Casey: From the OSS to the CIA*. New York: Viking, 1990.

Peterson, Christian Philip. "The Reagan Administration's Efforts to Promote Human Rights and Democracy in the Soviet Union." In *The Reagan Administration, the Cold War, and the Transition to Democracy Promotion*, edited by Robert Pee and William Michael Schmidli, 95–114. Cham, Switzerland: Palgrave Macmillan, 2019.

Phillips-Fein, Kim. "Conservatism: A State of the Field." *Journal of American History* 38 (June 2010): 367–92.

——. "'If Business and the Country Will Be Run Right': The Business Challenge to the Liberal Consensus, 1945–1964." *International Labor and Working-Class History* 72 (Fall 2007): 192–215.

———. *Invisible Hands: The Businessmen's Crusade against the New Deal.* New York: W. W. Norton, 2010.

Power, Samantha. *"A Problem from Hell": America and the Age of Genocide.* New York: Harper Perennial, 2002.

Prevost, Gary. "The Status of the Sandinista Project." In *The Undermining of the Sandinista Revolution,* edited by Gary Prevost and Harry E. Vanden, 9–44. New York: Palgrave Macmillan, 1999.

Rabe, Stephen G. *The Killing Zone: The United States Wages Cold War in Latin America.* New York: Oxford University Press, 2011.

———. *The Most Dangerous Area in the World: John F. Kennedy Confronts Communist Revolution in Latin America.* Chapel Hill: University of North Carolina Press, 1999.

Radchenko, Sergey. "The Sino-Soviet Split." In *The Cambridge History of the Cold War,* edited by Melvyn P. Leffler and Odd Arne Westad, 2:349–72. New York: Cambridge University Press, 2010.

Reding, Andrew A. "Governmental Institutions." In *Revolution and Counterrevolution in Nicaragua,* edited by Thomas W. Walker, 15–47. Boulder, CO: Westview Press, 1991.

Renouard, Joe. *Human Rights in American Foreign Policy: From the 1960s to the Soviet Collapse.* Philadelphia: University of Pennsylvania Press, 2015.

Ricciardi, Joseph. "Economic Policy." In *Revolution and Counterrevolution in Nicaragua,* edited by Thomas W. Walker, 247–73. Boulder, CO: Westview Press, 1991.

Robinson, William I. *A Faustian Bargain: U.S. Intervention in the Nicaraguan Elections and American Foreign Policy in the Post–Cold War Era.* Boulder, CO: Westview Press, 1992.

———. *Promoting Polyarchy: Globalization, US Intervention, and Hegemony.* New York: Cambridge University Press, 1996.

Rossiter, Caleb. "Human Rights: The Carter Record, the Reagan Reaction." *International Policy Report,* September 1984, 14–17.

Ryan, Maria. "Bush's 'Useful Idiots': 9/11, the Liberal Hawks and the Cooption of the 'War on Terror.'" *Journal of American Studies* 45, no. 4 (2011): 667–93.

Sánchez Nateras, Gerardo. "The Sandinista Revolution and the Limits of the Cold War in Latin America: The Dilemma of Non-intervention during the Nicaraguan Crisis, 1977–78." *Cold War History* 18, no. 2 (2018): 111–29.

Sandbrook, Dominic. *Mad as Hell: The Crisis of the 1970s and the Rise of the Populist Right.* New York: Anchor Books, 2012.

Sanders, Jerry W. *Peddlers of Crisis: The Committee on the Present Danger and the Politics of Containment.* Cambridge, MA: South End Press, 1983.

Sargent, Daniel J. *A Superpower Transformed: The Remaking of American Foreign Relations in the 1970s.* New York: Oxford University Press, 2015.

Schaller, Michael. *Reckoning with Reagan: America and Its President in the 1980s.* New York: Oxford University Press, 1994.

———. "Ronald Reagan and the Cold War." In *Deconstructing Reagan: Conservative Mythology and America's Fortieth President,* 3–40. Armonk, NY: M. E. Sharp, 2007.

Schifter, Richard. "Building Firm Foundations: The Institutionalization of United States Human Rights Policy in the Reagan Years." *Harvard Law Review* 2 (Spring 1989): 3–24.

Schlesinger, Arthur M., Jr. *A Thousand Days: John F. Kennedy in the White House*. Boston: Houghton Mifflin, 1965.

Schmidli, William Michael. *The Fate of Freedom Elsewhere: Human Rights and U.S. Cold War Policy toward Argentina*. Ithaca, NY: Cornell University Press, 2013.

———. "Human Rights and the Cold War: The Campaign to Halt the Argentine 'Dirty War.'" *Cold War History* 12, no. 2 (May 2012): 345–65.

———. "'The Most Sophisticated Intervention We Have Seen': The Carter Administration and the Nicaraguan Crisis, 1978–1979." *Diplomacy & Statecraft* 23, no. 1 (2012): 66–86.

Schmitz, David F. *Thank God They're on Our Side: The United States and Right-Wing Dictatorships, 1921–1965*. Durham, NC: University of North Carolina Press, 1999.

Schmitz, David F., and Vanessa Walker. "Jimmy Carter and the Foreign Policy of Human Rights: The Development of a Post–Cold War Foreign Policy." *Diplomatic History* 28, no. 1 (2004): 113–43.

Schoenwald, Jonathan. *A Time for Choosing: The Rise of Modern American Conservatism*. New York: Oxford University Press, 2001.

Schoultz, Lars. *Beneath the United States: A History of U.S. Policy toward Latin America*. Cambridge, MA: Harvard University Press, 1998.

———. *Human Rights and United States Policy toward Latin America*. Princeton, NJ: Princeton University Press, 1981.

Schulman, Bruce J., and Julian E. Zelizer, eds. *Rightward Bound: Making America Conservative in the 1970s*. Cambridge, MA: Harvard University Press, 2008.

Schulzinger, Robert D. "Détente in the Nixon-Ford Years, 1969–1976." In *The Cambridge History of the Cold War*, edited by Melvyn P. Leffler and Odd Arne Westad, 2:373–94. New York: Cambridge University Press, 2010.

Scott, James M. *Deciding to Intervene: The Reagan Doctrine and American Foreign Policy*. Durham, NC: Duke University Press, 1996.

Serra, Luis Hector. "The Grass-Roots Organizations." In *Revolution and Counterrevolution in Nicaragua*, edited by Thomas W. Walker, 49–75. Boulder, CO: Westview Press, 1991.

Sharnak, Debbie. "Reagan and the Waning Years of Uruguay's Military Rule: Democracy Promotion and the Redefinition of Human Rights." In *The Reagan Administration, the Cold War, and the Transition to Democracy Promotion*, edited by Robert Pee and William Michael Schmidli, 189–207. Cham, Switzerland: Palgrave Macmillan, 2019.

———. "Sovereignty and Human Rights: Re-examining Carter's Foreign Policy towards the Third World." *Diplomacy & Statecraft* 25, no. 2 (2014): 303–30.

Shestack, Jerome J. "An Unsteady Focus: The Vulnerabilities of the Reagan Administration's Human Rights Policy." *Harvard Human Rights Journal* 25, no. 2 (1989): 25–53.

Siekmeier, James. "The Iran-Contra Affair." In *A Companion to Reagan*, edited by Andrew L. Johns, 321–38. Malden, MA: John Wiley & Sons, 2015.

Sikkink, Kathryn. *Mixed Signals: U.S. Human Rights Policy and Latin America*. Ithaca, NY: Cornell University Press, 2004.

Simpson, Brad. "'The First Right': The Carter Administration, Indonesia, and the Transnational Human Rights Politics of the 1970s." In *The Human Rights Revolution: An International History*, edited by Akira Iriye, Petra Goedde, and William I. Hitchcock, 179–200. New York: Oxford University Press, 2012.

Smith, Allen. "Leadership, Orientation, and Rhetorical Vision: Jimmy Carter, the 'New Right,' and the Panama Canal." *Presidential Studies Quarterly* 16, no. 2 (Spring 1986): 317–28.

Smith, Christian. *Resisting Reagan: The U.S. Central America Peace Movement.* Chicago: University of Chicago Press, 1996.

Smith, Gaddis. *Morality, Reason, and Power: American Diplomacy in the Carter Years.* New York: Hill and Wang, 1986.

Smith, Steve. "U.S. Democracy Promotion: Critical Questions." In *American Democracy Promotion: Impulses, Strategies, and Impacts*, edited by Michael Cox, G. John Ikenberry, and Takashi Inoguchi, 63–85. New York: Oxford University Press, 2000.

Smith, Tony. *America's Mission: The United States and the Worldwide Struggle for Democracy in the Twentieth Century.* Expanded ed. Princeton, NJ: Princeton University Press, 2012.

———. *A Pact with the Devil: Washington's Bid for World Supremacy and the Betrayal of the American Promise.* New York: Routledge, 2007.

Snyder, Sarah B. "'A Call for U.S. Leadership': Congressional Activism on Human Rights." *Diplomatic History* 37, no. 2 (2013): 372–97.

———. "The Defeat of Ernest Lefever's Nomination: Keeping Human Rights on the United States Foreign Policy Agenda." In *Challenging US Foreign Policy: America and the World in the Long Twentieth Century*, edited by Bevan Sewell and Scott Lucas, 136–61. New York: Palgrave Macmillan, 2011.

———. *From Selma to Moscow: How Human Rights Activists Transformed U.S. Foreign Policy.* New York: Columbia University Press, 2018.

———. *Human Rights Activism and the End of the Cold War: A Transnational History of the Helsinki Network.* New York: Cambridge University Press, 2011.

———. "Human Rights and U.S. Foreign Relations: A Historiographical Review." *Passport: The Newsletter of the Society for Historians of American Foreign Relations*, April 2013, 16–21.

———. "'Jerry, Don't Go': Domestic Opposition to the 1975 Helsinki Final Act." *Journal of American Studies* 44, no. 1 (February 2010): 67–81.

Søndergaard, Rasmus Sinding. "Bill Clinton's 'Democratic Enlargement' and the Securitisation of Democracy Promotion." *Diplomacy & Statecraft* 26, no. 3 (2015): 534–51.

———. *Reagan, Congress, and Human Rights: Contesting Morality in US Foreign Policy.* Cambridge: Cambridge University Press, 2020.

Stiglitz, Joseph E. *Globalization and Its Discontents.* New York: W. W. Norton, 2003.

Strong, Robert A. *Working in the World: Jimmy Carter and the Making of American Foreign Policy.* Baton Rouge: Louisiana State University Press, 2002.

Suri, Jeremi. "From Isolation to Engagement: American Foreign Policy and the Opening to China, 1969–1972." In *Foreign Policy Breakthroughs: Cases in Successful*

Diplomacy, edited by Robert Hutchings and Jeremi Suri, 101–20. New York: Oxford University Press, 2015.

——. *Henry Kissinger and the American Century*. Cambridge, MA: Belknap Press of Harvard University Press, 2007.

Thomas, Daniel C. *The Helsinki Effect: International Norms, Human Rights, and the Demise of Communism*. Princeton, NJ: Princeton University Press, 2001.

Thompson, John A. *Woodrow Wilson: Profiles in Power*. New York: Longman, 2002.

Todd, Molly. "'We Were Part of the Revolutionary Movement There': Wisconsin Peace Progressives and Solidarity with El Salvador in the Reagan Era." *Journal of Civil and Human Rights* 3, no. 1 (Spring/Summer 2017): 1–56.

Travis, Philip W. *Reagan's War on Terrorism in Nicaragua: The Outlaw State*. Lanham, MD: Lexington Books, 2016.

Troy, Gil. "Reagan's 100-Day Revolution." In *Living in the Eighties*, edited by Gil Troy and Vincent J. Cannato, 10–21. New York: Oxford University Press, 2009.

Tulli, Umberto. "'Whose Rights Are Human Rights?': The Ambiguous Emergence of Human Rights and the Demise of Kissingerism." *Cold War History* 12, no. 4 (2012): 573–93.

Vaïsse, Justin. *Neoconservatism: The Biography of a Movement*. Cambridge, MA: Belknap Press of Harvard University Press, 2011.

Vanden, Harry E. "Democracy Derailed: The 1990 Elections and After." In *The Undermining of the Sandinista Revolution*, edited by Gary Prevost and Harry E. Vanden, 45–73. New York: Palgrave Macmillan, 1999.

Vanderlaan, Mary B. *Revolution and Foreign Policy in Nicaragua*. Boulder, CO: Westview Press, 1986.

Van Ommen, Eline. "Sandinistas Go Global: Nicaragua and Western Europe, 1977–1990." PhD diss., London School of Economics and Political Science, 2019.

Vaughan, Patrick. "Zbigniew Brzezinski and Afghanistan." In *The Policy Makers: Shaping American Foreign Policy from 1947 to the Present*, edited by Anna Kasten Nelson, 107–30. Lanham, MD: Rowman & Littlefield, 2009.

Walker, Thomas W. "The Armed Forces." In *Revolution and Counterrevolution in Nicaragua*, edited by Thomas W. Walker, 77–100. Boulder, CO: Westview Press, 1991.

——. *Nicaragua: Living in the Shadow of the Eagle*. 4th ed. Boulder, CO: Westview Press, 2011.

——. *Nicaragua: The Land of Sandino*. Boulder, CO: Westview Press, 1981.

Walker, Vanessa. *Principles in Power: Latin America and the Politics of U.S. Human Rights Diplomacy*. Ithaca, NY: Cornell University Press, 2020.

Westad, Odd Arne. *The Global Cold War: Third World Interventions and the Making of Our Times*. Cambridge: Cambridge University Press, 2005.

Weyland, Kurt Gerhard. "Neoliberalism and Democracy in Latin America: A Mixed Record." *Latin American Politics and Society* 46, no. 1 (Spring 2004): 135–57.

Wilentz, Sean. *The Age of Reagan: A History, 1974–2008*. New York: HarperCollins, 2009.

Wilford, Hugh. *The Mighty Wurlitzer: How the CIA Played America*. Cambridge, MA: Harvard University Press, 2009.

Williams, Harvey. "The Social Programs." In *Revolution and Counterrevolution in Nicaragua*, edited by Thomas W. Walker, 187–212. Boulder, CO: Westview Press, 1991.

Wilson, James Graham. *The Triumph of Improvisation: Gorbachev's Adaptability, Reagan's Engagement, and the End of the Cold War*. Ithaca, NY: Cornell University Press, 2015.

Winn, Peter. *Americas: The Changing Face of Latin America and the Caribbean*. 3rd ed. Berkeley: University of California Press, 2006.

Witcover, Jules. *Party of the People: A History of the Democrats*. New York: Random House, 2003.

Wright, Bruce E. *Theory in the Practice of the Nicaraguan Revolution*. Athens: Ohio University Center for International Studies, 1995.

Yaqub, Salim. *Containing Arab Nationalism: The Eisenhower Doctrine and the Middle East*. Chapel Hill: University of North Carolina Press, 2004.

Young, Marilyn B. *The Vietnam Wars, 1945–1990*. New York: HarperPerennial, 1991.

Zaretsky, Natasha. "Restraint or Retreat? The Debate over the Panama Canal Treaties and U.S. Nationalism after Vietnam." *Diplomatic History* 35, no. 3 (June 2011): 535–62.

Zelizer, Julian E. *Arsenal of Democracy: The Politics of National Security—from World War II to the War on Terrorism*. New York: Basic Books, 2012.

Zimmermann, Matilde. *Sandinista: Carlos Fonseca and the Nicaraguan Revolution*. Durham, NC: Duke University Press, 2000.

Index

CPSIA information can be obtained
at www.ICGtesting.com
Printed in the USA
LVHW101907250822
726871LV00017B/435/J